Global Drug Enforcement

Practical Investigative Techniques

CRC SERIES IN
PRACTICAL ASPECTS OF CRIMINAL AND FORENSIC INVESTIGATIONS

VERNON J. GEBERTH, BBA, MPS, FBINA *Series Editor*

Practical Homicide Investigation: Tactics, Procedures, and Forensic Techniques, Third Edition
Vernon J. Geberth

The Counterterrorism Handbook: Tactics, Procedures, and Techniques, Second Edition
Frank Bolz, Jr., Kenneth J. Dudonis, and David P. Schulz

Forensic Pathology, Second Edition
Dominick J. Di Maio and Vincent J. M. Di Maio

Interpretation of Bloodstain Evidence at Crime Scenes, Second Edition
William G. Eckert and Stuart H. James

Tire Imprint Evidence
Peter McDonald

Practical Drug Enforcement, Second Edition
Michael D. Lyman

Practical Aspects of Rape Investigation: A Multidisciplinary Approach, Third Edition
Robert R. Hazelwood and Ann Wolbert Burgess

The Sexual Exploitation of Children: A Practical Guide to Assessment, Investigation, and Intervention, Second Edition
Seth L. Goldstein

Gunshot Wounds: Practical Aspects of Firearms, Ballistics, and Forensic Techniques, Second Edition
Vincent J. M. Di Maio

Friction Ridge Skin: Comparison and Identification of Fingerprints
James F. Cowger

Footwear Impression Evidence, Second Edition
William J. Bodziak

Principles of Kinesic Interview and Interrogation
Stan Walters

Practical Fire and Arson Investigation, Second Edition
David R. Redsicker and John J. O'Connor

The Practical Methodology of Forensic Photography, Second Edition
David R. Redsicker

Practical Aspects of Interview and Interrogation, Second Edition
David E. Zulawski and Douglas E. Wicklander

Investigating Computer Crime
Franklin Clark and Ken Diliberto

Practical Homicide Investigation Checklist and Field Guide
Vernon J. Geberth

Bloodstain Pattern Analysis: With an Introduction to Crime Scene Reconstruction, Second Edition
Tom Bevel and Ross M. Gardner

Practical Aspects of Munchausen by Proxy and Munchausen Syndrome Investigation
Kathryn Artingstall

Quantitative-Qualitative Friction Ridge Analysis: An Introduction to Basic and Advanced Ridgeology
David R. Ashbaugh

Practical Criminal Investigations in Correctional Facilities
William R. Bell

Officer-Involved Shootings and Use of Force: Practical Investigative Techniques
David E. Hatch

Sex-Related Homicide and Death Investigation: Practical and Clinical Perspectives
Vernon J. Geberth

Global Drug Enforcement

Practical Investigative Techniques

Gregory D. Lee

CRC PRESS

Boca Raton London New York Washington, D.C.

Library of Congress Cataloging-in-Publication Data

Lee, Gregory D., 1953-
Global drug enforcement : practical investigative techniques / by Gregory D. Lee.
p. cm.— (CRC series in practical aspects of criminal and forensic investigations)
Includes bibliographical references and index.
ISBN 0-8493-1629-4
1. Drug traffic—Investigation. 2. Criminal investigation. 3. Narcotics, Control of. 4. Narcotics, Control of—International cooperation. I. Title. II. Series.

HV8079.N3L437 2003
363.25′977—dc22 2003058470

Direct all inquiries to CRC Press LLC, 2000 N.W. Corporate Blvd., Boca Raton, Florida 33431.

Visit the CRC Press Web site at www.crcpress.com

International Standard Book Number 0-8493-1629-4
Library of Congress Card Number 2003058470

Dedication

This work is dedicated first of all to my wife, Virginia, for her love, devotion and encouragement throughout this endeavor. It is also dedicated to the brave men and women of the Drug Enforcement Administration around the world who sacrifice so much for their country and fellow man.

Editor's Note

This textbook is part of the "Practical Aspects of Criminal and Forensic Investigations" series. This series was created by Vernon J. Geberth, New York City Police Department Lieutenant Commander (Retired), who is an author, educator, and consultant on homicide and forensic investigation. This series has been designed to provide contemporary, comprehensive, and pragmatic information to the practitioner involved in criminal and forensic investigation by authors who are nationally recognized experts in their respective fields.

Preface

Unlike other criminal investigation books that only devote a chapter or two to the topic, *Global Drug Enforcement: Practical Investigative Techniques* is devoted entirely to this specialized field of proactive criminal investigation. This book replicates and greatly expands on many of the topics both new and in-service employees of the Drug Enforcement Administration (DEA) receive in their training.

This book serves the needs of criminal justice majors, federal agents, police officers, detectives newly assigned to a drug unit, police training institutions, and members of the legal profession who want to expand their knowledge in the field. It serves equally well as a reference for many foreign police officials who are charged with enforcing their country's drug laws.

There are two major parts. The first deals in the fundamentals of drug investigation and includes comprehensive chapters on drug identification, undercover operations, and the handling of confidential informants. The second part is devoted to complex drug cases with chapters on conspiracy investigations, clandestine laboratories, intelligence, and money laundering.

There is also a glossary of common terms used in drug enforcement, as well as two chapters devoted to the similarities in conducting drug and terrorism investigations, and the nexus between drugs and terrorism. Drug agents know that winning the war on drugs contributes significantly to winning the war on terrorism since drug profits fund many terrorism events. Throughout the work, I use the term *drug agent*, which is synonymous with *investigator*, *detective*, *officer*, or any other title used by law enforcement personnel who perform drug investigations.

During my 30-year career in law enforcement, I have taught drug enforcement and terrorism topics both to new and in-service federal agents, state and local police officers, foreign police officials, and members of the U.S. intelligence community. While a special agent with the DEA's Office of Training at the FBI Academy in Quantico, VA, I traveled to Europe, Asia, Central and South America, and the Middle East as a member of an international training team. I discovered each region I visited had a common thirst for more, detailed knowledge on the subject that could not be found in print medium. This textbook was written, in part, to help provide domestic *and* international law enforcement officers with a one-stop reference source on contemporary drug enforcement. The investigative techniques revealed in this textbook should work well in most nations, regardless of their judicial system.

Author

Gregory D. Lee recently retired as a Supervisory Special Agent for the U.S. Department of Justice, Drug Enforcement Administration (DEA). Throughout his diverse government career, he has conducted and supervised numerous international drug investigations, and at one time was the resident agent-in-charge of the DEA's Karachi, Pakistan office. While in Pakistan from 1994 to 1998, Mr. Lee became involved in several notable terrorism investigations, and participated in the arrest of Ramzi Ahmed Yousef, the mastermind behind the 1993 World Trade Center bombings, and later testified at his trial. As a result of his experiences in Pakistan, he has lectured for and consulted with various agencies within the U.S. intelligence community. He taught conspiracy investigations, drug smuggling, informant management, and many other courses as a course developer/instructor at the DEA's Office of Training located at the FBI Academy in Quantico, Virginia. He spent a year as a member of one of DEA's international training teams, visiting many foreign countries providing drug enforcement training to foreign law enforcement officials. He is the author of several articles on drug enforcement topics for professional publications including the *FBI Law Enforcement Bulletin*, and *The Police Chief*. Lee also served as a counselor for the 160th session of the FBI National Academy in 1990. Prior to working for the DEA, he was a police officer for the cities of Salinas and Pasadena, California. He has a combination of over 30 years of active duty and U.S. Army Reserve service, and is a Chief Warrant Officer 5/Special Agent with the U.S. Army Criminal Investigation Command, better known as CID. As an army reservist, Mr. Lee is an associate instructor with the U.S. Army Military Police School as a subject matter expert in terrorism and counter-drug operations. Lee holds a master of public administration in justice administration degree from Golden Gate University, San Francisco, and a bachelor of science in sociology with a minor in vocational education from the University of Maryland. While attending graduate school, he taught a criminal investigation course for Monterey Peninsula College, Monterey, California.

Acknowledgments

I readily acknowledge that much of the information in this text stems from my training and experiences as a supervisory special agent with the world's premier drug law enforcement agency, the Drug Enforcement Administration. Thanks are also in order to the Military Police Corps and the U.S. Army Criminal Investigation Command (CID). I investigated my first drug case in 1973 as an active duty military police investigator. As an army reservist, I am proud to have been associated with this outstanding organization for over 30 years and am grateful for the opportunity to be an associate instructor for the U.S. Army Military Police School.

Contents

Section II

Section I

The Fundamentals

Introduction to Drug Law Enforcement

1

What distinguishes a drug law enforcement operation from traditional criminal investigations is that a drug case deals with crime *as it occurs*. In almost every occasion, before a formal drug investigation is launched, a suspect has already been identified, usually through an informant. The drug agent's challenge is to corroborate the informant's information, build a prosecutable case against the suspect, identify and arrest all the other members of the drug trafficking organization, and seize as much drug evidence and drug-related financial assets as possible.

Drug agents are first and foremost *criminal investigators*. Not only do they need to have the attributes of tenacious detectives, but they must also possess an abundance of specialized knowledge along with good communication and interpersonal relation skills. Having a good understanding of geography, different cultures, investments, banking, psychology, and in some cases foreign relations is also valuable. All this knowledge will be put to use during a drug agent's career conducting complex drug investigations.

International in Scope

Because most drugs abused in the United States come from outside its borders, drug investigations automatically become international in scope. Domestic drug operations are typically only a part of a much larger international conspiracy where the conspirators have agreed to violate the drug laws of the United States. It is the drug agent's mission to identify all the members of the conspiracy, confiscate their drugs, and seize the assets of the conspirators that were gained during their criminal enterprise. The international aspect of the crime distinguishes drug cases from many other criminal investigations.

Interpersonal Relationships

Almost all drug investigations are self-initiated. Citizens do not routinely call their local police department to report international drug conspiracies. Drug agents must rely almost exclusively on sources of information, or confidential informants, who are usually actively involved in the drug trade, in order to identify and build criminal cases against those persons engaged in the smuggling and distribution of illegal drugs. Because these persons are most likely criminals themselves, they must be handled differently than other witnesses criminal investigators encounter.

Finance and Banking

Drug agents are authorized to identify, locate, and seize drug dealers' financial assets in order to take the profit out of the crime. Federal and state asset forfeiture laws allow some of these ill-gotten gains to be used by law enforcement to supplement the cost of conducting drug investigations. Throughout their careers, drug agents will often seize assets valued many times their salaries, making their employment virtually cost free.

Psychology

Using a drug agent in an undercover role is a common investigative technique in drug cases. The agent must convince the criminal that he is dealing with another criminal involved in some aspect of the drug business. The specific role the undercover agent takes, and how convincing he or she is, will have a profound impact on the overall success of the investigation. Although it is the most effective technique there is in drug law enforcement, more drug agents are killed or injured while working undercover assignments than in any other enforcement activity. Many agents have been injured when the drug trafficker attempts to steal the money they were going to use to purchase the drugs. Good training and tactics help counter this potential danger.

Communication Skills

Modern drug agents are expected to have an extensive knowledge of drug identification, the physical and psychological effects on the user, as well as how to conduct effective drug education and demand reduction programs. The most frequently asked question of a drug agent is, "Are we winning the war on drugs?"

Foreign Relations

The U.S. Drug Enforcement Administration (DEA) maintains more than 78 offices in 56 foreign countries to facilitate international drug conspiracy investigations impacting the United States. These *country attachés*, as the agents-in-charge are known, and their fellow special agents establish and maintain relationships with their foreign counterparts, advise the ambassador on drug-related issues, and train and mentor their foreign counterparts. They are an important part of U.S. foreign relations in the field of global drug law enforcement.

Other Aspects

Drug agents must have a thorough understanding of the drug laws he or she has a duty to enforce, and how to effectively apply them. They rely heavily on the use of informants, surveillance, and historical intelligence to carve out an investigative product that will result in the convictions of those involved in the illegal drug trade. Unless the twenty-first century drug agent possesses a wide range of expertise in the fundamentals of drug enforcement, he or she cannot thoroughly debrief informants and suspects in order to gather the intelligence data necessary to attack organized drug criminal groups.

Summary

Successful drug agents are criminal investigators who possess the requisite specialized knowledge of the drug trade. He or she must have a good understanding of where illegal drugs originate, as well as how they are manufactured, smuggled, sold, and used. Furthermore, they need a working knowledge of how illicit drug profits are returned to these source countries, and how the money is laundered to appear to come from legitimate sources.

Drug agents are expected to have the answers to questions concerning drug abuse, symptoms users display, how drugs in the workplace affect productivity, drug trafficking trends, harsh mandatory minimum sentences, racial profiling, and the inevitable questions on drug legalization and if the war on drugs can be won.

Source Countries

2

For many reasons it is important for drug agents to know the countries where drugs are clandestinely manufactured, grown, and transited through. Agents will lose their credibility with drug informants, drug traffickers, and the public alike if they do not possess at least basic information about source countries and drug trafficking trends.

Drug informants will dismiss the agent as being too naive or inexperienced to act upon the information they have, especially since their lives may be on the line. Drug agents involved in undercover operations enhance their likelihood of success if they can express some knowledge about drug trafficking trends. Undercover agents who display ignorance will appear to the trafficker to either be a fool or a police officer since it is obvious he or she has never been involved in the drug business. The public expects drug enforcement professionals to have the answers to questions about the drug problem in general, and where drugs come from specifically.

Colombia

As the oldest democracy in South America, Colombia has many entrepreneurs with much experience in capitalism and the free enterprise system. Its vast, remote, sparsely populated fertile valleys, coupled with its longtime political struggles, make conditions ideal for the cultivation of marijuana, coca leaves, and opium poppies (Figure 2.1). Colombia's clandestine laboratories manufacture more cocaine than any other country. Members of the Revolutionary Armed Forces of Colombia (FARC) protect these laboratories in return for fees generating millions of dollars of income each year to spread their communist mantra (see Chapter 20 for details). Colombia is currently the third largest coca leaf producer in the world, only behind Peru and Bolivia.

Figure 2.1 Colombian opium poppy field. (Courtesy of the U.S. Drug Enforcement Administration.) (See color insert following page 36.)

Colombia has the distinction of being a truly poly-drug source country as it supplies the drugs most in demand: cocaine, marijuana, and heroin. Using well-established cocaine smuggling routes, Colombia now supplies more heroin to North America than any other source country, and its market share in Europe has steadily increased as well.

Where there is no demand, Colombians create it. When demand for cocaine began to wane in North America in the early 1990s, Colombians began introducing the drug in Europe. Prior to that time, cocaine was virtually never seen there. Now seizures of the drug are measured in tons. Colombians have aggressively expanded their cocaine and heroin distribution networks in Western Europe. In every year for the last decade it has vastly increased the flow of cocaine. Colombians have exploited what they perceive as weaknesses in European defenses against smuggling, and have used Portugal and Spain as their primary, but not exclusive, conduit for much of the cocaine entering Europe.

Colombian traffickers at one time relied heavily on nearby Peru and Bolivia to supply the raw material necessary for the production of cocaine, the coca leaf, to their laboratories in Colombia. But due to a variety of reasons, including stepped up eradication efforts and the desire to not have to rely on others for their essential ingredient, Colombians took it upon themselves to grow their own coca bushes in order to have an uninterrupted steady supply. Colombia now supplies about 70% of its own coca leaves for manufacturing cocaine. High-level corruption, coupled with Colombia's lack of political will and struggling with a decades-old civil war, has made this country an ideal haven for *drug cartels.*

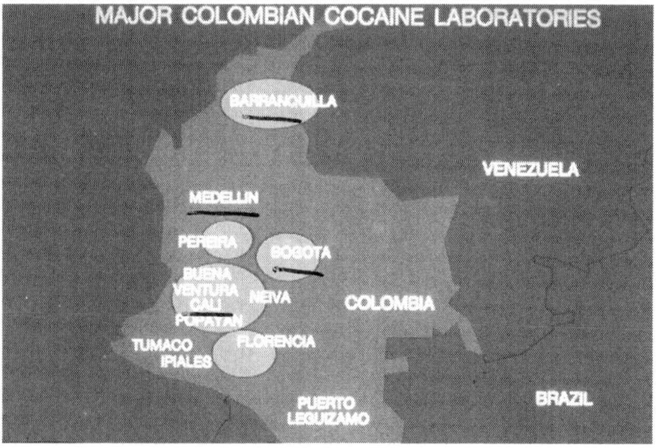

Figure 2.2 Major Colombian cocaine laboratories. (Courtesy of the U.S. Drug Enforcement Administration.)

As an example of how entrenched Colombian traffickers are in cocaine production, in 1997, authorities discovered a laboratory capable of producing 300 tons of cocaine a year. That is about half the amount of cocaine smuggled into the United States yearly. It was equipped with its own landing strip and housing for scores of workers. Despite the dismantlement of this huge laboratory, the wholesale price of cocaine in the United States did not change (Figure 2.2).

Chronic political unrest in Colombia has created an alliance between indigenous terrorists such as the FARC and the cocaine traffickers. The revolutionaries provide protection for the cocaine loads and in turn get necessary funding to continue their left-wing political agenda.

Bolivia and Peru

High in the Andes Mountains, which stretch through Peru and Bolivia, grows the coca bush. For centuries it has provided mild euphoria for peasants who chewed it to ward off the effects of working in high altitudes. Peru is the world's largest source of coca, with Bolivia a close second. These two countries sell their product almost exclusively to the cocaine laboratory operators in Colombia. There is some manufacturing of cocaine in both Bolivia and Peru; however, it is mostly for domestic consumption and is minute compared to the Colombian output. The much less sophisticated Peruvians and Bolivians are attempting to take a larger portion of the market share away from the Colombians, but they have had only limited success. Political corruption throughout the governments of Peru and Bolivia has hampered enforcement efforts in these two countries (Figure 2.3 to Figure 2.5).

Figure 2.3 Coca bush fields in Peru. (Courtesy of the U.S. Drug Enforcement Administration.) (See color insert following page 36.)

Figure 2.4 Peruvian coca farmer harvesting leaves. (Courtesy of the U.S. Drug Enforcement Administration.)

Mexico

Long a source country for marijuana, methamphetamine, and heroin, Mexico also has the distinction of being the main conduit for South American drugs, particularly cocaine, entering the United States.

Only Brazil and Argentina are larger than Mexico. Its area covers 761,602 square miles, or a quarter of that of the United States. Besides the United States, only Guatemala and Belize border Mexico, and both are also transit countries for drugs from South America. With almost 6000 miles

Figure 2.5 Coca leaves for sale in La Paz, Bolivia. (Courtesy of the U.S. Drug Enforcement Administration.)

of coastlines and about 2500 miles of borders, 2000 of which are with the United States, it is easy to see why Mexico is the main conduit of drugs to North America. An estimated 95% of the United States' southern border has neither fences nor barricades that can easily be crossed by unsophisticated smugglers.

At the end of the twentieth century, an estimated 6.8 tons of heroin and 21,700 tons of marijuana were produced annually in Mexico; and an estimated two thirds of all cocaine entering the United States is funneled through this country, almost always by land. Numerous sophisticated tunnels have been discovered under the U.S.–Mexican border, which have been used in the highly successful smuggling of billions of dollars worth of drugs into the United States.

Almost all the heroin produced in Mexico is exported to the United States; however, it falls well behind the amount produced and smuggled into the country from Colombia. Mexico is the exclusive producer of low priced but high potency *black tar heroin* that gets its name from resembling a glob of tar. Any heroin of this variety seized by law enforcement will be found to have originated from Mexico.

Upwards of 70% of all marijuana consumed in the United States comes from Mexico. The western Mexican states of Chihuahua, Sonora, Sinaloa, Guerrero, Zacatecas, Durango, Nayarit, Oaxaca, Michoacan, San Luis Potosi, and Jalisco are the primary growing areas of marijuana. Marijuana, sometimes spelled marihuana, is grown throughout the year; however, it is primarily planted in late spring and harvested in the fall. Little effort is made by Mexican traffickers to conceal the cultivation, relying instead on remoteness and payoffs to government officials to stay in business (Figure 2.6).

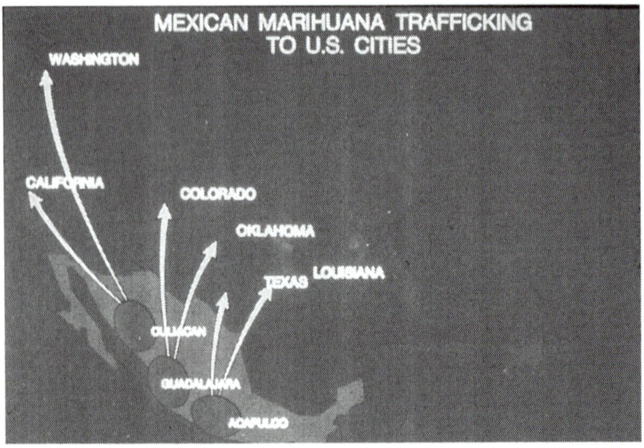

Figure 2.6 Mexican marihuana trafficking to the United States. (Courtesy of the U.S. Drug Enforcement Administration.)

The United States has strict controls on the sale of precursor chemicals necessary in the manufacture of the stimulant drug, methamphetamine. Within the past 15 years, Mexican traffickers have seized the opportunity to take away business from domestic clandestine laboratory operators in the United States. Using chemicals obtained within its own borders and elsewhere, Mexico now manufactures the drug for export mainly to the southwestern United States, where it is redistributed throughout the country. Mexican clandestine laboratory operators have been known to travel as far as the Middle East to secure precursor chemicals. Many of these chemical distributors have connections to international terrorist organizations.

Mexican trafficking organizations at one time only facilitated Colombians in moving drugs into the United States along its southern border; however, within the last decade they have demanded product instead of money for their services. The result has been the establishment of Mexican cocaine trafficking organizations that now actively compete with Colombians in the sale of cocaine.

Endemic corruption has plagued the Mexican government, preventing it from being more effective against its drug traffickers. The number and size of trafficking organizations within Mexico has steadily grown in the past two decades. With U.S. Customs only being able to inspect about 2% of all commercial shipments coming into the United States from Mexico and elsewhere, it is easy to see why this is a major smuggling route for drug traffickers.

The Golden Triangle

The area where Thailand, Burma, and Laos join constitutes the area known as the *Golden Triangle*. It produces the largest amount and highest quality opium poppy products second only to Afghanistan. This area of Southeast Asia is ideally suited geographically, topologically, and culturally for the production of heroin.

The producers of the opium are so entrenched and powerful that they are able to employ private armies to provide protection for their poppy fields and heroin laboratories. They market their product using names such as the *Lucky, Tiger,* and *Double-Uoglobe* brands, complete with distinctive colorful logos.

Although marijuana flourishes in the surrounding area, high quality *Thai* marijuana does not necessarily come from Thailand. *Thai* or *thai sticks*, as it is sometimes called, has become synonymous with marijuana originating from Southeast Asia but may have very well been grown in Cambodia or Vietnam.

Thai nationals are the predominate traffickers of heroin and marijuana originating from the Golden Triangle. They have formed an alliance with Nigerian smugglers who transport the drug to many parts of the world, predominately Western Europe and the United States.

For many years, Thailand and South Korea have been the source countries for methamphetamine tablets. These tablets are mostly manufactured for domestic consumption as well as for abusers in Japan, but their presence in the United States has increased substantially since 2000.

The Golden Crescent

The southwest Asian nations of Afghanistan, Iran, and Pakistan are collectively known as the *Golden Crescent*. The crescent comes from the crescent symbol of the Islamic faith that dominates the area.

Afghanistan is the world's largest producer of opium poppies. For the last 20 years, Afghanistan has been engaged in warfare and has not had a stable government, despite the overthrow of the Taliban. Its people have survived by their wits and tenaciousness. Unlike the rich, fertile valleys of the Golden Triangle, the Golden Crescent is mostly mountainous, dry, and remote. Farmers grow opium for economic and practical reasons. They are paid more for opium than any other cash crop, and claim heroin laboratory operators threaten them if they do not continue to produce. The Taliban routinely collected *taxes* on the production and transportation of poppy. Osama bin Ladin's al-Qaida terrorist network received vast revenues to finance their operations through the production of poppy and heroin in Afghanistan (Figure 2.7).

Most of the opium produced in Afghanistan is smuggled into Turkey where long-standing laboratories use it to produce refined heroin. Heroin laboratories also exist along the Afghanistan-Pakistan border, which produce a smoking variety of heroin that is used for domestic consumption. These same laboratories have the capacity to produce heroin that can range from

Figure 2.7 Opium poppy field in Afghanistan. (See color insert following page 36.)

low potency brown to high potency white for export to Europe, Australia, and the United States. Early indicators suggest that the war on terrorism, which began in late 2001, has had little effect on the total production of opium and heroin in Afghanistan.

Only between 5 and 20% of all heroin found in the United States comes from the Golden Crescent. Almost without exception, these traffickers are Pakistanis, Afghans, or Iranians with long-standing ties with relatives or friends already living in the United States. The majority of all heroin found in Europe comes from this part of the world and is predominately trafficked by Turks.

Afghanistan and Pakistan also produce the world's largest amount of hashish. These two countries produce around 600 tons of the drug annually; much of which is used for domestic consumption. However, multi-ton shipments of hashish are frequently smuggled out of Pakistan to Western markets, including Europe, Australia, the United States, and Canada.

Pakistan has four provinces, one being the Northwest Frontier, sometimes referred to the Federally Administered Tribal Areas (FATA). It is a semi-autonomous area where the government of Pakistan has limited authority. The FATA is the home of many of the country's heroin laboratories as well as its most prolific drug traffickers. Some live in lavish surroundings and employ thousands of armed guards that protect them from the government.

Corrupt public officials are routinely paid a stipend to keep major traffickers informed about the government's activities directed toward them. Some tribal leader-traffickers have entered politics and have become members of Pakistan's national assembly. Corruption is endemic in Pakistan, and it will continue to be a large contributing factor in the country's inability to stymie the production and distribution of controlled substances.

Western Europe

The Netherlands' port of Amsterdam has long been a transiting point for hashish and heroin entering Europe and the United States. Liberal drug laws and lack of enforcement have made this country a haven for drug users and the manufacturing of hallucinogens, especially MDMA, better known as Ecstasy. An estimated 2,000,000 tablets of Ecstasy are manufactured in The Netherlands and Belgium each week and are distributed throughout Europe and the United States.

Canada

A hybrid marijuana known as *B.C. Bud* is grown in British Columbia and exported to the United States and throughout Canada. The *tetrahydrocannabinol* (THC) content of the plant meets or exceeds any other variety of marijuana in the world and is often bartered for cocaine from Mexican traffickers operating in the United States for resale in Canada.

United States

The United States has long been a source country for marijuana to Australia, Canada, and parts of Europe. Illicit marijuana growers in California produce most of this export quality crop. Methamphetamine laboratories located in California produce the drug for redistribution throughout the country. The vast majority of these labs are owned and operated by illegal Mexican aliens. Laboratories that manufacture MDMA, cocaine, and heroin are sometimes found in the United States, but they are an anomaly. *Crack cocaine* is almost exclusively a product of the United States made for domestic consumption. However, the essential ingredient is cocaine, which is smuggled from Colombia. Lysergic acid diethylamide (LSD) is primarily manufactured in the San Francisco bay area of California for domestic consumption, but can also be found in some European cities from domestic sources.

Summary

Most drugs sold in the United States originate in foreign countries, making the investigation of their trafficking international in scope. Even domestic illegal drugs such as methamphetamine and crack cocaine, which have been manufactured in the United States, have their origins in other countries. As an example, methamphetamine traffickers in the United States are predominately Mexican nationals who use domestic and foreign chemicals frequently smuggled by Middle Easterners, many of which are connected with terrorist organizations. The essential ingredient of *crack* is cocaine that originates in South America and is controlled predominately by Colombian and Mexican traffickers.

Marijuana and LSD sold in the United States are frequently domestic products; however, LSD can also originate from Europe, and marijuana can be grown just about anywhere in the world. Drug agents need to know where specific drugs originate in order to be cognizant of which organized drug trafficking organizations may be controlling the distribution network.

Drug Identification and User Recognition

3

Although there are many substances that are either abused or have the potential for abuse, this chapter will primarily focus on the drugs of abuse law enforcement officers will most frequently encounter during their careers. What these drugs have in common is that they affect the user's *central nervous system* (CNS), produce a euphoric state, and in some cases cause physical and or psychological dependency.

Physical dependence is the reliance on a particular substance in order to function normally, and its continued use is required to prevent *withdrawal symptoms.* Psychological dependence is a compulsion to use a particular substance for its pleasurable effects. Many drugs, such as heroin, inflict both physical and psychological dependency on the user. With physical dependence comes tolerance, requiring the user to take increasing amounts of the drug in order to produce the same euphoric effect as the original dose. Many hard-core heroin addicts need to take at least a dose equal to the last taken in order to *maintain*, or prevent horrific withdrawal symptoms.

Drug Scheduling

Most drugs of abuse can be categorized as being depressants, stimulants, hallucinogens, or inhalants. There are drugs that have medical purposes, but have a high risk of abuse due to their euphoric effects. The *Controlled Substance Act* (CSA) of 1973, the same act that created the U.S. Drug Enforcement Administration (DEA), lists *schedules* of drugs. To simplify a complex process, drugs are categorized from schedule I to V. For a complete listing of controlled substances, see Table A.1 (schedules) and Table A.2 (drugs listed alphabetically) in Appendix A.

Schedule I drugs are those that have a high probability of abuse and have no currently acceptable medicinal use in treatment in the United States. Also, there is a lack of accepted safety for use of the drug or other substance under medical supervision. Included in schedule I are such substances as heroin, marijuana, methaqualone, and LSD.

Schedule II drugs also have a high potential for abuse; however, they have a currently accepted medical use in treatment in the United States or a currently accepted medical use with severe restrictions. Abuse of any of these drugs may lead to severe psychological or physical dependence. Schedule II substances include morphine, phencyclidene (PCP), cocaine, methadone, and methamphetamine.

Schedule III drugs have a potential for abuse less than the drugs in schedules I and II. These drugs have a currently accepted medical use in treatment in the United States. Abuse of any of these drugs may lead to moderate or low physical dependence or high psychological dependence. Anabolic steroids, codeine and hydrocodone with aspirin or Tylenol, and some barbiturates are schedule III substances.

Schedule IV drugs have a low potential for abuse relative to the drugs in schedule III. These drugs have a currently accepted medical use in treatment in the United States. Abuse of any of these drugs may lead to limited physical dependence or psychological dependence relative to the drugs in schedule III. Included in schedule IV are Darvon, Talwin, Equanil, Valium, and Xanax.

Schedule V drugs have a low potential for abuse relative to the drugs in schedule IV. These drugs may lead to limited physical dependence or psychological dependence relative to the drugs in schedule IV. Cough medicine with codeine is an example of a schedule V drug.

The Comprehensive Crime Control Act of 1984 amended the CSA. This act included a provision that allows the administrator of the DEA to place a substance, on a temporary basis, into a schedule when necessary to avoid an imminent hazard to the public safety.

This emergency scheduling authority permits the scheduling of a substance that is not currently controlled, is being abused, and is a risk to the public health to become controlled while the formal rule-making procedures described in the CSA are being conducted. This emergency scheduling applies only to substances with no accepted medical use. A temporary scheduling order may be issued for one year with a possible extension of up to 6 months if formal scheduling procedures have been initiated. The proposal and order are published in the Federal Register, as are the proposals and orders for formal scheduling. The general rule of thumb is the trafficking of lower schedule drugs produce higher prison sentences. See Table A.1 and Table A.2 in Appendix A, which list commonly abused drugs and their schedules.

Narcotic Depressants

The pharmacological definition of a narcotic is any natural, synthetic, or semi-synthetic substance that acts on the central nervous system (CNS) in a manner similar to morphine. Morphine is the active ingredient of the opium poppy (*Papaver somniferum L.*), and is the most effective pain reliever there is. It is also effective in the treatment of diarrhea and coughs. The plant can be found with both white and red leaves that surround the poppy plant bulb, which is distinguishable from other plants by its *crown*. The leaves naturally fall off the bulb at maturity (Figure 3.1 and Figure 3.2).

Heroin and Opiates

Many people refer to all drugs of abuse as *narcotics*. However, only heroin and opiates are true narcotics, and both have a high potential for abuse. Opiates include opium, morphine, heroin, and codeine. The poppy *Papaver somniferum L*, is the main source of nonsynthetic narcotics. It is an essential element of heroin.

Heroin's appearance ranges in color from a pure white powder with the consistency of flour, to various tan and brown shades, up to tar-like black. Southwest Asian heroin has the consistency and color of chocolate

Figure 3.1 *Papaver somniferum L.*, also known as the opium poppy. (Courtesy of the U.S. Drug Enforcement Administration.) (See color insert following page 36.)

Figure 3.2 Opium poppy bulb and crown. (Courtesy of the U.S. Drug Enforcement Administration.) (See color insert following page 36.)

cocoa due to its processing, but can also be white, and is mostly reserved for export to the United States (Figure 3.3). Southeast Asian heroin has the consistency and look of flour and is almost always white. It is often sold at wholesale in *units* that are 700 grams. Mexican heroin, popular mostly in the southwestern United States, is called *black tar* based on its black, gummy appearance. Colombian heroin is white with purity levels in the 90th percentile (Figure 3.4).

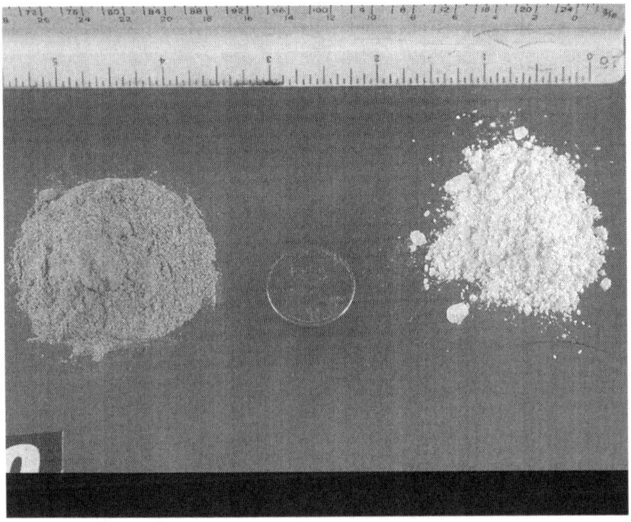

Figure 3.3 Varieties of Asian heroin. (Courtesy of the U.S. Drug Enforcement Administration.) (See color insert following page 36.)

Figure 3.4 Mexican black tar heroin. (Courtesy of the U.S. Drug Enforcement Administration.)

History of Heroin in the United States

Heroin accounts for 90% of the opiate abuse in the United States. The drug was first synthesized from morphine in 1874 and was thought to be free of side effects. The Bayer Chemical Company of Germany first introduced *Heroin* as a new headache and general pain remedy in the United States in 1898 (Figure 3.5 and Figure 3.6). It was widely used and abused due to its highly addictive properties, which lead to the enactment of the Harrison Narcotic Act of 1914 controlling it for the first time. Heroin is listed under schedule I of the CSA.

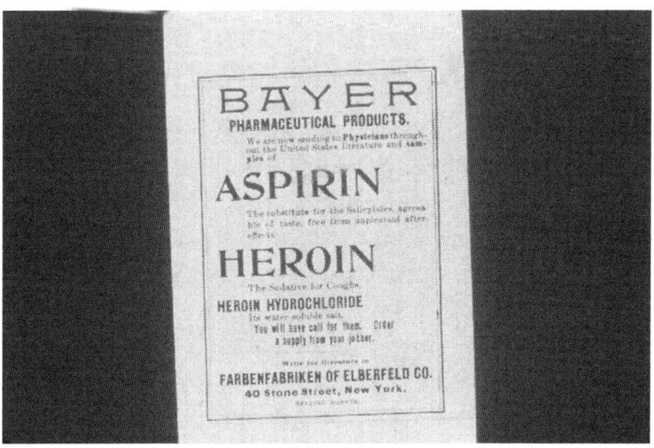

Figure 3.5 Bayer Pharmaceutical advertisement for heroin. (Courtesy of the U.S. Drug Enforcement Administration.)

Figure 3.6 Opium-based syrups were popular for treating children.

The poppy seems to grow best at higher altitudes and in mild climates and has been traditionally planted and harvested for the illicit market in Southeast and Southwest Asia where it has been abused for centuries (Figure 3.7). Southeast Asian countries that cultivate poppy include the Golden Triangle region of Burma, Laos, and Thailand. Southwest Asian poppy production is found in the Golden Crescent areas of Turkey, Lebanon, and Pakistan but largely in Afghanistan where it has been grown and smoked since as early as 300 B.C. Heroin's popularity in the United States coupled with high profit margins, has given rise to a significant production in South and Central America, notably Mexico, Guatemala, and most recently Colombia where sophisticated drug traffickers use well-established, traditional cocaine smuggling routes to supply approximately 80% of the heroin used in the United States. Colombian heroin is considered the world's finest.

Heroin Production

The heroin extraction process begins with the gathering of raw opium gum, as it is called, by making either horizontal or vertical incisions in the opium bulb, and later scraping the dried gum from the plant. Southwest Asian cultivators always scrape the bulb of the opium poppy vertically from the bottom up, whereas the Southeast Asian farmer always scores the bulb horizontally. They have been doing this practice for hundreds of years (Figure 3.8 to Figure 3.10).

The opium gum is then broken down chemically, turning it into morphine that is later converted into heroin. It takes 10 kilograms (about 22 pounds) of raw opium gum to make one kilogram (2.2 pounds) of morphine that is converted one-to-one (1 kilogram of morphine = 1 kilogram of heroin) to make heroin. One acre of poppies can produce between 6 and 8 kilograms of raw opium gum (Figure 3.11).

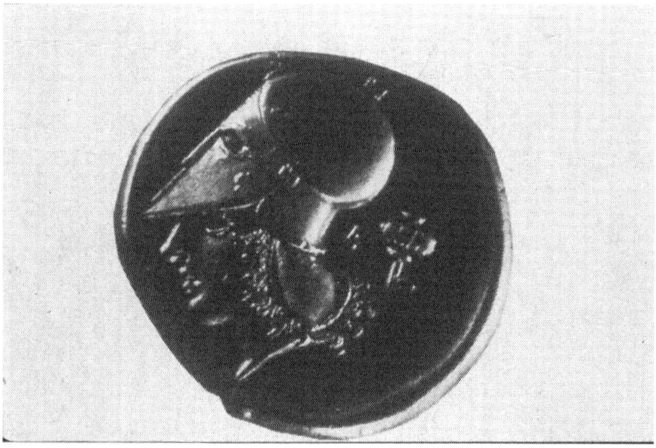

Figure 3.7 Roman coinage depicting opium poppy. (Courtesy of the U.S. Drug Enforcement Administration.)

Figure 3.8 Vertical incisions made by southwest Asian poppy cultivator. (Courtesy of the U.S. Drug Enforcement Administration.) (See color insert following page 36.)

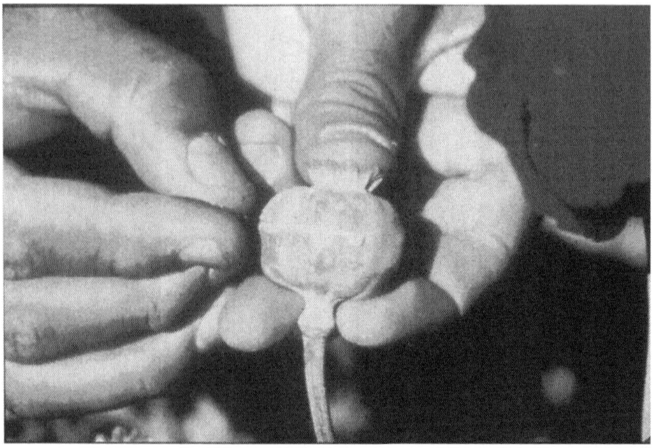

Figure 3.9 Southeast Asian poppy cultivator scoring opium poppy. (Courtesy of the U.S. Drug Enforcement Administration.) (See color insert following page 36.)

Figure 3.10 Cultivator harvesting raw opium from scored opium poppy. (Courtesy of the U.S. Drug Enforcement Administration.)

Despite heroin being illegal globally, Southeast Asian heroin producers are proud of their product. They package their finished product inside unit-sized plastic bags that display their logos. Below are some of the most frequently encountered logos found on packages of seized heroin in Thailand and the United States (Figure 3.12 to Figure 3.17). Making brand names for finished heroin products is not unique to Southeast Asia, as evidenced by a kilogram package of Southwest Asian heroin seized by the DEA (see Figure 3.18).

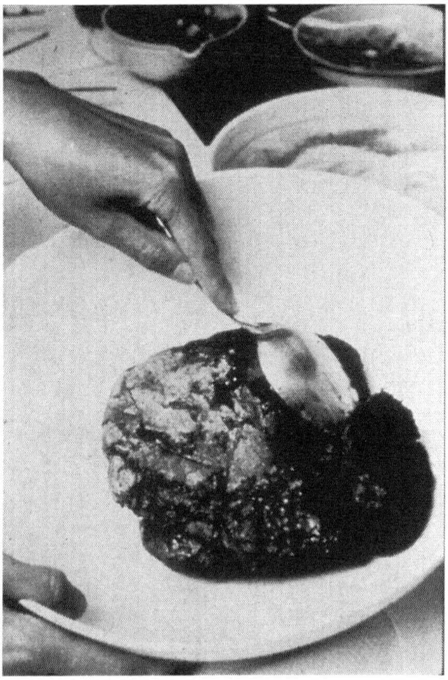

Figure 3.11 Approximately 1 kilogram (2.2 pounds) of raw opium gum. (Courtesy of the U.S. Drug Enforcement Administration.)

Figure 3.12 Double Uoglobe brand of heroin. (Courtesy of the U.S. Drug Enforcement Administration.)

Figure 3.13 Super Number One brand of heroin. (Courtesy of the U.S. Drug Enforcement Administration.)

Figure 3.14 Good Luck To You brand of heroin. (Courtesy of the U.S. Drug Enforcement Administration.)

Figure 3.15 Yong Yee brand of heroin. (Courtesy of the U.S. Drug Enforcement Administration.)

Figure 3.16 Tiger and Globe brand of heroin. (Courtesy of the U.S. Drug Enforcement Administration.)

Figure 3.17 Dragon brand of heroin. (Courtesy of the U.S. Drug Enforcement Administration.)

Figure 3.18 An example of a Southwest Asian heroin logo. (Courtesy of the U.S. Drug Enforcement Administration.)

How Heroin Is Used

Although it can be snorted or smoked, in the United States the most popular method of use is through injection. Heroin injection paraphernalia includes a bent spoon or bottle cap and a hypodermic needle often attached to an eyedropper in lieu of hard to obtain hypodermic syringes, using the bulb to push the drug into the vein. Other items include a razor blade to turn the often granular substance into a fine powder, matches to liquefy the heroin once it is mixed with water, a cotton ball to filter out the drug's impurities, and either a belt or rubber tubing to use as a tourniquet to expose the vein. Heroin addicts usually have their *works* as they are called, nearby for ready access when withdrawal symptoms set in. Many heroin addicts say the drug produces the best feeling they have ever experienced and have described it as better than sexual intercourse (Figure 3.19).

Physical Effects of Heroin

Upon injecting the heroin, the user is immediately relaxed and soon experiences a euphoric state, which abusers describe as they best feeling they have ever experienced, which is one explanation for the high rate of abuse among users. This feeling becomes so psychologically dominant that all other priorities in their lives, including food, clothing, shelter, family, work, religion,

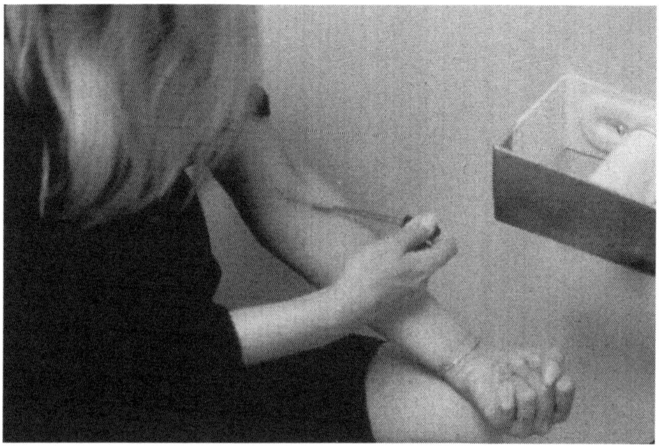

Figure 3.19 Heroin addict *shooting* heroin into her vein. (Courtesy of the U.S. Drug Enforcement Administration.)

and sex, become secondary. The powerful depressant immediately induces an overwhelming urge to sleep. Many describe the intense euphoric state as a *rush* as it travels quickly through the vein when the drug enters. Some will withdraw the blood from the vein to inject it again, and become fixated on the needle, hoping to duplicate the rush feeling.

The usual vein of choice is located where the forearm and upper arm meet on the nondominant side of the user, however any vein that can take a needle will do. After continued use, the vein will collapse necessitating the user to go to others. Since collapsed and abused veins will show *tracks*, or highly visible markings running alongside the vein, addicts will disguise their drug habit by wearing long-sleeved shirts and frequently alternating veins. Addicts have been known to inject heroin between their toes, in the cardiac veins of their neck, or even their penis or vagina.

Heroin addicts must be careful not to use too much heroin since their body may become so relaxed it shuts off the autonomic nervous system, which regulates breathing and heart rate, causing instantaneous death. Overdose victims will always have signs of pulmonary edema where body fluids will foam and be expelled through the nose and mouth (Figure 3.20). Continued use will cause infections of the lining of the heart and its valves. Other infections, including skin abscesses, AIDS, and hepatitis can arise from using nonsterile needles that are often shared among users. Many addicts will soon become nauseated and may vomit shortly after taking the drug. The relaxed state induces an intense desire to sleep, and fighting this urge is referred to as being *on the nod* (Figure 3.21). The drug almost immediately produces extremely constricted pupils, which is indicative of many depressants.

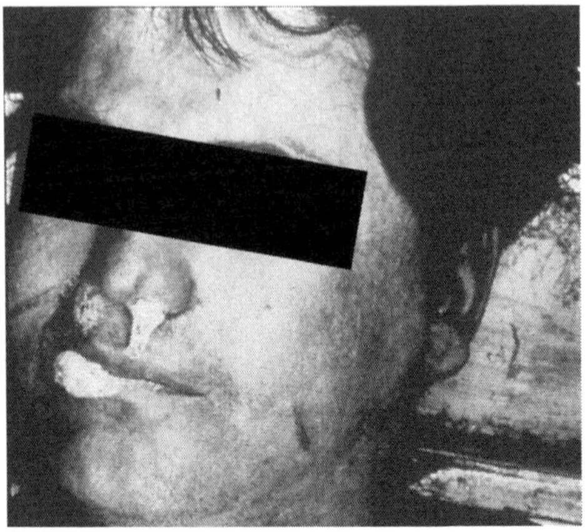

Figure 3.20 Pulmonary edema in dead heroin addict.)

Heroin Withdrawal Symptoms

After continued use, heroin users lose their ability to readily achieve a euphoric state and are forced to concentrate instead on avoiding horrific withdrawal symptoms.

Stage one — Within 8 to 12 hours after withdrawal, the addict's eyes become watery, their nose begins to run, and they have fits of yawning, perspire at any temperature, and exhibit nervousness.

Stage two — From 12 to 36 hours after withdrawal, stage one symptoms are intensified, plus the user becomes increasingly irritable, has insomnia, irritability, sneezing, tremors, goose flesh, and their pupils begin to dilate.

Figure 3.21 Heroin addict *on the nod* after using the drug.

Stage three — Within 36 to 72 hours after their last heroin injection, the addict exhibits signs of weakness, aching, cramps, nausea, diarrhea, chills alternating with excessive perspiration, and involuntary muscle spasms, especially in the legs, which is sometimes called *kicking the habit.*

Without treatment, most symptoms will disappear in 7 to 10 days. No one has ever died from heroin withdrawal.

Heroin User Recognition

Heroin users are often portrayed in movies and television as being unemployable, undereducated residents of a ghetto or barrio that associate with others of the same mindset. The reality is that anyone a drug agent encounters could be a heroin addict, many of whom are professionals or others from high socio-economic neighborhoods. Addiction will most likely affect anyone who abuses heroin.

Recognizing a heroin user can be difficult if they are not under the influence of the drug at the time they are encountered by law enforcement. Many abusers make it difficult for drug agents to recognize them since some states have laws mandating jail time for abusers that would deprive them of their drug.

Smoking — Heroin is most commonly injected, but it can also be smoked and snorted. Some heroin abusers falsely believe that if they smoke the substance instead of injecting it, they cannot become addicted. Others smoke heroin because they have phobias about hypodermic needles and do not want to be burdened with the possibility of contracting communicable diseases such as AIDS or hepatitis. Many new users to heroin start this way, but later turn to hard-to-find reusable needles that are often hard to keep sterile in a nonclinical environment. Smoking heroin is accomplished by what is called *chasing the dragon*. The user takes a small piece of tin foil, often from a stick of gum wrap, and places a small amount of heroin on it. While holding the foil, the user will activate a cigarette lighter and place the flame under the foil heating up the heroin until it vaporizes. A straw is held close to the heroin as a vehicle to gather the vapors that are inhaled deeply into the lungs to receive the desired effect. Glass pipes are also used in lieu of tin foil, and they can also be used for crack cocaine and methamphetamine, which will be discussed later. When a glass pipe is used, the source of flame may come from a butane canister from a small camping stove, attached with the appropriate tip to focus the flame. The problem the addict encounters with glass pipes and butane canisters is that they create telltale evidence of drug abuse, something they almost always attempt to disguise. Drug agents and police officers who encounter someone they suspect may have been smoking heroin should look for burned tin foil, butane canisters with no accompanying stove, along with glass pipes that are used specifically to inject controlled substances.

Slurred speech — Any depressant, especially heroin, will induce slurred speech in the user, which is similar to a drunk. Speech patterns will improve as the drug wears off.

Constricted pupils — Whether smoked or injected, heroin use will cause the person's eyes to become what can be described as *pinpoint*; they are not, but they appear to be much smaller than anyone's pupils under the same lighting condition. Drug agents should compare the size of the pupils of a suspect under the influence of heroin with their partner or anyone else not under the influence of the drug. The Pasadena, CA Police Department issues a *pupilometer* that shows various diameters printed on a wallet card so the officer can articulate in a report about his or her findings when confronting the suspect. Even when one shines light into the eyes of a heroin addict, or when the light is removed, there is little, if any visible difference in the constriction of the pupil (Figure 3.22 and Figure 3.23).

Droopy eyelids — Along with the urge to sleep and slurred speech are droopy eyelids as if the user is struggling to keep his eyes open. It is often easier for the addict to tilt his head back to look at someone than to raise his eyelids to see.

Flushed face — A light skinned person will exhibit signs of flushing, or the skin around the face appearing reddish.

Slowing down of vital signs — Addicts will exhibit slowed heart rate and breathing. Taking a suspected heroin user's pulse for 6 seconds and multiplying by 10 will reveal the suspect's number of heart beats per minute, a number that should be way below the norm of between 70 and 100 beats per minute. Addicts that accidentally overdose actually have their heart stop from the effects of the narcotic.

Dry mouth — Heroin users have an intense desire for liquids. The lack thereof will almost always produce dry mouth.

Constipation — Although not apparent, users also experience constipation as opiates are often used in prescribed drugs to control diarrhea.

Craving for sweets — The constant use of heroin will produce a craving of sweets, which is often satisfied by eating many candy bars in between doses. Empty candy wrappers in the addict's possession may be an indication of heroin abuse when coupled with other signs. Although there are other explanations for these symptoms, the drug agent or street police officer must take the totality of the symptoms into account before concluding that the person probably is under the influence of heroin.

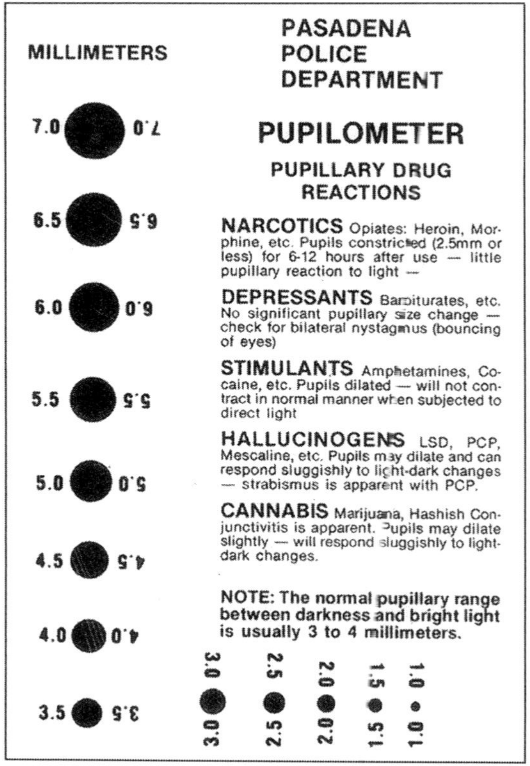

Figure 3.22 *Pupilometer* front. (Courtesy of the Pasadena Police Department.)

HEROIN, MORPHINE — *Boy, stuff, H, junk, smack.*
• Stupor, drowsiness, needle marks on body, watery eyes, loss of appetite, bloodstain on shirt sleeve, "on the nod," constricted (small) pupils — do not respond to light — inattentive, slow pulse, and respiration, crave sweets, chills.

COCAINE — *Rock, Snow, girl, coke, cola, goop.*
• Redness to nose, increased pulse, muscular twitching, convulsive movements, strong swings of mood, exhilaration, hallucinations, dilated pupils, rapid speech, weight loss, hyperactive.

CODEINE OR OPIUM ADDITIVES —
• Drunk appearance, lack of coordination, confusion, excessive itching . . . all from large doses. Small doses exhibit little effect.

MARIJUANA — *Joints, sticks, reefers, pot, weed, grass, muggles, moolers, Indian hay, locoweed, Mu, Mary Jane, griffo, mohasky, gigglesmoke, jive.*
• Sleepiness, or talkative and a hilarious mood, enlarged pupils, lack of coordination, craving for sweets, increased appetite, "high" feeling, erratic behavior, loss of memory, distortions of times and space.

LSD — *Phencyclidine, PCP, Acid, Dust, (Hallucinogens) Sherm, water.*
• Severe hallucinations, feelings of detachment, incoherent speech, cold sweaty hands and feet, vomiting, laughing, crying, exhilaration or depression, suicidal or homicidal tendencies, shivering, chills, with goose pimples, irregular breathing, (PCP-Nystagmus, odor, muscle rigidity.)

PEP PILLS — *Bennies, co-pilots, ups, footballs, hearts, speed, crystal (Amphetamines, Methamphetamine), Crank.*
• Aggressive behavior, giggling, silliness, rapid speech, confused thinking, no appetite, extreme fatigue, dry mouth, bad breath, shakiness, dilated pupils, sweating, licks lips and rubs and scratches nose excessively, chain smoking, extreme restlessness, and irritability, violence, and a feeling of persecution, abcesses.

Figure 3.23 *Pupilometer* back. (Courtesy of the Pasadena Police Department.)

Cocaine

Cocaine is a CNS stimulant extracted from the coca plant, which is grown primarily in Bolivia, Peru, and most recently in Colombia. At one time Colombia grew very little coca for its cocaine laboratories, relying instead on the raw material from neighboring Bolivia and Peru. However, in the late 1980s and early 1990s, mostly because of eradication efforts spearheaded by the United States and embraced by the governments of Bolivia and Peru, coca production in these countries plummeted. What coca that was left was being used for cocaine production laboratories in those countries in an effort to compete with Colombian traffickers. These well-established traffickers decided they could no longer rely on these countries for their essential ingredient, so instead encouraged peasant farmers in Colombia to grow the crop exclusively for them. As a result, Colombia is now one of the largest coca producing countries in the world.

Cocaine is one of the most potent naturally occurring stimulants known. Because pharmaceutical cocaine is used as an anesthetic for eye and dental surgery, but has a high potential for abuse, it is listed in schedule II of the CSA.

History of Cocaine Abuse

The first recorded use of cocaine dates back 2000 years to the Inca civilization of Peru. Nobility and priests first used cocaine to create a trancelike state for religious ceremonies. The masses soon followed, widely using cocaine to fight fatigue, as an appetite depressant, and for its euphoric effects. The experience in Bolivia parallels that of Peru (Figure 3.24).

In the sixteenth century, Spaniards discovered coca and introduced it to Europe. About 1859, Albert Neiman isolated cocaine from the coca plant, and around 1864 a popular wine and cocaine beverage called "Vin Mariani" was introduced. In 1873, Alexander Bennett discovered the anesthetic properties of cocaine. Between 1884 and 1905 cocaine became a flavoring agent for many beverages in the United States, including Coca-Cola, which coined its name after the drug (Figure 3.25).

To meet the demand for cocaine-laden products, a significant amount of cocaine was imported to the United States in 1905. In 1977, the Pure Food and Drug Act eliminated cocaine from most patent medicines and soft drinks because of its potential for abuse. In the same year, the Harrison Narcotic Act classified cocaine as a narcotic, and the drug went underground about 1914. In 1970, the CSA was enacted classifying cocaine as a schedule II controlled substance.

Harvest and Yield

The coca bush (*Erythroxylon coca*) is grown from seed and is essential to the production of cocaine (Figure 3.26). It is grown primarily in South America

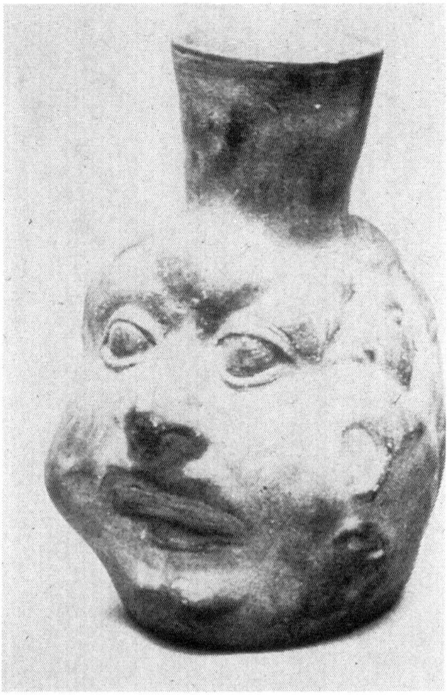

Figure 3.24 South American artifact depicting man chewing coca leaves. (Courtesy of the U.S. Drug Enforcement Administration.)

Figure 3.25 Early Coca-Cola advertisement. (Courtesy of the U.S. Drug Enforcement Administration.)

Figure 3.26 Coca bush. (Courtesy of the U.S. Drug Enforcement Administration.) (See color insert following page 36.)

in extremely remote locations along the Andes Mountains of Peru and Bolivia, but it is also planted and harvested in Colombia to insure a steady supply to cocaine processing laboratories located there. Other clandestine cocaine production occurs in Bolivia and Peru, but their numbers are miniscule compared to those found in Colombia.

The coca plant reaches maturity in about 18 months and grows between 3 and 4 feet per year. It can reach 8 feet tall; however, farmers prune it to shoulder height for easy harvesting. The plant will produce for about 50 years with three or four harvests per year. Before U.S. government initiatives took hold in the early 1990s, Peru produced between 100,000 and 125,000 metric tons of coca leaf per year, with Bolivia close behind at 60,000 to 80,000 during the same time period. It takes approximately 350 pounds of coca leaf to produce 1 kilogram (2.2 pounds) of cocaine hydrochloride.

Cocaine Extraction

After coca leaves are harvested they are soaked in a solution of chemicals. The outcome is a cocaine paste that is chemically turned into cocaine base. The base, in turn, is transformed into cocaine hydrochloride (HCl), which is the finished product sold by traffickers. It takes 240 kilograms of dried coca leaves to produce 1.9 kilograms of coca paste, and 0.96 kilograms of coca base is required to produce 1 kilogram of cocaine HCl (Figure 3.27).

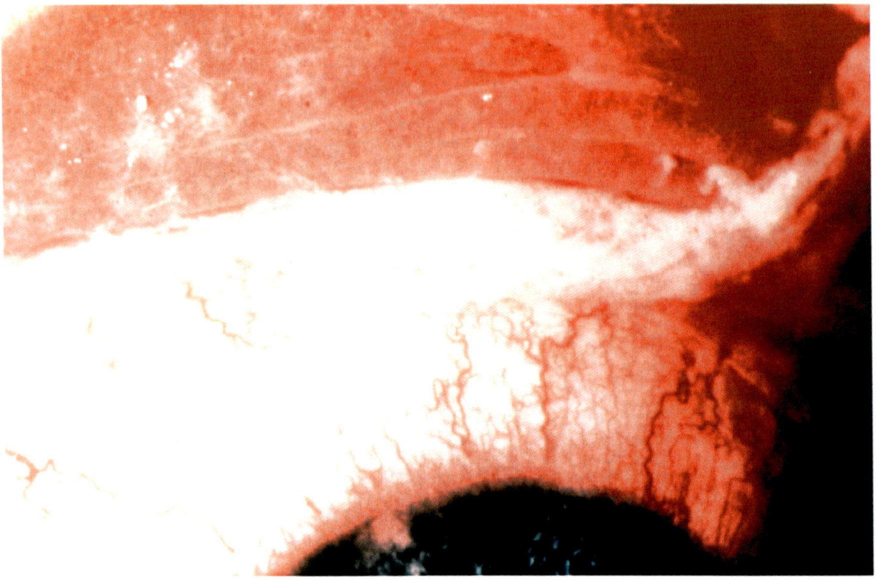

COLOR FIGURE 3.37 People under the influence of marijuana will exhibit deep reddening of their eyes under the lids. (Courtesy of the U.S. Drug Enforcement Administration.)

COLOR FIGURE 3.42 Variety of blotter acid. (Courtesy of the U.S. Drug Enforcement Administration.)

COLOR FIGURE 3.32 Marijuana bud. (Courtesy of the U.S. Drug Enforcement Administration.)

COLOR FIGURE 3.36 Variety of hashish. (Courtesy of the U.S. Drug Enforcement Administration.)

COLOR FIGURE 3.26 Coca bush. (Courtesy of the U.S. Drug Enforcement Administration.)

COLOR FIGURE 3.31 Marijuana plants. (Courtesy of the U.S. Drug Enforcement Administration.)

COLOR FIGURE 3.8 Vertical incisions made by Southwest Asian poppy cultivator. (Courtesy of the U.S. Drug Enforcement Administration.)

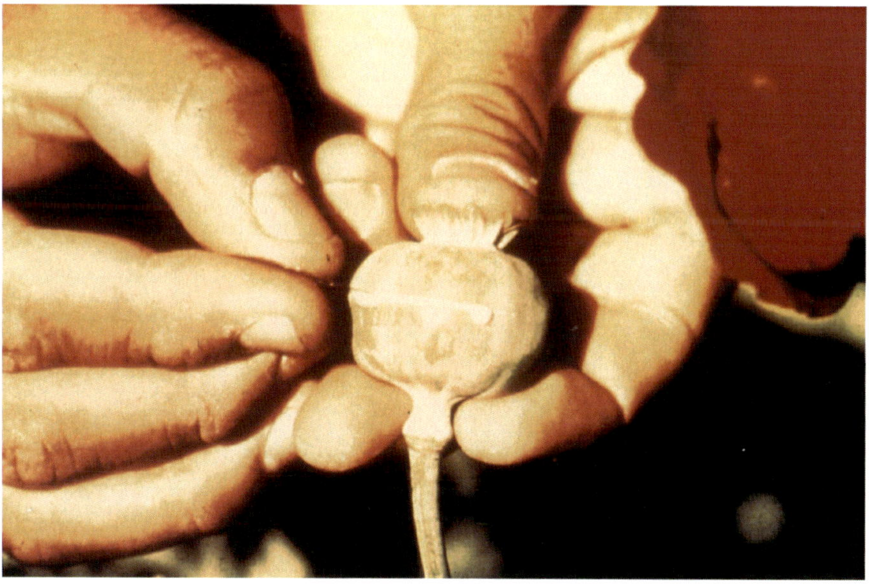

COLOR FIGURE 3.9 Southeast Asian poppy cultivator scoring opium poppy. (Courtesy of the U.S. Drug Enforcement Administration.)

COLOR FIGURE 3.2 Opium poppy bulb and crown. (Courtesy of the U.S. Drug Enforcement Administration.)

COLOR FIGURE 3.3 Varieties of Asian heroin. (Courtesy of the U.S. Drug Enforcement Administration.)

COLOR FIGURE 2.7 Opium poppy field in Afghanistan.

COLOR FIGURE 3.1 *Papaver somniferum L.*, a.k.a. the opium poppy. (Courtesy of the U.S. Drug Enforcement Administration.)

COLOR FIGURE 2.1 Colombian opium poppy field. (Courtesy of the U.S. Drug Enforcement Administration.)

COLOR FIGURE 2.3 Coca bush fields in Peru. (Courtesy of the U.S. Drug Enforcement Administration.)

Figure 3.27 Cocaine hydrochloride. (Courtesy of the U.S. Drug Enforcement Administration.)

Cocaine Abuse

The euphoria experienced by cocaine users is produced as the cocaine travels through the major emotional centers of the brain producing rapid heart rate and stomach churning. Unlike heroin, the pupils become dilated, sexual desire is enhanced, and the mood is greatly elevated. Cocaine produces minor physical addiction, but its primary addictive property is psychological.

Paranoia — Regular users of cocaine experience paranoia and often panic while under the influence of the drug. They suffer from unjustified fears that oftentimes produce feelings of aggression. They become talkative and experience loss of sleep and irritability.

Chronic cocaine users find it difficult to concentrate, suffer memory loss, and sometimes lose interest in their appearance compared to before abusing the drug. In addition, they run the risk of general health deterioration.

Psychosis — Long-term cocaine use will often lead the abuser to turn to other drugs such as alcohol, tranquilizers, marijuana, or heroin to calm them down. Abusers will sometimes mimic symptoms of manic-depressive types. They become blind to reality, can experience blackouts, conjure up thoughts of suicide, and have been known to hallucinate and experience delusions. They often exhibit compulsive behavior such as the tapping of feet and constant hair combing.

Cocaine Abuse in the Workplace

Drug agents are often sought out to educate employers on how to spot employees who may be under the influence of drugs, specifically cocaine. Many of these symptoms can be attributed to the abuse of other drugs, and no single employee is likely to experience all of these symptoms. The following are some of the indicators of an employee using cocaine and other drugs:

- Dilated pupils (in the case of cocaine abuse)
- Erratic or unusual behavior
- Failure to meet schedules and deadlines
- Missed appointments and meetings
- Increased rate of lateness
- Unexplained or lengthy disappearances
- Irritability
- Negativism
- Engages in constant arguments
- Exhibits sharp mood swings
- Decreased energy and confidence
- Less caring about personal appearance and hygiene
- Frequent sick leave
- Loss of interest in competition for promotion

Employers should be cautioned that some of these indicators could derive from other external factors such as emotional problems and personal life crises. The totality of the signs and circumstances of the employee should be taken into consideration before anyone is accused of using drugs that are affecting job performance. If an employer has a standing policy on employees submitting to random or unscheduled drug testing, they may want to exercise this option while simultaneously referring them to a company-provided counseling professional.

Cocaine's Physical Side Effects

Long-term cocaine users pay a high price. They can expect to experience a general health failure resulting from the combined effects of the following:

- Overall loss of energy
- Insomnia
- Reoccurring sore throat
- Unexplained nose bleeds
- Nasal septum damage when ingestion is through the nose and not smoked
- Frequent headaches

- Unexplained loss of sex drive
- Occasional unexplained trembling
- Seizures or convulsions that cannot otherwise be explained medically
- Nausea or vomiting
- Licking of lips or grinding of teeth
- Constant sniffling and rubbing of nose
- Unexplained loss of consciousness
- Trouble breathing or swallowing
- Heart palpitations and heart attacks

Not all cocaine abusers will experience all of these symptoms, but sadly many of them do. Some of these symptoms are life threatening, but as a general rule, people do not die from cocaine use. They do, however, develop physical problems that may later lead to death, especially when using a variety of cocaine known as *crack cocaine*, which will be discussed later in this chapter.

Pharmacological Effects and Symptoms of Cocaine Abuse

Police officers and drug agents are expected to know the telltale signs of cocaine use. The first thing they should be cognizant of is that cocaine, in any form, is a powerful natural stimulant. When cocaine is snorted or inhaled, the symptoms are similar to amphetamine. These symptoms may include increased heart rate and breathing, edginess, and the inability to sit still. When it is smoked or injected, however, these symptoms are more prevalent and often mimic those of methamphetamine ingestion, which will be described later in this chapter.

The effects of cocaine last only for a period of 15 to 20 minutes. Often users will associate with other users and ingest cocaine over several hours, or until their supply runs out.

Cocaine can be used orally, intravenously, or snorted and smoked. The coca leaf, when mixed with a small amount of ash is chewed by peasants in coca producing nations to ward off the effect of high altitudes. Hard core users sometimes inject a combination of cocaine and heroin, known as a *speedball,* which can quickly lead to death if not prepared in exacting dose quantities. The late *Saturday Night Live* comedian John Belushi died as a direct result of a speedball he had injected while in a hotel in Hollywood, CA in the 1980s.

By far, the most popular method of ingestion is through the nose by means of a straw or rolled up piece of paper, often a dollar bill, or smoked in its *crack* form (Figure 3.28). Many longtime users would never consider injecting the drug, however heroin users are most likely to ingest the drug this way.

Figure 3.28 Abuser *snorting* cocaine through a straw. (Courtesy of the U.S. Drug Enforcement Administration.)

The most common give-away to cocaine abuse is the dilated pupils of the eyes. Again, as discussed previously, a *pupilometer* should be used to compare the suspect's eyes with a person not under the influence, or if alone, by using the officer's own eyes using a mirror. The difference in the size of the pupil should be obvious and pronounced. Often cocaine users will wear sunglasses at inappropriate times to disguise their recent cocaine use.

Crack Cocaine

This variety of cocaine derives its name from the crackling sound it makes when heated to smoke. It effectively took the place of *freebasing*, where the user was forced to use volatile liquids to produce essentially the same effect.

Crack was introduced in the United States in the mid-1980s and immediately created a firestorm for drug agents because of its dramatically cheaper cost coupled with the violence it created between criminal drug organizations vying for position in its distribution, particularly in the inner cities.

The drug, which in essence is cocaine that has had its impurities removed by the introduction of a heat source, creates an intense euphoric state, only for shorter durations of 5 to 10 minutes. The intensity of the high enhances the potential for addiction among its users.

Ease of Manufacture. Crack cocaine is nothing more than cocaine base adhered to baking soda. The receipe is simply three parts of baking soda to one part of cocaine, which is mixed in a pan of heated water. The solution is stirred until the water is nearly all evaporated. This removes the impurities and cutting agents. It is then filtered and allowed to dry. The baking soda acts as a binding agent for the cocaine, thus resulting in its transformation

Figure 3.29 Street-level dose units of crack cocaine. (Courtesy of the U.S. Drug Enforcement Administration.)

into pebble-sized pieces that look very similar to macadamia nuts in size, color, and shape. The *cook* then takes a razor blade or similar instrument and cuts the pieces into pea-sized shapes for sale on the street (Figure 3.29).

How Crack Cocaine Is Ingested. Crack is designed to be smoked. The user will take the pea-sized piece and place it inside the bowl of a glass pipe. Glass is used since it is a good conductor of heat. Under the pipe a flame from a butane cigarette lighter or small butane torch is used to heat up the substance until fumes appear. The fumes are deeply inhaled through the stem of the pipe and held until the euphoric effect takes place. Methamphetamine is also often used this way (Figure 3.30).

Potential For Death. Because of the drug's intensity with the absence of cutting agents, it becomes an extremely powerful stimulant that can lead to many physical ailments that could cause death.

Suffocation — Crack cocaine can cause massive brain seizures that disrupt breathing and stop the lungs.

Cardiac arrest — Crack can disrupt the brain's electrical messages to the heart initiating irregular heartbeats that cannot be controlled.

Heart attack — Crack increases heartbeat and constricts arteries. The overworked heart cannot get the needed oxygen, potentially causing attacks.

Stroke — Crack elevates blood pressure and can burst blood vessels in the brain causing death.

Overdoses and accidents — In rare cases, users die from overdose, and they are susceptible to accidents while under the influence.

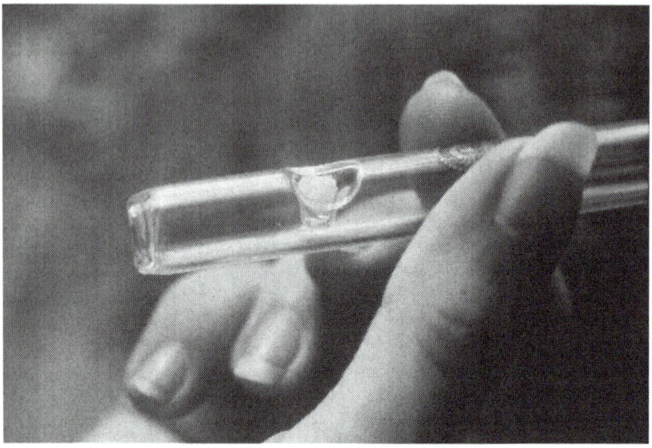

Figure 3.30 Crack cocaine in bowl of glass smoking pipe. (Courtesy of the U.S. Drug Enforcement Administration.)

Crack Babies. A side effect of crack cocaine first seen in the 1980s was the introduction of *crack babies*. About 100,000 are born in the United States annually, 50% of which end up in foster care homes. The powerful crack affects both the mother and fetus, resulting in higher rates of miscarriage and premature labor. Some fetuses suffer prenatal strokes. Crack babies are more susceptible to sudden death syndrome, and they have a higher rate of kidney and breathing difficulties. They also have visual coordination problems as infants and may later develop learning disabilities.

Marijuana

Marijuana use in the United States has remained fairly consistent since the early 1980s, and is the most commonly used illicit drug today. It remains popular with all ethnic groups and people from different socio-economic classes. The term marijuana, as commonly used, refers to the leaves and flowering tops of the cannabis-sativa plant.

Marijuana is usually smoked in the form of loosely rolled cigarettes called joints or hollowed-out commercial cigars called blunts. Joints and blunts may be laced with a number of adulterants including phencyclidine (PCP), substantially altering the effects and toxicity of these products.

Plants can grow upwards of 20 feet in height, and are usually harvested during late August through mid-October. For statistical purposes, when a law enforcement agency seizes a marijuana field, one plant should be considered to average one kilogram in weight. The number of plants seized times 2.2 pounds will reveal the approximate number of pounds of marijuana seized during a given operation. The sold product is a combination of dried leaves and flowering tops of the plant that are packaged in kilogram incre-

Figure 3.31 Marijuana plants. (Courtesy of the U.S. Drug Enforcement Administration.) (See color insert following page 36.)

ments before being smuggled into the United States (Figure 3.31 to Figure 3.33). Each leaf is thin and serrated, and always comes in clusters of odd numbers, usually seven. On average, Mexico produces approximately 5970 metric tons (13,134,000 pounds) of marijuana to the country each year, with Colombia second in production with 1650 metric tons. Tiny Jamaica has been known to produce upwards of 300 metric tons in a year.

Tetrahydrocannabinol (THC) is the active ingredient of the plant. Although marijuana grown in the United States was once considered inferior because of its low concentration of THC, advancements in plant selection and cultivation have resulted in highly potent domestic marijuana. In 1974, the average THC content of illicit marijuana was less than 1%; in early 1994, potency averaged 5%. Today's percentages of THC content between plants vary from 0.5% for wild marijuana to over 20% for the modern hybrid varieties.

Marijuana contains known toxins and cancer-causing chemicals that are stored in fat cells for as long as several months. Marijuana users experience

Figure 3.32 Marijuana bud. (Courtesy of the U.S. Drug Enforcement Administration.) (See color insert following page 36.)

Figure 3.33 Kilogram of marijuana. (Courtesy of the U.S. Drug Enforcement Administration.)

the same health problems as tobacco smokers, such as bronchitis, emphysema, and bronchial asthma. Some of the effects of marijuana use also include increased heart rate, dryness of the mouth, reddening of the eyes, impaired motor skills and concentration, and frequent hunger and an increased desire for sweets. Extended use increases health risks to the lungs and reproductive system, as well as suppression of the immune system. Occasionally, hallucinations, fantasies, and paranoia are reported.

Because of its immense popularity among people who are inclined to use drugs, law enforcement and antidrug organizations often refer to marijuana as the *gateway* drug. This refers to strong evidence suggesting that the vast majority of hard-core drug users, those who either use cocaine and heroin, almost invariably began their drug experience using marijuana.

Marijuana's popularity took hold during the volatile 1960s when young people turned to drug use in large numbers as part of the *counter-culture* preached by anti-Vietnam war advocates, rock and roll artists, and members of the *hippie generation*. It has remained popular since, and some connoisseurs of marijuana have developed a following, and thereby a market for the drug, which they are willing and able to supply. An organized criminal drug group actively involved in marijuana cultivation, transportation, and sale is the *Brotherhood of Eternal Love*, which is a loosely connected group of hippies from the 1960s who still engage in the cultivation and sale of marijuana and other drugs for profit. Marijuana is singularly the most profitable illicit drug, carrying with it less chance of a long prison sentence that may be associated with other drugs of abuse.

Marijuana smuggling organizations flourished in the 1970s and 1980s when federal drug law enforcement's efforts were concentrated on cocaine and heroin. Marijuana went by almost entirely unnoticed by federal law enforcement. As a result, many more users were introduced to this gateway drug, and its popularity grew. Many of these users went on to other drugs of abuse.

Marijuana Source Countries

Colombia, Mexico, Jamaica, Thailand, and now Canada are the main sources of foreign supply for marijuana in the United States. The United States itself produces vast amounts of marijuana to satisfy the demand. Some of the best marijuana in the world, according to users in the United States, originates in California and Canada. The California variety, known as *sin semilla*, Spanish for *without seeds*, is one of the most potent varieties found and has a THC content in the 20th percentile.

Another form of marijuana introduced in the late 1990s is a variety called *B.C. Bud*. British Columbia, Canada produces a potent variety of marijuana that is popular on the west coast of the United States. Its level of THC content is among the highest there is. It is often traded by Canadian drug traffickers in the United States for cocaine that is then sold in Canada.

Indoor Growing

Because of recent increased efforts to eradicate marijuana from clandestine fields, growers have shifted their operations indoors (Figure 3.34). Many growers will produce plants using the *hydroponics* method of cultivation. This method does not require topsoil, but relies instead on a system of moistening the plant to keep it alive and flourishing. Hydroponics has been used in the desert and during space exploration to test its dependability to produce in unnatural environments. The marijuana trafficking community, as a way to

Figure 3.34 Marijuana indoor grow operation. (Courtesy of the U.S. Drug Enforcement Administration.)

avoid detection from law enforcement aircraft, embraced this method of cultivation.

The problem marijuana cultivators face with hydroponics is the required increased amounts of energy for continued operation. Many cultivators run up tremendous electricity bills, in comparison to their neighbors, because of the amounts of electrical energy required to operate the hydroponics systems. Other growers will simply erect heat lamps over potted marijuana plants to mimic sunlight.

Further, many cultivators will rent or lease a home in a middle-class neighborhood as a cover for their operation to hide hydroponic systems for the cultivation of marijuana. Many focus their entire attention on their task and let other things go by the wayside, such as the lawn, outdoor lighting, and the like. These homes may stand out from others in the neighborhood because of their appearance. Couple this with an extraordinary energy bill, and these could be indicators of the house being used exclusively for the purpose of marijuana cultivation.

Hashish

Hashish is the THC-rich resinous secretion of the cannabis plant that is collected, dried, and compressed into *plates* and individually bagged and sold primarily in western Europe and Canada. The THC content only reaches between 3 to 5%.

The largest producers of hashish are Afghanistan and Pakistan with Turkey, Morocco, and Lebanon far behind. Hashish is produced from massive fields of typically low percentage THC marijuana. The resin from the marijuana is extracted from the plant and compressed into plates (Figure 3.35

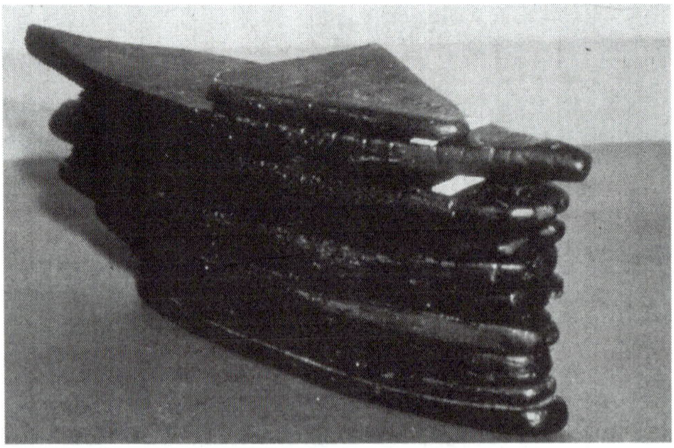

Figure 3.35 Plates of hashish. (Courtesy of the U.S. Drug Enforcement Administration.)

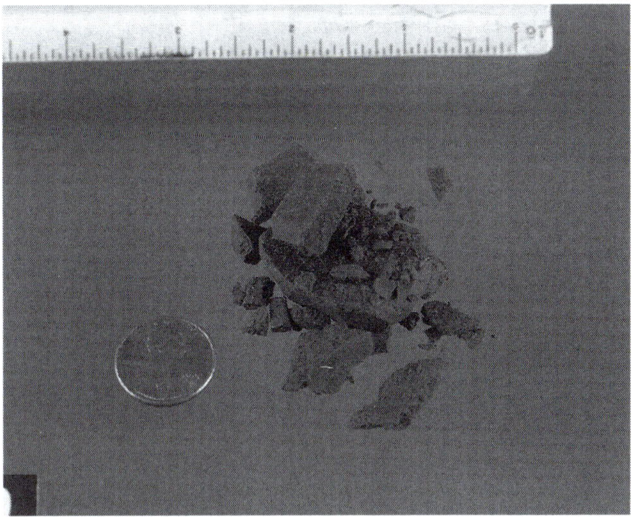

Figure 3.36 Varieties of hashish. (Courtesy of the U.S. Drug Enforcement Administration.) (See color insert following page 36.)

and Figure 3.36). Hashish is transported by the ton via camel caravan from Afghanistan and Pakistan to the Macron coast of Pakistan, where it is ferried to a mother ship by smaller craft and then smuggled to another country. It is also smuggled through commercial cargo for destinations in western Europe, primarily The Netherlands.

Effects of Cannabis

Marijuana produces a mild state of euphoria that often relaxes inhibitions. Its one side effect is known to produce an increased appetite in the user or, as many users refer to it, the *munchies*. The physical effects of THC are not fully understood, but they clearly are mild. Physical dependence on the drug is also unknown, but scientific studies seem to suggest there may indeed be evidence of it.

Persons under the influence of marijuana have judgment lapses similar to being under the influence of alcohol. At best, there is a moderate psychological dependency on the drug by its users. A telltale sign of someone having recently used marijuana is the deep reddening of the eye hidden by the eyelid (Figure 3.37).

Methylenedioxy-*N*-Methylamphetamine (MDMA)

Although it was discovered in 1912 and briefly became popular in 1985 for a short while, in the late 1990s, *Ecstasy* (the common street name for MDMA)

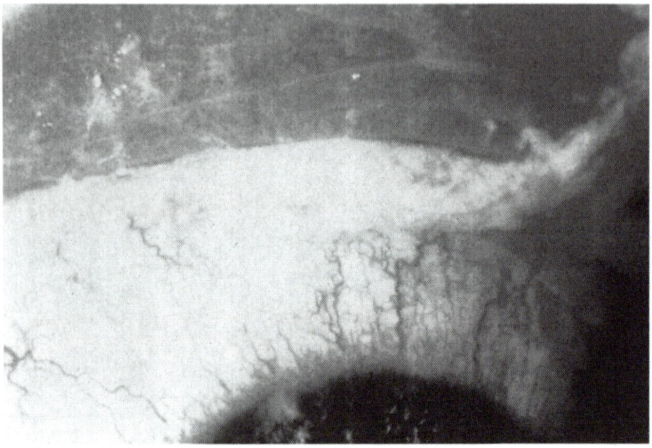

Figure 3.37 People under the influence of marijuana will exhibit deep reddening of their eyes under the lids. (Courtesy of the U.S. Drug Enforcement Administration.) (See color insert following page 36.)

exploded onto the drug scene in Europe and the United States primarily through *rave parties*. In 1985 it was permanently listed as a schedule I synthetic, psychoactive drug. Its popularity created major concerns by law enforcement agencies that were ill equipped to handle the sudden surge in the popularity of the drug.

This *designer drug*, or *club drug*, is a chemical derivative of methamphetamine in tablet form that initially became popular in the club scene in London. It later took root among teenage and early twenty-year-olds in the United States, first on the East Coast and then rapidly spread across the country, where it blossomed in California.

Many of its users compare its effects as being similar to methamphetamine with hallucinogenic properties. Others describe the effects as a constant adrenaline rush. Users claim that the drug increases awareness, sharpens perception, produces mood swings, and increases performance. Some describe the drug experience as a separation of mind and body. The drug compels users to talk and communicate excessively with others and join in dancing to the point of complete exhaustion, sometimes after several days of abuse.

The average oral dose of 100 mg is felt 30 to 45 minutes after ingestion, peaks in 60 to 90 minutes, and wears off after 6 to 8 hours. It takes up to 3 full days for the user to fully recover from the effects of the drug. Higher doses of 200 mg or more produce severe side effects such as nausea, confusion, and difficulties in concentrating, reasoning, and speech. Users sometimes use a method called *stacking* in which three or more pills are ingested at a time, or *piggyback* doses, which is taking one pill an hour for 3 consecutive

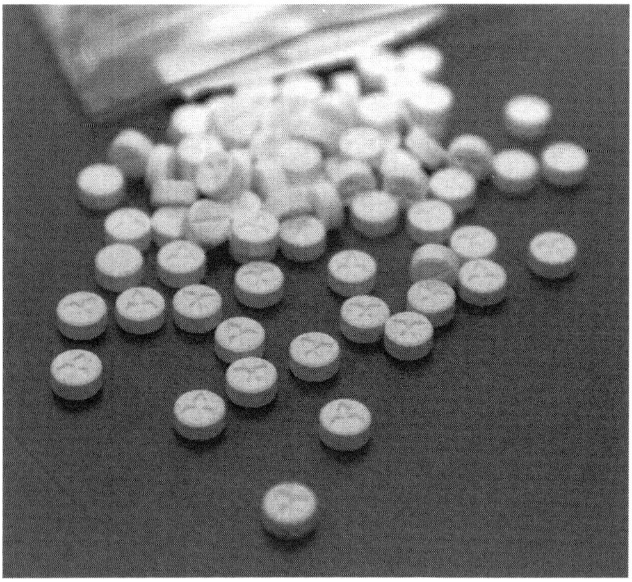

Figure 3.38 Ecstasy tablets seized by U.S. Customs. (Courtesy of U.S. Immigration and Customs Enforcement.)

hours. Marijuana is frequently used in conjunction with the substance. MDMA has a high potential for psychological dependence among its users, and is life threatening even with one dose. Most users take at least three tablets (Figure 3.38).

Users will experience a rapid heart rate — up to 220 beats per minute — and those in poor health run the risk of brain hemorrhaging or heart failure by taking the drug. Body temperature of users can vary from 106 to 117°F. Ecstasy has been shown to cause damage to nerve cells and the degeneration of the muscular system. Prolonged use may cause liver and kidney malfunctions. In 1998, the National Institute of Mental Health conducted a study of a small group of habitual MDMA users who were abstaining from use. The study revealed the abstinent users suffered damage to the neurons in the brain that transmit serotonin, an important biochemical involved in a variety of critical functions including learning. This study revealed that recreational MDMA users may be at risk of developing permanent brain damage that may manifest itself in depression, anxiety, memory loss, and other neuro-psychotic disorders.

The body develops a tolerance for the drug with prolonged consumption. However, the regular user cannot overcome the tolerances by increasing the dosage. He must abstain for a period of several days or weeks to achieve the desired euphoric state.

Drug Recognition

Ecstasy tablets are slightly smaller than aspirin tablets, frequently, but not always scored, come in many different colors and almost always have recognizable logos stamped on one side, some of which are well known. There are currently over 600 cataloged logos on the illicit market. It is sometimes found in capsule and powder forms. The logo the manufacturer chooses often creates the *street name*, or moniker, of their particular variety of Ecstasy and also serves as an investigative lead in conspiracy investigations. Logos have been extensively used on Ecstasy tablets seized in Europe and the United States. Logos include shamrocks, butterflies, lightning bolts, Disney cartoon characters, comic book superheroes, windmills, and stars, as well as luxury car and restaurant logos.

Ecstasy users almost always have drug paraphernalia with them that they use to enhance their experience while under the influence of the drug. Items such as chemical light-sticks, small flashlights, and other flashing colored lights, which when shown in the eyes of the user supposedly create a more intense euphoric state.

Baby pacifiers attached to necklaces worn by the users are popular in the prevention of their jaw muscles from seizing up during exhaustive dancing while under the influence (Figure 3.39). Leg and back muscles are subject to seizure, requiring massaging by fellow users.

Ecstasy rapidly creates body dehydration, especially when the user dances for hours at a time, which is often the case while under the influence. Users will frequently possess large amounts of bottled water for their use while under the influence of Ecstasy.

Ecstasy Source Countries

Ecstasy is almost always manufactured in western Europe, predominately The Netherlands, Belgium, and Germany. Only a few domestic MDMA laboratories have been discovered in the United States. The DEA estimates that over one million tablets of the drug is manufactured per day in Europe, with a significant amount of the finished product being smuggled to the United States.

Figure 3.39 Baby pacifiers sold at rave parties. (Courtesy of the U.S. Drug Enforcement Administration.)

Traffickers sell the drug in various quantities, up to what is called a *boat*, or one thousand tablets. Some traffickers have access to several boats for sale at one time. Drugs shipped from Europe to the United States come in *boat-sized packages* and are then broken down in smaller quantities for resale.

It appears that many large quantity traffickers in the United States have direct ties to ecstasy sources in Europe. Israeli organized crime syndicates, some composed of Russian émigrés associated with Russian organized crime, have forged relationships with western European traffickers and gained control over a significant share of the European market. The Israeli syndicates are currently the primary source to U.S. distribution groups, but overlaps of the two organizations have been seen. Mexican drug traffickers have recently attempted to manufacture their own ecstasy in Mexico for immediate sale in the United States, giving competition to their Russian and Israeli counterparts. The drug is most frequently smuggled into the United States by commercial air smugglers, airfreight shipments, and express mail services.

Rave Parties

Frequently referred to simply as *X*, Ecstasy has spawned an entirely new industry of *rave parties*. A rave party is where Ecstasy users gather at often-huge events to dance and listen to the music played by popular disk jockeys while surrounded by other like-minded drug users who feel relatively safe from intervention by law enforcement.

Rave parties initially were small underground gatherings advertised by word of mouth, but by the turn of the century they emerged into well-advertised blockbuster events attracting tens of thousands of people. Many of these raves have occurred on municipal property, where city administrators unwittingly promote the use of the drug by allowing these events to take place. However, the cities collect revenue through the renting of their publicly owned facilities.

The promoters of these events often earn money in several ways. Money collected at the admission gate can run upwards of $25 to $50 per person. They hire scores of security guards to ward off criticism they are promoting drug use, when in reality they are. However, these guards often confiscate drugs and rave party paraphernalia like baby pacifiers, light sticks, and bottled water from ticket holders entering the rave area, and then lead them inside to persons who can provide them with the same items for sale, including the drugs.

Because the rave party-goers become dehydrated quickly from the effects of the drug and long hours of dancing, promoters have been known to cut off drinking water dispensers in order to sell bottled water at extravagant prices for extra profits.

Gamma Hydroxybutyrate (GHB)

Gamma hydroxybutyrate (GHB), also known as *Liquid X* or *Grievous Bodily Harm*, is another *club drug* that became popular at the turn of the century. It is a central nervous system depressant abused for its ability to produce euphoric and hallucinatory states, and its alleged ability to release a growth hormone and stimulate muscle growth. It is frequently found at rave parties where ecstasy is being abused. Ecstasy abusers will often use GHB to counter the effects of the MDMA.[1]

GHB was originally considered safe and was sold in health food stores as a food supplement. Soon after, the medical community realized GHB caused many health problems and overdoses. GHB can produce drowsiness, dizziness, nausea, unconsciousness, seizures, severe respiratory depression, and coma. It is most often found in liquid form, but can also be in white powdered material. It is taken orally and is frequently combined with alcohol. Abusers include high school and college students and rave party attendees who use GHB for its intoxicating effects.

Numerous cases throughout the United States have documented the use of GHB to incapacitate women for the commission of sexual assault. Suspects will spike the substance into an unsuspecting woman's beverage, and within 15 to 30 minutes, she will be rendered unconscious. Upon awakening 3 to 6 hours later, the victim often has no recollection of what occurred.

Gamma Butyrolactone (GBL)

GBL is a chemical used in many industrial cleaners and is the precursor chemical for the manufacture of GHB. When consumed, the body synthesizes it into GHB. Several Internet businesses offer kits that contain GBL plus the proper amount of sodium hydroxide or potassium hydroxide, along with litmus paper and directions for the manufacture of GHB. The process is quite simple and does not require complex laboratory equipment. The kits sell for between $48 and $200. As with GHB, GBL can be added to water and is nearly undetectable.

Drug agents will often find GHB and GBL in their clear liquid form disguised in plastic water bottles at rave parties. By vigorously shaking the bottle, police officers can detect the presence of these substances when the clear liquid, unlike water, will readily create foam.

Ketamine[2]

Also known as *Special K*, *K*, and *Cat Valium*, ketamine is another substance abused by rave partygoers. Ketamine is a prescribed veterinarian pharmaceutical

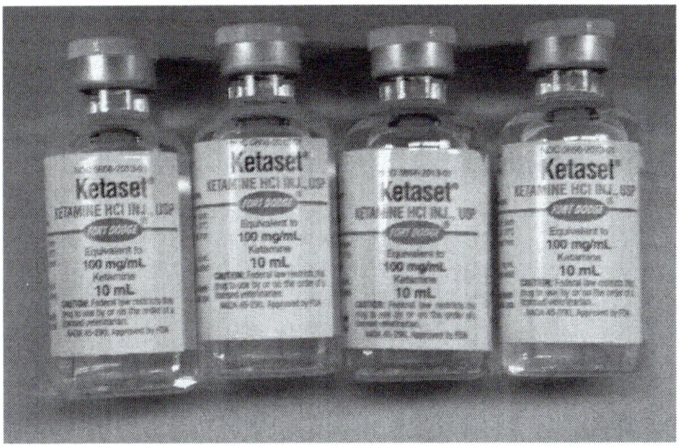

Figure 3.40 Ketamine 10 ml bottles. (Courtesy of the U.S. Drug Enforcement Administration.)

product that is diverted from legitimate sources of supply such as animal hospitals and veterinarian offices.

The liquid form of ketamine can be injected, applied to material that is smoked, or consumed in drinks. The powdered form is made by allowing the solvent to evaporate, leaving a white or slightly off-white powder that, once pulverized, looks very similar to cocaine. The powder can be put into drinks, smoked, or injected.

Ketamine produces physical effects similar to PCP, which is an animal tranquilizer, and has the visual effects of LSD. Users report that it is better than PCP or LSD because the euphoric effect lasts for only an hour or less. Higher doses produce an effect referred to as an *out-of-body* or *near-death* experience.

Use of the drug can cause delirium, amnesia, depression, long-term memory and cognitive difficulties, and fatal respiratory problems. Due to its disassociate effect, it is reportedly used as a date-rape drug. Ketamine was placed on schedule III of the CSA on August 12, 1999 (Figure 3.40).

Methamphetamine

Methamphetamine, or *Meth*, is a powerful chemically produced CNS stimulant. It can be taken orally or snorted, but the most popular method of ingestion is from smoking the drug in the same manner as crack cocaine. It can be milky white to brown in color, and sold at the wholesale level in pound rather than kilogram increments. Much of the methamphetamine sold in the United States is manufactured here, with the rest originating in Mexico.

The price for methamphetamine varies widely. At the wholesale level, prices can range from $3500 per pound in California to over $20,000 per

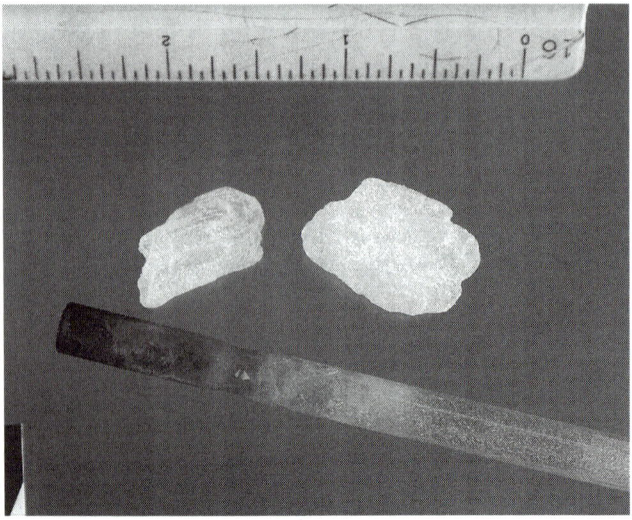

Figure 3.41 Crystal ice methamphetamine with smoking pipe. (Courtesy of the U.S. Drug Enforcement Administration.)

pound in urban areas in the Northeast. Retail prices can range from $400 to $3000 per ounce.

An even more potent variety of methamphetamine is known as *Crystal Meth* or *Ice* because of its appearance (Figure 3.41). It commands a significantly higher wholesale and retail price than methamphetamine.

Methamphetamine use produces rapid heart rate and an increase in blood pressure, breathing rate, and body temperature. Persons under the influence frequently exhibit violent behavior, increased energy, tremors, and hyperactivity. Higher doses have caused unjustified nervousness, irritability, and paranoia among abusers.

Because it is a powerful stimulant, chronic, high-dose users may experience no sleep for several days and then suddenly fall into deep sleep. Users are unpredictable and have a high propensity of violence towards police.

Methamphetamine is also found in a tablet form that is manufactured exclusively in Southeast Asia (SEA). Thailand and South Korea are the major source countries for these tablets, which are manufactured for consumers throughout the region, especially Japan. The seizures of these tablets in the United States have increased steadily, and are predominately smuggled through the mail. In 2000, authorities seized 301,697 SEA methamphetamine tablets in U.S. Postal Service facilities in Oakland, Los Angeles, and Honolulu. This represents a 656% increase from the 1999 seizure total of 39,917.* This trend will

* Drug Enforcement Administration, Intelligence Division, Drug Trafficking in the United States, September 2001.

probably continue for the foreseeable future. SEA methamphetamine tablets are aspirin size, multi-colored, and often have distinctive logos pressed on them.

Lysergic Acid Diethylamide (LSD)

LSD is the most potent hallucinogen known. Dr. Albert Hoffman originally synthesized it in 1938, but its hallucinogenic effects were unknown until 1943 when Dr. Hoffman accidentally consumed the drug. Since LSD is similar chemically to a chemical present in the brain and similar in its effects on certain aspects of psychosis, LSD was used decades ago as a research tool to study mental illness.

After a decline in its illicit use after its initial popularity in the 1960s, LSD made a comeback in the 1990s. However, the current average oral dose consumed by users is between 30 and 50 micrograms, a decrease of nearly 90% from the 1960 average dose of 250 to 300 micrograms. This lower potency probably accounts for the relatively few LSD-related emergency room incidents during the past several years and its present popularity among young people.

LSD is sold in tablet form, usually small in size referred to as *microdots*, on sugar cubes, or in thin squares of gelatin. It is widely referred to by users as *acid*. LSD is most frequently found on blotter paper that has been soaked with LSD and perforated into one-quarter-inch squares, each one being a single dose unit. These *blotter acid* sheets may be colored brightly, or have cartoon figures or logos on them (Figure 3.42).

Physical Reaction

Users may exhibit dilated pupils, lowered body temperature, nausea, goose bumps despite profuse perspiration, and rapid heart rate. Users are usually

Figure 3.42 Variety of blotter acid. (Courtesy of the U.S. Drug Enforcement Administration.) (See color insert following page 36.)

talkative about what they are experiencing and will articulate their visions of distorted perceptions of the size and shape of items, movements, color, sound, and touch. Users may also experience *flashbacks* where they have a recurrence of the effects of the LSD days or even months after taking their last dose.

LSD Traffickers

Much of the LSD manufactured in the United States originates from northern California, specifically the San Francisco Bay area. Most drug investigations elsewhere will almost always find a nexus to this area of the country. These traffickers tend to be white Americans who may be second-generation users.

Methylphenidate (Ritalin®)

Methylphenidate (MPH), also known as Ritalin is a schedule II stimulant that produces pharmacological effects similar to those of cocaine and amphetamine. Doctors prescribe it to treat attention-deficit disorder (ADD) and other conditions. Unlike other popular drugs, Ritalin has not yet been produced in clandestine labs.

The dramatic increase in abuse of this drug recently can largely be attributed to its increased use for the treatment of ADD in children. A growing number of abuse cases have been associated with adolescents and young adults who are using MPH for its stimulant effects: appetite suppression, wakefulness, and increased focus/attentiveness, usually for long nights of studying, and euphoria.

Pharmaceutical tablets are most frequently taken orally or by crushing the tablets and snorting the powder. Some addicts dissolve the tablets in water and inject the mixture. Complications arising from this practice are common due to the insoluble fillers used in the tablets. When injected, these materials block small blood vessels, causing serious damage to the lungs and retina of the eye. MPH also produces increases in heart rate and blood pressure and is capable of producing severe psychological dependence.

Phencyclidine (PCP)

In the 1950s, phencyclidine, or PCP, was developed as an anesthetic, however since the side effects of confusion and delirium were present, its research for human medical use was discontinued. It later became commercially available as a veterinary anesthetic in the 1960s under the trade name Sernylan®, and was placed in schedule III of the CSA. In 1978, due to considerable abuse of

Figure 3.43 Foil wrappers containing marijuana laced with PCP. (Courtesy of the U.S. Drug Enforcement Administration.)

PCP, it was transferred to schedule II, and its commercial manufacturing stopped. Today, virtually all PCP seized by police agencies in the United States is produced by clandestine laboratories (Figure 3.43).

PCP is marketed under a number of other names including *Angel Dust*, *Supergrass*, *Killer Weed*, *Embalming Fluid*, and *Rocket Fuel, each name reflecting* the range of its bizarre and volatile effects. In its purest form, it is a white crystalline powder that is water soluble. However, most PCP contains a number of contaminants as a result of makeshift manufacturing, causing the color to range from tan to dark brown, resembling motor oil. Its consistency ranges from a powdery form to a gummy mass.The required chemicals needed to manufacture the drug are readily available and inexpensive, and the production process requires little knowledge of chemistry or elaborate laboratory equipment.

The drug is sold primarily in urban neighborhoods in a limited number of U.S. cities. The liquid form of PCP is actually PCP base dissolved in the highly flammable solvent ether. Traffickers typically dip rolled cigarette paper containing parsley, mint, or marijuana into the solution for later smoking. *Sherman* brand cigarettes, or *Sherms* were used extensively to dip into the PCP solution in the early 1980s.

PCP's effects are as varied as its appearance. Even a moderate dose of PCP can cause users to feel detached, distant, and estranged from their surroundings. Numbness, slurred speech, and loss of coordination are often coupled with a feeling of strength and invulnerability. The feeling of strength is derived from the user's inability to feel pain. Persons under the influence have been known to break out of handcuffs, often injuring themselves because of their inability to detect pain. Users often have a blank stare, rapid and involuntary eye movements called *nystagmus*, and a stupor gait. Auditory hallucinations, image distortion, severe mood disorders, and amnesia frequently occur. Some PCP users may experience acute anxiety and a feeling of impending doom; many turn violent in the presence of the police. Users are often misdiagnosed as being schizophrenic; however, the telltale vanilla-like odor of the drug will permeate the user's clothing and distinguish him from someone who is mentally ill. PCP is one of the most dangerous drugs of abuse because of the violence attributed to it.

Steroids

Congress passed the Anabolic Steroid Control Act in 1990, classifying 27 steroids as CSA schedule II substances. As a result, street prices for the drug have substantially increased. Health clubs have traditionally been the primary distribution centers for steroids since weightlifters and bodybuilders are the majority of the abuser population. Steroids have since spread to professional and amateur athletes as well as boys in junior high and high school (Figure 3.44 to Figure 3.46).

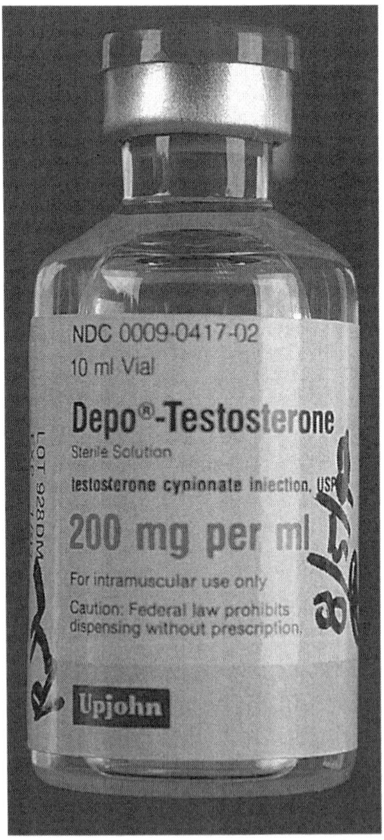

Figure 3.44 Ten-milliliter bottle of injectable steroids. (Courtesy of the U.S. Drug Enforcement Administration.)

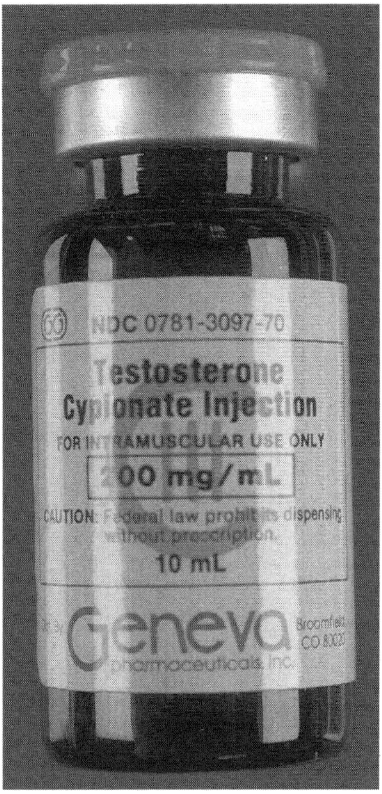

Figure 3.45 Common variety of injectable steroid. (Courtesy of the U.S. Drug Enforcement Administration.)

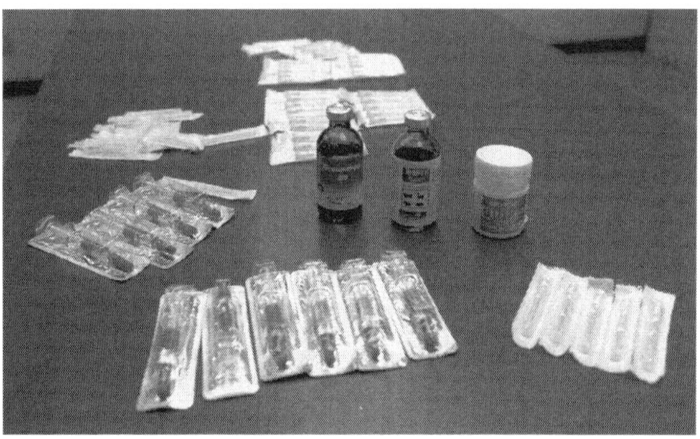

Figure 3.46 Variety of steroids seized by the U.S. Customs Service. (Courtesy of U.S. Immigration and Customs Enforcement.)

Anabolic steroids are smuggled from European countries as well as Mexico to the United States by individuals as well as by bulk traffickers from eastern Europe and Russia. The lack of international control over foreign sources of supply makes it nearly impossible to attack the trafficking at its source. Studies show that, over time, anabolic steroids can indeed take a heavy toll on a person's health. The abuse of oral or injectable steroids is associated with higher risks for heart attacks and strokes, and the abuse of most oral steroids is associated with increased risk for liver problems. Steroid abusers who share needles or use nonsterile techniques when they inject steroids are at risk for contracting dangerous infections, such as HIV/AIDS, hepatitis B and C, and bacterial endocarditis.

According to the National Institute on Drug Abuse, anabolic steroid abuse can also cause undesirable body changes. These include breast development and genital shrinking in men, masculinization of the body in women, and acne and hair loss in both sexes.

Other Drugs of Abuse

Other drugs commonly abused in the United States include: alcohol, prescription medications, methaqualone, peyote mushrooms, plus a variety of inhalants such as glue, gasoline, and other common household products. This list is not meant to be exclusive, as changes in drug abuse can occur suddenly with little warning (Figure 3.47 and Figure 3.48).

Figure 3.47 Glue as an inhalant. (Courtesy of the U.S. Drug Enforcement Administration.)

Figure 3.48 Solvent used as an inhalant. (Courtesy of the U.S. Drug Enforcement Administration.)

Summary

Drug agents in the 21st century are more likely to encounter traffickers dealing the popular drugs of marijuana, cocaine, ecstasy, methamphetamine, and heroin than any other drugs during the course of their law enforcement careers. Although there are many other drugs on the market, their popularity has dwindled over time. Drug trafficking trends may change, but the economic theory of supply and demand remains constant in the drug world.

What all abused drugs have in common is they affect the user's CNS, produce a euphoric state, and in some cases cause physical or psychological dependency. Drug agents should be thoroughly familiar with the physical symptoms associated with each drug, and be able to educate others on how to recognize drug users.

They should also be familiar with where these drugs originate, and what criminal organizations are most likely involved in their trafficking. This chapter intentionally did not mention much about wholesale and retail prices of drugs. This is because market conditions can change rapidly, and many factors such as transportation, distribution, storage, etc. have to be factored into the ultimate price on the street. Street prices can change dramatically from one part of the country to another. Drug agents need to know the price of these drugs from intelligence gleaned from informants in order to be knowledgeable for undercover negotiations.

References

1. Ecstasy and Predatory Drugs, U.S. Drug Enforcement Administration, February, 2003.
2. Drug Intelligence Brief, Drug Enforcement Administration, September 2000.

Confidential Informants

4

Drug law enforcement operations rely heavily on the use of confidential informants as the general public does not usually report drug crimes. A drug agent's professional accomplishments are directly related to his or her ability to recruit and manage a steady stream of diverse confidential informants (CIs).

Drug informants are arguably the most difficult among all informants to control and manage. However, the chances of successfully managing them are increased significantly when drug agents know what motivates them to provide information to the police.

Although CIs are a necessary tool in drug law enforcement, they must be carefully scrutinized for hidden motives. Drug agents are cautioned not to take anything a CI has to offer at face value, and to always corroborate their information either through surveillance, records, or even polygraph examinations, if warranted.

The nature of drug cases often requires a CI to become closely involved with traffickers and their police handlers alike. They are asked to befriend drug dealers for the purpose of gaining their confidence so they may later be arrested. The personal relations drug informants develop with criminals can sometimes lead them into unethical, immoral, or illegal conduct.

Some egotistical informants have personalities that make them difficult, if not almost impossible to manage. These individuals often have questionable motives for offering their services to law enforcement. When drug agents do not tightly control their informants, safety problems arise, placing department resources and personnel at risk. Each time an informant offers information, drug agents should question his motives and discontinue using him if he is not willing to accept his handler's specific direction.

This chapter explains the most common motivational factors leading people to become informants, the professional working relationships that must exist, and the steps that must be taken to successfully manage them. Methods of keeping the informant's identity confidential are identified in order to protect him from retaliation and keep him a viable asset for future counter-drug operations. The chapter also explains how to properly use a CI to make a controlled purchase of drugs.

Purpose of Informants

Drug informants are used most frequently for the following reasons:

To gather information from sources not readily available to law enforcement officers. Police have long depended on informants to provide them with information they would never otherwise receive. Because of the clandestine nature of the drug world, specific information about upcoming drug transactions, where drugs are being manufactured, and how they are transported is only known by those involved in the crime. Informants within drug organizations play a vital role in obtaining this needed information for law enforcement.

To make observations in places where strangers would immediately be suspect. Many drug investigations require that surveillance operations be conducted within communities that are suspicious of strangers. Using informants who are accepted within these communities will lower the level of suspicion that a police operation is underway, and makes criminals operating in the area feel more comfortable. Unfamiliar faces in an area may raise suspicions that might force them to go deeper underground or change their modus operandi.

To conduct undercover negotiations. Since drug dealers realize that a common drug law enforcement investigative technique is to infiltrate their organization with undercover agents, they frequently will not interact with strangers. Many dealers build up their businesses by not dealing with strangers, and they are not willing to take a risk with a new person, regardless of what he or she may have to offer. With proper direction and guidance, informants can take the place of an undercover drug agent in negotiating the purchase of drugs from a targeted drug dealer. When doing so, the drug agent should electronically record the conversation to corroborate exactly what the informant told the dealer, and what the dealer told the informant. Informants may be reliable in many cases, but they are not infallible. A recording device will capture all that was said, and nothing will be lost through faulty memory. A tape recording of the informant's conversation with the drug dealer will also keep him honest.

To gain firsthand, timely intelligence. Since informants have the ability to interact with criminals in both professional and social settings, they are in an excellent position to obtain information about crimes that have occurred or are about to occur. Police must still corroborate the informant's information before any action is taken. Timely intelligence information provided by informants may later be the basis for search warrant affidavits, arrest warrants, or seizure warrants for drug proceeds, property, or money.

Motivational Factors

Like many people, informants need motivation to produce. The more motivated they are, the more likely they are to apply themselves to the task at hand and remain committed to achieving success. Identifying an informant's true motives for providing drug agents with information increases the chances of conducting an effective and safe drug operation. If a drug agent believes that the informant is providing information because he is repentant for past crimes, when in actuality he is there to learn police intelligence and their methods of operation in order to avoid detection himself, a disaster is in the making.

Informants commonly voice a specific motive for providing information, however as the case progresses, other more compelling reasons may surface. Some of the more common motivational factors encountered by drug agents are fear, revenge, money, repentance, and sometimes altruism. However, often times an individual's ego and compulsion to play a role in something important and exciting drives the individual to become an informant.

Walk-In/Call-In Informants

Drug agents need to be good listeners and carefully evaluate a first time informant's information being offered over the telephone. Someone who visits the drug agent's office offering information must be scrutinized for what is motivating him or her to take this initial step. A thorough interview will often reveal clues as to what is motivating this person to come forward. Their information cannot be discounted simply because the person is not willing to meet with a drug agent in person. Drug agents should obtain identifying information and a callback telephone number whenever possible. The informant should be encouraged to submit to a face-to-face meeting if the informant's information appears actionable.

Fear

The most frequent motivation leading someone to provide information is the fear of going to prison. Fear is a strong motivator when someone has just been arrested and faces the probability of years of imprisonment for committing drug crimes.

Drug agents will attempt to convince a newly arrested suspect to immediately provide information leading to other arrests in the ongoing investigation. Drug agents must convince the potential informant that this may be his only opportunity to help himself in his pending legal matter. The agent must never promise a reduced sentence or other consideration, but can assure the person that his cooperation will be made known to the prosecutor and the court at a future date. He should know that his lack of cooperation will also be brought to the attention of the prosecutor and court.

A typical scenario may be this: a suspect has agreed to deliver a quantity of drugs to an undercover drug agent. Upon delivering the drugs, the suspect is arrested and taken into custody. Drug agents will frequently question the suspect at the scene of the arrest, and solicit his cooperation in helping them immediately expand their investigation. They will ask the arrested person who his drug source of supply is and where more drugs are located.

Drug agents know that fear will often motivate a suspect to cooperate in the investigation once he realizes how much punishment he is likely to receive if convicted of the crime, especially if the person has prior drug arrests (see Chapter 10). This fear tactic may induce him to make a recorded telephone call to his drug source in the hopes of getting him to acknowledge furnishing the drugs, thereby making him also subject to indictment.

Depending on the particular circumstances, drug agents may ask the arrested person to immediately telephone his source to set up a meeting on the pretense of paying for the drugs just delivered, or to deliver more drugs for another sale. If the drug agents are successful in luring the source of supply out in the open and can arrest him, they will attempt to convince him to also cooperate. The technique of convincing a person to cooperate against co-conspirators is commonly known as *flipping the suspect.*

It should be noted that once it becomes public knowledge that someone has been arrested on drug charges, other members of the conspiracy often assume the suspect is cooperating with drug agents and may identify other members of the conspiracy. Because of this assumption, co-conspirators will usually avoid the arrested suspect and cut off all forms of communication with him for fear he is setting them up to be arrested. Swift action must be taken by drug agents to seize the opportunity before other co-conspirators realize what has happened. Defendant-informants, however, may still be valuable in testifying against other members of the conspiracy in return for legal consideration.

Informants may also be motivated to cooperate with drug agents to protect them from their criminal associates. Some may think that by having their criminal associates arrested, they will protect themselves from retribution and will not have to pay for any drugs their source of supply advanced or *fronted* them on consignment.

Fear in the mind of a drug dealer can also stem from a member of a drug conspiracy falsely accusing him of being an informant and cooperating with the police. In order to seek self-preservation, money, or both, they will often become informants.

Revenge and Jealousy

Both revenge and jealousy have historically motivated people to do things they might not normally do. Jealousy may stem from love or money, but business disputes between competing drug criminal organizations may prompt revenge.

Drug agents should be wary of informants who seek to eliminate their own drug dealing competition. Nothing prevents a drug agent from using this information to target the competing drug dealer. However, once the competitor is arrested, the drug agent should solicit his help in eliminating the informant's drug enterprise as well.

Repentance

Informants often claim they are repentant for past crimes, but this is rarely the case. Expressions of repentance are sometimes used to convince the drug agent he or she is now a good person and wants to make amends for past deeds. However, this is seldom their only motive for cooperating. When drug agents encounter an informant who claims repentance as their sole reason for providing information, they must be cautious of hidden and sometimes devious motivational factors.

Altruism

Some individuals are motivated by a sense of self-sacrifice. People with professional obligations or feelings of responsibility frequently provide information to the police. Examples of altruistic informants include airline employees when they see something suspicious about a passenger or his baggage, or express delivery service employees who detect drugs in packages they are delivering. These informants are rarely involved in criminal activity, and their usefulness is limited.

Mercenaries

Some individuals provide information or services simply for money. These money-motivated informants, known as *mercenaries*, are usually the most willing to follow a drug agent's direction. They frequently have a history of criminal activity prior to their relationship with law enforcement. This familiarization with crime and criminals make them a valuable asset for drug agents who must rely on them to make frequent and personal contacts with drug traffickers to glean criminal intelligence. They often serve as a means of introducing an undercover drug agent to drug dealers on the pretense of being a buyer of narcotics or someone who can provide a specific service in the drug trade such as a transportation specialist or money launderer.

Money-motivated informants are expected to accompany the targeted drug dealer alone for much longer periods of time than would be practical for an undercover drug agent. Drug agents should be aware that they frequently possess other motives besides remuneration that must be explored. They are professionals deserving of respect and appropriate compensation if agents want them to continue providing information in the future. Payments to informants will be discussed in detail later in this chapter.

Egotism

These commonly encountered informants often have low self-esteem and may not have received positive reinforcement from their parents, authority figures, or peers when growing up. Consequently, as adults they seek positive reinforcement wherever they can get it and sometimes rely on anticipated positive feedback from their handlers for doing a good job. Drug agents who provide egotistical informants positive reinforcement motivate them to continue supplying quality information. Unfortunately, these informants are often the hardest to handle because their egos prevent them from relinquishing control of the investigation to their handlers.

Egotistical informants wish to have an aggressive role in the undercover investigation in order to justify as much praise or money as possible. They will sometimes prolong an investigation unnecessarily in order to justify more money or praise. They are quick to remind their handling agent that if it were not for them, the case would never have happened. An informant in this category may demand payment for services rendered, but in reality, the praise he expects to receive from authority figures is the primary motivator for him becoming and staying an informant.

Drug agents who recognize egotistical informants for what they are should heap the praise he desperately seeks. To deny these informants praise could jeopardize future working relationships with him and may drive him to work with another drug agent or go to an entirely different agency to offer his services. The ego of the informant should not be in competition with the ego of the handling agent.

James Bond Syndrome

Some drug informants see their role as an opportunity to have their life imitate art. While working as informants they imagine themselves in a particular police or spy drama. Sometimes they will even orchestrate events to parallel a scene from a movie or chapter of a novel. Being especially hard to handle, these informants often exaggerate their knowledge of drug activity to enhance the likelihood of becoming an informant so they can play the role of their life. When an informant insists that an undercover operation be conducted in a particular or peculiar way or demands that he be issued a weapon, identification, or fancy vehicle, these are indicators he may be more interested in his role than the objective of the investigation.

These informants are rarely motivated to work for the police to make amends for past criminal activity, but rather give their motive for becoming an informant as something as noble as wanting to help win the war on drugs. Drug agents are advised to handle this type of informant carefully. Although the information they provide may be credible and easily verifiable, the informant cannot be allowed to take control of the investigation and dictate how it will be conducted. To do so wastes valuable time and resources while the informant plays out his fantasies. The informant's insistence on how to carry out a particular phase of the case may raise unnecessary safety concerns for drug agents and the informant alike. The informant's handler must control him by making it clear that although his suggestions will be seriously considered, the agent is the decision maker and his or her supervisor is the final authority on how the investigation will be conducted.

The Wannabe

Wannabe informants are usually people that from a very young age, wanted to become a law enforcement officer. For whatever reason though they did not qualify, either because of physical or psychological defects, and believe that becoming an informant is the only way left for them to fulfill their life's desire. Because they usually lack criminal associates, these individuals usually cannot provide specific information about drug traffickers, and thus do not make good informants.

Indicators that the drug agents may be dealing with a *wannabe* are when the prospective informant asks to see what the drug agent's badge and identification card look like or asks what the likelihood of him becoming a sworn officer is. Drug agents who use wannabe informants run the risk of the informant purposely implying to third parties they are actually police officers. These informants also have a tendency to reveal their role to unconcerned parties, implying they have some sort of governmental authority, which they do not.

Perversely Motivated Informants

Perhaps the most dangerous and disruptive person a drug agent will encounter in drug law enforcement is a perversely motivated informant. They offer their services to law enforcement agencies for the purpose of identifying undercover agents, learning the department's methods, targets, and intelligence, or eliminating their own competition in the drug business. Sometimes criminal organizations, especially outlaw motorcycle gangs, instruct these individuals to infiltrate departments as informants and employees to learn whatever they can to assist the traffickers. These individuals may even provide genuine information about a specific event as a decoy to divert resources from a much more significant trafficking activity elsewhere.

Drug agents must constantly guard against providing more information to informants than the informants are providing to them. The information informant's gain from law enforcement agencies about their personnel, undercover vehicles, tactics, equipment, and particularly targets, is a valuable commodity that can be sold to traffickers or traded for drugs. These informants may also be seeking information to help in their own drug dealings in the future.

Drug agents should always minimize the exposure of undercover officers, their vehicles, and other informants to all informants in order to minimize damage to their operations in case they are working for drug traffickers or intend to do so. Criminals may threaten some informants or their families if they do not provide them with details on what information the police have concerning their drug trafficking activities.

Drug agents must question all walk-in and call-in informants, e.g., individuals who volunteer their services without prompting, because they may be, or have the potential of becoming perversely motivated. These potential informants should be told that their backgrounds will be thoroughly investigated, and that their fingerprints and photograph will be maintained in a file that will be established. Knowing that their backgrounds will be investigated may be enough to sway a potential informant from carrying out his perverse mission. Merely asking an informant to submit to a polygraph examination in order to substantiate his claims that he is not working for drug traffickers will often reveal his perverse activities.

Restricted-Use Informants

Some informants, by virtue of their extensive criminal backgrounds or status, pose special management challenges to both drug agents and supervisors. Drug unit supervisors should carefully scrutinize these individuals prior to using them as informants. Examples include juveniles, individuals on probation or parole, individuals currently or formerly addicted to drugs, felons with multiple convictions, and individuals known to be previously unreliable.

Drug agents should not use these individuals as informants without supervisory approval. Because these informants require special scrutiny and rigorous handling, only senior investigators should be assigned to manage them. Drug agents must constantly reevaluate the motives of these individuals.

Informants known to be previously unreliable should not be used except in the most extraordinary circumstances. They have shown, through their past actions, that they cannot be trusted or relied on to follow the directions of their handler. They will often exaggerate their knowledge of drug activity in order to regain their informant status, which in itself is a reason to question their use.

Developing Confidential Informants

Every person a drug agent comes into contact with is a potential informant. As stated earlier, the most common pool of informants are criminals recently arrested that want to *work off* their legal dilemma. Informants are often shared by police agencies. Sometimes when an informant has specific information about a crime that cannot be investigated by his handler's agency, the handler will turn the informant over to the appropriate law enforcement agency to conduct the investigation. An example would be an informant for the U.S. Secret Service who comes across drug information that the DEA would be interested in.

Drug agents can also locate informants by reviewing closed drug investigative files and contacting persons involved in the case who are either now in prison or were somehow affected. Sometimes these people, especially those incarcerated, will either seek revenge or provide information to enhance their chances of parole. Even though they are in prison, they can make telephone introductions to dealers for undercover investigators so that they can discuss future drug transactions.

Sometimes targets of opportunity arise for the drug investigator. If a targeted drug dealer harms someone's spouse, parent, significant other, or business partner, the drug agent should visit the victim to solicit their help in the investigation. The injured party may use the drug agent as the means of seeking revenge and punishing the dealer for harming them.

Supervisor's Role in Informant Management

Police agencies should not leave the management of drug informants exclusively to nonsupervisory drug agents. Formulating a written policy, approved by the agency head, ensures consistency in the use and management of informants and serves as a guide for inexperienced investigators.

The informant policy should indicate which investigators may maintain informants as well as who will supervise them. In addition, the policy should clearly establish that informants are assets of the entire department and not the individual agent/handler. In this regard, management should both authorize and encourage investigators to share informants with others within the department. Also, checks and balances must be in place to ensure that the policy is followed. Violations of the policy can leave the department vulnerable to severe criticism from the public and prompt lawsuits by persons affected by the informant's information.

Policy concerning the management of CIs should establish procedures in several areas. These include creating and documenting informant files, debriefing and interacting with informants, and determining methods and amounts of payments for services rendered.

Protecting the Informant's Identity

Society has always been negative toward informants. "Tattletales" and others who provide information to authorities have always been looked down on. The number one concern of informants is the protection of their identities. Generally in drug investigations, a guarantee that the identity of the informant will never be revealed cannot be made. In fact, due to the nature of these investigations, there is much more likelihood that the informant's identity will be revealed than not, and that he will possibly be later called to testify in court. This is because of the intense personal involvement of the informant with the suspect during the course of the investigation. Everything he sees, hears, or does is subject to cross-examination by a defense attorney.

Avoid Making the Informant a Percipient Witness

There are methods, however, that can help prevent the identity of the informant from being revealed. One such method is not exposing the informant to actions that make him a percipient witness to the event. Another is to conceal exactly when the informant provided information to the police.

As an example, an informant notifies the police that open drug sales are being conducted at a given location. Drug agents establish surveillance at the location, and from their experience and training conclude that in all likelihood, drugs are being sold at this location. The surveillance lasts for one week. In the middle of the week, the informant is sent into the location to make a controlled purchase of drugs to establish that controlled substances are, in fact, being sold at the location. Surveillance continues for several more days until an affidavit for a search warrant is presented to a judge who grants the police authority to search the premises, based partly on the actions of the informant. The affidavit may not have to be specific as to when the informant made the drug purchase. Since numerous drug sales most likely will continue up to the moment the search warrant is executed on the premises, it would be impossible for the traffickers to know, with certainty, who informed the police. To further protect the informant, an agreement should be made ahead of time with the prosecutor not to file charges against the defendants for the controlled purchase of drugs made by the informant. This will help guarantee his identity will not be revealed to the suspect or the public in general.

Report-Writing Techniques

Another way to minimize the informant's exposure is to not reveal his name in police investigative reports. These reports can be written in a way to conceal the gender of the informant by substituting a number for his or her name. Be mindful that even though the name of the informant may not be in the police report, the drug trafficker will most likely remember who was involved in the activities revealed in the police report. It may become obvious to the trafficker who the informant is, however, no one outside the investigation will know who was involved.

Using the Informant to Introduce Undercover Agents

Informants must be percipient witnesses to events in order to be called to testify in court. If an informant is used solely to introduce an undercover agent to the targeted drug trafficker and has no further involvement, the likelihood of the informant being identified by being called to testify in court is diminished greatly. If the informant is later confronted by the trafficker and accused of being an informant, he can provide a plausible story denying he knew the person he introduced to the trafficker was a drug agent.

Wall-Off Method

Another highly successful method of concealing the identity of the informant is using a technique known as a *wall-off*. Here an informant is ready to consummate a drug deal with the suspect. This drug deal is likely to be the third in a series of *confidence buys* where the suspect was allowed to leave with the *buy money*, giving him no reason to suspect the informant was involved with the police. During a final meeting, the informant may display money to the trafficker to prove he can purchase additional drugs.

The trafficker departs the meeting with the intent of returning with the drugs at a given time to deliver them to the informant. After retrieving the drugs, but before arriving back at the original meeting spot, drug agents arrange for a marked police car to follow the trafficker until the uniformed police officers can develop independent probable cause to stop the vehicle, which is usually a minor traffic offense.

The officers may either see the drugs in plain view, or ask the driver/drug trafficker for permission to search the car. Many suspects grant permission for the search feeling they have hidden the drugs well enough that they cannot be found. The search is conducted and after the drugs are found, the suspect is arrested.

If the dealer later makes bail, the CI will be instructed to telephone the trafficker. To reinforce in the trafficker's mind the informant had no prior knowledge of his arrest, he will ask the trafficker why he never returned to the delivery point with the drugs. If the trafficker admits to being arrested, the informant can suggest they stay away from each other since law enforcement must be investigating him. The informant can also feign anger at dealing with someone that the police were interested in, and state how lucky he was to have escaped arrest. Also, the informant can ask the trafficker if he mentioned he was going to deliver the drugs to him, and if he gave the police any information about the CI.

This charade has been highly effective in keeping drug informant's identities confidential. To further conceal the identity of the informant, drug agents can arrange with the prosecutor not to prosecute any prior controlled purchases between the informant and the trafficker in order to minimize the likelihood of the informant being exposed.

By using these methods, drug agents will successfully build a wall that will hopefully prevent the drug trafficker from discovering who the CI is. This wall-off technique also works well in concealing the involvement of an entire law enforcement agency. One agency may ask another to stop and conduct a search of a drug trafficker's vehicle in order to disguise its involvement.

Camouflage Techniques

In order to camouflage the relationship between the informant and the police, several techniques can be used. At the time the suspect is arrested, the informant can also be handcuffed and "arrested," reinforcing the notion he is not an informant. The informant can be initially lodged in the same jail cell with the drug dealer immediately after the arrest and allowed to wear a transmitter to record their conversations about other suspects, drug hiding places, and the like.

Another method is when the trafficker delivers drugs to the informant and he "escapes" without the drugs followed by drug agents in hot pursuit. Later the pursuing agents return to the arrest scene and question the suspect about the identity of the person who fled thereby giving him the impression that they have no idea who the person is or that he is an informant.

Other Considerations

Drug agents should refrain from providing their informants with their department business cards. Providing them with business cards shows that a relationship exists between the drug agent and the informant. There is also a possibility that targeted drug dealers will inadvertently see the card and accuse him of being an informant. Any connection drug traffickers can establish between the informant and law enforcement will jeopardize the ongoing investigation, and possibly create safety problems for both the drug agents and the informant.

Another good reason not to provide an informant with a business card is to eliminate the possibility of the informant posing as a drug agent. Informants have been known to pose as police and *seize* drugs from unsuspecting drug dealers to later sell. Producing an authentic police business card may facilitate this or other crimes. This also prevents the informant from posing as a drug agent in social situations.

To further protect the identity of the informant, drug agents should provide an informant with the investigator's telephone contact numbers on a plain piece of paper in the informant's own handwriting. The numbers can be arranged in such a way to resemble a mathematical problem, where the numbers in the equation make up the office or pager number of the handler (Figure 4.1).

$$\begin{array}{r} \mathbf{2025} \\ \mathbf{5512} \\ \underline{+\ \mathbf{12}} \\ \mathbf{7549} \end{array}$$

Figure 4.1 Example of disguising telephone number (202) 555-1212.

The Informant File

Investigators should formally establish files on CIs who regularly provide information or expect compensation for information they supply. Informant files chronicle their work performance, background data; and personal history. Investigators should not use any CI that has not been documented.

Although drug agents should document every contact with informants, not everyone in the department has a need to know an informant's identity or have access to informant files. Access should be on a strictly need-to-know basis, including only those drug agents and their supervisors who deal directly with the informant.

To further protect the CI's identity, investigators should use code numbers in lieu of his name in all investigative reports. Informants should keep the same number throughout their working relationship with the department.

The informant file should include information pertaining to the informant's vital statistics. Information such as his photograph and fingerprints, physical description, work and home addresses, vehicles driven, contact telephone numbers, including cellular, home, business, fax, pager, and email address. Also next of kin information needs to be documented to help find the informant if he should later be wanted for a crime.

Equally important are periodic checks through the FBI National Crime Information Center (NCIC) for any wants or warrants for the informant. Also needed are FBI and state police rap sheets reflecting past arrests and convictions. This information needs to be consistently updated and documented in the file. A wanted informant should never be used, and any drug agent who knowingly uses an informant who is a fugitive from justice should be severely censored. The likelihood of any case being prosecuted that was developed by a fugitive informant is remote at best.

Taking a CI's photograph and fingerprints, and other documentation sends a clear message to the informant that he should be straightforward and honest with his handlers. The informant will also realize that he is dealing with professionals who leave nothing to chance. He will know drug agents have sufficient personal information about him to enable them to find him quickly if he should ever commit a crime or maliciously expose information about undercover agents and police operations. Such documentation may deter perversely motivated informants.

In addition, informant files enhance the credibility of the department in the eyes of the court and the public who view informants as inherently unreliable. Every time the informant provides information concerning an actual or potential criminal event, the agency should create a written report detailing this information in the file.

The department must also document what steps it takes to corroborate information provided by the informant. This is especially important when informants act unilaterally. As a matter of policy, all informant information should be verified regardless of the informant's past reliability.

Informant Debriefings

Before drug agents initiate an investigation based on information received from an informant, the designated handler should debrief the informant in order to ascertain his motive or motives and to advise him about the department's rules and regulations concerning the management of informants. For example, informants should know that they carry no official status with the department, that the department will not tolerate their breaking the law or entrapping suspects in any investigation, and that the department cannot guarantee that they will not be called as witnesses in court.

At the end of the initial debriefing, the drug agent should document this information in an *informant agreement*. This agreement should be signed by the informant, witnessed by the handler and supervisor, and placed in the informant's newly created permanent informant file. Investigators should debrief their informants on a regular basis, usually every 30, 60, or 90 days, to show they are active, or if necessary, to terminate their association with the department due to lack of productivity.

Agent–Informant Contact Procedures

The department must establish drug agent–informant contact procedures, and train employees in their use. For instance, the handler should meet with the informant in private and always in the presence of another drug agent or sworn police officer. The department should either strongly discourage or prohibit drug agents from contacting informants alone, especially if the drug agent intends to pay the informant. Meeting or paying an informant alone leaves the drug agent and the department vulnerable to allegations of wrongdoing.

Although informant handlers often develop special working relationships with their informants, department policies should preclude drug agents from contacting their informants outside the scope of official business. Drug agents must keep their relationships with informants strictly professional. This is particularly important when the informant and the drug agent are not of the same sex. Policies should also expressly prohibit socializing with informants and their families, becoming romantically involved with them, having off-duty business relationships with them, and accepting informant's gifts or gratuities.

To ensure adherence to department policy, supervisors should review informant files regularly. In addition, they need to attend debriefings periodically to oversee the entire informant management process.

Finally, department managers must establish procedures for investigating alleged policy violations by drug agents or informants. Thorough investigations of this type maintain the integrity of the department by dispelling any notion that the department does not enforce its own policies.

Informant Payments

Informant payments can be divided into two distinct categories: *awards* and *rewards*.

Monetary awards are often based on a percentage of the net value of a drug dealer's assets seized during an investigation as a result of informant's information. Advising the informant what percentage he can expect to receive at the beginning of the case provides an incentive for the informant to seek out hidden assets that might otherwise go undetected.

Rewards, on the other hand, do not represent a percentage of the value of the seized assets. Rewards are specific amounts of money usually determined by the type and quantity of drugs seized. Other determining factors include the overall quality of the case, his level of cooperation, the number of defendants indited and convicted, the amount of time and effort expended, and level of danger the informant was exposed to during the course of the investigation. Unlike awards, rewards come directly from the agency's budget. Informants should be eligible for both awards and rewards.

While an informant may receive money as a reward, many cooperate with law enforcement agencies to receive a reduced sentence for a pending criminal matter. Regardless of the form of compensation the informant receives, police departments must have a policy addressing under what circumstances an informant qualifies for an award or reward, who can authorize such payments, and under what conditions payments will be granted.

A defendant-informant should only be reimbursed for actual expenses incurred during the investigation. His reward is judicial consideration for his cooperation. Once the informant works off his legal situation, drug agents should continue to use him with the promise of awards and rewards in future investigations.

Although many informants can receive substantial awards by locating the assets of drug dealers, agency policy and budget restraints may limit the dollar amount informants receive. For this reason, investigators should exercise caution when explaining the payment policy to informants. They should never mention a specific dollar amount the informant will receive. Otherwise, the informant will hold the department to that amount, regardless of future budgetary constraints. Departments should never pay informants based solely on the amount of drugs they recover. Informants have been known to tell dealers to add adulterants to their drugs that are about to be seized as a way of justifying a larger money reward.

In addition to providing awards and rewards, departments should reimburse informants for expenses incurred during an investigation. The department may wish to round up the reimbursement the informant is entitled to as an added incentive to continue working.

It is highly recommended that informants be paid only in the presence of witnesses, with the final payment being made only after all court proceedings have been completed to ensure the informant's presence at the trial. Every time an informant payment is made, a record documenting the date, exact amount, and who made and witnessed the payment must be included in the informant's file in anticipation of future court inquiries.

How to Make a Controlled Purchase Using an Informant

An investigative technique known as a *controlled purchase*, or a *controlled buy*, is frequently used in modern drug enforcement operations. By definition, a controlled purchase is when an informant or undercover drug agent buys drugs or other contraband from a suspect in order to use it as evidence in trial. The first sale of the contraband itself is a crime the suspect can be arrested for, but usually several purchases are made within several days or weeks, in progressively larger amounts, in order to defeat the *entrapment defense*. Entrapment is a legal defense where the defendant claims that either the informant or police convinced him to commit a crime he would not otherwise be predisposed to commit, solely for the purpose of arresting him. In other words, the defendant claims the police planted the idea of him committing the crime. By making several controlled buys, additional physical evidence is obtained, and the prosecution can dispel any notion that they entrapped the defendant.

CIs are frequently used to make controlled purchases of drugs, stolen property, weapons, and other contraband when using an undercover police officer would be impractical. Generally, informants provide law enforcement with the initial information pertaining to the illegal activities of the suspect. In a typical drug case scenario, investigators will first conduct a thorough debriefing of the informant that will most likely reveal that the informant has bought drugs or other contraband from the suspect in the past. The drug agents will determine if the suspect will continue to deal with the informant. If he will, an undercover meeting is planned.

Drug agents may learn the suspect refuses to take on new customers for fear they may be undercover police officers. Using a drug agent should be the first choice in investigating this type of case, but in light of his refusal to meet new customers, investigators may have to rely on the CI to make these controlled purchases instead.

The objective of the controlled buy investigative technique is to be able to prove in court that the suspect sold drugs to the informant. This is accomplished by taking precautions to lessen, if not eliminate, any other possibility. Below is the step-by-step procedure that should be followed to enhance the informant's safety during the operation, and to convince a reasonable man that the informant could only have obtained the drugs from the defendant.

Thoroughly Debrief the Informant

Drug agents must conduct a thorough debriefing of the informant in order to ascertain all known facts about the suspect. Questions the informant must answer include:

1. What is the physical description of the suspect? Where does he live and work? What are his contact telephone numbers? What type of vehicle does he drive?
2. Does the suspect have a propensity towards violence? Does he have access to a weapon?
3. How does the informant know the suspect? How long have they known each other?
4. Who is the source of supply (SOS) for the suspect's drugs? Does he have more than one SOS? What other items of contraband does he deal in? Is he a poly-drug dealer or does he specialize in one particular drug? When was the last time the informant saw the suspect deal drugs?
5. What is the price for the drugs he is selling? Are the prices reasonable, or exceptionally high or low for the area? (A low price could be indicative of either a planned robbery, or the sale of counterfeit drugs.)
6. Will the suspect meet new customers? Is he part of a larger organization needing assistance, e.g., couriers, enforcers, transporters, money launderers? Can an undercover agent be introduced to fill one of the organization's needs?
7. Where does he deal his drugs? What quantities does he deal in? Where does he like to make the exchange of drugs for money?
8. Does he deal alone or with others? Does he use counter-surveillance during his drug deals? If so, what do these people look like? What are their names, addresses, work places, vehicles they drive, etc?

Check Law Enforcement Indices

Once this preliminary information is obtained, a thorough check of various law enforcement and public records should be made. The FBI's NCIC can quickly determine if the suspect is wanted, has ever been arrested, what he was arrested for, and if he has ever been in prison.

If the suspect has been arrested, a review of the arrest report may reveal known associates, if he was armed, methods of operation, vehicles driven at the time of the arrest, etc. all of which are helpful in the beginning stages of a drug investigation. If a check reveals the suspect has a warrant for his arrest, it may make more sense to abandon the drug deal in favor of arresting him for the warrant instead. There is also a chance the suspect could be arrested by another police agency for the warrant prior to the completion of the drug investigation.

Checking with the state's Department of Motor Vehicles will identify all vehicles registered to the suspect, what mailing addresses he uses, as well as his driving record and photograph from his driver's license.

Requesting information from the local utility and telephone companies will reveal what locations he pays for gas and electric service as well as long distance telephone numbers he calls. Cellular telephone companies can provide credit information used to secure the service, as well as billing addresses, and a listing of all telephone numbers dialed from that instrument. From an analysis of telephone numbers he calls, the drug agents may be able to show connections between the suspect and other known or suspected drug dealers.

Monitor Phone Calls and Personal Visits between the Informant and the Suspect

To further corroborate the informant's information, monitor and record all telephone conversations between the informant and the suspect. It should be noted that in most states, conversations recorded with the consent of at least one involved party do not require a warrant. However, because consensual eavesdropping rules vary from state to state, agents not employed by the federal government should consult with their state attorney's office before using this technique.

The objective of these initial phone calls is to schedule a face-to-face meeting between the informant and the drug dealer. Monitoring these conversations accomplish several important things: it corroborates that the informant personally knows the suspect, it shows the informant that the drug agents are thorough in their methods, and it makes it clear that they intend to verify unsubstantiated information.

Before a telephone call is made to set up a face-to-face meeting, the drug agents should have an investigative plan that includes the clear objectives of the investigation, including where the meeting will take place. The selection of the location of the meeting should be made in advance to insure the location is conducive to easy surveillance.

The objectives of the investigation may change depending on the development of the case. The suspect may reveal to the informant a location where drugs are being stashed, or may ask him to assist in a future drug transaction. By monitoring all contacts between the informant and the suspect, the drug agents know all the unfiltered information the informant has about the suspect. It also prevents the informant from secretly taking part in an unauthorized side deal with the suspect.

Provide the Informant with Official Funds That Have the Serial Numbers Recorded

Just before leaving the office to follow the informant to the meeting location, drug agents should provide him with the monies necessary to purchase the drugs in question. In order to document how much money investigators gave to the informant, a signed receipt for the money must be obtained and included in the case file. Any monies not spent to purchase evidence must immediately be returned. Serialization of the money is important for three reasons: (1) It clearly demonstrates that the money originated from law enforcement, (2) it discourages the informant from stealing it, and (3) in the event the serialized money is seized from the suspect at a later date, it further corroborates he received the money from the informant. These funds may later be recovered at the time of the suspect's arrest or during the execution of a search warrant at the suspect's home, business, or vehicle.

The physical appearance of the money to be given to the suspect is important. Freshly printed notes banded in a wrapper provided by the Federal Reserve Bank, may alert the suspect that he is dealing with government authorities. However, used bills, in a variety of denominations, secured by rubber bands, will help convince the suspect that he is dealing with another drug dealer, because these are the types of bills drug dealers usually encounter (see Chapter 8).

Wire the Informant for Sound

Make sure the device used to transmit and record the informant's conversations with the suspect is operational before leaving the office. The informant must be cautioned not to turn off the transmitter under any circumstances since this will leave the investigation open to criticism and the issue will likely be raised in future court proceedings. Informants must be made to understand that if the transmitter is switched off the suspect may allege in court that while it was off, the informant threatened him harm if he did not go through with the drug deal. To avoid this situation, drug agents should attempt to only use transmitters that cannot be turned off, intentionally or accidentally.

Another rule of thumb about recording and transmitting devices is that if drug agents decide to record the first meeting, they should be prepared to record all subsequent meetings and telephone calls between the informant and the suspect during the entire investigation. By selectively recording only certain conversations, questions will be raised about the integrity of the case, and this may dampen the enthusiasm of the prosecutor to file charges against the suspect.

Designate Verbal and Visual Distress and Arrest Signals

Drug agents must discuss with the informant what signals to give in the event he is in trouble or he is being robbed of the agency's money. Both verbal and visual signals are needed since the transmitter cannot be relied upon. The informant must be trained that in the event of a transmitter failure, he should provide previously agreed upon visual signals designating distress or when drug agents should make their arrest.

Telephonic pagers greatly assist the drug agent in discretely communicating with the informant. Sending the informant a certain code number may mean to wrap up his conversation and leave the area. Another code may indicate surveillance is following him. Cellular telephones are also extremely useful in giving direction to the informant, provided the suspect cannot overhear the conversation, and the informant does not say something that would identify the caller.

Search the Informant and His Vehicle

Before leaving the office to go to the meeting location, it is vital that drug agents thoroughly search both the informant and his vehicle. This allows the drug agent to testify he did not find any drugs, weapons, or other contraband in the informant's immediate possession that could be used to either frame the suspect, or coerce him into selling drugs. If the informant refuses to allow himself or his vehicle to be searched, halt the operation immediately, and do not proceed until it can be established why the informant refuses to follow direction.

Surveillance Team to Follow the Informant

The surveillance team follows the informant to the predetermined meeting place so drug agents can later testify that the informant did not leave their sight and have an opportunity to pick up drugs or weapons at another location. Upon arrival at the meet location, drug agents should set up surveillance of the location to not only determine if the suspect has arrived, but when he arrives, and to also protect the informant from the suspect.

If the meeting place is at a public location such as a resturant, placing a drug agent inside to pose as a customer will further corroborate the informant's statements and will reveal if anyone joined the suspect during the conversation. The inside surveillance agent may be able to detect persons acting as counter-surveillance for the suspect. (For more details on this, see Chapter 6.)

Informant Is to Go to a Designated Cold Spot after the Meeting

Immediately upon completion of the meeting, the informant should go to a designated *cold spot* that is far enough away from the location to not be seen by the suspect.

There drug agents should retrieve the drug evidence that the informant just purchased, and they should also search the informant and his vehicle again to look for any other contraband the suspect may have given him. Informants have been known to receive more drugs than expected, and keep the excess amount for their own personal use or resale later.

Instruct the Informant to Immediately Return to the Office

The informant should return to the drug agent's office where he can be thoroughly debriefed on what transpired and to make a written statement detailing the events. Every time an informant makes a controlled buy, regardless of how many times he has done it before, these same procedures must be followed. If an undercover drug agent is making the controlled buy instead of an informant, there is a presumption of integrity that precludes the necessity to search him or her. However, because of officer safety concerns, he or she should always be under constant surveillance by a team designated to provide him with protection. (For more information on this, see Chapter 7.)

The Seven Steps to Successful Informant Management

Identify potential informants. Recognize persons who may be potential informants. Drug agents will develop this skill with experience.

Recruit informants. Establish a rapport with the person and explain the department's policy on awards and rewards in order to recruit a diversified stable of informants.

Document all contacts with informants. Document and maintain informant files to give a true picture of his work performance. Update files whenever changes occur.

Develop relationships. Know the limitations of individual informants, but do not accept anything less than their maximum effort.

Maintain relationships. Keep informants active by exposing them to situations that enhance, not limit or restrict, their ability to perform at their maximum potential.

Use informants to their fullest. Continue to use informants to keep them from losing interest. Encourage other drug agents to task these informants whenever possible.

Control informants. Manage informants successfully by controlling them. Drug agents cannot allow informants to run investigations, regardless of how insistent or assertive they become. Drug agents and their supervisors ultimately make the decisions during cases, and informants must be made to realize this.

Keys to Success in Informant Management

Control

Drug agents must learn to control their informants in order to keep a handle on their investigation. Informants need to know that the drug agent is in charge of the investigation, and their supervisor is the ultimate decision-maker and they are not. Keeping control of the informant will prevent him from making unauthorized contacts with the targeted drug dealer and keep him in focus. Drug agents who lose control of their informant will soon lose control of their investigation.

Honesty

If the controlling drug agent is not honest with the informant, why should the informant be honest with the agent? For the sake of safety and maintaining control of the informant, the investigator must be honest with him. If the investigator exaggerates about the amount of money his agency will pay the informant for his services, the informant is probably not going to work for the agency again. He may become disgruntled to the point of not cooperating during trial preparation or courtroom testimony. Honesty is certainly the best policy when working with drug informants.

Fairness and Respect

Informants, like anyone else, appreciate being treated fairly. Drug agents should consistently treat their informants fairly throughout their relationship, and they should be treated the same as any other employee.

Show respect for the informant and refrain from calling him names such as *snitch*, *fink*, *rat*, and the like. Chances are he would not be an informant if it were not out of necessity. Show your appreciation for his long hours and hard work on the job.

Clarity in Direction

Many mistakes can be avoided when the drug agent takes the time to clearly explain directions to the informant. By being clear and specific with the informant, he cannot claim, rightly or wrongly, that he did not know he could not do a particular thing. Making mistakes due to misdirection or carelessness can cause tremendous safety problems for the informant and drug agents as well.

Provide Training for the Informant

Informants must be trained in some legal aspects of drug enforcement to avoid violating a suspect's rights and to prevent the informant from committing unintentional criminal acts. Unless trained, informants may believe they have law enforcement authority, when they do not; that they can carry concealed weapons, when they cannot; and that they can entrap people who normally would not be predisposed to commit a drug crime for the purpose of arresting them. All these areas as well as departmental policies concerning informant interaction must be gone over with the informant.

Informants must also be taught to know they cannot violate the law in an effort to enforce it. The informant must know that violations of the law will not be tolerated, and that he will be arrested for doing so. For instance, breaking into a drug dealer's home to find evidence of a crime will result in the informant's arrest and prosecution for burglary. The informant must be clear on what he is expected to do, and more importantly, what he shall not do.

Summary

Since the public does not usually report drug crimes, it is imperative that drug agents collect a steady flow of actionable criminal intelligence in order for them to be effective. This requires the constant recruitment, use, and proper management of drug informants and their information. The purpose of informants is to gather information from sources not readily available to law enforcement officers; to make observations in places where strangers would immediately be suspect; to conduct undercover negotiations; and to gain firsthand, timely intelligence.

Most informants either still are, or once were a part of the drug underground, which gives them access to highly valuable criminal information. At the same time, this association with drug dealers makes them inherently unreliable due to their criminal pasts and desire for anonymity.

All informants provide information to the police in order to get something in return. Their motives range from being paid to playing the role of a fictional crime-fighter. Regardless of what motivates an informant to provide information, the drug agent must identify the true reasons early on. An informant who states he is being motivated by money when in reality is motivated by revenge, will ignore direction from his handler and orchestrate events that will fulfill his motivation. Perversely motivated informants are dangerous and destructive.

Informants need to be kept under tight control. They need to know who is in charge and that they are not. The case agent and his or her supervisor must make every decision on what direction the drug investigation will take, never the informant. The informant's input should be solicited and carefully considered, but the drug agent and his or her supervisor ultimately decides how the investigation will be conducted.

5 Sources of Information

Sources of information include both people and institutions. Drug agents need a steady flow of information in order to be effective in their jobs. Information is the lifeblood of any investigation, and drug cases rely more on information than any other form of criminal investigation.

Everyone a drug agent comes into contact with is a potential source of information. Those people and institutions most frequently encountered include:

- Airline ticket agents
- Travel agents
- Baggage handlers
- Car rental employees
- Hotel clerks
- Utility companies
- Telephone service providers
- Real estate agents
- Internet service providers
- Bank employees
- Taxi drivers
- County Assessor's Office
- Credit bureaus
- Private express shipping companies
- Yacht club employees
- Boat sales personnel
- Flight service station employees
- Private airplane sales personnel

These potential sources of information can provide drug agents with documentation of the suspect's travel, banking, and telephone habits. This information frequently produces leads to other members of the conspiracy, and may help locate hidden assets and drug proceeds.

Most people employed in these occupations provide information to drug agents either because they are compelled to by court order, or they have altruistic motives. Offering to pay these sources of information may result in some being offended, while others are eager to earn extra money while helping law enforcement.

Airline Ticket Agents

Many basic drug investigations have the potential of being expanded into a complex smuggling case. Smuggling cases have the goal of identifying not only the smugglers involved with introducing the drug into the United States, but also with identifying those who move the drugs from one part of the country to the other.

Drugs are commonly moved from one place to another via commercial airline. Both passengers and employees of airlines in all categories have been arrested for actually smuggling controlled substances, or for facilitating the transfer of these illegal drugs. Airline ticket agents, as well as other categories of employees, can help tremendously in cases of this type. Airline ticket agents, when trained by drug agents on the profile of a commercial air smuggler, can provide specific information about passengers, how their tickets were paid, as well as when and where they were purchased. Sometimes a simple computer check accessing this type of information can provide drug agents assigned to airport interdiction operations with information that frequently leads to arrests and seizures. See Chapter 15 for specific information.

Travel Agents

Unlike airline ticket agents who usually only have access to specific information pertaining to their own airline, travel agents can access information from not only airline computers, but those maintained by rail, bus, and cruise ships, plus hotels throughout the world.

These agents can provide drug law enforcement officers with vital information in the tracking of individuals involved in drug trafficking. Leads generated from travel agencies can provide drug agents with the opportunity to glean telephone toll information from calls made at hotels stayed at by the trafficker, as well as the method of payment for the room. The credit card information from payment of the hotel stay can lead to the development of other information in connection with the credit card application.

Car Rental Employees

Employees of car rental agencies can provide drug agents with information pertaining to when and where a suspect rented a vehicle, how he paid for it, and the expected date of return of the car. They can also provide agents with information pertaining to prior history of car rentals by a particular suspect. With a court order, rental companies will allow drug agents access to the vehicle the suspect will be renting in order to install tracking or other devices inside.

Hotel Registration Clerks

These valuable sources of information can provide drug agents with not only the occupant of a certain room, but can search reservation computers for recent and future stays. Nationwide hotel chains and especially international hotel chains can provide information about the airline and flight on which the suspect will be arriving, and its origin. Also, the hotel can provide the international telephone numbers that were called from the room, and what hotel services, including Internet and other business center services, that may have been provided. Having this type of information may lead to the development of valuable leads in identifying sources of supply and co-conspirators.

Utility Companies

Drug agents can quickly ascertain the names of persons paying for water, electric, and gas service at a particular address by contacting the appropriate utility company. Based on the huge volume of requests that are generated from law enforcement agencies in major metropolitan areas, these companies sometimes devote employees specifically for this purpose and sometimes require a subpoena before releasing this information.

Surveillance agents should contact more than one of the utility companies providing service to a specific address in order to compare names of subscribers. Some utilities, such as electric companies, may have initiated service in a man's name, and the water and gas may be subscribed either in the name of the man's wife or in an entirely different name. The names and the credit applications submitted to the utility companies to initiate service can lead to the identity of other members of the drug conspiracy. Furthermore, by furnishing a suspect's name to a utility or local telephone company, the drug agents can determine if the suspect is a customer, and at what address services are being provided.

Drug agents in major metropolitan areas may find many different municipal and regional electric power companies within their jurisdiction. Often, agents will have to contact each company directly to ascertain the information they seek.

Telephone Service Providers

One of the most important tools in a drug agent's box is access to information pertaining to telephone calls made by suspects. Suspects rely on residential, business, pager, and cellular telephone service to communicate with other members of their criminal conspiracy and take steps to disguise their use of the telephone when possible.

Many suspects activate one or more cellular telephones only to discontinue the service or discard the actual telephone within a few days or weeks fearing law enforcement has obtained their number and may be listening in on their conversations. The reality of the situation is that there are many more telephones being used to facilitate drug transactions then there are drug agents to monitor them. Despite this, most drug traffickers do not take the chance, and will frequently cancel service, change subscriber names, or abandon cellular telephones altogether.

Under subpoena, telephone companies are required to provide drug law enforcement with the subscriber information and any particular detailed information called for in the subpoena. Typically, drug agents will ask for a record of all toll, or long-distance telephone calls made from a particular number for the past 6 months. After receiving this information, drug agents and intelligence analysts can see the relationship between the suspect and others that he calls. An analysis of telephone calls made by a particular subject can frequently identify members of the same conspiracy, and locate hiding places, stash houses, and the like. Telephone companies can also provide subscriber information on an emergency basis to law enforcement. For specific information pertaining to telephone analysis, see Chapter 17.

Real Estate Agents

Real estate agents can perform a variety of services for drug agents during the course of an investigation. They have the ability to conduct property searches to locate properties owned by a particular individual. They can also, in some cases, provide the price the home or building was purchased for, if it was financed, and with what lender. They can identify the real estate office responsible for the sale, as well as the escrow company that completed the transaction.

This type of information may be helpful in determining the assets of a particular drug trafficker when attempting to seize his property as drug proceeds. They may also be able to identify the architect who built the home or building, which may be of help if serving a high-risk search warrant. Architectural drawings may reveal unique or hidden compartments within the home.

Internet Service Providers

Drug agents are encountering an increasing number of traffickers that rely on their own web sites, email, and the Internet to sell drugs, chemicals, and laboratory supplies. Internet service providers can provide law enforcement with the names and billing addresses of all subscribers to their services. They can also provide technical assistance in helping to track email, as well as email addresses used by subscribers.

Banking Institutions

Banks are compelled to provide information to a drug agent who is armed with a grand jury subpoena. Requests can range from verifying whether a trafficker maintains an account at the bank, to the balance he maintains, and copies of applications for loans he may have made. They can also provide names of safety deposit box holders, as well as when they last had access to the boxes.

Security at banks require constant videotaping of customer transactions, and still photos can be obtained from the tapes. Making a deposit or withdrawal of drug proceeds may be an overt act in proving a conspiracy case, and these tapes may provide invaluable evidence.

Taxi Drivers

Long a source of information for police officers, taxi drivers can provide suspect descriptions, where they were picked up and taken to, and possibly call back telephone numbers maintained by their dispatchers. Taxi drivers are a natural part of the landscape in any neighborhood they frequent. Drug agents may solicit trusted sources to drive by certain locations during different times of the day to look for a particular vehicle. A taxi company or independent driver may also allow drug agents the use of their vehicle for particular surveillance assignments.

County Assessor's Office

This governmental office can provide drug agents with the names of the owners of properties within the county, and advise when and if a certain property is in the process of changing ownership.

Credit Bureaus

There are several large credit bureau organizations operating within the United States. Each maintains an extensive record of anyone who has ever established credit, as well as the payment history of an individual. The security management of credit organizations have assisted drug agents in the past in creating a credit history under an undercover name that will be used by an agent. Creating such a history, which will show employment, using totally fictitious information helps tremendously in gaining the confidence of traffickers while working undercover.

Express Shipping Companies

Many drug traffickers have used express shipping companies such as Federal Express and United Parcel Service to transport drugs to customers. These companies, as well as others, have proven to be extremely cooperative in drug investigations. In addition to providing tracking information on packages, they may assist by lending uniforms, vehicles, and other items for use during special surveillance operations and controlled deliveries.

Yacht Club Employees

Employees of yacht clubs may have inside information pertaining to the travels of particular boats and yachts, and who was aboard the vessels at the time they arrived at the club. They can also serve as lookouts for specific vessels drug law enforcement may be interested in.

Many employees hear rumors or are themselves asked to participate in certain aspects of maritime drug smuggling. They can provide leads into how services were paid for, who accompanied the trafficker during his visit at the club, how long his vessel was docked, etc. They can alert drug agents to furtive activity and suspicious persons that may be visiting with members of the yacht club or are waiting for them to arrive from a sailing voyage.

Boat and Yacht Sales Personnel

These professional sales people will be able to provide information to drug law enforcement agents about the sales of popular vessels used in the smuggling of drugs. With a court order, they can provide law enforcement with access to vessels for the placement of tracking devices. They will also have access to financing information, bank loans, insurance carriers, and other companies and individuals involved in maritime businesses. Many drug smuggling cases are initiated based on information provided by yacht salesmen and women.

Flight Service Station Employees

These employees work in offices at airports that provide private and commercial pilots with a place to rest, file flight plans, buy fuel, food, maps, rent aircraft, and other necessities for air travel. Like yacht clubs, but to a smaller degree, these employees can ascertain when a certain plane arrived or took off, who was flying the plane, and its destination. These employees can also look out for particular airplanes drug law enforcement knows are involved in air smuggling.

Private Airplane Sales Personnel

Much like their yacht sales counterpart, private airplane sales personnel can provide listings of all sales of aircraft or who was interested in purchasing planes or modifying existing ones that may accommodate smugglers. These people could prove to be a wealth of information pertaining to air smuggles occurring in any particular area of the country.

Conclusion

This list of sources of information is not all-inclusive, and not all the sources will be able to provide criminal information on a continuing basis. Drug agents should, however, make contacts at these establishments to cultivate informants who can provide specific, timely information about the activities of drug traffickers.

Summary

Drug agents, like any criminal investigator, need to cultivate and develop sources of information from a variety of places. This can be accomplished by seeking out people in certain professions that may be privy to the goings-on of drug traffickers and smugglers.

Many of these sources can provide a wealth of information about particular sales transactions, what was purchased, how it was paid for, and the like. This information may prove vital in identifying co-conspirators and lead to the location of drugs and drug proceeds.

Surveillance and Counter-Surveillance

6

Throughout the career of any drug agent, he or she will spend a substantial amount of time conducting surveillance. This is due to the fact that drug crimes are investigated as they happen as opposed to after-the-fact crimes such as burglary or robbery where the suspects are normally not known. Traditional police investigations do involve surveillance activities, however not nearly as often as drug cases because of the nature of the crime. Drug agents working as a surveillance team will develop into a highly effective force to gather intelligence information about suspects and identify co-conspirators in the drug trafficking organization.

Definition and Purpose of Surveillance

Surveillance is the secretive and continuous or periodic watching of persons, vehicles, places, and objects to obtain information concerning the activities and identities of the individuals.

Surveillance is often the only investigative technique drug agents can use to identify *stash pads* where drugs are stored, couriers, and sources of supply. It also frequently identifies buyers and distributors as well as codefendants and co-conspirators.

There is no substitute for traditional, hands on surveillance. Following the primary suspect to learn his activities on any given day may lead drug agents to where he lives, who he associates with, what vehicles he had access to, where he socializes, and where he works. This information may be invaluable later when trying to locate him in order to make his arrest or to prevent him from committing another crime.

Frequently CIs (confidential informants) will tell their drug agent handlers that they have met a drug dealer willing to sell a particular drug to them with one caveat; he does not know the identity of the dealer. The drug agents should direct the informant to arrange a meeting in a public place with the man in order to allow the agents to place surveillance on him. From there, the agents potentially can identify what vehicle he is driving, where he lives, what his full description is, and possibly where he stores his drugs.

Types of Surveillance

There are three basic types of surveillance used in modern drug enforcement: mobile, stationary, and electronic.

Mobile

Conducted either on foot or using a vehicle, drug agents have an opportunity to follow the suspect to determine who he meets, where he goes, and what he does.

Stationary

Stationary surveillance is conducted from a fixed point; often from within a building or parked vehicle.

Electronic

Twenty-first century drug investigations often involve the use of technical listening equipment and cameras to keep suspects under constant surveillance or to alert them when they have arrived at a particular location. Law enforcement technicians are creative in ways of concealing cameras that are used by agents to maintain surveillance on suspects. A common piece of equipment used is a hollow transformer container, which can be found on telephone and power poles, that has a video camera inside that transmits microwave signals to a receiver at the drug agents' office. There the signal is recorded on videotape where it can be reviewed for activity overnight or at other times. The *pole-cam*, as it is called, is usually installed by drug agents posing as employees of the telephone or electric company servicing the area, and is nearly impossible to detect by the suspects. They have been used successfully for many years.

Other forms of electronic surveillance equipment may include hidden cameras in furnishings commonly found in any hotel room in the United States, including thermostats, alarm clocks, table lamps, and televisions. Cameras have also been installed in the brake lights of unoccupied automobiles for recording suspects and the coming and goings of other vehicles that drive up to a particular address. Use of such devices should be discussed with local prosecutors to insure they do not violate any particular state statue forbidding the use of such devices, even by law enforcement.

Objectives of Surveillance

There are many good reasons to conduct surveillances of suspected drug traffickers. As previously stated, drug trafficking involves many persons working in concert to achieve their goal. The drug agent's objective is to identify as many persons as possible who are involved in the conspiracy and surveillance will go a long way in achieving this goal.

Identify the Main Target of the Investigation

Conducting surveillance often leads to the full identify of the suspects involved in the drug trafficking organization. Sometimes, simply observing the license plate of the vehicle he drives and later determining the registered owner through records maintained by the state department of motor vehicles can lead to the true identity of the suspect. However, sometimes it becomes more challenging, particularly if the suspect has made efforts to thwart drug law enforcement. More on this will be discussed in the counter-surveillance portion of this chapter.

Even if the vehicle the suspect is driving is not his own, the leads developed from obtaining the registered owner information may later determine that the owner of the vehicle is also involved in the drug crime. If the registered owner is not involved directly, he or she can later be interviewed, which may lead to other persons who are involved.

If, for example, the unidentified suspect, when first observed, is driving a rental vehicle, his name, a driver's license number and address can be ascertained from the car rental company. The company can also tell agents when the vehicle is due back, and possibly if the suspect arrived from out of town on a particular flight. The point is that surveillance creates investigative leads for drug agents that would not normally be available by any other means.

Identify Other Members of the Drug Organization

Conducting surveillance of the suspect will often lead to the identification of other members of the criminal conspiracy. Many drug dealers work at his or her trade on a full-time basis, and the likelihood is good that every person they contact could be involved as well. All persons the main target of the investigation meets with should be fully identified. Drug agents can make record checks of these individuals to determine if they have a criminal background. If they do, especially if they have a history of drug trafficking, this means the surveillance agents should continue their surveillance on these persons. Once surveillance agents begin to see that the suspects are only associating with each other, and no one new, it is probable that all members of their organization have been identified.

Locate *Stash* Locations

Drug agents strive to seize large amounts of drugs during the course of their investigations. In many urban, suburban, and rural areas, huge quantities of drugs may be stored in innocent looking dwellings or commercial storage facilities. Suspects will travel to these locations to check on co-conspirators who are providing security for the drugs, determine the amount of the supply on hand, or remove a quantity for sale later. They will also be on the alert for anything out of the ordinary to alert them that drug agents are investigating their activities.

During the undercover phase of an investigation, the undercover agent or informant may order a quantity of drugs they believe the suspect cannot produce at the moment, forcing him to travel to where the drugs are stored. Sometimes to increase the likelihood of forcing the suspect to travel to get the drugs, the undercover agent will not order a specific amount of drugs until he or she meets personally with the suspect. Another technique is to pay for the drugs the suspect delivers, and then immediately order a similar quantity forcing him to return to the original location or go somewhere else to retrieve the drugs. Doing this gives the surveillance agents another opportunity to locate the stash pad if they happen to lose the suspect during their first attempt (Figure 6.1).

Obtain Probable Cause for a Search Warrant

Surveillance agents may be able to articulate in an affidavit certain facts they observed that may lead a judge to issue a search warrant. For example, during a drug investigation surveillance agents observe the suspect meeting with an undercover agent at a restaurant to discuss a drug transaction. At the conclusion of the meeting, the surveillance agents follow the suspect to a house where he is observed entering the dwelling empty-handed. A few minutes later, surveillance agents observe the suspect leave the house carrying a shopping bag, which he places in the trunk of his vehicle. Surveillance agents then follow the suspect back to the original meeting location, where he delivers the bag that contained drugs to the undercover agent.

Thanks to the surveillance agents, they now know where the suspect probably stores his drugs. Without their observations, they would have no chance of obtaining a search warrant for the house to look for more drugs. If a search warrant is issued and agents find more drugs along with other suspects in the house, these additional people may be arrested as co-conspirators, or they may wish to cooperate with drug agents in providing information

Figure 6.1 Kilos of cocaine seized after a successful surveillance operation. (Courtesy of the U.S. Drug Enforcement Administration.)

about the original suspect. In either event, surveillance agents would have made a difference in expanding the investigation to its fullest potential.

Locate Wanted Persons

Often surveillance agents will identify people the main target of the investigation meets with and determine that they are wanted by police authorities in other jurisdictions. This information should be passed on to these authorities so that they may coordinate the arrest in such a way as to not jeopardize the ongoing drug investigation.

Verify the Reliability of an Informant

Surveillance can add to the reliability of newly established CIs. Surveillance agents can corroborate certain information provided by the informant by verifying certain things during the course of a surveillance operation. If the informant says the suspect drives a certain type of vehicle, surveillance can verify this information if the suspect is seen driving the vehicle. Surveillance agents could also corroborate informant information pertaining to the description and location where the suspect lives, and the names and descriptions of people the suspect associates with. Documenting this corroboration of the informant's information will add to the informant's history of reliability. As the number of occasions where the informant's information is corroborated increases, it may later sway a judge to issue a search warrant based in part on the past proven reliability of the informant.

Obtain Detailed Information

Search warrants require not only probable cause to be issued, but the warrant must include a detailed description of the location to be searched. Surveillance agents can drive by or position themselves to see the location long enough to obtain a detailed, accurate description of the premises to be searched.

Prevent the Commission of a Crime or Arrest a Suspect in the Act

Drug traffickers are often engaged in other criminal activity. If it should come to the attention of drug agents that the suspect intends to commit a nondrug crime such as burglary or robbery, surveillance agents can follow the suspect and make an arrest of the suspect in the act, or prevent the crime entirely.

Many police departments around the country will set up surveillance teams on recently paroled violent offenders on the assumption they will commit another violent crime. These surveillance teams often catch parolees in the act of committing a robbery or similar crime.

Obtain Information for Later Use during an Interrogation

During the course of surveillance, agents will record the activities of those they follow. Later during an interrogation, if a suspect denies knowing someone or being at a particular location, surveillance notes, photographs, and videotapes may convince the suspect that it is fruitless to lie because they were seen with certain people doing certain things during a surveillance.

Develop Clues and Information from Other Sources

When surveillance agents follow a suspect to locations such as a bank, stockbroker, or post office, agents can conduct a follow-up investigation to determine what relationship the suspect has with these businesses. By following the suspect to these and other locations, agents are afforded the opportunity to develop clues and information about the suspect that would not have normally been possible without surveillance. Agents may determine the suspect has a bank account at a particular bank, has an account with a stockbroker, or uses a post office box to receive personal mail. This type of information may not have been available to the informant who initiated the case and is frequently learned only through the use of surveillance.

Qualities of a Surveillance Agent

Drug agents conducting surveillance must be able to fit into a crowd and avoid being noticed by their target. Besides having a normal appearance and acting naturally in their surroundings, they must be able to remain alert during long, sometimes arduous hours of work, and be resourceful when necessary. Patience and stamina are qualities they must exhibit during most of their time spent on a surveillance team.

Normal Appearance

Surveillance agents must adapt to their surroundings. If they know in advance that they will be covering a meeting between a CI and the target of the investigation at an opulent hotel, the majority of them should dress accordingly. Since people from all walks of life and socio-economic backgrounds frequent hotels, even opulent ones, the manner of dress and appearance must match what they expect to find there.

Some drug agents choose to have long hair, a beard, and wear blue jeans, t-shirts, and running shoes. Agents appearing this way can still effectively conduct surveillance at upscale locations, but in limited capacities, such as street people, laborers, and the like. Common sense dictates that surveillance agents should approximate the same appearance as the suspect they are following. If the weather is warm, surveillance agents should not be the only ones on the street wearing a jacket (to conceal their weapons). Adjustments need to be made to rid themselves of the telltale signs of being the police. Ankle holsters, butt packs, notebooks, portable radios, car radio microphones, emergency lights, binoculars, cameras, handcuffs, etc. should be concealed from view and even covered up inside the agent's vehicle. The suspect's movements may change suddenly and the agent could find him or herself parked near the suspect as he walks by, giving him the opportunity to see surveillance equipment inside the vehicle.

Act as Naturally as Possible

Inexperienced surveillance agents sometimes act as if they are wearing their badge on their shirts or have *POLICE* tattooed on their forehead. This is a natural response that comes from unrealistic fear that they have been spotted by the suspect, and that he knows that surveillance agents are following him. Many of these fears are later determined to be unfounded. The subject of the surveillance has no way of verifying that he is being followed by the police, and in most cases will be reluctant to confront surveillance agents.

Many suspects firmly believe they are the subjects of around-the-clock surveillance by government entities. They cannot be convinced that the government has not tapped their telephones, fax machines, homes, and businesses. These suspects are extremely fearful of going to prison for their criminal activity, and sometimes have a boost to their egos knowing that the government is devoting so much time in apprehending them. Because of the paranoia of constantly being followed, many suspects will take surreptitious routes to frequently visited places and will attempt to lose any surveillance agents that may be following them before they park at their intended destination. When such a suspect encounters a surveillance agent who is acting normally for the surroundings, he can never be sure he is being followed. More on this will be discussed later in this chapter.

In order to blend in with other people in public, surveillance agents should attempt to appear as normal as possible within their surroundings. They should not wear flashy jewelry or colorful clothing, and they should be careful not to expose any firearms or other equipment they may have on their person. Their clothing should fit prevailing weather conditions. Having several different colored caps and sunglasses to change their appearance helps them remain invisible to the suspect they are following.

Alert

Often surveillance assignments can last the entire day and into the night. Agents need to prepare for such an event and have adequate amounts of water, coffee, food, and clothing to endure the day. The lack of these essential items will necessitate the agent being taken away from the rest of the surveillance team until they can be obtained.

Agents need to be alert to any sudden actions by the suspect that may change the course of the investigation. They need to be aware of telephone calls he makes at public telephone booths, businesses he visits, and people he meets with.

Surveillance agents need to obtain the telephone number of any public telephone booths the suspect makes outgoing telephone calls from. The telephone company can later determine if a toll call was made at that exact time, and what telephone number was called. This information can possibly lead to the identity of other conspirators, or provide a useful investigative lead.

When the suspect meets with an individual never encountered before, the surveillance team leader needs to make a decision about following the new person. He or she must decide if following this new person will risk draining available resources to identify him. A good rule of thumb is to make an effort to identify the new person since the opportunity may not present itself again.

Resourceful

Expert surveillance agents have been known to use their surroundings as natural camouflage. Using a fold up windshield sunscreen with slits cut in it to see out of while observing a suspect in a parking lot is just one example of resourcefulness exhibited by surveillance agents. Putting the hood up on a vehicle to make it appear to be disabled while positioned at a particularly good vantage point is another example of resourcefulness.

Observant

Surveillance agents must be good observers. Experienced drug agents and police officers can see things that citizens without police experience cannot. Some police officers seem to have a sixth sense that aids them in anticipating what might happen next after observing the body language and demeanor of a suspect they are following. Drug agents can also often tell when a drug deal is about to take place, or when one has just occurred. Since many drug dealers assume they are constantly under surveillance, drug agents must be especially observant to see with whom they come in contact and what packages are exchanged.

Patience and Stamina

Any surveillance potentially could conclude much later than the drug agents originally intended. The time spent on a surveillance depends on how successful the agents are in following the suspect, and exactly what the suspect is doing while being followed.

No two surveillance operations are alike, and because of their unpredictability, drug agents should be prepared for lengthy assignments that will require stamina. When a team of agents follow a suspect into a restaurant, most of that team will be outside in their vehicles waiting for the suspect to exit and will not have the ability to refresh themselves with food or drink. When it appears the suspect will be at a particular place for a predictable length of time, e.g., after he has ordered a meal, surveillance agents should take advantage of this time to make food runs.

Categories of Surveillance

There are five categories of surveillance: intelligence gathering, prebuy and postbuy surveillance, reconnaissance, and physical survey. Each has an important role in leading to a successful drug operation and in keeping undercover agents safe.

Intelligence Gathering

The whole purpose of surveillance is to gather intelligence about the suspect. The goal is for the drug agents to learn whom the suspect meets, where he lives, whom he visits, and where he socializes, etc. Conducting surveillance may discover previously unknown details concerning drug crimes, locate fugitives, or enhance the credibility of any informant involved.

Prebuy Surveillance

Before any undercover agent or informant is sent to a location to purchase drugs during the course of the investigation, surveillance agents must be on hand ahead of time. The conducting of prebuy surveillance may aid in the identification of co-conspirators and may reveal the presence of counter-surveillance. For the protection of the undercover agent or informant, surveillance agents must be on hand before, during, and after the purchase of drugs in order to insure their safety.

Prebuy surveillance agents may be able to see accomplices that are armed, or identify who may be in possession of the drugs the traffickers intend to sell. Not conducting prebuy surveillance is abandoning an effective investigative tool and may result in safety problems for undercover personnel.

Postbuy Surveillance

Even after the drugs have been purchased by the undercover agent or informant, and he or she has left the location, surveillance agents should remain on scene for a short while in order to see if the suspects return for any reason, and if so, who they meet with.

Simultaneously, other agents must keep surveillance on the undercover agent, who should not drive directly back to his or her office, to determine if suspects may be following. If suspects are following, their intention may be to rob the agent of the drugs, or possibly kidnap him or her to later extort more money from his "partners." Any notion that the undercover agents are being followed should immediately be communicated to the agents so they can initiate counter-surveillance driving techniques to avoid being seen returning to their office.

Reconnaissance

Surveillance agents can *recon* the scheduled meeting spot with an undercover agent, and determine if there are suitable places to conduct stationary surveillance undetected. The case agent or surveillance team leader can assign surveillance agents to these locations in order to get a full field view of the activities that will take place there. Other surveillance agents familiar with the suspects, their cars, and where they live and work should show other agents who will be participating in the surveillance or stakeout.

Physical Survey

Surveillance agents conduct preplanning activities to familiarize themselves with the topography of the area, and basic information regarding the neighborhood and its residents. Local police officers in the city where the surveillance is going to be conducted are an excellent source of information to determine what type of neighborhood the suspect lives in, and what the likelihood of encountering counter-surveillance by sympathetic neighbors is. They can also advise where the best local hospitals are in the event that they are needed. Physical surveys also determine typical traffic conditions in certain areas that may affect the ability of surveillance agents to maneuver while at the same time allowing agents to familiarize themselves with local streets and alleys.

Other Considerations

Every surveillance agent should carry an adequate amount of cash to handle any emergency that may arise during a planned or unscheduled surveillance. Agents do not have time to go to an automatic teller machine or stop inside a bank to write a check while the surveillance is being conducted. Agents will need funds to quickly pay for meals if they are assigned to follow the suspect inside a restaurant, or to possibly purchase something if they go into a store. Using a credit card may take too long to allow the surveillance agent to rejoin his or her surveillance team members in a timely fashion.

Agents should always have in their vehicles a packed bag containing personal hygiene items and a change of clothing in case an overnight stay is necessary. The bag also doubles as a prop if they have to follow a suspect into an airport, train station, or hotel.

Surveillance team members also need to have all their communication equipment with them including:

- Cellular telephones programmed with the telephone numbers of other agents and their supervisor in the event assistance is needed
- Cellular telephone car battery cord
- Charged portable radios with extra batteries
- Pager
- Binoculars or monocular
- Bottled water

- Fruit or snacks
- Flashlight
- Map of the area
- Pen and notepad or small tape recorder or digital recording machine to dictate time, date, places, and events observed
- Several different styles of hats
- Sunglasses
- Jacket or coat appropriate for the weather
- Umbrella
- Shoulder bag for equipment storage or use as a prop

Agents should remember that it does not take the entire team to see when a suspect comes out of a building or returns to his car. One agent is usually sufficient to see the suspect exit a building, assuming he or she has an unobstructed view. During this time, other agents should be set up to follow the suspect away in any direction he may travel.

Rules of Surveillance

There can be only one team leader during a surveillance operation. Each surveillance agent must have a specific assignment given by the team leader. When following a suspect in his vehicle into a store parking lot that is part of a strip mall, the surveillance team leader must immediately insure that members of the team are covering each driveway in anticipation of the suspect exiting there. The team leader can assign an agent to go into the business the suspect is visiting to determine who he is making contact with.

Furthermore, agents need to be positioned on the street in all possible directions of travel the suspect may go. Once the suspect returns to his car and is committed to driving away in one particular direction, the other agents will quickly catch up to continue the surveillance.

Surveillance agents should work out a form of communicating with each other while on foot and in sight of each other. Cellular telephones work well for this purpose, as do alphanumeric pagers that receive lines of text. Agents can call their office from the scene of foot surveillance and have someone transmit a page to these types of pagers telling other agents precisely where the suspect is. Using this system is preferred to using hard-to-conceal radios with limited range. Supervisors and surveillance team leaders need to make arrangements for a shift relief in the event the surveillance should need to go on for longer than expected.

Fundamentals of Surveillance

- Agents should avoid eye-to-eye contact with the suspect. Most suspects will immediately be convinced they are being followed if someone makes eye contact with them. Surveillance agents should not fear being discovered by the suspect, even if eye contact is made, since the suspect can never be positive drug agents are watching them.
- Agents should have a rehearsed reason for being where they are. In the event the suspect should confront a surveillance agent and ask him why he or she is following him, they can deny such activity and tell them the reason for their presence. The agent should not leave the area immediately in an attempt to act natural, but they should no longer participate in the surveillance that day.
- Surveillance agents can avoid attention and detection by acting as naturally as they can for their surroundings. If the suspect is followed into a restaurant and he is going to order a meal, the agent should also order something to justify his stay in the restaurant for as long as the suspect does.
- Agents should not rely on information provided by persons who provide a service to the suspect. Asking the suspect's barber, doorman, bartender, gardener, waiter, or housekeeper a question about the suspect usually will prompt them to immediately report their contact with the police, usually in hopes of a reward.
- Surveillance agents need to be prepared to telephone the suspect at his home or business using a false pretense. Telephoning the suspect's home or business asking for him is one way of verifying he is there. Suspects may answer these calls themselves and may be reluctant to say where they are. A convincing story may cause the suspect to relax his guard.
- Checking the suspect's mailbox to see who he is getting mail from, and what businesses he has a relationship with, may generate investigative leads. Checking his garbage, or taking it once it is placed on the sidewalk area of his residence for collection can be a treasure trove of information. Often cutting agents, small baggies, drug paraphernalia with drug residue, empty boxes of baking soda for the production of crack cocaine, duct tape to reseal kilogram packages of cocaine, etc. can be found in a suspect's garbage.
- When following the suspect in a vehicle, surveillance agents should not be afraid of being too close, especially in areas of heavy traffic. Large urban areas produce heavy traffic that calls for vehicles being close to one another at most times of the day and night.

ents should not be ashamed of losing the suspect. Often a single red traffic light will prevent the agent from following the suspect through an intersection. Agents who violate traffic laws with impunity while the suspect watches are telegraphing their presence, thereby jeopardizing the surveillance. Losing a suspect during a surveillance sometimes cannot be helped, regardless of the amount of preplanning that was done. If the agents are convinced the suspect is aware of their presence, they should not immediately return to their office, but rather drive in different directions to avoid being followed themselves by any mobile counter-surveillance accomplices.

Using Air Support during Surveillance

Many law enforcement agencies utilize aircraft to support surveillance operations. These airplanes or helicopters have proven invaluable in assisting ground surveillance follow a suspect, especially in urban areas, or over long distances.

Surveillance aircraft, manned by a pilot and a dedicated trained observer, should take the bulk of the responsibility in keeping tabs on the suspect, while ground units will be valuable once the suspect arrives at his destination.

When following the suspect on a freeway or expressway, the lead ground unit should call out landmarks and the names of exits for the benefit of the other units. In many cases, the helicopter or airplane observer will be unable to read the highway signs and will never be able to read residential street signs.

Unfortunately, aircraft have limitations such as flying in controlled airspace, running low on fuel, and the need for periodic maintenance. However, they have proven to be highly effective and successful in drug law enforcement investigations. If drug agents have the opportunity to get air support, use it!

Surveillance Notes and Reports

The team leader should assign a specific agent before the surveillance is conducted to be responsible for writing a report about the activities they observe the suspect engaged in. The specific report writer should also be responsible for gathering all notes taken by other surveillance agents from which he or she will formulate the report (Figure 6.2).

Counter-Surveillance

Drug agents should never underestimate the sophistication of some drug dealers. Drug traffickers realize they are in a high-risk business between

State Police
Drug Investigation Unit

Surveillance Log

Case Number	Agent	Date	Page ____ of ____

TIME	SUBJ	VEH	OBS	ACTIVITY

Figure 6.2 Surveillance log.

dealing with other criminals to make money and having to watch out for drug agents. Drug dealers seem to be the most paranoid about being arrested or killed doing their illegal activities than any other class of criminal.

Many traffickers attempt to lay their fears to rest by hiring persons to conduct counter-surveillance for them during critical, and some noncritical stages of an ongoing drug deal. Many of these same counter-surveillance types also double as body guards or provide security for the trafficker and his drugs. They are often paid in drugs instead of cash. Many are armed, all seem to have criminal backgrounds, and some are violent. Drug agents must always be cognizant of the presence of counter-surveillance at any drug deal in which they are participating.

Counter-surveillance accomplices may use hand or other visual signals such as adjusting a cap or taking off a jacket to warn others of the presence of the police. Some counter-surveillance accomplices will be on foot, others in cars and on bicycles where they can cover a larger area and be more mobile. These counter-surveillance associates of the trafficker are there to inform him what they see during the meeting, and if they detect the presence of surveillance agents.

Some traffickers themselves will sit a short distance away from the location and watch the parking lots before parking to do either a drug transaction or have a meeting with a buyer. They may telephone the undercover agent or CI after seeing them arrive at the meeting location, and lie about being several minutes away due to heavy traffic, just to see their reaction. The trafficker is looking for any contact with probable surveillance agents, no matter how slight, or anything else that will confirm he is dealing with the police. In smuggling investigations, it is increasingly common to see counter-surveillance accomplices acting suspicious at airports, train stations, and other transportation nodes hoping to attract the attention of any covert drug agents to draw attention away from the actual courier of drugs.

With cellular telephones being as prevalent as they are, traffickers will counter the efforts of electronic wiretap surveillance by changing telephone numbers frequently, or by having several telephones activated at the same time so he can rotate their use. Others use prepaid telephones and dispose of them when their time credits expire.

Counter-Surveillance Driving

Many drug dealers will take a surreptitious route of travel from point A to point B. While driving, these paranoid drug dealers assume they are either always being followed, or could be followed by drug agents at any given moment. Some of their driving techniques are dangerous, others just annoying.

Drug traffickers may drive normally during a ten-mile trip, but once they come within a mile of their destination, the counter-surveillance activity commences. Surveillance agents will often observe traffickers pull into dead end streets and park to see who follows them. They will make sudden, often dangerous U-turns to see if vehicles will follow them, and drive through parking lots and corner gas stations as shortcuts.

Some traffickers painfully follow the posted speed limit to prevent being stopped by a uniformed police officer, while others use excessive speed to evade any surveillance there may be. Traffickers who enter an apartment complex will often park on the opposite side of where they live to disguise which apartment they intend to enter.

Counter-Surveillance Equipment

Many stores in the United States and elsewhere specialize in selling equipment capable of detecting the presence of transmitters and wiretaps. They sell products that are purported to detect the presence of any wireless transmitter that may be on the person of someone, or can detect the presence of a listening device or *bug*. Many of these devices are worthless, however a growing number of them actually work well, and provide significant problems for undercover agents, informants, and surveillance agents.

A growing number of drug organizations, including money launderers, are using sophisticated electronic devices, including video equipment, mounted in the rear window of a vehicle to record any surveillance vehicles that may be following them in the hopes of observing the driver use a radio or do other things indicative of being a police official.

Pin-hole cameras are known to be mounted in flower pots, bird houses, molding, smoke detectors, and other common items to warn them that the police are present. Others may use motion detectors that activate flood lights near their homes or laboratory sites.

Suspects have also been known to use modified audible car alarms that a person conducting counter-surveillance will activate to warn persons inside a residence of the presence of the police. Pushing the button on such a device while the counter-surveillance operative has his hand in his pocket can be almost impossible to detect.

Drug dealers have also been known to purchase transceivers that not only can be programmed to monitor the frequencies of body transmitters worn by police, but can also transmit on actual police department frequencies. Suspects have been known to use police radio codes to learn the registered owners of vehicles used by police officers. This includes privately owned vehicles undercover agents use to drive to and from work everyday.

It is important when debriefing informants for the case agent to ask if the targeted drug dealer has a history of using any of these devices. If the trafficker has used these devices in the past, the undercover agent should not wear any body transmitter or recorder at the initial meeting with him. The agent may even ask to search the trafficker for any body wires he may have, just to throw him off-guard and to convince him he is not dealing with the police.

If an undercover agent knows ahead of time that the suspect will be carrying a detection device, he or she should not wear any electronic recording equipment to the initial meeting. However, if subsequent meetings take place and a recording is made, the undercover agent should make mention of the previous meeting and what was discussed to make up for the previous shortcoming. This is done in an attempt to get the suspect to acknowledge that the initial meeting took place, and that certain things were discussed and agreed upon. This will go a long way in the eyes of prosecutors and jurors in making up for the fact the original meeting was not recorded.

Summary

Surveillance is used extensively by drug law enforcement to obtain intelligence information about the suspect they are following. Surveillance can be conducted either from a stationary position, while mobile, or through electronic means.

Drug agents assigned to a surveillance must be resourceful, alert, natural acting, and have an appearance that will not attract undue attention. They must be well equipped for any situation that may arise. Surveillance operations can reveal many aspects about the suspect's life and associates he interacts with that could not otherwise be determined. Surveillance operations often lead to the identities of co-conspirators and stash houses. Many drug traffickers are on guard to detect surveillances placed upon them and will conduct countermeasures. Findings from surveillance are often used as the basis for arrest and search warrants.

Drug agents must be cognizant of counter-surveillance measures being adopted by traffickers in their jurisdictions. They have been known to use sophisticated audio and video equipment as well as scanners and transceivers to learn the identity of undercover agents. These devices are used to detect the presence of police and thwart their efforts to investigate them.

Drug dealers have also been known to employ counter-surveillance accomplices to look for the presence of strangers who may be police officers or drug agents in the neighborhood. They use hand and other signals to alert their employers of the presence of drug agents.

Undercover Operations

7

Definition of Undercover

The use of undercover agents is a time-tested investigative technique where disguises and pretexts are used to gain the confidence of known or suspected criminals in order to undermine their illegal activities. Working undercover in a drug investigation does not mean that the drug agent will be living and working with drug dealers full-time. To the contrary, undercover drug agents should strive to minimize the amount of exposure they have with a drug dealer. Short-term undercover operations are the norm in modern drug investigations. Long-term undercover operations do take place, but they require extensive planning and preparation and expose the agent to risks not encountered in short-term undercover roles. The longer the undercover agent is exposed to the suspect, the greater the odds he or she will be discovered to be a law enforcement official.

Drug agents should avoid going inside drug dealer's residences and other dwellings since surveillance officers cannot immediately respond to help the agent if the need arises. Surveillance agents are ultimately responsible for the safety of the undercover agent, and operations that degrade safety should be avoided.

Undercover agents should never allow suspects to go to their personal homes for any reason. A furnished undercover apartment will help ease the suspicions of the drug dealer who asks to visit the agent at his or her home. If an undercover apartment or house is not available, numerous excuses can be given to deny the suspect's request to conduct business there. Most drug dealers accept the fact that the undercover agent does not want to expose his family to other drug traffickers.

Purpose of Undercover Operations

The undercover investigative technique is used to infiltrate criminal organizations to determine their intentions. Infiltration of a criminal organization is extremely dangerous and is used sparingly by most law enforcement agencies.

Drug agents chosen for long-term undercover roles must weigh their personal lives against the demands of such an investigation. Supervisors and managers of long-term undercover agents must consider the risks along with the affect it will have on their employees and their families. Managers must decide if the risks posed to the employee are worth any potential information gained through a long-term undercover assignment.

One of the objectives of an undercover operation is to identify as many members of a drug conspiracy as possible, and determine what their particular role in the organization is. By interacting with these persons, undercover agents can sometimes predict, with some accuracy, which members of a criminal organization may later cooperate with law enforcement after they are arrested.

Undercover agents obtain evidence for court. Through their roles, they have the opportunity to learn where drugs and evidence are located. In addition to drugs and evidence of the crime, undercover drug agents should be alert to determine where drug proceeds and items purchased with ill-gotten gains are located.

One of the most important responsibilities an undercover agent has is to determine the suitable time and place for the execution of arrest and search warrants. His or her intimate knowledge of the drug traffickers will be beneficial in helping locate persons subject to arrest, and predicting if these persons will resist arresting officers.

Undercover agents frequently pose as customers of drug traffickers. An informant introducing an undercover agent to a drug trafficker usually accomplishes this. In complex investigations, more sophisticated undercover roles may be required. The agent may be required to pose as someone who possesses a special skill the drug trafficking organization needs, such as a pilot or money launderer.

Through thorough debriefings of informants, the case agent determines where the criminal organization is most vulnerable to the introduction of an undercover agent. Since traffickers have to rely on the recommendations from trusted associates, they may ask a confidential informant (CI) to find a pilot or big-rig truck driver to move drugs from one location to another. This is an ideal opportunity to introduce an undercover drug agent into the organization. The selected agent must possess the necessary skills required to convince the traffickers he or she can perform the job. They may be quizzed extensively about their experience in these skills, something the undercover drug agent must be prepared for.

Other areas where drug trafficking organizations often need persons with particular skills to carry out their objectives are: boat captains, flight attendants, travel agents, real estate agents, bank employees, investment consultants, chemists, chemical suppliers, automobile dealers, enforcers, countersurveillance personnel or lookouts, corrupt law enforcement officials, private investigators, and house sitters. A house sitter is someone who will reside in a residence where a substantial amount of drugs and or money are stored. The house sitter not only provides security, but also maintains the overall appearance of the residence so to not raise suspicions from the neighbors. Sophisticated Colombian cocaine trafficking organizations have been known to provide written instructions to house sitters on how to give the appearance of being a normal American family by attending local churches and having barbeques on Sunday afternoons.

Qualifications for Undercover Work

The drug agent selected for an undercover role must first possess the necessary sophistication for the assignment. Supervisors and managers need to insure that the candidate has sufficient knowledge about drugs in general, and specifically how they are bought, sold, diluted, transported, smuggled, concealed, and used. They must also speak the trafficker's "language" and know street terminology for different drugs. He should be an experienced investigator who has a good working knowledge of street and wholesale prices in the area.

He or she must have the appropriate appearance for the role. An investigator normally assigned to surveillance work who has a disheveled appearance may have to become well groomed and tailored if he is needed to play the role of an investment banker anxious to launder a drug dealer's money. On the other hand, a clean-cut investigator must alter his appearance if he hopes to convince a drug dealer he is a homeless person who is addicted to drugs. Appearance is equally important as knowledge and skill.

Undercover drug agents must understand the metric system. Drugs are dealt in quantities of grams, ounces, pounds, kilograms, and metric tons. The undercover drug agent needs to understand that some drug trafficking organizations use a variation of this system for drug sales. For example, Mexican heroin organizations sell 25 gram ounces of heroin, instead of the true weight of 28.35 grams, simply because a large number of their customers are Americans, and it is easier to separate a kilo into 40, 25-gram *pieces*. Mexican heroin traffickers also deal in 20-ounce half-kilos. The latter two equal the correct metric measurement for a half-kilogram and kilogram.

Investigators working undercover assignments targeting Mexican heroin traffickers who do not know these nuances between different trafficking organizations will demonstrate their lack of experience in the drug business, and may possibly expose themselves to dangerous situations. A quick primer on the drug dealer's metric system is:

Kilogram = 1000 grams or approximately 2.2 pounds
Gram = 0.03527 ounce
Ounce = 28.35 grams
Pound = 0.4536 kilograms
Metric ton = 1000 kilograms (2200 pounds)

The experienced undercover officer knows what drugs are sold in what increments. For example, methamphetamine at the wholesale level is always sold in quarter-pound to pound quantities. Retail sales of methamphetamine can be in any quantity, but is usually sold in ounces. Cocaine is commonly sold at the wholesale level in kilogram increments whereas retail sales are usually ounces, half-ounces, and grams. It would be a tactical error for an undercover drug agent to ask a drug trafficker for a kilogram of methamphetamine. The trafficker would immediately recognize this person as someone who did not know what he or she was talking about. This is why preparation is so important before performing any undercover assignment.

Some trafficking organizations are reluctant to deal at the wholesale level with someone outside their own ethnicity or nationality. However, street level sales to persons of different ethnic groups are commonplace. This is one reason a well-trained, ethnically diverse drug investigation unit is most effective against drug traffickers. Dealers are naturally leery of strangers who may be undercover agents or informants. They become more cautious as the stakes are raised. Informants can often ease the fears of the drug trafficker by vouching for the undercover agent, but ultimately the agent must convince the trafficker he is not affiliated with law enforcement.

Drug agents selected for undercover assignments should not be from the same area where they will be working. Smaller police departments can overcome this dilemma by having an *undercover exchange program* with other departments to insure covert law enforcement officials are not recognized.

Undercover Agents' Traits

Intelligence

Obviously, drug agents who perform undercover operations have to be intelligent. They must also have an abundance of common sense, and be able to think quickly on their feet and make sound judgments while under stress. They must be able to recognize criminal acts when they are committed in their presence, and identify those persons responsible for the crimes later in court.

The undercover agent must be able to work with others on his team and know how to gain their full support during difficult surveillance operations, keeping their needs in mind. An undercover drug agent who unnecessarily prolongs a meeting with a suspect for the sake of "playing the role," will find his surveillance team less enthusiastic the next time they cover him. The undercover drug agent must be cognizant of the telltale signals suspects give when they intend to rob him of his "buy" money instead of selling him drugs.

Self-Confidence

Successful undercover agents frequently display an abundance of self-confidence. Self-confidence is gained through having a thorough knowledge of the case, the drugs in question, and the suspects he or she is targeting. Self-confidence will rub off on both the informant and the suspect who will both feel comfortable working with the agent during his undercover role.

Someone with no self-confidence will communicate to the traffickers he or she couldn't possibly be the person the informant led them to believe. Creating a doubt in the criminal's mind may not only jeopardize the undercover operation, but could pose safety problems for the informant and agent alike.

Courage

It takes courage for a drug agent to meet with a known criminal to discuss buying drugs. The suspects undercover agents meet are people they would never otherwise associate with in either professional or social settings. Yet, he or she is flung into a situation where they must now socialize with these criminal types, and gain their confidence.

Undercover work is extremely dangerous. More DEA special agents have been killed or injured while working undercover than in any other assignment. If the agent selected for the undercover assignment expresses reluctance because of fear or uneasiness, supervisors should not allow him or her to perform that particular assignment. Undercover work is not for everyone. On the other hand, drug agents who only want to perform undercover roles need to experience other duties as well.

Some drug dealers may attempt to rob a customer if they feel there is an excellent chance of getting away with it. Dealers know that any customer they rob of their money to purchase drugs would be reluctant to report such an incident to the police. The undercover agent must constantly ask him or herself why the suspect insists on doing a drug transaction a certain way or at a particular location. Could robbery be the motive? Even well established drug dealers may decide to rob a customer if they think they can get away with it.

The most dangerous situation for the undercover agent is when money and drugs are together to be traded. The danger level is relatively low when there is only a meeting to discuss an upcoming drug transaction, but the danger level rises significantly when drugs or money is shown to the other party. The danger level also rises significantly when the drug dealer believes the undercover agent has access to a large amount of money to be used in a future purchase.

Even if the undercover agent has no plans of showing the trafficker money, there may be problems. If the agent has told the trafficker he or she has access to the money, there is a possibility the dealer may attempt to hold the agent hostage until someone delivers the money in exchange for the agent's release. Undercover drug agents must constantly be on guard against robbery or kidnapping attempts by the drug trafficker he or she is negotiating with.

Often undercover drug agents will not carry weapons during their undercover roles for fear of them being seen. They do not want to be thought of as either someone who intends to rob the drug trafficker or as a drug agent. The presence of a firearm for self-protection may be easy to explain to the drug dealer, but it increases the likelihood that the dealer will bring a weapon to future meetings. The undercover agent must assume at all times that the drug trafficker is armed or may have someone who is nearby.

When the time comes for the surveillance team to arrest the drug dealer, the undercover agent should remove himself from the scene and resist the temptation to participate. Arrest situations are an exceptionally dangerous aspect of the undercover agent's job. The suspect may initially believe he is being robbed and may attempt to defend himself. Or if he realizes he is about to be arrested, he may mistakenly assume the drug agent is an informant, and attempt to immediately retaliate against him. Ruthless drug dealers are much more likely to kill an informant than a law enforcement officer. Undercover agents have successfully avoided being killed by drug traffickers when they were able to convince them they were actually law enforcement officers.

Good Judgment

Undercover drug agents need to exercise good judgment at all times. They need to be experienced law enforcement officers who can anticipate trouble before it happens.

Dealers frequently insist on receiving the money before delivering the drugs. Their insistence is usually a test to see if the drug agent is foolish enough to do such a thing. Undercover agents and their supervisors need to recognize that *fronting*, or advancing departmental funds to the drug dealer on the promise he will return later with the drugs is not a good idea, no matter what the informant says, or how convincing the dealer may be. There is no guarantee that the dealer will return with either the money or the drugs, or at all. Giving money to the dealer in advance is a foolish decision that exhibits poor judgment.

Many departments have policies addressing when an undercover drug agent may, under extraordinary circumstances, advance monies to the drug dealers, and when, where, and under what circumstances official funds will be displayed to the drug dealer to prove he or she has the means to purchase the drugs under negotiation. The drug dealer is usually satisfied the undercover agent has the means to purchase the drugs by conducting a *money flash*. (See Chapter 8 for details.) These written policies usually come as a result of an undercover officer or supervisor exercising poor judgment during a past drug investigation.

Drug agents working undercover must know their perimeters and limitations before engaging in negotiations with drug dealers. They must follow their department's guidelines and last minute instructions from their supervisors. Deviation from a supervisor's instruction, or a departmental policy could, at a minimum, jeopardize the outcome of the investigation and cause severe safety problems for the undercover agent and back up teams.

Undercover drug agents should never get so personally involved in the investigation that they believe their reputations rest on the outcome of the case. Agents with the *gotta go syndrome* will say or do anything the drug dealer wants to convince him to deliver the drugs. These agents are so focused on the outcome of the investigation that they cease to exercise good judgment. Some will ignore a supervisor's direction fearing it will jeopardize the delivery. Supervisors need to counsel these agents and reevaluate if they should continue their undercover role.

Initiative and Resourcefulness

Undercover officers need to show initiative during undercover operations. They need to develop new and safer ways of doing their jobs. They need to have several public locations preapproved by their supervisor that are suitable for conducting future undercover negotiations and drug deliveries before initially meeting the drug dealer. This way, if during negotiations the trafficker suggests a location for a drug delivery that is totally unacceptable, the undercover officer can immediately suggest an alternative without having to seek permission from a supervisor before agreeing to a meeting there.

Undercover investigators often need to develop ways of convincing the drug dealer they have no connection with the police, or that they are from out of the area. If a drug dealer wants the undercover agent to accompany him over the weekend to attend parties, the agent needs to have a good reason why he cannot. It is unrealistic for an agency to allow the undercover investigator to have unnecessary long-term exposure to the suspect. Surveillance teams are often scarce or not available. Resourcefulness is shown when the agent responds that he has a commitment out of state, and then gives the drug dealer the telephone number where he can be contacted. What the dealer does not realize is the number connects to an undercover telephone line at another law enforcement office in that particular state that is automatically forwarded to the agent's home telephone number giving the appearance he actually is out of town. The blocking of the caller ID function on the telephones is a must.

A good undercover agent needs to take the initiative and learn about every modern means of electronic communication, and how to use these tools to enhance his credibility with the criminals, as well as how to defeat these items when they are used against him.

Good Memory

Despite the use of recording devices and transmitters, the undercover officer should have a good memory for details. The clothing worn by the suspect, the license plate of his vehicle, and the name of the person the drug dealer called from his cellular telephone are all important bits of information the drug agent needs to memorize. Fortunately the use of recording devices greatly enhances the accuracy of what transpired during undercover meetings, but there is no substitute for an officer who possesses a good memory to recall of the events for later courtroom testimony.

Good Communication Skills

Successful undercover agents have the ability to clearly communicate with others. A miscommunication with informants or traffickers will cause severe delays in the development of the investigation and could lead to safety problems. If unsure of the particular time or location of a meeting, the undercover agent must clarify the information. Nothing should be assumed. If an informant acts as the interpreter for the undercover agent, he should take extra precautions to ensure the translation is correct.

If during an undercover meeting the suspect uses slang or terms not familiar to the drug agent, he must later thoroughly debrief the informant about them, or ask reasonable questions during the meeting to make clear what the dealer meant. Slang terms are often unique to a particular area and can change considerably from region to region. The undercover agent should be familiar with the local terminology, but should not use such terms unless he is certain what they mean.

When an undercover agent assumes a role of a money launderer or corrupt employee of a financial institution, he must have a good working knowledge of the profession. His or her knowledge of stocks, letters of credit, bonds, banking, investing, other financial instruments, and in particular wire transfer of funds to offshore banks, is essential. He cannot assume the suspect has little to no knowledge, but rather he or she should assume the suspect has vast knowledge on the subject matter.

Proper Experience for the Role

When possible, investigators with experience in undercover operations should be the first choice for any undercover assignment unless they lack an essential talent needed for that role, e.g., foreign language, financial background, licensed pilot, etc. For example, a lesser-experienced investigator who speaks Spanish may be a better choice for an undercover role over an experienced investigator who does not when dealing with a Spanish-speaking suspect. Even though a CI may be able to provide translation for the non-Spanish speaking investigator, they cannot always be trusted. There has to be a balance between experience working undercover operations and the skills necessary to successfully complete the mission. Novice undercover agents can gain experience playing minor support roles in undercover operations.

Good Common Sense

There is no substitute for good common sense. No matter how talented, multi-lingual, experienced, or courageous a drug agent may be, if he does not exhibit an abundance of common sense, he should not be considered for an undercover assignment.

Common sense is an essential element in undercover operations and has a direct bearing on the safety of the agent as well as the surveillance teams providing his or her protection. Common sense does not come from textbooks or training courses. It is a part of a person's makeup. Supervisors need to identify drug agents who will exercise common sense in undercover assignments, as well as those who will not.

Undercover agents who assume the personality and characteristics of criminals to the point where they have a hard time reverting back to being themselves, need to be considered for reassignment. Further, an agent who is willing to take unnecessary risks, does not follow their supervisor's directions, or deviates from the agreed upon operational plan, should have their undercover role terminated.

Necessary Preparations for Undercover Assignments

Once selected to perform an undercover assignment, the drug agent should review the file of the CI involved in the case before a thorough debriefing takes place. The review should focus on the informant's past performance and manageability. If the informant has a history of perjury, or is known for embellishment or exaggeration, a supervisor or prosecutor should review the facts and decide whether this informant should continue to be used. If the decision is made to use the informant, the undercover agent may want to minimize the informant's role, if possible, and must continuously verify information the informant receives outside the agent's presence. Further, the case agent must insist the informant record every phone call he has with the suspects.

The drug agent must research the criminal history of the informant, and the degree of his past relationship with the suspect. The motivation for the informant to provide information to the police must be determined. In short, the undercover agent must know as much as he can about the informant's background so he or she can feel comfortable working with him. The agent should consult with other agents who have handled this informant in the past.

The informant must be fully debriefed. When formally debriefing the informant, the undercover agent must determine the trafficker's limitations in respect to the quality and quantity of drugs he usually deals in, and the modus operandi he uses. The undercover agent must stay within the boundaries of the suspect's limitations. To significantly exceed these limitations would raise suspicions by the dealer and could seriously jeopardize the case. The dealer may also feel he is not in the same league as the undercover drug agent. It would be unrealistic for the informant to introduce someone to the suspect who wants to purchase far more drugs than the informant knows the suspect is capable of handling.

Research must be conducted by the undercover agent to ascertain the known associates of the suspect. They should be fully identified and their photographs obtained before any undercover operation begins. These associates are likely to be the persons the suspect will solicit to conduct counter-surveillance, act as runners for drugs or money, or provide protection to the suspect during the conduct of the drug deal. The identities of these persons can possibly be made through recent arrest reports, intelligence databases such as the DEA's Narcotic and Dangerous Drug Intelligence System (NADDIS), Western States Intelligence Network, Treasury Enforcement Computer (TECS), and many others.

The undercover agent must ascertain the suspect's propensity for violence. Intelligence reports and arrest records may shed light on the suspect's violent nature, or lack there of. The undercover agent must never assume because the suspect did not exhibit violent behavior during past encounters with other drug dealers or the police, he will not do so this time. The suspected level of violence the drug agents will most likely encounter from the trafficker will dictate the need for additional security, surveillance, and other manpower. If the informant believes the suspect has a history of violence, specifically robbing drug buyers of their money, whether or not the suspect is a genuine drug dealer, this information needs to be corroborated prior to any face-to-face meetings between the suspect and the undercover agent. If it cannot be corroborated because the trafficker's victims never reported the crime to the police, it must be assumed.

Drug enforcement supervisors must weigh the risks of having either an undercover agent or CI attempt to make controlled purchases from a suspect who may be more inclined to rob the buyer than sell drugs. The risks increase proportionately with the amounts of drugs and money being discussed. They need to bear in mind that undercover assignments are the most dangerous aspect of investigating drug crime.

Just prior to the scheduled meeting with a drug trafficker, the CI should be debriefed again to ascertain any additional information that may have come to mind, or any changes that may have occurred since the last debriefing.

The Cover Story

Drug traffickers are keenly aware of the use of CIs and undercover agents being deployed against them. Because of this, they are constantly on the alert for indications their associates, especially new members of the organization, may be working with law enforcement. One way to ease the suspicions of drug traffickers and enhance the safety of the undercover agent is to devise a solid *cover story.*

Cover stories are used to prepare the CI and undercover agent in answering questions the drug traffickers may ask so they are consistently the same. Some background information that must be agreed upon and memorized by the undercover agent and informant is: How did the two meet? When did you meet? Where are you from? What previous experience do you have in drug trafficking? Undercover agents are advised not to say they met their informant in jail since contacts within penal institutions may easily confirm this is not true. If an informant is involved and he has already answered seemingly innocent questions about the background of the undercover agent, he must be thoroughly debriefed on exactly what was asked, and what answers he gave before an introduction is made.

To further ease the suspicions of the traffickers, the undercover agent must know as much about the methods of transportation, smuggling, and price of the drug in question as possible. He must give the appearance of being either a desperate novice in need of money, willing to learn the business for the first time, or a skilled professional who has never been arrested. He may be required to know how to street-test drugs to determine if they are genuine. He must know how drugs are normally packaged for the quantity he is purchasing, and be able to talk about fictitious sources of supply.

The cover story must make sense to the trafficker when he hears it for the first time. The differences in age, race, socio-economic background, etc., with the informant may have to be addressed. A black undercover agent and a white informant, who might not otherwise socialize, may have to convince a trafficker that they first met each other while in the military or while attending school. They may have met through a mutual "friend" that is created. Whatever story is used, it must leave the trafficker comfortable. Undercover agents are advised not to be too specific in detail with their cover stories, and they should not mention their pasts unless quizzed by the trafficker. The informant must alert the undercover agent when he has been questioned about certain details such as when and how they met, so that the agent can be prepared to answer the same questions the same way if asked by the trafficker.

The undercover agent should not volunteer any cover story information to the suspect, but can expect to engage in conversation that will "break the ice." Many suspects are paranoid about being arrested, and they all want to feel comfortable with a new person when discussing their drug business. A suspect may go far beyond having a friendly conversation, and begin to ask many specific questions in an attempt to trip up the agent. If this occurs, an appropriate response is to sternly tell the suspect it is none of his business, and put him on the defensive by asking him if his curiosity is because he is working for the police. This usually halts further questioning. The more information the drug agent volunteers to the suspect, the greater chance he or she will say something contradictory to what was said previously.

Undercover Identity

Although an undercover agent may never have to prove his identity to a drug trafficker, he or she must prepare for the event. A used wallet containing documents that will satisfy an inquisitive suspect should be prepared well in advance for future undercover assignments.

Sophisticated drug dealers have been known to either personally investigate, or hire private investigators to delve into the background of the undercover agent to find any law enforcement connection. Many demand that they visit the undercover agent at his or her home, believing that a police officer would never allow such an event to take place.

Since the sophistication level of many drug dealers has risen, investigators should never assume drug dealers would not investigate their backgrounds. For this and other reasons, investigators should avoid using any part of their real names while working in an undercover capacity. Suspicious drug traffickers have been known to telephone various law enforcement organizations asking for a drug agent by first name, hoping he or she will answer the phone in an attempt to recognize the voice. If this happens, the trafficker could retaliate against the informant who introduced the agent to him.

To help convince the traffickers that the undercover agent is not associated with law enforcement, he must be equipped with documents and other items that coincide with his undercover identity. An undercover driver license is the most important document the agent can possess in convincing the trafficker he is not associated with law enforcement, and it serves as a foundation for other supporting documents. Many states will provide law enforcement personnel with genuine driver licenses displaying the chosen undercover name and address of the agent. These records are usually segregated from other records within the department of motor vehicles at the state capital, and only a few select employees have access to them. DMV employees in some cases will alert the undercover agent in the event a member of the public or another law enforcement agency queries information pertaining to the undercover driver license.

In picking an address to use for the undercover driver license, a post office box, whether from a U.S. post office or a private company, works well. These boxes lend an aura of authenticity since drug dealers often use them to disguise where they actually live. An advantage in using a private box office allows the undercover agent the use of an actual street address, using the box number as an *apartment* or *suite*. Even if the undercover agent's law enforcement agency cannot pay for the use of a private post office box, the address of an actual private post office box can still be used. If the agency is to pay for the private post office box, the undercover agent must fill out the rental application with information identical to the cover story he or she assumes, in all areas required in the application, e.g., employment, home and work telephone numbers, etc. The undercover agent cannot risk having the proprietor of the business furnishing this information to the suspect either voluntarily or unwittingly. Further, the undercover agent making application for a private post office box should never identify himself or herself as a law enforcement officer seeking an undercover address.

Using the address of a large apartment complex, leaving off the apartment number, may work equally well, however it could pose problems if a suspect demands to know why an apartment number is not shown on the license. Using a vacant lot should be avoided since in many states, the only way a driver license can be obtained is through the mail. If a purely fictitious address is used, questions can be raised on how the license was obtained without government intervention. Using the actual address of someone in the telephone directory should never be done because civil liability could fall on the department in the event the suspect later attempts to retaliate or otherwise confronts the occupants of the residence.

When deciding an undercover name, the selected family name should match the agent's ethnic background unless a feasible story can be concocted to explain otherwise. The selected name should be one the undercover agent will readily recognize the first time he or she hears it. The use of a mother's maiden name, or close relative or friend's last name may serve this purpose. The use of the names of actual persons, living or dead, should be avoided.

The date of birth used in an undercover drivers license or other document should be different from the actual date of birth of the undercover agent. Like the undercover name, the date of birth should be readily recognizable, and memorized by the agent. Using the date of birth of the spouse or mother of the undercover agent may help in remembering this important date under the stress of an ongoing operation.

When selecting a city of residence that will appear on the drivers' license, it should be one that the undercover agent is thoroughly familiar with. Ideally, it will be a city the suspect knows little about. The undercover agent must be prepared to talk about famous restaurants, landmarks, news events, and weather for the city they select as their hometown.

The undercover agent must be comfortable with the background information he or she is going to present to the suspect. These are facts that should be difficult to verify. The selected neighborhoods, residential areas, schools attended, and employment history for the area must be well rehearsed prior to any contact with the suspect.

Undercover Vehicles

Hand in hand with an undercover driver license is an undercover vehicle registration certificate. In cooperation with state departments of motor vehicles, genuine registration certificates in the chosen undercover name can be issued. The name and address of the registered owner of the vehicle should be identical to the name and address that appears on the drug agent's undercover driver license. Under no circumstances should an undercover agent's privately owned vehicle be used in an undercover operation. If a government owned undercover vehicle is not available, one should be rented for the specific operation, using the agent's undercover identity on the rental application. Using a rental vehicle for undercover meetings and the purchase of controlled substances is readily acceptable to drug dealers who frequently do the same in an effort to prevent their expensive privately owned vehicles from being confiscated under federal or state asset forfeiture laws.

If the undercover agent is posing as someone from out of the area, he or she should rent a vehicle at a car rental agency that services a major airport. Efforts to make another vehicle appear to be a rental car, or renting a vehicle from other than a transportation hub may raise serious questions with the suspect. If during an undercover operation the suspect is left alone in the agent's vehicle for any length of time, he can be expected to go through glove box and common areas of the vehicle looking for anything connecting the agent with law enforcement. A good technique to ease the fears of the drug trafficker is to allow him time alone in the vehicle to look for documents that coincide with the undercover agent's cover story.

Whatever type of undercover vehicle is selected for an operation, it must be cleared of all official documents, markings, and accessories that might be associated with law enforcement. It is possible to equip undercover vehicles with concealed microphones and cameras to record meetings between drug agents and suspects. Professionally installed devices can be concealed well enough to not raise any suspicion on the part of the suspect. Supervisors should insure that undercover vehicles under their control cannot be identified as being connected with law enforcement.

Undercover Documents and Credit Cards

Other documents that should be in agent's undercover wallet can be credit cards issued in the covert name, membership in a health club, library card, undercover business cards, commercial airline frequent flier memberships, discount store membership cards, etc. Checks from a cancelled checking account with the undercover name printed on them will further add to credibility.

Undercover credit cards can be obtained through cooperative credit reporting agencies that will create a fictitious credit history under a covert name. In this way if a credit history should ever be requested on the undercover agent, the credit reports will confirm the undercover agent's date of birth, place of birth, place of employment, and undercover social security number.

Upon application, agent's can easily obtain additional credit cards in their undercover names tied to their existing personal Visa, Mastercard, Discover, and American Express accounts. However, if a trafficker should steal a credit card receipt resulting from a purchase the agent makes, and later checks with a credit-reporting agency, the connection to the primary cardholder being employed by a law enforcement agency will be discovered.

Planning the Undercover Operation

Investigators selected to perform undercover roles must discuss the overall strategy and objectives with the case agent and their supervisor. The *case agent* is the individual responsible for the overall outcome of the investigation, and with supervisory concurrence, will make decisions and direct the day-to-day activities connected with the case. Together the case agent and undercover agent should meet with the informant frequently to discuss and rehearse the cover story. An operational plan must be formulated for any planned undercover meetings with suspects to fully brief surveillance team members who may not be knowledgeable about the investigation, and to identify clear goals that have been established for the operation.

Undercover agents must search their vehicles for anything connected with a law enforcement agency. They must insure that identification placards, parking and building passes, payroll slips, etc. have been removed from the vehicle before leaving on an undercover assignment.

Many undercover agents feel comfortable carrying their departmental identification with them during covert meetings; however, obvious problems will arise if the suspect somehow discovers it. It may be appropriate to carry official police identification if the operational plan calls for the suspect's arrest at the conclusion of an undercover meeting. There have been occasions when the lives of undercover agents have been spared because they were able to convince the suspect they were law enforcement officers. A drug suspect may be less inclined to murder a police officer or federal agent during a drug transaction for fear of the death penalty, if he is convinced the undercover agents are law enforcement officers and not informants or other drug dealers.

Undercover agents should be mindful of leery drug dealers who might want to search their persons to check for body transmitters, especially during the initial meeting. If police identification is located, this will cause obvious problems for the undercover agent and the informant who introduced him or her to the suspect. Drug agents must evaluate each situation before deciding whether or not to carry official identification.

Carrying an excessive amount of keys is a sign of responsibility. All keys to handcuffs, police buildings that are marked "do not duplicate" and other areas connected with the agent's workplace must be stored. The undercover agent should only carry a minimum amount of keys on a separate key ring for the purposes of the operation. This key ring, which should be nondescript, should only have keys to the undercover vehicle, a post office box, and another key designed to look like a common house key.

The undercover agent must decide for him or herself, whether or not to carry a firearm. Special care should be made if the weapon is of a type typically carried by law enforcement agencies. If a nonstandard weapon is not available for use in undercover operations, the agent should seriously consider not carrying a weapon at all, regardless if the suspect is going to be arrested during the planned operation since undercover agents should not participate in the actual arrest of the suspect. If a weapon is going to be carried, the agent must be able to explain why he is carrying a weapon if it is noticed. The presence of a weapon may frighten a suspect and make him believe the undercover agent plans on robbing him of his drugs. If the suspect knows the undercover agent is armed, he may be more inclined to carry a weapon to future undercover meetings.

The Written Operational Plan

An *operational plan* is an important document created by the case agent that should be approved by a supervisor prior to distributing it to the other agents who will be participating in the operation. It should contain general information about what the objectives of the operation are, who the suspects are, their descriptions, home addresses, and what assignments each participant will have. The areas that should be addressed in any approved, written operational plan include (Figure 7.1 to Figure 7.6):

- Date, time, and place of the operation.
- The objective of the operation (e.g., arrest, purchase, money flash, meeting, etc.).
- Brief synopsis on what has led to this undercover meeting.
- Specific personnel involved in surveillance, and what their particular assignments are.
- If counter-surveillance is expected or anticipated.
- If the suspect is expected to be armed.
- Estimated duration of the meeting or operation with an established cut-off time.
- Whether the undercover agent has been approved to or prohibited from traveling with the suspect or to a second location.
- The anticipated actions of the informant.
- If body transmitters will be used, and who will be responsible for recording the undercover conversation.
- Listing of known vehicles associated with the suspect along with their addresses and physical descriptions.
- Known associates of the suspect that may appear on the scene unexpectedly.
- Distress signals, both audible and visual.
- Photos of suspect.
- Photocopies of maps showing the exact location of the undercover meeting.
- The cellular telephone and pager numbers of the undercover agent. Radio call signs, telephone numbers, and pager numbers for all surveillance agents.
- The location and telephone numbers for the local police, as well as police agencies with jurisdiction where the undercover meeting will take place.
- Thc nearest hospital emergency room.

Some operational plans have more information, but too much information may detract from information deemed essential and make it hard to

Drug Enforcement Administration - Pasadena Resident Office

TACTICAL SAFETY PLAN

☐ Buy/Bust ☐ Buy/Walk ☐ Surveillance ☐ Reverse
☐ Search Warrant ☐ Arrest Warrant ☐ Money Flash ☐ Other

Case Number: G-DEP: Case Agent: Date: Time: ☐am ☐pm

OPERATION

Narrative:

Objective:

Background:

Weapons:

Counter-Surveillance:

SUSPECTS

	NAME	AGE	RACE	HGT	WGT	EYES	HAIR	MISC	CLOTHING
S1									
S2									
S3									
S4									
S5									

VEHICLES

	PLATE	COLOR	YEAR	MAKE	MODEL	DESCRIPTION	R/O
V1							
V2							
V3							
V4							
V5							

LOCATIONS

	ADDRESS	APT.	CITY	THOMAS BROS.	DESCRIPTION
L1					
L2					
L3					
L4					
L5					

KEL AUTHORIZATION:

SUPERVISOR APPROVAL: GS _______ RAC _______ ASAC _______

Figure 7.1 Operational plan.

UNDERCOVER

	NAME	AGENCY	CALL SIGN	VEHICLE	PAGER	CELLULAR	ASSIGNMENT
1.							
2.							

SURVEILLANCE

		NAME	AGENCY	CALL SIGN	VEHICLE	PAGER	CELLULAR	ASSIGNMENT	TEAM
☐	1.	GREG	DEA	101	Gld Lexus	877-555-1234	626-555-2345		
☐	2.	STEVE	DEA	102	Blk Camry	877-555-5144	626-555-0873		
☐	3.	GEORGE	DEA	103	Slv T-Bird	877-555-5116	626-555-0875		
☐	4.	ROGER	DEA	104	Blk Mustang	877-555-5117	626-555-0874		
☐	5.	MIKE	DEA	105	Gry Intrepid	877-555-9403	626-555-8354		
☐	6.	RAY	DEA	106	Wht Sebring	877-555-5145	626-555-9469		

		NAME	AGENCY	CALL SIGN	VEHICLE	PAGER	CELLULAR	ASSIGNMENT	TEAM
☐	1.	ALLEN	DEA	107	Blk Grand Am	877-555-5104	626-555-6884		
☐	2.	ROBERT	DEA	108	Blk Grand Am	877-555-5149	626-555-4886		
☐	3.	DAVID	DEA	109	Slv Taurus	877-555-5148	626-555-9506		
☐	4.	MATT	APD	110	Wht Astro van	877-555-5120	626-555-4295		
☐	5.	TOM	PPD	111	Gld Camry	877-555-5119	626-555-4614		
☐	6.	BRENT	LASO	112	Tan Camry	877-555-8554	626-555-4496		

		NAME	AGENCY	CALL SIGN	VEHICLE	PAGER	CELLULAR	ASSIGNMENT	TEAM
☐	1.	DAN	DEA	201	Blk Gran Prix	877-555-0067	626-555-0881		
☐	2	LLOYD	DEA	202	Slv Gran Prix	877-555-6543	626-555-3944		
☐	2.	CINDY	DEA	203	Wht Landcruiser	877-555-5150	626-555-2052		
☐	3.	JOSE	DEA	204	Blk Grand Am	877-555-5114	626-555-2924		
☐	4.	LINDA	DEA	205	Blk Firebird	877-555-5105	626-555-0883		
☐	5.	BILL	DEA	206	Blu Grand Am	877-555-5113	626-555-0877		
☐	6.	ERIC	DEA	207	Grn Camaro	877-555-5152	626-555-0884		

		NAME	AGENCY	CALL SIGN	VEHICLE	PAGER	CELLULAR	ASSIGNMENT	TEAM
☐	1.	KEN	PPD	208	Blu Grand Am	877-555-5147	626-555-0882		
☐	2.	NANCY	PPD	209	Grn Accord	877-555-5106	626-555-4498		
☐	3.	WAYNE	PPD	210	Wht Cherokee	877-555-5122	626-555-1998		
☐	4.	ALICIA	APD	211	Mar Monte Carlo	877-555-5151	626-555-5981		
☐	5.	RUDY	SGPD	212	Brn Blazer	877-555-5146	626-555-7443		
☐	6.	BRIAN	LASO	213	Wht Taurus	877-555-5121	626-555-4717		

		NAME	AGENCY	CALL SIGN	VEHICLE	PAGER	CELLULAR	ASSIGNMENT	TEAM
☐	1.								
☐	2.								
☐	3.								
☐	4.								
☐	5.								

LOGISTICS

Verbal Arrest Signal:							
Visual Arrest Signal:							
Emergency / Help Signal:							
Arrest Location:							
Pager Codes:	21-	call asap	22-	terminate	101-	kel down	911 urgent
Frequencies:		primary		secondary	171.450	KEL	LAFD ☐
Administrative:		10-28's		Notes		Evidence	WSIN ☐
Notifications:		NIN		Locals		RAC/GS	Locals ☐

EMERGENCY

Nearest Trauma Center:	

SUPERVISOR APPROVAL: GS _______ RAC _______ ASAC _______

Figure 7.1 (continued) Operational plan.

United States Department of Justice
Drug Enforcement Administration
Pasadena Resident Office

Operational Plan
SUMMARY

INVESTIGATION

Case Number:	G-Dep	Case Agent:	Date:	Time:	☐ am ☐ pm

OPERATION

Type of Operation:	☐ Buy/Walk ☐ Buy/Bust ☐ Knock/Talk	☐ Arrest Warrant ☐ Search Warrant ☐ O/D Warrant	☐ Surveillance ☐ Consent Search ☐ Reverse	☐ Money Flash ☐ Drug Flash ☐ Other
Drug Type:		Quantity:		
Prosecution:	☐ State	☐ Federal	Prosecutor:	
Narrative:				
Objective:				
Background:				

LOGISTICS

Verbal Arrest Signal:				
Visual Arrest Signal:				
Emergency / Help Signal:				
Arrest Location:				
Pager Codes:	21- [call asap]	22- [terminate]	101- [kel down]	911 [urgent]
Frequencies:	[primary]	[secondary]	171.450 [KEL]	LAFD ☐
Administrative:	[10-28's]	[Notes]	[Evidence]	WSIN ☐
Notifications:	[NIN]	[Locals]	[RAC/GS]	Locals ☐

AUTHORIZATIONS

☐ KEL:	☐ telephonic	Date:	Time:
☐ Group Supervisor:	☐ telephonic	Date:	Time:
☐ RAC:	☐ telephonic	Date:	Time:
☐ ASAC:	☐ telephonic	Date:	Time:
☐ A/SAC:	☐ telephonic	Date:	Time:
☐ SAC:	☐ telephonic	Date:	Time:

EMERGENCY

Nearest Trauma Center:
EMT Available:
Transport Responsibility:

- Contact Control 1 on RED channel (998) or call 911; Contact DEA Comm Center on 7 (10-99) or call 626/555-2704
- DEA Center will follow-up with Local Police; Trauma Center; Duty Group; LAFD Trauma Team; GS; RAC; ASAC; SAC; HQ
- Invoke Miranda and ***do not make any statements to anyone***, including DEA, for at least 24 hours; if necessary, sequester in a local hotel
- Surrender all involved weapons to one senior DEA agent only, who will keep log; S/A should accompany all injured to hospital

Figure 7.2 Operational plan summary.

United States Department of Justice
Drug Enforcement Administration
Pasadena Resident Office

Operational Plan
SUSPECTS

SUSPECT 1 **Name**

☐ Probation	☐ Warrants	☐ Juvenile	☐ Guns Registered
☐ Parole	☐ Crime/Bail/Crime	☐ Drug User	☐ Felony "Strikes":
☐ Search/Seizure	☐ P.A.L.	☐ Gang Member	☐ Other:
Height	Weight	Eyes	Hair
Race	Sex	Age	DOB

Associated Subjects:	Photograph
Associated Locations:	
Associated Vehicles:	
Scars, Marks, Tattoos:	
Facial Hair:	
Clothing Description:	
Additional Description:	
Prior Arrest History:	
Other:	

SUSPECT 2 **Name**

☐ Probation	☐ Warrants	☐ Juvenile	☐ Guns Registered
☐ Parole	☐ Crime/Bail/Crime	☐ Drug User	☐ Felony "Strikes":
☐ Search/Seizure	☐ P.A.L.	☐ Gang Member	☐ Other:
Height	Weight	Eyes	Hair
Race	Sex	Age	DOB

Associated Subjects:	Photograph
Associated Locations:	
Associated Vehicles:	
Scars, Marks, Tattoos:	
Facial Hair:	
Clothing Description:	
Additional Description:	
Prior Arrest History:	
Other:	

Figure 7.3 Operational plan list of suspects.

United States Department of Justice
Drug Enforcement Administration
Pasadena Resident Office

Operational Plan
VEHICLES

VEHICLE 1 — **vehicle plate**

Year	Color	Make	Model
Body Type	VIN	Registration Year	Registration Type

Owner:	Photograph
Driver	
Additional Description:	

VEHICLE 2 — **vehicle plate**

Year	Color	Make	Model
Body Type	VIN	Registration Year	Registration Type

Owner:	Photograph
Driver	
Additional Description:	

Figure 7.4 Operational plan list of vehicles.

United States Department of Justice
Drug Enforcement Administration
Pasadena Resident Office

Operational Plan
LOCATIONS

LOCATION 1 — **address**

☐ Single Family ☐ Duplex ☐ Townhouse	☐ Condominium/Apt. ☐ Fortified Door(s) ☐ Fortified Windows	☐ Dogs ☐ Fence/Locked Gate ☐ Storage Buildings	☐ Garage – attached ☐ Garage – detached ☐ Garage – converted
Telephone Number	Thomas Guide	Cross Streets	Gate/Alarm Code
Manager – Name	Manager – Number	Color of House:	Color of Roof:

Owner:	Photograph
Roof Description:	
Construction:	
Location/Description of House Numbers:	
Fence Description:	
Garage Description:	
Location on street:	
Location in complex:	
Additional Description:	

LOCATION 2 — **address**

☐ Single Family ☐ Duplex ☐ Townhouse	☐ Condominium/Apt. ☐ Fortified Door(s) ☐ Fortified Windows	☐ Dogs ☐ Fence/Locked Gate ☐ Storage Buildings	☐ Garage – attached ☐ Garage – detached ☐ Garage – converted
Telephone Number	Thomas Guide	Cross Streets	Gate/Alarm Code
Manager – Name	Manager – Number	Color of House:	Color of Roof:

Owner:	Photograph
Roof Description:	
Construction:	
Location/Description of House Numbers:	
Fence Description:	
Garage Description:	
Location on street:	
Location in complex:	
Additional Description:	

Figure 7.5 Operational plan list of locations.

United States Department of Justice
Drug Enforcement Administration

Operational Plan

Pasadena Resident Office

Additional PERSONNEL

PERSONNEL

NAME	AGENCY	CALL SIGN	VEHICLE	PAGER	CELLULAR	ASSIGNMENT	TEAM
1.							
2.							
3.							
4.							
5.							
6.							

NAME	AGENCY	CALL SIGN	VEHICLE	PAGER	CELLULAR	ASSIGNMENT	TEAM
1.							
2.							
3.							
4.							
5.							
6.							

NAME	AGENCY	CALL SIGN	VEHICLE	PAGER	CELLULAR	ASSIGNMENT	TEAM
1.							
2.							
3.							
4.							
5.							
6.							

NAME	AGENCY	CALL SIGN	VEHICLE	PAGER	CELLULAR	ASSIGNMENT	TEAM
1.							
2.							
3.							
4.							
5.							
6.							

NAME	AGENCY	CALL SIGN	VEHICLE	PAGER	CELLULAR	ASSIGNMENT	TEAM
1.							
2.							
3.							
4.							
5.							
6.							

NAME	AGENCY	CALL SIGN	VEHICLE	PAGER	CELLULAR	ASSIGNMENT	TEAM
1.							
2.							
3.							
4.							
5.							
6.							

ASSIGNMENTS

Team	:
Team	:
Team	:
Team	:
Team	:

Figure 7.6 Operation plan listing other personnel.

find important information quickly. Many plans are preprinted with check marks next to the names of those agents who will be participating. In any event, a supervisor should thoroughly review the plan and discuss it with both the case and undercover agents. The supervisor should make it clear whether or not the undercover agent is authorized to deviate from the approved operational plan, and any consequences for doing so.

Before approving the undercover agent to travel to a secondary meeting location, the location should be known, and surveillance agents already in place to look for other persons associated with the suspect. The location of an undercover meeting should never be approved that gives the suspect a tactical advantage.

An undercover agent's unilateral decision to deviate from the approved investigative plan can cause serious problems. If the suspect wants the undercover agent to travel with, or follow him to a secondary location, the agent should refuse to do so unless it was approved beforehand by a supervisor and discussed during the operational briefing. If the undercover agent leaves with the suspect without the knowledge of the surveillance team, they will naturally think the agent is under duress and view it as a possible kidnapping or robbery attempt and would be expected to take action to rescue the agent.

It is unwise, for several reasons, to furnish government money to a suspect on his promise to return later with drugs. The suspect could change his mind and keep the money without fear of retribution from the undercover agent or the police since in his mind he is dealing with another drug dealer. Even if the trafficker sincerely intends to return with the drugs, he may be robbed of the money before he can obtain them. Fearing retribution from the undercover agent, he may flee. Either way, only under extraordinary circumstances in a tightly controlled environment should undercover agents or their supervisors allow money to be advanced to dealers.

The undercover agent should ask but not insist on seeing the drugs to be purchased before any money is displayed. Once the location of the drugs is revealed the arrest can be made without ever jeopardizing the loss of official government funds.

Undercover agents should avoid accompanying the suspect in his vehicle since control cannot be exercised over the moving vehicle. The suspect could drive the car into an area where surveillance agents would immediately be detected, or he could drive to a deserted location where accomplices are waiting to rob the undercover agent. Allowing the suspect to travel in the undercover vehicle is preferable, but only if the agent is driving, knows ahead of time where he is going, reasonably believes the suspect is unarmed, and adequate surveillance agents are available to follow.

If the operational plan forbids the undercover agent from traveling anywhere with the suspect, regardless in what vehicle, and this occurs, the surveillance team must assume the agent is being kidnapped for the purpose of robbing him or her. Even if the surveillance team is electronically monitoring the conversation between the undercover agent and suspect, and distress does not seem obvious, the surveillance team must still assume the worst and be ready to rescue the agent. If the undercover agent is under distress and can communicate with the surveillance team through a wireless transmitter, he should attempt to alert them as soon as possible to what is happening. For example, the undercover agent can simply state, "Why are you pointing that gun on me?" or "Don't shoot me!" as obvious signs of distress. Under these circumstances, the undercover agent should immediately identify him or herself as a law enforcement officer and tell the suspect other agents are following them. Drug dealers are less likely to kill or injure a law enforcement officer than an informant or other drug dealer.

The Operational Briefing

The case agent should conduct an *operational briefing* immediately after the approved operational plan has been distributed to each agent or officer participating in the operation. The informant and case agent should be personally introduced to the surveillance team members to insure they are not mistaken to be the suspects.

If possible, an undercover agent should always be equipped with a cellular telephone in order for him or her to have instant communication with the case agent and supervisor. This also allows the case agent to inform or warn the undercover agent, during the actual operation, things that the surveillance team has detected. Cellular telephone communication with the undercover agent also allows supervisors to direct the undercover agent to discretely shut the operation down if they deem it necessary.

Undercover operational plans and briefings cannot be taken lightly since the agent or informant will potentially be exposed to extreme danger. Everyone associated with the operation must be thoroughly briefed on the plan and know who the participants are. Supervisors should approve all such plans, as well as the concept of the operation. There must be an adequate amount of surveillance agents to cover the meeting, and they must be trained and equipped to handle any eventuality.

The Undercover Meeting

Undercover agents, meeting a drug trafficker for the first time, will naturally feel uneasy and nervous. Not only is he nervous about being away from his fellow officers in the presence of the unsuspecting drug dealer, he will feel pressure knowing his performance will be judged by his peers. This should not matter, but it is a natural occurrence. The objective of meeting undercover with a drug trafficker is to gather evidence and build a prosecutable case against the suspect. Even though the undercover agent may appear anxious and nervous, the drug trafficker will probably mirror the same anxiety and nervousness.

When an informant is involved in an undercover meeting with a suspect, he will be the key to the success of the operation. If the suspect believes the informant when he says the undercover agent is a genuine drug dealer, then he will most likely deal with the agent. If the informant does not have a great deal of credibility with the suspect, he may never lose his suspicion that the agent is a law enforcement officer.

Formal meetings with suspects should be in public, especially the initial meeting. During this first meeting, the undercover agent will get a feel for the suspect, and begin to learn about his personality. The agent should attempt to establish a rapport with the suspect as soon as it is practical. They should not jump into to talking about drugs within a short time of meeting the suspect. The agent should let the trafficker bring up the topic of drugs first, if possible. If not, when the appropriate time arrives, the informant can take the lead by mentioning the topic.

Undercover meetings can be held in restaurants, hotel lobbies, parking lots, restaurants, and bars. Hotel rooms should only be used when the undercover agent wants the suspect to feel comfortable enough to go into detail about his drug trafficking operations. The suspect often suggests a hotel room when large amounts of money and drugs are going to be exchanged. However, because hotel rooms are secluded and confining, they pose a significant amount of danger for the undercover agent. Because of their seclusion, drug traffickers may be more inclined to rob the undercover agent. Robbery is something the undercover agent must always be conscious of when negotiating with the drug trafficker. Undercover agents must constantly ask themselves why the suspect insists the drug transaction be conducted a certain way or at a particular location.

Suspects are highly suspicious of new people they are introduced to. Undercover agents should remember the suspect is always looking for a reason not to do a drug deal with them. Because of their suspicions, they may withdraw their offer to sell drugs and never contact the agent or informant again.

Many lower-level drug dealers routinely abuse the drugs they sell, creating paranoia. Some are extremely paranoid of being arrested, and will take extraordinary means to detect police informants and undercover agents. Some paranoid drug dealers are convinced the government is tapping their phones, and that they are under constant observation by satellites, none of which is true.

One way to make the trafficker feel comfortable is by not asking too many questions. Traffickers believe that the more questions asked, the more likely the person he is dealing with is associated with the police. By not asking a lot of questions, credibility rapidly builds up in the eyes of the trafficker who may feel comfortable enough to boast about his drug trafficking successes. Undercover agents can never ask too few questions.

The undercover agent should not volunteer any personal information from his or her cover story, and only answer those questions that have the appearance of being harmless. Undercover agents, as well as their informants should be attentive as well as be a good listener. Everything he says and does may later help in identifying other members of his organization.

Undercover Negotiations

The objective of the undercover agent is to successfully negotiate the price and delivery of drugs to him or her without having to display money first. If during negotiations the suspect insists on seeing money before bringing out drugs, this can be done safely, under controlled circumstances, but should be avoided if at all possible. (See Chapter 8 for details.)

As mentioned earlier, during actual negotiations, the undercover agent should always keep robbery in mind. The agent should never agree to meet in an area where he or she is known or where the suspect frequents.

Undercover agents should have at least three specific locations in mind that have been prescreened by a supervisor as being acceptable for a drug operation. If the first location mentioned by the undercover agent is unacceptable, he or she will have two or three others as alternatives.

The agent should never allow the trafficker to talk him or her into doing something inherently dangerous. Some undercover agents are so determined to be successful in their negotiations they will sacrifice their personal safety to increase the chances of the suspect delivering drugs to them. They have found themselves caught up in with the *gotta go syndrome* in that no matter what, the deal has got to go. To counter this, supervisors should review all audiotapes of the negotiations between the agent, informant, and suspect to insure the agreed upon terms provides safety for the undercover agent and surveillance team.

During undercover negotiations, surveillance and arrest teams must be kept in mind. Where the agent parks his vehicle, where he sits in a restaurant, and where he stands in the lobby of a hotel is important, and can raise security concerns if surveillance teams are unable to constantly observe him or her.

The undercover agent should be thoroughly familiar with the use of modern mobile telephones, pagers, and other communication devices. Codes can be used on pagers to designate certain events and to pass on information that will not be obvious to the suspect during the negotiations. Supervisor's can send a simple page of "10-22" to order the undercover agent to end the undercover meeting soon.

Prebuy and postbuy surveillance should be established during the actual transaction to look for counter-surveillance accomplices, sources of supply, and where the drugs may be hidden.

The undercover agent should strictly stick to self-imposed time limitations during meetings with the suspect. Surveillance agents will naturally become curious why the meeting that was supposed to last for 30 minutes is dragging on for over an hour. Further, the longer the undercover agent is exposed to the suspect, the greater the likelihood he or she may say something that will be contradictory to what he or she earlier said, raising the suspicions of the suspect.

Drug Samples

Usually before the purchase of a substantial amount of drugs, an undercover agent will ask for a sample of what he is going to be purchasing. Drug sample weights range from a gram to a kilogram according to amount of drugs being negotiated for sale.

Requesting a sample serves several purposes. Providing a sample to the undercover agent is a crime in and of itself, making the suspect subject to arrest. It may also provide surveillance agents with the opportunity to follow the suspect to the person he obtains drugs from, and where drugs are being stored. This information may become the basis for a search warrant in the future.

It is perfectly acceptable for the undercover agent to purchase the sample of drugs being negotiated. This changes, however when huge amounts of drugs are being negotiated for purchase. In this situation, the sample will sometimes be cost free. A sample does not guarantee that the drugs being purchased will be the same quality and purity. Many suspects have multiple sources of supply, which can generate several samples, each one providing an opportunity for surveillance agents to follow the suspect to where he obtains them.

Requesting a sample during an undercover meeting with the suspect provides an opportunity to identify other members of the drug trafficking organization. The suspect may be convinced to travel from the meeting to his source of supply to retrieve the sample while the agent waits for him to return. This gives surveillance agents an opportunity to follow him from the meeting location to his source of supply. The source of supply can then be followed and surveillance may determine where drugs are being stored, possibly resulting in the issuance of a search warrant later.

If the undercover agent is negotiating the purchase of multi-kilogram amounts of a drug, he should ask to see the drugs beforehand and be allowed to remove a small sample himself from a kilogram package to gauge the quality of the drug. The agent should tell the suspect that any sample he cannot personally retrieve is meaningless since it may not have come from the drugs the trafficker intends to sell him. In the event the trafficker allows the undercover agent to see the drugs to prove he has them, usually after the displaying of a flash roll, the objective of the investigation has been met and the suspects can be arrested and the drugs seized.

Any sample that is obtained by an undercover agent should immediately be sent to a crime lab for both a *qualitative* and *quantitative analysis*. These examinations will not only tell the agent if the sample is in fact a controlled substance, but how pure the drug is. If the sample is of such low purity to almost render it worthless for resale, the undercover agent can tell the suspect later that he was dissatisfied with the drug sample he received. If the agent does not complain about the sample's purity, the trafficker will perceive the undercover agent as either a fool, or a drug agent since the trafficker probably knew the quality of the drugs was poor. If the trafficker did not know the quality of the sample was poor, he will probably confront his supplier about the quality, which may give agents an opportunity to identify him through telephone calls or surveillance.

Use of Controlled Substances by Undercover Agents

Suspects on occasion will ask, or sometimes demand, that the undercover agent take a controlled substance in their presence before they are willing to sell drugs to them. Agents should have a convincing story ready to tell the suspect why he or she will not take drugs at that time. Some examples of responses are:

- "I want to save the drug to take it at a later time."
- "I want to give the dope to my girlfriend."
- "I don't take drugs when I'm doing business."
- "We can party when the business is over."
- "I'm allergic to the drug; it almost killed me the last time I took it."
- "I'm a businessman/woman and don't do drugs."
- "I only sell the stuff; I don't take it."
- "I have to take a drug test for my probation/parole agent, and I don't want to come up positive."
- "I'm scheduled to take a drug test tomorrow for a job and don't want to come up positive."

If these excuses do not work, the undercover agent should refuse and depart the area. He or she should call the suspect after a few days allowing the informant an opportunity to again vouch for the undercover agent's truthfulness.

If this fails to change the mind of the suspect, the agent should contact the suspect and tell him he or she is now willing to take the controlled substance in order to do the deal. The agent should also tell the suspect to have the drugs to be sold nearby so the transfer can be completed before the affects of the drug kicks in.

Upon the delivery of the single dose of the drug to the agent, the suspect should be arrested and his vehicle and person searched for other drugs. A search warrant for other locations may be justified under these circumstances since the suspect told the agent he was in possession of a larger amount of drugs than he intended to sell.

Undercover agents are generally prohibited from taking controlled substances while performing undercover operations for many good reasons. There is no case worth getting an agent hurt or killed. Taking an unknown substance from a drug dealer is an unacceptable risk for any employee of the agency. Only under the direst of circumstances could the undercover agent justify such an act. One circumstance would be if the suspect pointed a gun at the unarmed undercover agent and demanded he took drugs to prove he was not the police, and if he did not, he would kill the agent. Absence a horrific event as this, there is no way to justify the use of drugs by an undercover agent.

For the protection of the operative, some jurisdictions absolve state peace officers from prosecution if they use drugs in conjunction with undercover assignments. There is no such comparable federal law. These laws are designed to protect the undercover agent from prosecution if he or she is forced by the suspect to ingest a controlled substance while under duress. Proper planning and preparation will minimize the undercover agent's exposure to violent drug criminals who force their new customers to ingest controlled substances before conducting business.

Confidence Buys or Buy–Walk Operations

Drug dealers are naturally leery of new customers for fear of them being undercover agents. One proven way to ease the fears of the trafficker, as well as defeat the entrapment defense, is to make a series of *confidence buys*.

A confidence buy usually starts with relatively smaller amounts of drugs and progresses to larger quantities. The objective is to make the suspect feel comfortable selling drugs to the undercover agent later since he was not arrested after the initial transaction. The theory is that the more confidence buys that are made, the more convinced the buyer is that he is not selling to an undercover agent.

Coordination should be made with the local, state, or federal prosecutors to determine when sufficient evidence has been gathered to ensure an indictment and conviction of the suspect. The amount of money left in the department's budget for *buy money* also factors into how many confidence buys are made from the suspect before he is eventually arrested.

The following is an example of a logical progression of a typical methamphetamine drug investigation conducted by a local municipal police department. Starting off with a one ounce purchase, the second *buy* increases to four ounces, followed by a third purchase of five or six ounces, and ending with the final delivery of one pound. It would be unrealistic for a person who normally purchases four ounces of methamphetamine to suddenly jump to a ten-pound quantity. The final quantity of drugs delivered to the agent depends on how confident the suspect is the undercover agent is not connected with the police.

It also depends on what quantities of the drug the suspect has access to. Many boast of being able to obtain drugs in any amount, when they actually cannot. They may, in fact, have access to large quantities of drugs, however their source of supply may not trust them with the drugs unless they pay for them first. This will prompt the suspect to ask the undercover agent to furnish or front the money with his promise to immediately obtain the drugs and deliver them to the agent. Many departments, including the DEA, have policies against fronting money for drug purchases except under extraordinary circumstances. Many times the undercover agent and suspect come to an impasse due to the suspect's inability to obtain drugs without paying for them first.

A successful technique used to give surveillance agents an opportunity to identify the suspect's source of supply is to make two separate orders of drugs the same day from the same suspect. The undercover agent first meets the suspect at a public place, such as a restaurant. The agent orders a sufficient quantity of drugs beyond the dealer's capabilities that prompts him to travel to his source of supply to obtain them. Surveillance agents will follow the suspects, but if they are unsuccessful in finding out where he went, they will notify the undercover agent. Upon taking delivery of the drugs, the undercover agent will tell the suspect that while he was gone, he received a telephone call requesting a second, equal amount. He or she asks the suspect to retrieve the same amount again immediately. Surveillance agents will now have experience following the suspect and may be successful in following him a second time to his source of supply.

Buy–Bust Operations

This frequently used technique is similar to a confidence buy operation, except the suspect will be arrested upon delivery of the drugs to the undercover agent. The preparation involved is identical to any other planned undercover encounter with the suspect, however the danger level rises when surveillance agents suddenly appear and take the suspect into custody.

Undercover agents should not be physically involved in the actual arrest of the suspect since he or she will most likely not have the equipment necessary in making such arrests, e.g., handcuffs, bulletproof vest, gun, spare ammunition, badge, identification, etc.

At the time of the arrest, the undercover agent should back away from the situation and take cover in the event of a shooting, and remain out of the way of the arresting agents. Once the situation is under control, the undercover agent should be made available to assist the case agent in the postarrest questioning of the suspect. The presence of the undercover agent during such questioning verifies that the suspect was dealing with a government agent and not an informant. It also makes lying about what he said or did in the undercover agent's presence fruitless and unnecessary.

If after being advised of his constitutional rights, the suspect agrees to talk with agents, he should be questioned in detail as soon as practical after the arrest. Because of the heat of the arrest and psychological trauma the suspect will experience, questioning him at the scene of the arrest rather than at the office may prompt him to cooperate before he has more time to think about it. His cooperation may reveal his source of supply and where more drugs and money/drug proceeds are located.

Federal and many state laws allow law enforcement officers to tape-record telephone conversations when they have the consent of one of the parties. Undercover agents, CIs, and cooperating suspects can each give their consent to the recording of their telephone conversations with drug suspects. Due to this, case agents should always be equipped at the scene of the arrest with a tape recorder to record any voluntary cellular telephone conversation between the suspect and his source of supply.

The case agent should give the suspect specific instructions on what to say to his source, and that the objective of the conversation is to get the source to acknowledge his involvement in the conspiracy. This can usually be achieved by instructing the suspect to inform his source that the drug delivery went well, and that he now has money to either purchase more drugs, or to pay for the drugs he received on consignment. This recorded evidence may later be detailed in an affidavit in support of the source of supply's arrest warrant, and later a search warrant that may yield more drugs, money, and documentary evidence of other members of the organization.

Postbuy Debriefings

After the undercover operation is completed, the designated report writer should collect all the notes from those agents who participated in the surveillance so an accurate account of the events that took place can be documented. If drugs were obtained, the evidence should be weighed in front of a witness and placed in an evidence container, usually a transparent plastic bag, that is sealed and placed into the evidence room. A presumptive field test of the drugs can be performed. This is where an agent places a small amount of the drug into a clear, plastic ampoule that contains chemicals designed to change colors when a particular controlled substance is introduced. If the substance is what it was purported to be, the chemical reaction will produce a certain color substantiating this. These tests, however, are not a substitute for a thorough examination by a certified chemist, and their results are not admissible in court.

As cautioned earlier, this field test cannot be substituted for an examination that will reveal the purity of the drug. The field test does not reflect drug purity, regardless of how fast the chemicals change color in the ampoule. Future undercover meetings to talk about the sample should wait until a qualitative examination has been conducted.

Whatever the drugs were contained in by the suspect should be preserved for fingerprints. The suspect's source of supply may have handled the container, substantiating his involvement in the crime. A single fingerprint may reveal the identity of the source of supply if he has been arrested before. Evidence forms are designed to clearly establish the *chain of custody* of the drugs from the moment they were obtained by the undercover agent to their transfer to the crime laboratory and introduction in court.

Proven Undercover Techniques and Strategies — Playing Mind Games with the Suspect

Traffickers have preconceived notions about police in general, and undercover drug agents specifically. They draw these notions from personal experiences in the drug trade, conversations with other dealers, and from television and movies that portray police tactics.

All drug traffickers are paranoid of being arrested, and many of them think they have an uncanny ability to detect undercover agents. Sometimes the traffickers outsmart themselves by mistakenly believing they know police tactics well enough to avoid detection.

Experienced drug agents know that drug traffickers are rarely on time for meetings to negotiate prices or to actually deliver drugs. Recognizing they are chronically late for important meetings, some suspects believe that anyone who is on time could be an undercover agent.

To further convince the trafficker that he is dealing with another drug dealer, surveillance agents should arrive at the meeting location in time to see when the suspect arrives. They can then alert the undercover agent to then drive into the parking lot a few minutes later, giving the illusion that he was also late for the meeting.

If surveillance agents cannot positively place the suspect at the meet location, the undercover agent should arrive a minimum of 15 minutes late for any meeting with the suspect in case the suspect has counter-surveillance in place to tell the trafficker when the undercover agent arrived. If the suspect is not there, the agent should wait no more than 15 to 20 minutes for the suspect to arrive, and then depart the area. Drug dealers have been known to hire counter-surveillance persons specifically to tell them how long the undercover agent waited at the meeting location before leaving. Traffickers believe that undercover agents not only have the responsibility to arrive on time, but will also remain at the location until the suspect arrives, regardless of how long that may be. In the mind of some suspects, the longer the drug customer remains waiting for them to arrive, the greater the likelihood this customer is an undercover drug agent.

With this in mind, supervisors should set a strict time limit for the suspect to arrive at the meeting, as well as for the suspect to return to the undercover agent with the drugs. In the case of a delivery, if the suspect is late by 20 to 30 minutes, the undercover agent should be instructed to leave the area and not return without first hearing from the suspect. In the mind of the suspect, the longer his customer waits for the drugs to be delivered, the greater the likelihood he is dealing with an undercover agent. Further, undercover agents should always leave the meeting location and return later to meet the suspect to take delivery of drugs rather than wait at the location the entire time. This will help prevent the suspect's accomplices from robbing the undercover agent and keeps him or her away from possible counter-surveillance at the location.

Some drug suspects firmly believe that if they ask the undercover agent if he or she is a law enforcement officer, and he or she denies it, that anything they say from that point cannot be used against them in court. This, of course, is nonsense, but it can be used by the undercover agent to further convince the suspect he or she is not a police officer.

Another technique designed to reinforce in the drug trafficker's mind that he is not dealing with an undercover agent, is for the agent to ask the trafficker if he is a police officer. Most traffickers immediately become defensive, and this can help dispel the notion the undercover agent is anything other than another drug dealer.

The undercover agent can also ask the trafficker's permission to physically check him for the presence of wire transmitters or tape recorders. This can be accomplished in a public restroom, or in the undercover agent's vehicle. This again will put the trafficker on the defensive, and it also allows the agent to search the suspect for weapons he may be carrying. Also, if a transmitter or tape recorder is found on the suspect, it will mean that the suspect is probably a police informant targeting the undercover agent in a *reverse sting operation*. A reverse sting is when an undercover agent or informant poses as a drug seller, instead of drug buyer, for the purpose of seizing the suspect's money he intended to use to purchase the drugs, therefore depriving him of the means to do so. Suspects the police arrest can be charged with attempting to commit a drug crime or drug conspiracy, if applicable.

Some traffickers also believe that drug agents do not work at night, weekends, or especially holidays. They are convinced that if an undercover agent will not agree to consummate a drug transaction on any of these days, he must be working for the police.

What these traffickers do not understand is that many drug agents often work at night, on weekends, and on holidays when necessary, although many undoubtedly would prefer not to. An undercover agent can defeat the trafficker's intention of completing the drug deal on a weekend or holiday by the agent being the first to suggest it. The agent should tell the suspect he knows that drug agents do not work at night, weekends, or holidays, and he would prefer to do a drug transaction then to help avoid detection. The suspect will most likely agree. As the agreed upon date approaches, the agent should call the suspect and reemphasize the importance of doing the deal on that particular day.

A day or so before the event, in what will seem to be a sudden, unexpected change, the agent should either personally meet with or telephone the suspect and tell him that something has suddenly come up, e.g., insistent girlfriend, sick relative, conflicting drug deal, etc., requiring his or her presence elsewhere for the entire weekend or holiday period. The agent promises that immediately upon his or her return, the deal will be consummated.

The agent can go so far as to furnish the suspect with a telephone number he can be reached while out of town for the weekend or holiday period. By providing the suspect with an undercover telephone number used by an out of town or out of state police agency, the suspect should be further convinced the agent's excuse is valid. What the suspect does not realize is that the agent has already made arrangements to have all incoming calls to that out of town number forwarded back to his home telephone number, so he or she can talk to the suspect if need be.

If the suspect believes the undercover agent's feelings about doing a drug transaction on a weekend, he will most likely agree to sell the drugs to the agent during normal working hours. Most drug dealers know that undercover agents will never provide them with their home address or telephone number. To overcome this, an undercover agent can provide the suspect with a telephone number purported to be his or her home phone number. The suspect will not realize the number is actually to an undercover telephone, located at the office, with an attached answering machine featuring the undercover agent's voice urging the caller to leave a message or to page him. In cooperation with the local telephone company, an out-of-town area code can be installed in the office. The agent can periodically check the machine for messages while either at the office or remotely from the undercover agent's residence. The suspect can then be called back from the agent's home telephone, provided the *caller I.D.* feature the suspect may have has been blocked by the agent.

The agent can also have his or her undercover telephone forward all telephone calls directly to his or her actual home telephone number after duty hours. With dramatic technical advances in personal communication devices, undercover agents must become familiar with them before using them in any undercover operation.

The Seven Critical Factors Leading to Undercover Violence

Undercover violence is defined as any violence directed towards the undercover agent or support personnel during an undercover operation. This violence may include injuries sustained by undercover or support personnel by friendly fire coming from surveillance agents.

Robbery is the most common reason behind undercover violence, whether it is to steal the agent's *flash roll* or drugs used during a reverse sting operation. Whenever money or drugs are exposed, the risk of robbery climbs dramatically.

Violence is sometimes directed towards undercover agents in retaliation for them causing the arrest of a suspect. Undercover agents should always be alert for defendants who may seek retribution after they have been identified as law enforcement officials, whether they are at work or home.

The DEA conducted a study to determine what factors contribute to violence after five special agents were murdered while performing undercover roles during investigations over a three-year period. The DEA correctly identified that factors such as increased trafficker paranoia stemming from the use of mind altering drugs, coupled with a significant increase in mandatory prison sentences, created an incentive for the dealer to either fight or flee. Further, the proclivity toward violence from some foreign trafficking groups and the large amounts of money involved during drug transactions were all included in the recipe of violence during undercover operations.

Poor Operational Planning

A complete operational plan should be mandatory for any undercover operation. Supervisors should discuss and approve such plans with the undercover and case agents before any briefing is conducted. At a minimum, the plan should reflect the potential risk the undercover agent will be exposed to, and how it will be countered. It should always include prebuy surveillance of the suspect and the location of the meeting, surveillance of the undercover agent and flash roll, preapproved alternate meeting locations, distress signals, the arrest signal, and an arrest plan. The approving supervisor, who will be at the enforcement operation, should allow for some flexibility in the operational plan.

Making the Arrest

Arguably the most dangerous action the undercover agent could perform is to attempt to personally arrest the trafficker immediately after taking possession of the drugs he has just purchased. The trafficker has obviously been convinced he has been dealing with another drug dealer or user, and for the undercover agent to suddenly revert to his law enforcement identity will confuse and disorient the suspect. He will immediately believe he is being robbed of the money he just received and may act in self-defense. For this reason, the undercover agent should maneuver him or herself as far away from the scene of the arrest as possible. If the arrest team arrives before the undercover agent has had the opportunity to depart the area, he or she must take a defensive position to prepare for any violent actions that may immediately follow.

Managing the Flash Roll

Mismanaging flash rolls is the single most critical factor in undercover violence. The drug trafficker will constantly assess the undercover agent for his vulnerability to robbery. Most traffickers are in the business to make money, but some believe they can get away with *rip-offs* if the circumstances are right since the victim is not likely to report the robbery to the police. Even without ever seeing money, if the trafficker realizes that the undercover agent has access to a large sum of money, he may attempt to kidnap the agent to hold him hostage until the money is exchanged for his freedom.

To avoid these problems, the undercover agent should never let the trafficker know, or even assume where the money is being kept either before or after a displaying of the money has been completed. The undercover agent should make it clear to the trafficker through his or her conversations with him that he will not have access to the money again until the drugs are delivered to him.

When drug agents elect to conduct a scheduled flash of the money instead of a surprise flash, they are unnecessarily exposing the undercover agent to danger. Drug agents should always strive to display money using the surprise tactic, thereby preventing the trafficker from formulating a plan to steal it. For further details, see Chapter 8 on flash roll management.

Poor Communication

Every undercover agent should be equipped with, at a minimum, a pager or a cellular telephone so his or her supervisor and surveillance team can remain in constant communication. The undercover agent needs to be alerted in the event the surveillance team detects counter-surveillance or other indicators of a possible robbery.

The use of such devices is so important to agent safety to justify canceling or delaying the scheduled undercover meeting until such time they can be obtained. Even if the undercover agent is engaged in conversation with the trafficker inside a restaurant, it would not be unusual for him or her to receive a call on a cellular telephone from his "money man" or some other person. Certain codes can be displayed on pagers that will alert the undercover agent to immediately leave the area or make a telephone call to the case agent for updates on the observations made by the surveillance team.

Complacency

Complacency is a real danger that is especially prevalent with more experienced drug agents. Although many undercover operations are similar, none are ever the same. Each undercover meeting and operation has a high potential for danger, and the undercover agent cannot predict the intentions of the drug trafficker based on his or her past experiences with him.

Complacency coupled with the attitude that "it will never happen to me," is a dangerous combination for an undercover agent. He must constantly be on guard and approach each undercover situation as an entirely new challenge where surprises are the norm. Supervisors should look for signs of complacency among his or her subordinates and consider removing them from undercover roles until a new attitude emerges.

Inaccessibility of Undercover Weapons

The decision to carry a weapon while undercover should be the sole discretion of the agent. However, if a weapon is going to be carried, then he or she should make it readily accessible if the need should arise. Various commercially made holsters are on the market that provide complete concealment, however, they are not always easily accessible. Unexpected situations can arise in which the undercover agent may need immediate access to a firearm. He or she should use these hidden holsters while qualifying at the pistol range to insure they are familiar with their operation and reduce the time needed to draw their weapons.

Making Inaccurate Conclusions from Accurate Observations

Danger can arise when drug agents draw inaccurate conclusions based on accurate observations, and then make operational decisions based upon them. Drug agents must remain aware, stay alert, and keep an open mind during undercover operations. Experienced agents may see something entirely different from an inexperienced one. There is no substitute for experience, especially when the undercover agent's life may be on the line.

Drug agents must have constant, free flowing intelligence information from surveillance, technical listening devices, and open sources in order to make appropriate conclusions about the intentions of drug traffickers. Constant, thorough debriefings of any informants involved will help drug agents make accurate conclusions.

Summary

Undercover agents face the most dangerous aspect of drug law enforcement. They come face to face with drug criminals as the crime is occurring. They are exposed to dangerous criminals who may be bent on robbing them of their money. The suspects the undercover agents encounter may not think twice about robbing or even killing someone they perceive as being another drug dealer. Suspects reason that their victims will either not report the crime to the police or their death will not generate much police interest.

Undercover agents need to adequately prepare for every assignment they face. If the agent is exposed as a police officer, it could create serious safety problems for the CI who introduced the drug dealer to the agent. They must have sufficient documents in their undercover identities to convince a suspect he is not dealing with the police. His or her cover story must be rehearsed with the informant to further credibility.

Agents selected for undercover assignments should have those traits most seasoned police detectives have and, above all, be willing to accept the inherent dangers associated with this type of work. Agents unable or unwilling to perform undercover assignments should not be forced by supervisors into these roles.

All operational planning must be designed with the safety of the undercover agent in mind. Supervisors must review and approve these plans before any operation is conducted. Even if drug agents always follow proper procedures and strictly adhere to the seven critical factors of undercover violence, they will still be exposed to an element of danger inherent to the job. However, following the steps identified by the research conducted by the DEA minimizes this risk.

Flash Roll Management

8

A *flash roll* is a sum of money displayed to a drug trafficker by an undercover agent, for a brief amount of time, to prove he or she has the means to purchase a quantity of drugs under negotiation. When, where, and how to display departmental funds to known criminals is something drug enforcement supervisors need to fully understand.

The objective of doing a *money flash* is to convince the suspect the undercover agent can buy the drugs, while at the same time protecting the money from theft or robbery. There are several sound reasons for displaying money to drug suspects: (1) money flashes prove the undercover agent is serious about purchasing the drugs under negotiation; (2) it proves he or she has the means to purchase the drugs; (3) the need to later show the money to the suspects again is eliminated; (4) the suspect is forced to verify he has access to drugs by showing them to the undercover agent; and (5) the displaying of money has a tendency to move the case rapidly.

Surprise Flashes vs. Scheduled Flashes

When contemplating displaying money to any criminal, the safety of the undercover agents must always be taken into account. To minimize the danger the undercover agents are exposed to, a technique known as a *surprise flash*, usually works well.

A surprise flash is when an agent displays money to the drug trafficker, without his prior knowledge, that he believes will be used to purchase drugs at a later time. The money only needs to be shown long enough for the suspect to count it or otherwise be convinced that all the money needed for the pending drug transaction is there.

One drawback to surprise flashes is that the money may be displayed to a suspect who does not have credibility with his source of supply. The suspect may vouch for the undercover agent, but if the source of supply does not believe him, the technique will not work in getting the drugs delivered, no matter how many times the money is shown to the suspect. The undercover agent must convince the source of supply to attend a meeting where he and his middleman can both see the "buy" money simultaneously.

Scheduled flashes are when the suspect knows in advance he is going to see the money that will be used to purchase drugs. This should only be done in extraordinary circumstances and only in an extremely controlled environment. Because of the obvious dangers involved, scheduled flashes should be avoided whenever possible.

Creating a Controlled Environment

The challenge to the case agent is to devise a scenario that will minimize the dangers the undercover agent will be exposed to when displaying money to a known criminal. A tightly controlled environment should be created to deter the suspect from ever attempting to steal the money. An example of a controlled environment would be the scheduling of a money flash inside a bank vault where the money is stored in a safety deposit box. Surveillance agents should be positioned inside the bank posing as customers and employees. In general, because of the inherent dangers associated with this technique, scheduled flashes should be avoided.

Surprise flashes in public places help to deter the suspect from robbing the agent of the money. A restaurant, public parking lot at a shopping mall, or similar place works well; however, the suspect will now know that the undercover agent has access to the money. When the amount of money is large enough to temp the suspect to steal it, this will cause significant safety problems that must be overcome. The suspect may later consider kidnapping the informant or the agent, holding him or her hostage until the money is delivered to them. In order to deter this from happening, the undercover agent must make it clear to the suspect that the money does not belong to the agent, but rather it is money pooled from many different investors. Further, that the money will be given back to the investors immediately until such time an agreement is reached on how to take delivery of the drugs. Anything the agent can say to convince the suspect he or she will no longer have access to the money afterwards will go a long way in deterring a robbery.

Using a Second Undercover Agent

Using a second undercover agent in a money flash enhances the safety of the operation and shows the suspect he is dealing with a professional who takes his business dealings seriously. Money that is displayed to any suspect must leave the area as soon as practical. Money flashes can be done in such a manner to reach this objective.

For example, an undercover agent meets with a suspect in a restaurant to further negotiate the price and method of delivery of drugs. The previous agreed upon amount of money needed for the purchase of the drugs is $100,000.

During the negotiations, the undercover agent uses his cellular telephone to call a second undercover agent and tells him or her to meet him at the restaurant. At this point the suspect does not know what the agent is planning.

A few minutes later, the second agent arrives and is seen in the parking lot by the first agent. The primary undercover agent asks the suspect to accompany him outside. When they approach the second agent's vehicle, the agent places a gym bag on the front passenger seat of the vehicle. The door is locked and the window is closed. He or she unzips the bag and shows the suspect the money inside. The agent fans the bills of each *bundle* to prove they are all one hundred dollar bills, and *bundle counts* the ten stacks, each containing ten thousand dollars. He or she then immediately drives off as the first undercover agent and suspect return to the restaurant to continue their discussion about the delivery of the drugs.

To reemphasize, once the money is displayed to the suspects, the agent controlling the money should immediately depart the area. Having the money on hand will increase the danger level to an unacceptable level and make the agents prone to robbery.

In 1988 in Pasadena, CA, two DEA special agents were murdered by a suspect who knew he was going to see $80,000 in cash to buy heroin and insisted the agents accompany him, with the money, to his source of supply's home. Instead they arrived at a residence picked at random, whereupon, exiting the undercover vehicle, the suspect shot and killed the two agents, shot another one, and stole the flash money.

Once the money is flashed, the question of whether or not the undercover agent has the money to purchase the drugs or not is no longer an issue. The ball, so to speak, is now in the suspect's court. At this time the primary undercover agent should tell the suspect he will not see the money until he or she sees his drugs.

Many greedy suspects will become motivated to immediately go to their source of supply to ascertain the availability of the drugs. During this time in between the flash and the delivery of the drugs, the primary undercover agent should depart the area to become inaccessible to the suspect except by telephone. Surveillance agents should be standing by to follow the suspect to his source of supply in an effort to identify him and possibly later obtain a search warrant for the premises.

Toll records of telephone numbers called by the suspect immediately after the money flash may reveal the identity of his source of supply.

Use of an Informant to Display the Money

CIs should never be trusted with the government's funds for money flashes. Informants cannot be trusted to this point and should be told that policy prohibits them from performing this role. Some informants have been known to be in collusion with the suspects for the sole purpose of stealing the flash money.

Informants can, however, do the negotiating and call an undercover agent to conduct the surprise money flash. Any scenario is permissible so long as the informant does not have control and dominion over the flash roll.

Seeing Drugs before Displaying the Money

Both suspects and experienced undercover agents know that the element of danger increases when money and drugs are brought out in the open. Undercover agents should first ask the suspect to prove he has drugs before considering displaying money. Usually, suspects will decline, but they have been known to do so. In any event, the undercover agent should be prepared to show money, especially if the suspect appears reluctant to deal with the agent.

Case agents should keep in mind that many suspects negotiating drug deals do not have the authority to show drugs without first seeing money. Others will bring drugs out with the understanding that the money is in the immediate area, held by another, waiting for word on when to deliver it to the suspect. One of the goals of money flashes is to force the suspect into revealing where his drugs are so law enforcement can seize them.

Flash Roll Preparation

Preparation is key to convincing the suspect he is not dealing with the police. Suspects believe that law enforcement has access to unlimited resources, money, and manpower to carry out their mission, none of which is usually true. If the traffickers see a flash roll of newly printed currency, neatly stacked and banded in brand new paper band adhesives, it will raise suspicions that the money came from a government source. The money flashed to the suspect must appear to be the proceeds of other drug transactions or criminal activity.

Drug dealers amass large amounts of cash, in various denominations, and usually use rubber bands to hold various amounts of money together. This same thing must be done when preparing money for a flash. Any paper adhesive bands provided by the city treasurer or Federal Reserve Bank must be removed and replaced with various colored rubber bands. The agents should insist on a variety of denominations and then count out bundles, or stacks of money, for quick and easy bundle counts, e.g., stacks of $1000, $5000, or $10,000 are normal.

Some agencies have sealed flash rolls that have been precounted with the serial numbers recorded for use in an operation on short notice. If the precounted flash roll consists of $100,000 and only $50,000 is needed, the balance should remain in a safe and not taken out to the street. Undercover agents should never display more money than the suspect expects to see. Showing more money than absolutely necessary telegraphs to the suspect that he is dealing with someone who is inexperienced and, therefore, prone to making judgment errors. If the situation was reversed, the suspect would never do it, and he will not show you more drugs than he expects to sell.

Summary

Money flashes have long been a successful tool in undercover drug operations. They help convince the suspect that the undercover agent has the means to purchase the drugs he is negotiating for. Displays of money need to be done in a safe manner and in controlled environments.

Using a second undercover agent will enhance the safety of the flash, and show the suspect the undercover agent is professional when it comes to handling and safeguarding money. Because they cannot be trusted, informants should never be allowed to handle the money. A sworn law enforcement officer is a much better choice.

Drug agents should only show the money to the suspect once, and refuse any attempts by him to see it without first insisting on seeing his drugs. Once the flash occurs, the money should immediately be removed from the premises. A second money flash may be the time the suspect intends to rob the undercover agent. Agents should ask to see the drugs before agreeing to show the money again. Once the drugs are shown, the suspects should be arrested.

9 Evidence Collection and Preservation

Categories of Evidence

As in other criminal investigations, evidence will either prove or disprove that an offense took place and the defendants are guilty of the crime. In most drug investigations, there are generally two categories of evidence agents deal with: drug and nondrug. It would be highly unusual for agents to ever collect hair or fiber samples, fingernail scrapings, DNA samples, and the like. These types of scientific evidence are usually reserved for crimes committed by unknown perpetrators. Drug investigations, as previously stated, are crimes that are being investigated while they are being committed. The suspects are generally known at the time of the offense, and the evidence collected by drug agents reinforces the prosecutor's theory that the defendants are involved.

Collection of Evidence

Most drug evidence is collected through purchase or seizure. Undercover agents purchase drug evidence to later use against the suspect. During the course of an investigation, search warrants are often obtained for homes, businesses, storage lockers, and vehicles.

Systematic Searching

Whatever is being searched for controlled substances, whether it is a vehicle or a residence, the key to success is being systematic. Using a systematic search method will ensure that no area of the vehicle or building was overlooked, and increases the likelihood of success.

Searches should always be conducted in conjunction with other personnel who provide protection and can act as witnesses when items of evidence are found. Before any search is conducted, drug agents should wear gloves to protect themselves from needle punctures and volatile substances they may come into contact with. Gloves are a necessity to ward off possible contamination of HIV; puncture resistant varieties are available for law enforcement.

If a home is going to be searched, after the agents have announced their presence and intention, and everyone inside has been accounted for and detained, the search can begin. One or two agents should be assigned the responsibility to search a particular room or common area. The room can be visually divided in half, or in fourths, or similar to pieces of a pie. Whatever method is used, it must be consistent to insure all areas have been searched.

Because vehicles offer little space to maneuver, an agent should be assigned to either the front or back seat, and then they should switch sides to search the opposite side of the car just in case something was overlooked. Together they can search the trunk and under the hood of the vehicle to look for concealed drugs in air filters, under hoses, and many other hiding places.

Vehicles are often fashioned with custom made hidden compartments that require an electronic switch to open. Unless the agents have prior intelligence information about the vehicle being equipped with such a device, they cannot be detected, in most cases, by the human eye.

Drugs can be hidden in either buildings or vehicles in many uncommon places. Agents must be meticulous in their search since traffickers have devised many clever hidden compartments in furniture, behind walls, behind easily removed medicine cabinets, and the like.

Drug Detection Dogs

Drug agents should seek the assistance of a trained drug detection dog (K-9)to narrow their search for controlled substances. Dogs are not infallible and sometimes tire and become bored with their surroundings. Most K-9s do a tremendous job in locating drugs; however, they are not a substitute for the agents looking for documents and other items of nondrug evidence. Many nondrug items of evidence are contaminated with trace amounts of controlled substances that the K-9 can find, including money. It is very common to find dog "hits" on currency found in suspects' possession.

When using K-9s, agents should clear the area and allow the dog and its handler unfettered access to the home, building, or vehicle being searched. Dogs do not have the ability to distinguish between law enforcement and suspects, and agents are advised not to make any moves toward the dog's handler that might be interpreted as threatening. Many of these dogs will react to protect their handler and have caused unnecessary injury to agents and suspects alike.

Drug Evidence

Any controlled substances purchased undercover or seized during search warrants or other searches constitute drug evidence. Seized drug evidence should immediately be transported to the office where it can be weighed and sealed in a sturdy transparent plastic bag. The weight should not reflect any container the drugs were concealed in. If the drugs were found in a suitcase, bag, or other item, these nondrug items should be logged separately as *containers* and made available for court later. Crime laboratories will remove the substance and weigh it for the exact amount. Any weighing conducted at the office is solely for the purpose of obtaining a good faith estimate for report writing purposes.

As an example, if a kilogram of cocaine is seized from a drug trafficker, that kilo package should be weighed as is. The gross amount is the total weight of the cocaine plus its original wrapping. The crime laboratory will later determine the exact net amount before it is analyzed.

Smaller individual packages of drugs should also remain in their original container when being weighed (e.g., paper fold, balloon, etc.), but not anything these containers were stored or concealed in such as a bag or a sock. Including these items would skew the true amount of drugs seized and could make a significant difference in formulating charges against the defendant.

Tablets seized as drug evidence, if practical, should be counted as well as weighed. Ecstasy tablets are sometimes found in large, sealed plastic bags, amounting to multi-hundreds or thousands in number. This type of evidence should remain sealed and weighed only. The laboratory is capable of accurately counting the tablets and will determine the exact amount and weight submitted.

Handling Drug Evidence

Unlike what is depicted on some popular television shows and movies, drug agents do not, under any circumstances, taste, smell, or sample drugs to determine if they are in fact controlled substances. To do so would be pointless and create immense safety issues.

When handling drug evidence, agents should wear latex or similar gloves to avoid placing their fingerprints on containers, as well as eliminating the possibility of absorption of chemicals through the pours of their skin. Special care needs to be taken when handling all controlled substances since they could be laced with caustic chemicals designed specifically to injure or kill law enforcement personnel.

Chain of Custody

Whether seized or purchased by a drug agent or confidential informant, all drug evidence must be accounted for at all times, and a *chain of custody* must be established. Drug evidence forms usually reflect who the seizing agent was and documents what he or she did with the evidence. These important forms also indicate who seized the drugs, when they were booked as evidence and sent to the laboratory, who examined the evidence, and when it was returned to the submitting agency. Other logs and records most departments maintain will indicate who later signed for the evidence for court purposes, and when it was returned. In order to maintain the integrity of the evidence, these procedures must be followed in every case involving evidence, whether it involves drugs or nondrug items. Strict accountability must be maintained to defeat any notion by defense attorneys that the substance was tampered with after it came into police custody.

Bulk Evidence

Drug agents frequently seize large amounts of marijuana that can be categorized as *bulk evidence*. Law enforcement agencies should photograph and videotape the gathering of bulk evidence, and ask the permission of the prosecutor and court to dispose of the vast majority of the material prior to any court proceedings. If necessary, the bulk evidence will be maintained in locked storage containers located at a law enforcement facility. For statistical purposes, each mature marijuana plant, absent stock, seeds, and stems, can be considered to weigh one kilogram (2.2 pounds). This is a rule of thumb that most court jurisdictions will accept. It also takes into account that cut marijuana will lose a large percentage of its weight from lack of hydration, time, and heat. The weight of the bulk evidence is important for sentencing guidelines in federal matters, and several kilograms of marijuana can make a significant difference in the sentence a defendant receives.

Field Testing of Drug Evidence

Chemical companies make a variety *field test kits* that drug agents use to make a presumptive determination that the substance in question is what it was purported to be. They are available to test for specific drugs, including marijuana, cocaine, amphetamine, and heroin. These kits include heavy transparent plastic pouches that usually contain small vials of chemicals. The agent will place a fingernail-size amount of the suspected controlled substance into the pouch and clamp it shut. By breaking the small glass vials in a particular order, the chemicals, mixed with the suspected controlled substance, will turn color. What color the liquids from the vials turn will indicate whether the substance, in all likelihood, is a controlled substance.

These kits have a limited value to drug agents. Despite the chemicals turning the correct color to indicate the presence of a controlled substance, there is no guarantee of their accuracy. Many additives to cocaine, heroin, methamphetamine, and other substances may cause these chemicals to react in a different manner. Other noncontrolled substances, or those disguised as a controlled substance, may contain properties that will also cause a false reaction. Further, even if the substance being analyzed by the kit is truly a controlled substance, how fast or slow the colors appear have no relationship to the purity of the drug.

The test kit can be used by undercover drug agents to prove the substance they are about to purchase is genuine. While an undercover meeting takes place in a public place, a surveillance agent can conceal a test kit in the restroom. Before the undercover agent purchases the substance, he or she may want to "sample" the drug and excuse themselves to the restroom, presumably to take the substance in private. While in the restroom, the agent retrieves the kit, tests a small amount, and conceals the rest. Upon returning to the trafficker, the agent can report, with a degree of certainly, that the drug appears to be good. If the substance did not test positive, the agent could argue the drug had no effect, and accuse the dealer of trying to sell a counterfeit.

In any event, drug agents should rely instead on the quantitative analysis of the drug conducted by their crime laboratory to determine the purity of the substance. If the analysis reveals the purity level to be 20% or below, drug consumers would normally complain to their dealer. Fifty percent and above is the norm, and the higher the purity usually dictates the asking price for the drug.

Undercover drug agents should avoid being placed in the position of rendering an opinion to the drug trafficker about the quality of the drugs they purchased before receiving confirmation from the laboratory that what was purchased was in fact a controlled substance. If the agent prematurely praises the quality of the drug to a trafficker who knew he sold either a highly diluted substance or an outright counterfeit, he will realize the agent has little or no experience in the drug business. The dealer's perception of the undercover agent could have a profound impact on the outcome of the investigation. The trafficker will realize he is dealing with either a fool or a drug agent (Figure 9.1).

Nondrug Evidence

Other evidence developed during the course of a drug trafficking investigation must also be accounted for and will later be made available for examination by the defense attorney, court, and jury.

It is not unusual for drug agents to create numerous audiotapes of telephone conversations between drug agents, confidential informants, and the

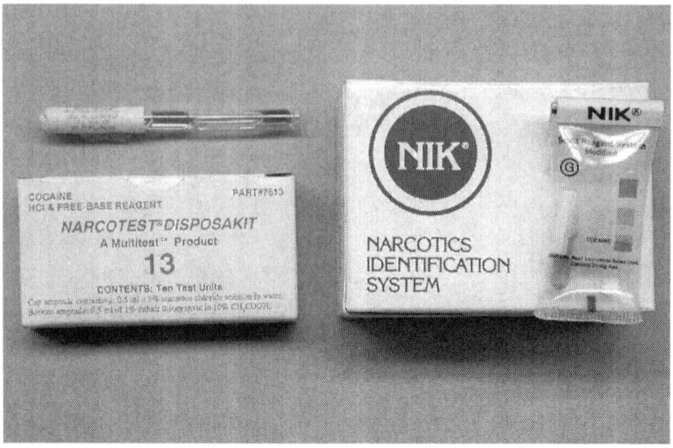

Figure 9.1 Drug testing kit.

defendants. Videotapes may also have been created depicting the sales of drugs or meetings in hotel rooms between the traffickers and drug agent.

Other nondrug evidence associated with modern drug investigations may include:

- Airline tickets
- Travel agency records
- Hotel registration cards and toll call records
- Car rental agreements
- Telephone billing records
- Cash
- Lease agreements
- Sales receipts for laboratory equipment, cellular telephones, and pagers
- Firearms
- Ammunition
- Miscellaneous documentation
- Weigh scales, balloons, plastic bags, cutting agents, etc., indicative of sales
- Laboratory equipment, baking soda boxes, chemical containers, hydroponic equipment, etc. indicative of manufacturing

All of these items should be booked as evidence to establish a chain of custody.

Fingerprints

Fingerprint technology has significantly improved over the years to the point where a single fingerprint found on drug packaging can often lead to the identity of a co-conspirator. Drug agents should consider fingerprinting packages and containers where drugs were located in order to help identify other persons involved in the conspiracy. Automated fingerprint files often quickly identify the person whose fingerprints are found on drug packaging, and may sway a prosecutor to indict him without any other physical evidence.

Frequently, undercover drug agents will negotiate the purchase of drugs from a suspect who will later return with the drugs and an accomplice to act as counter-surveillance or security for the drugs. Once the drugs are delivered to the undercover agent and both men are arrested, their fingerprints should be compared to any fingerprints found on the packaging in order to solidify the case. Many accomplices claim they had no idea what was transpiring or that they had any prior knowledge about a drug transaction. Finding their fingerprints on any packages where drugs were located defeats the *blind mule* defense, and may sway that person to later testify against the primary suspect.

Summary

Drug and nondrug evidence play an important part in convicting traffickers. Drug evidence is often purchased or seized through search warrants. Nondrug evidence can materialize from a variety of sources, mostly legitimate.

A chain of custody must be established in order to maintain the integrity of the evidence. There should be no question about the status of evidence from the moment it is seized until the end of the appeals process.

Drug field testing kits are available to perform a presumptive test on the substance seized to determine the presence of any controlled substances. Although these kits may be helpful in some areas, they are limited in their abilities and cannot be heavily relied on for accuracy. They cannot determine the percentage of a controlled substance present in any item tested. Fingerprint evidence should not be overlooked and can prove helpful in solidifying a case against a particular individual as well as identify other conspirators in the crime.

10 U.S. Sentencing Guidelines for Drug Offenses

It is important for drug agents, no matter which law enforcement agency they work for, to not only know the elements of proof for controlled substance statutes, but also what the punishment for drug trafficking is. Knowledge of these tables of punishment will assist drug agents in obtaining the cooperation of traffickers they arrest, and may lead to expanding their investigation, or opening entirely different ones.

Local law enforcement officers who believe the punishment for a state drug crime will have little or no impact on a particular trafficker can approach the U.S. Attorney's Office in their area either directly or through the DEA and seek federal prosecution. When the defendant learns he is liable for substantially more severe punishment for the same offense, he may be more inclined to cooperate.

Unlike many states, the federal government has a sentencing commission, a nine-member panel working as an independent agency of the federal judiciary. The commission's seemingly monumental task initially was to overhaul the sentencing policies of the federal criminal justice system. Since that was accomplished, it now serves to fine tune sentences on its own or when Congress mandates that such changes take place.

Background

Prior to 1987, defendants in similar federal cases but different judicial districts often received substantially different sentences, ranging from probation to several years in prison. Then, after being sent to prison, defendants became eligible for parole automatically after serving only about one-third of their sentences. Thus, a 5-year prison sentence became, in reality, less than 2 years incarceration.

The Sentencing Reform Act of 1984, part of Title II of the Comprehensive Crime Control Act of 1984, took steps to prevent such scenarios from occurring. The Comprehensive Crime Control Act established the U.S. Sentencing Commission. Its mission was to achieve uniformity and proportionality in sentencing in the federal criminal justice system. It achieved that and ended parole in the federal system as well.

Because of the latitude given federal judges prior to 1987, there was a wide disparity in sentencing. The guidelines were designed to close this gap by requiring that defendants be sentenced according to their criminal histories and the seriousness of the crime committed. Thus, a defendant with two prior convictions who commits a crime will, not may, will receive more prison time than a defendant with no criminal record that commits the identical crime.[1]

As part of the same legislation that created the U.S. Sentencing Commission, Congress established mandatory minimum sentences for certain federal crimes, including drug offenses. Mandatory minimum penalties also limit the discretion of federal judges by requiring that sentences be based solely on the type and amount of drugs involved, the criminal history of the defendant, and other aggravating circumstances, such as possession of a weapon during the crime. Unlike the sentencing guidelines, however, mandatory minimums give judges little flexibility in sentencing.

Federal Parole Abolished

Previously, the U.S. Parole Commission could, and often did, authorize the early release of federal prisoners. The Sentencing Reform Act limited this authority by abolishing federal parole. As a result, defendants serve their count-imposed sentences, with a minimum sentence reduction of approximately 15% for good behavior, if applicable. Such sentence reductions may not exceed 54 days per year. Other types of early release are prohibited.

Longer Prison Sentences

The sentencing guidelines, in conjunction with federal mandatory minimum sentences, have resulted in longer prison sentences for offenders who violate federal drug laws. According to the Bureau of Justice Statistics, from 1980 to 1989, the average sentence for federal drug offenders increased by 59%. In 1980, drug traffickers received an average sentence of 48.1 months; in 1985, 60.8 months; in 1988, 71.3 months; and in 1990, 84 months.[2] Furthermore, without parole, federal prisoners now serve almost their entire sentences.

The Sentencing Table

Federal judges sentence offenders according to a table established by the guidelines. Using a two-dimensional grid, the table categorizes offenses according to the seriousness of the crime (level 1 through level 43) and the defendant's criminal history (category I through category VI). The higher the level of offense, the longer the possible sentence. The maximum offense mandates a life sentence. Lower figures represent the minimum a defendant with no criminal history would receive. (See Table 10.1 through Table 10.3 for details.) The sentencing tables used in drug cases base punishments on the type and the amount of the drug, as well as the criminal history of the defendant. Heroin and methamphetamine violations receive greater punishments than those involving cocaine or marijuana. Also, offenses involving crack cocaine receive substantially higher sentences than those dealing with cocaine in its powdered form, due to crack's higher addictive qualities. Defendants convicted of conspiracy or an attempt to commit any offense involving a controlled substance warrant the same level as if they had completed the object of the conspiracy. For example, if two or more people conspire to import 500 kilograms of cocaine, but the plane containing the drugs crashes into the Gulf of Mexico, the defendants would be punished the same as if they plane had landed safely in the United States.

Drug Offense Sentencing Tables

Table 10.1 Cocaine

Base Offense Level	Amount	Sentence Range
26	500 grams < 2 kg	63–150 months
28	2 < 3.5 kg	78–175 months
30	3.5 < 5 kg	97–210 months
32	5 < 15 kg	121–262 months
34	15 < 50 kg	151–327 months
36	50 < 150 kg	188–405 months
38	150 < 500 kg	235 months–life
40	500 < 1500 kg	292 months–life
42	1500 < kg or more	360 months–life

Note: Base offense levels, which range from 1 to 43, correspond to the seriousness of the crime committed. In drug cases, they depend on the type and the amount of the drug. Level 43 commands a life sentence in all cases. The sentence range represents the minimum category I sentence, for a defendant with no criminal history, and the maximum category VI sentence, for a defendant with an extensive criminal background.

Table 10.2 Marijuana

Base Offense Level	Amount	Sentence Range
26	100 < 400 kg	63–150 months
28	400 < 700 kg	78–175 months
30	700 < 1000 kg	97–210 months
32	1000 < 3000 kg	121–262 months
34	3000 < 10,000 kg	151–327 months
36	10,000 < 30,000 kg	188–405 months
38	30,000 < 100,000 kg	235 months–life
40	100,000 < 300,000 kg	292 months–life
42	300,000 kg or more	360 months–life

Table 10.3 Heroin

Base Offense Level	Amount	Sentence Range
32	1 < 3 kg	121–262 months
34	3 < 10 kg	151–327 months
36	10 < 30 kg	188–405 months
38	30 < 100 kg	235 months–life
40	100 < 300 kg	292 months–life
42	300 kg or more	360 months–life

Departures from the Guidelines

In formulating the guidelines, the commission analyzed thousands of cases and based punishments on scenarios considered typical for certain crimes. Still, in some instances, aggravating or mitigating circumstances may warrant departure from the guidelines.

Based on its research, the commission anticipated when departures likely would occur. The guidelines provide for adjustments, up or down, in cases where, for example, the defendant obstructs justice, physically restrain the victim, or plays a major or minor role in the crime. Thus, if a defendant organizes, leads, manages, or supervises a criminal activity, the sentence increases, depending on the specific role and the number of codefendants involved. On the other hand, if a defendant clearly plays a minor role, the sentence decreases accordingly.

The punishment also increases if a defendant abuses a position of public or private trust or uses a special skill to commit or conceal an offense. By definition, a *special skill* is not possessed by members of the general public and usually requires substantial education, training, or licensing to learn and use. Examples of individuals with special skills include accountants, attorneys, boat captains, pilots, chemists, and demolition experts.[3]

A hypothetical situation may serve to illustrate sentences based on a defendant's role in a crime. A group of people conspire to smuggle 12 tons of marijuana into the United States from Thailand. They use a fishing vessel to transport the contraband to a deserted beach where they off-load it. Drug agents arrest the organizers, managers, supervisors, and the boat captain, as well as the individuals who off-loaded the drugs onto the beach. Assuming identical criminal backgrounds, according to the guidelines, the organizers would receive more prison time than the managers and supervisors, who would receive more time than the captain or those who merely unloaded the illicit cargo. But, the captain would receive a greater sentence than the off-loaders, because of the special skill required to navigate a boat. Regardless of their skills and abilities, defendants who complete drug transactions within 1000 yards of a school or college,* or who use pregnant or juvenile accomplices,[4] also receive increased sentences.

In contrast, defendants may receive reduced sentences for clearly accepting personal responsibility for their criminal conduct. That is, defendants who, for example, cooperate with authorities, express remorse to their victims, or make restitution for their crimes may receive reduced sentences. However, merely entering a guilty plea does not entitle a defendant, as a matter of right, to a reduced sentence.

Court Ordered Departures

The commission recognizes that some cases will not fit the guidelines, even with adjustments, and will require departures. Still, judges who depart from the guidelines must provide written justification for doing so.

Some offenses mandating an increase above the guidelines include significant disruption of a governmental function, extreme conduct by the defendant, substantial property damage or loss, and extreme psychological injury to the victim.[5] In drug cases, death or serious bodily injury resulting from the use of controlled substances that the defendant distributed would warrant an increase in the sentence. In cases that carry mandatory minimum penalties, the sentence doubles, at least. If an individual commits such a violation after a prior felony drug conviction, the sentence doubles again. Coupled with mandatory minimum sentences, the sentencing guidelines may provide a strong deterrent to drug law violators.

Defendants can receive a shorter sentence if they provide substantial assistance to authorities, defined as providing investigators and prosecutors with information leading to the indictment of other offenders. Only the

* USSG, Section 2D1.2 applies an enhancement for defendents convicted under 21 U.S. Codes § 859, 860, and 861.

prosecution can motion for a reduced sentence based on the substantial assistance clause of the guidelines.

The possibility of receiving a reduced sentence often provides a powerful incentive for defendants to cooperate. The assistance they provide often results in the arrest and prosecution of previously unknown accomplices and the seizure of hidden assets that would have gone undetected otherwise.

Criticism of the Guidelines

Although the guidelines have brought uniformity to federal sentencing, they initially generated considerable controversy. From 1987, when the guidelines took effect, to 1989, when the U.S. Supreme Court upheld their constitutionality,[6] over 150 federal judges claimed that the guidelines violated the Constitution and refused to follow them.[7] Even today, some federal judges and citizens groups criticize the guidelines, mainly because they limit their discretion in sentencing, especially in drug matters.

Evolutionary Process

The sentencing guidelines have evolved since their inception in 1987 and continue to do so today. As judges sentence according to the guidelines, and as they depart from them, the commission gains insight into what areas require modification. The group meets at least once each year to review the guidelines, and revisions are published in the Federal Register. The changes become effective after 180 days, unless Congress enacts a law to the contrary.

With the passage of the Violent Crime Control and Law Enforcement Act of 1994, Congress hopes to reduce punishments for individuals convicted of low-level drug violations. The act waives mandatory minimum sentences in cases in which offenders did not act as organizers, leaders, managers, or supervisors and did not use guns, commit violence, or harm others while committing their crimes. In addition, the offender must have only minor criminal histories and must cooperate with authorities.[8]

Summary

Sentencing guidelines in the United States have changed the way judges sentence federal offenders. They mandate consideration of the defendant's criminal history, the severity of the crime, and other aggravating or mitigating factors. The guidelines place a limit on the sentencing discretion of judges and provide harsher sentences where warranted.

Some view the guidelines as too harsh and inflexible. Others believe they are not strict enough, and still others champion them as a necessary deterrent to crime because of the certainty of the sentence to be served. Despite the debate, the sentencing guidelines, coupled with mandatory minimum penalties, clearly have raised the ante for individuals contemplating violating federal drug laws.

State and local drug agents can bring significant violators to the attention of the U.S. Attorney's Office to seek prosecution in lieu of state charges. When faced with what could be significantly higher punishment when compared to a state court, it may serve as a way in obtaining the cooperation of the defendant in his and other drug cases.

References

1. 28 U.S. Code § 994(b)(2).
2. Federal Criminal Case Processing, 1980–89, with preliminary date for 1990, Bureau of Justice Statistics, October 1991, p. 17.
3. U.S. Sentencing Commission, *Guidelines Manual*, Section 3B1.3 (November 1991), comment. (n2).
4. U.S. Sentencing Commission, *Guidelines Manual*, Sections 2D1.2, 3A1.1.
5. U.S. Sentencing Commission, *Guidelines Manual*, Ch. 3, Pt. k.
6. *Mistretta v. United States*, 488 U.S. 361, 109 S. Ct. 647, 1989.
7. Torry, S., Some Federal Judges Just Say No to Drug Cases, *The Washington Post*, May 17, 1993, p. F7.
8. The Violent Crime Control and Law Enforcement Act of 1994, Publ. No. 103-322, Sec. 80001, 108 Stat. 1985.

Raid Planning and Execution

11

A raid is the lawful attack of a location by law enforcement. Raids can occur at any time during the course of a drug investigation, although they most frequently are conducted in conjunction with the execution of either a search or arrest warrant. They are conducted for two primary reasons: safety and recovery of evidence before it can be destroyed.

The vast majority of search warrant executions do not require a special weapons and tactics team (SWAT) to gain entry safely, however drug agents need to be prepared and should have some idea what they are going up against before serving search and arrest warrants. If a supervisor deems the situation is too dangerous to conduct a search without the assistance of a SWAT team, and one is not available, the execution of the warrant should be delayed until either the circumstances change, or the appropriately trained officers are available to assist.

The elements of raids are *speed*, *surprise*, and *violence of action* in order to make the location safe and secure for drug agents, and to preserve any evidence that may be in the location before it is intentionally destroyed by the suspects inside. Raids can be one of the most dangerous, yet rewarding experiences in the course of any drug investigation.

Reading this chapter is not going to make the reader an expert in the field. Conducting raids is part of a broad range of accepted police tactics that are deployed by professional police and military organizations throughout the world. Specialized equipment and constant practice is necessary to perform safe and efficient raids. Smaller police departments should select raid team members who volunteer for such an assignment and have at least some basic knowledge of police tactics. Once drug agents are assigned as raid team members, regular practice will develop them into an effective tool, and will minimize injury to both themselves and suspects alike.

There are about 40,000 police and sheriff departments in the United States. Very few of these maintain a full-time SWAT team, or others trained in high-risk entries, or even have access to them. Even departments that have SWAT trained members who are not dedicated to SWAT missions full-time usually find many of their team members unavailable when the need arises. This chapter is designed to provide only general information to drug agents who do not have access to full-time SWAT or entry teams and have to rely on themselves to perform the task.

Raid Planning

Unlike the military, in drug law enforcement there are no acceptable losses. Performing what amounts to an armed assault on a building is not a military operation where success or failure is determined by the number of casualties that were suffered.

Case agents and supervisors need to develop as much information about the location as possible beforehand. Supervisors should assess the situation and determine if a *raid* is necessary to begin with. Are there safer alternatives that will accomplish the same results? Could a proposed raid to arrest a heavily armed drug trafficker at his home be modified to arresting him while he is shopping for groceries? Can a ruse be used to get the suspect out of the residence or to go to a different location? These types of decisions have to be made in advance in order to enhance the safety of the officers and the suspect, as well as help preserve evidence.

Types of Raids

There are two types of raids: proactive and reactive. In a proactive raid, long-term planning is required to develop intelligence about the suspect, where he will be at the time of the raid, and what is the likelihood of his putting up resistance. The more information that can be gathered through records, informants, and surveillance, the greater the odds that the operation will conclude successfully and safely.

Reactive raids are those where the circumstances dictate the immediate action of the drug agents. An example may be a freshly arrested suspect granting permission to search his home where other suspects are waiting for him, or exigent circumstances require entering a building to *freeze* it while a search warrant is being obtained. In either event, little time is available to adequately plan, and this lack of time can result in injury or death of drug agents who are not prepared.

Site Surveys

Site surveys of the place to be raided are to drug law enforcement what reconnaissance missions are to the military. Both attempt to ascertain the strengths and weaknesses of the enemy, and compare them to the resources that are going to be led against them.

Steps to take:

1. Photographs. Still and video photographs should be taken of the targeted location in order to familiarize both supervisors and participants with the general layout of the establishment as well as the surrounding neighborhood. Studying these pictures will lessen the possibility of the raid team assaulting the wrong location, and can insure that the physical description of the dwelling or building to be search is detailed and specific for any search warrant affidavits that are filed. Aerial photographs further help in determining what may be in the back area of the building and may reveal the presence of any dogs or other animals. It will also indicate the location of vents or skylights that may show where certain rooms within the building are, such as kitchens and bathrooms.
2. Surveillance. Agents should conduct drive-bys and surveillance of the building to verify the existence or lack of obstructions such as barred windows, metal mesh screen doors, and vents in the roof. The amount of traffic on the street, and how many cars are parked on it, may necessitate police officers blocking off traffic on both sides of the street when the agents arrive. Parking may be another consideration.
3. Assess probable floor plan. As mentioned above, vents may reveal where certain rooms are located within a building, and this could be a key to devising a probable floor plan of the structure. Mobile homes have vehicle identification numbers (VINs) that will identify the manufacturer who can provide copies of floor plans to law enforcement.
4. Thoroughly debrief informant or undercover agent. Informants and undercover agents who have been inside the dwelling or building in question can reveal specific details about the floor plan as well as furnishings and other items that may be present. Particular attention should be made to the presence of firearms and any items that could be used as weapons.
5. Be conscious of booby-traps. Drug agents have experienced on occasion the presence of booby-traps in dwellings and buildings they intended to search. Agents should ascertain if the targets of their investigation have any history of using such devices or if they are prone to use them. Informants should be asked specific questions about the suspects use of booby-traps, vicious dogs, or any exotic animal such a poisonous snake to guard the premises.

Raid Briefing

A written operational plan should be distributed to each member of the raid team. The plan should clearly identify the place to be raided, what legal authority the team will be acting under, e.g., search or arrest warrant, and what agents and outside departments will be participating. The plan should name the suspect and others thought to be inside the building, as well as the description of what vehicles they have access to (see Figure 7.1 to Figure 7.6 for details).

The operational plan should also have the emergency contact numbers for local hospitals, fire departments, and police departments in case of injury, fire, or additional assistance being needed. Photographs of the suspects as well as a map leading to the location should be attached to the plan.

Equipment

Supervisors should insure each team member has the necessary safety equipment to conduct the operation. Some of the equipment should include:

- Firearm(s)
- Bulletproof vests
- Ballistic helmets
- Handcuffs
- Flashlights
- Pepper spray
- Expandable baton
- Flash bangs
- Breaching equipment including sledge hammer, prying tools, crow bars
- Ballistic shields

Agents should always notify the local police if in a different jurisdiction and have adequate communication equipment, including radios and cellular telephones if possible.

Raid Execution

More than half of all law enforcement officers shot at raid sites are shot by fellow officers. With proper planning and training, raids can be carried out successfully without injuries to suspects or fellow drug agents. Part of the process of being prepared is to know what elements will enhance the success of a raid.

Elements of a Successful Raid

The following elements must be present in order to ensure the success of any aggressive law enforcement action. These elements not only apply to drug agents, but to detectives and patrol officers as well.

Tactics

Drug agents who do not have a plan of action before assaulting a dwelling or other building are destined to fail. Each agent should have at a minimum, a general understanding of police tactics in entering a building and searching it for suspects. Entering a building tactically with a purpose as opposed to rushing in and hoping for the best are two different matters entirely. There is no substitute for proper tactics, and agents should not be made to feel pressured to conduct a raid until they are thoroughly prepared to do so.

Physical Fitness

Agents should maintain a good level of physical fitness throughout their entire law enforcement career. It is especially important when part of his or her duties is to conduct raids. Each raid party is only as strong as its weakest member.

Many drug suspects that agents arrest have criminal backgrounds and have spent time in state or federal prisons where they had almost unlimited access to weights and other body building equipment. They spend their days lifting weights and pound per pound, are usually more physically fit than police officers in general. To help offset this, agents and officers who are going to be members of a team that demands physical dexterity and endurance should exercise regularly to maintain fitness.

Mental Conditioning

Being physically fit is obviously important, but drug agents also need the mental conditioning on how to handle situations that will arise during any raid. They must have a clear understanding of their department's use of force policy and not hesitate to defend themselves or their partners in the event they encounter resistance. The agents conducting the raid have to expect the unexpected and react immediately when they perceive a threat or encounter violence.

Equipment

Drug agents need to be equipped properly to conduct a raid in the same way a diver needs certain equipment to perform his or her job. If agents do not possess the required equipment to successfully conduct a raid, they should not be expected to execute it since they would be placed in unnecessary danger. There is no substitute for the right equipment that is properly maintained.

Firearms

In addition to issued handguns, drug agents need access to and training with other firearms that may be required to execute raids safely and successfully. Shotguns, compact sub-machine guns, and long weapons that have accuracy at great distances should be part of any arsenal used by agents to conduct drug raids.

Training

Drug agents should engage in regular training in raid tactics and be exposed to a variety of methods in how to conduct them. Many books, professional magazines, and videotapes by experts from major law enforcement organizations can help in this regard. Federal agencies like the DEA and FBI regularly conduct such training for local law enforcement.

Consciousness Modes

There are four consciousness modes, white, yellow, orange, and red, which agents will experience while conducting raids. The mode changes up or down the scale based on what the agent sees, hears, or anticipates. The concept was originated by the legendary Jeff Cooper, who is recognized as one of the founding fathers of contemporary combat pistol shooting.

White

Somebody dead to the world who has no idea where he is, who he is, or why he is there can best be described as in condition white. Drug agents and police officers should never experience this while working, but instead should be at the next level, which is yellow.

Yellow

Most police officers are constantly aware of their surroundings and in tune with their environment. In this mode, they are much closer to the next level up the scale, orange, than if they were in the white mode. It can take 6 to 10 seconds for a drug agent conducting a raid or facing a life-threatening situation, to transform from white to red modes of consciousness.

Orange

Drug agents and police officers who are in the process of executing a high-risk entry into a dwelling, making an arrest, or who otherwise anticipate that danger may be imminent should find themselves automatically in conscious mode orange. By being in this mode law enforcement officers require less time to react to any dangerous situation they may encounter and will increase their odds of survival. Drug agents and police officers who are in dangerous situations and are in consciousness modes yellow or white pose an unnecessary risk to themselves and others.

Red

Here the agent is in a fighting mode. He or she is experiencing tunnel vision where all the agent's concentration is focused on the subject of his rage. He or she also experiences hearing attenuation where noises, such as gunfire, may not be recognizable by the affected agent since all his attention is devoted to the task at hand. Some agents also report seeing all motion slow down while in this stage. Drug agents who experience this condition should be allowed to regress slowly back to the yellow stage with the assistance of verbal and emotional support of other agents.

Escalation of Force

During drug raids agents will sometimes encounter resistance from suspects, and on occasion neighbors, friends, and associates of the suspect. This resistance can range from lying about the whereabouts of the suspect to using deadly force to help the suspect evade custody.

Drug agents on raid parties must be prepared for the entire range of resistance that they may face. Information gathered through reconnaissance, as discussed above, may provide the agents early warning about what, if any resistance to expect when assaulting the location.

There are basically six levels of force, ranging from the mere presence of the drug agents up to the administering of deadly force. The appropriate level of force is determined by the actions of the suspects, however, in raid situations, weapons are always drawn and verbal commands are constantly being given. The following are the different levels of the escalation of force scale:

- **Mere presence.** The appearance of the drug agents at the scene of a raid may be sufficient to convince the suspect to comply. A team of agents acting in a cohesive manner with the appropriate equipment and show of weapons can be intimidating.
- **Verbal commands.** These verbal commands, when coupled with the presence of the drug agents, are sufficient to handle most situations. However agents should not be lulled into complacency since the situation can change dramatically within a very short period of time. Commands given to the suspect in a firm and clear no-nonsense manner reinforce in the suspect's mind that the agents have a purpose

they intend to carry out. If possible, only one agent should be giving commands to the suspect to avoid confusing him. This minimizes the possibility of the suspect being told by the agents to not move and put his hands up at the same time. The agent giving the commands should be designated ahead of time.

- **Personal weapons.** If an unarmed suspect refuses to comply with verbal commands, agents will have to resort to physically restraining the suspect in order to place him into custody. The use of personal weapons may be impractical due to confined space or other circumstances. Personal weapons use at this level includes expandable batons and night sticks. The use of personal weapons and physically restraining the suspect are both considered to be at the same level of the escalation of force scale.
- **Pepper spray or other subduing devices.** Pepper and chemical sprays are considered one step up the level in subduing a suspect. Only trained personnel who know the limitations of such devices should use these items. Care must be made to not contaminate other agents at the scene who can easily be incapacitated if accidentally sprayed. Many situations, such as being in a confined space, may make the use of such devices impractical.
- **Cardiac restraint.** Many law enforcement personnel are trained in the use of the cardiac restraint hold. This, in essence, is when an agent, standing behind the violent suspect, pinches off the two cardiac arteries located on both sides of the neck below the ears, by the agent's forearm and biceps, cutting the flow of blood to the brain and causing lose of consciousness. Agents then have the opportunity to place handcuffs on the suspect while he is unconscious. The uneducated observer may call this a *choke hold*, but it clearly is not. This level of force is highly effective with physically violent suspects and if applied properly, will minimize injury to the agent as well as the suspect. Agents are advised not to attempt such a maneuver if they have never been formally trained in its use. For those agents or officers not trained in the use of the cardiac restraint hold, they may be forced to revert to the highest level of the scale, deadly force.
- **Deadly force.** Most police and all federal agencies have deadly force policies. Some are very detailed and specific, others are purposely vague and general. Essentially, deadly force should only be used to protect the life of the agent or someone else's life. If the situation the agent encounters does not fall into that category, he or she must maintain a level below deadly force. In any event, agents must be able to clearly articulate why deadly force was used. The agent's physical

strength, or lack there of, may be a factor in the decision making process why deadly force was used on an unarmed suspect. The totality of the circumstances will dictate when an agent should use deadly force. Drug agents should be thoroughly familiar with their own department's policy on deadly force.

British SAS Six-Man Snake Method

In the early 1990s the DEA adopted a modified British Special Air Services (SAS) method of high-risk entry that was thought to be both simple yet effective. The DEA has attempted to train every agent and task force officer within the organization to be familiar with this method, reasoning that agents on temporary assignment to a different office could, therefore, easily assimilate into a raid team because everyone has had the same training. There may be better ways of conducting high-risk entries, however it was impractical to turn all special agents into SWAT members (Figure 11.1).

The SAS snake method consists of six agents, each with a specific role. When they are about to enter a residence, they are lined up together facing in one direction. Number one calls for number six to break from the line and using a battering ram or similar tool, forcing open the door. Number six then drops the ram and falls in as the last man in line as the others pass him going inside. The number one agent dictates the direction of the snake as number two keys off of number one. Number three, the team leader, covers number two. Number four covers the team leader while number five covers number four.

Figure 11.1 U.S. Customs agents arrest suspects in their vehicle. (Courtesy of Immigration and Customs Enforcement.)

As suspects are found in the residence, number six handcuffs them and places them in a central location, usually the living room of the house or apartment. The team goes into every room of the house until the team is certain that all occupants have been found. Number six is designated to watch them as the search is conducted, if a uniformed police officer is not available.

Summary

Drug agents must be prepared to conduct high-risk entries of dwellings and buildings in order to make arrests and execute search warrants. These *raids* consist of a combination of speed, surprise, and violence of action in which there are no acceptable loses.

Agents must plan before attacking a building, and do reconnaissance in order to have some idea what to expect so they can be prepared for the worse. Planning includes photographing the location, conducting surveillance, thoroughly debriefing any informants involved, and attempting to obtain the floor plan of the residence.

A briefing before the raid is conducted to ensure each team member has his or her equipment, that local police authorities have been notified of the pending event, and that the agents have adequate communication equipment. Successful raids come from team members being familiar with tactics, being physically fit, having the appropriate equipment, and having the mental conditioning and firepower to carry out the objective. Team members must be alert to their surroundings and know how to use the appropriate level of force if resistance is encountered.

The DEA uses a modified six-man snake technique to clear buildings of suspects and render the area safe, however many techniques are used throughout the United States. Whatever method is used, drug agents should be familiar with that method and practice the maneuvers with other drug agents in order to form a cohesive, effective team.

Section II

Complex Drug Investigations

12 Drug Conspiracy Investigations

Drug traffickers increase their likelihood of success when they organize. A person acting alone is more likely to change his mind about committing a crime than someone who is involved with others in a criminal conspiracy. Because of their far-reaching effects, conspiracy laws have been the most potent and effective tool in dismantling entire criminal drug organizations.

Arresting a simple street level drug dealer does nothing to stop the criminal drug organization and its top management from continuing its criminal enterprise. A concerted effort must be made by law enforcement agencies at all levels to also arrest and convict the suppliers of controlled substances, the people who launder their money, and those who facilitate their criminal activity, no matter where they are. The most effective way of doing this is by enforcing age-old conspiracy laws against every member of a drug trafficking organization. It is a tool in the drug enforcement agent's bag that enables him or her to reach out and strike a devastating blow to these criminals. These laws are the most important legal weapon in global drug enforcement to bring the heads of these criminal organizations to justice.

The concept of conspiracy originated in England circa 1305, and later evolved into criminal statutes from common law around the seventeenth century. The U.S. Controlled Substance Act codified drug conspiracy laws in 1973.

As a result of the United Nations 1988 Geneva Convention against illicit trafficking in narcotic drugs and psychotropic substances, many nations have adopted drug conspiracy and money laundering statutes. They have also agreed to cooperate in *controlled deliveries*, which is a recognized investigative technique used to determine who is receiving drugs smuggled from one country to another (see Chapter 16).

Traditionally, police departments have arrested drug offenders for street level distribution. This often entails cultivating an informant to introduce an undercover officer to a drug dealer who poses as a drug consumer. The officer may make several confidence buys to build credibility with the seller, and then orders a larger amount of drugs, hoping to seize as much contraband as possible. Often this method proves successful; sometimes it does not.

Conspiracy cases on the other hand have the potential of expanding existing drug investigations to their maximum extent, and are "user-friendly" to law enforcement and prosecutors alike. Examples of this will follow later in this chapter.

One reason why U.S. conspiracy laws are so effective is that many foreign heads of criminal drug organizations have been brought to the United States for prosecution of these laws, even though they have never stepped foot in the country. This is because these federal drug laws are *extra-territorial*, which means that they apply to anyone, anywhere, even outside the boundaries of the United States. Once indicted, located, and arrested, they can be tried in the United States. Without conspiracy laws, drug lords in foreign nations would be able to operate their business within the United States with impunity.

Conventional drug cases require an inordinate amount of time, personnel, and above all, money when attempting to secure a conviction for simple distribution. Many of these cases go far beyond what is necessary to convict these suspects for the often-overlooked crime of conspiracy.

Supervisors and managers concerned with budget restraints should realize that drug conspiracies constitute a separate and distinct offense and do not depend on whether the subjects accomplished the conspiracy's objective: selling drugs. Undercover police officers do not have to spend large amounts of money to buy drugs during conspiracy cases. Accordingly, drug investigations that concentrate on the simple elements of proof for conspiracy can achieve many of the same results as more elaborate investigations, but with much less cost.

Conspiracy investigations are not intended to take the place of aggressive, long-term, multi-jurisdictional cases that have the promise of large drug and money seizures. However, they often achieve the same results as more traditional drug cases. Using conspiracy laws to identify people, drugs, and assets can be accomplished using fewer departmental resources. In short, conspiracy cases provide an innovative way to extend existing budgets while possibly eliminating an entire drug organization.

Definition of Conspiracy

U.S. District Court Judge John Martin of the southern district of New York used the following as a portion of his unpublished jury instructions in conspiracy cases:

> Simply defined, a conspiracy is an unlawful agreement by two or more persons to violate the law. Whether or not the persons accomplished what they conspired to do is immaterial to the question of guilt or innocence in regard to a conspiracy. The success or lack of success of the conspiracy doesn't matter, for a conspiracy is a crime entirely separate and distinct from the substantive crime that may be the goal of the conspiracy. A conspiracy has sometimes been called a partnership in crime in which each partner becomes the agent of every other partner. However, to establish the existence of a conspiracy, the prosecution is not required to show that two or more persons sat around a table and entered into a formal agreement, orally or in writing, stating that they have formed a conspiracy to violate the law, setting forth the details of the means by which it was to be carried out or the part to be played by each conspirator. Indeed, it would be extraordinary if there were such a formal document or specific agreement. Thus, it is sufficient if two or more persons, in any manner, through any contrivance, either implied or tacitly, came to a common understanding to violate the law. Express language or specific words are not required to indicate assent or attachment to a conspiracy.

In investigating conspiracies, agents need to focus on the *agreement* that was made between the parties. They merely have to prove that an agreement was made between two or more persons to violate drug laws. Conspirators are not accessories to the crime; they are equal partners under the law. Agents should know that an individual street-level dealer who sells drugs to individual customers cannot be charged with conspiracy because they are not parties to the same agreement.*

Punishment for Conspiracy

The laws of the United States and many individual states provide that if a defendant is convicted of a conspiracy to commit any offense involving a controlled substance, the punishment is the same as if the object of the conspiracy had been completed.[2] In other words, the punishment is identical to the crime the conspirators sought to commit. Conspiracy is not a lesser-included offense of the object of the conspiracy; it is a separate crime within itself. If the conspiracy ended before the goal of the conspiracy could be accomplished, this fact alone does not absolve the conspirators of their crime,

* The Wharton Rule may preclude a conspiracy charge when there is only one buyer and one seller agreeing to violate he law. See *Iannelli v. United States,* 420 U.S. 770 (1975).

namely conspiracy, since it is a separate and distinct offense in addition to any substantive crimes they may have committed.

Elements of Proof

Most statutes in the United States require that *two or more people* must have made an *agreement* to commit a criminal act, and that *overt acts* were committed in furtherance of the conspiracy. Through experience and training, drug agents know that it is practically impossible to commit a drug crime without the help of others. Most drugs of abuse in the United States originate from outside its borders, and it takes many people to plant, cultivate, harvest, process, package, transport, smuggle, store, protect, and sell the drugs. With the possible exception of a domestic marijuana grow that only involves a cultivator who sells his wares, there *has* to be a conspiracy. The drug agent's job is to identify those persons who participated in the crime.

Plurality Requirement

It is important for drug agents to understand that in order to prove a conspiracy, the prosecution must show that two or more people reached an agreement to commit a crime. What is equally important to know is that agents and informants are not part of that equation.

During an undercover operation, it is common for an undercover agent to meet with a drug trafficker from an introduction by an informant. By example, during an initial meeting between an undercover agent and a drug trafficker, discussions take place about the sale of heroin to the undercover agent. The trafficker departs the location to obtain it. He returns shortly afterwards with the heroin, and sells it to the undercover agent, and the trafficker is arrested. In this example, even though three people discussed committing a crime, two of the three are *agents of the government*. The trafficker cannot be charged with the crime of conspiracy since the agent cannot prove the existence of other members of a conspiracy, despite knowing from his training and experience that others must be involved.

Agents must be able to show that at least two suspects are involved in the drug crime in order to arrest the suspect for conspiracy. Agents do not have to fully identify the other member of the conspiracy; they simply have to prove he exists.

In a U.S. Supreme Court case, the court ruled that a defendant's mere admission to engaging in the drug trade with others is sufficient to sustain a conviction for conspiracy,[3] even if the co-conspirator was never identified or indicted.[4] In the example, in order to prove the existence of a conspiracy, the undercover agent could have merely asked if the trafficker had consulted with his source of supply about the quality or availability of the heroin he or she was about to purchase. If the trafficker remarks that he knew the heroin was available since he had called his source earlier that day, then that admission in itself would be sufficient to prove the existence of a conspiracy.

Conspirators do not have to know each other. There is no requirement that the prosecutor prove that each conspirator knows all the other members of the same conspiracy. Further, conspirators do not have to know what the role of each conspirator is, nor does the prosecutor have to show what their role was. All conspirators are agents for each other, and each is responsible for the actions of each other (see "Pinkerton Theory of Vicarious Liability" below).

The Agreement

The prosecutor must prove that an agreement was made to consummate the conspiracy. The crime of conspiracy is separate and apart from any other crimes committed during the life of the conspiracy. The crime the conspirators agreed to commit does not have to be accomplished by them in order to be charged with conspiracy. The sincerity of the agreement is accomplished through uncovering overt acts.

Overt Acts

Even though it may not be required by some statutes, prosecutors will not charge traffickers with conspiracy unless agents can prove the conspirators committed *overt acts* in furtherance of the conspiracy. An overt act is anything done to carry out the object of the conspiracy. Overt acts need not be criminal in nature. Purchasing a truck to transport drugs from one state to another is an over act made in furtherance of the conspiracy.

All participants need not know the overt acts committed by members of the conspiracy. When prosecutors prepare indictments to present to the grand jury, they will list major overt acts uncovered during the investigation to support the prosecution theory that these particular defendants were engaged in a conspiracy.

Pinkerton Theory of Vicarious Liability

Conspirators can be charged with substantive offenses committed by co-conspirators throughout the life of the conspiracy provided: (1) they were in the conspiracy at the time the offense was committed; (2) the offense was committed in furtherance of the conspiracy; and (3) the offense was a foreseeable consequence of the conspiracy.[5]

As an example, defendants A and B solicit C and D to transport drugs from California to Chicago by truck. A and B intend to fly to Chicago to receive the drugs upon the arrival of C and D. Unknown to A or B, instead of using the money A and B gave them to purchase a truck to be used in transporting the drugs, C and D steal an 18-wheel tractor-trailer rig they told A and B they had purchased with their money for the trip. C and D are caught during a traffic stop in Texas in the stolen truck with the drugs. They cooperate in a controlled delivery of the drugs to A and B, and they are taken into custody. All are charged with conspiracy to possess drugs with the intent to sell them. Because of the Pinkerton theory of vicarious liability, all of them can also be charged with the theft of the truck. A and B claim they had no knowledge that the truck was stolen, but readily admit they furnished C and D with the money to purchase a truck. This fact makes no difference and is no defense. A and B can still be indicted along with C and D for the theft of the truck in addition to the drug charge.

Each member of the conspiracy acts as an agent for other members and is liable for crimes committed in furtherance of the original conspiracy. Whether other members of the conspiracy knew the crimes were going to be committed or even if they discouraged other members from committing these crimes is irrelevant.

Members of the conspiracy can only be charged with future crimes committed by other members *after* they enter the conspiracy. They cannot be held responsible for crimes committed by other members before they joined the drug conspiracy.

The prosecution must only show that these crimes were committed to further the goal of the conspiracy. The prosecutor does not have to prove that as a member of the conspiracy, the defendant either participated in, or even knew of the existence of these crimes, only that he was a member of the conspiracy at the time they were committed.

However, mere association or knowledge of the existence of the conspiracy does not constitute joining the conspiracy. Those held liable for the actions of the other conspirators are those who made a specific or implied agreement to carry out the scheme.

Withdrawal from the Conspiracy

The most common legal defense in a conspiracy case is that the defendant withdrew from the conspiracy before any substantive crimes occurred. In other words, he may be guilty of the crime of conspiracy, but is not guilty of the substantive crimes other members of the conspiracy may have committed.

In order to withdraw, a conspirator must either: (1) inform the police about the conspiracy or (2) inform the other known co-conspirators of his intention to withdraw. The conspirator who wishes to withdraw from a conspiracy must do something affirmative to show his intent to withdraw. Merely staying away from or avoiding the other conspirators does not constitute withdrawal.

There is little chance that a member of a conspiracy will voluntarily inform the police about his involvement in a drug conspiracy. These admissions generally come after the person is caught up in a legal problem prompting him to cooperate with the authorities. However, if during the course of a conspiracy investigation agents learn through undercover meetings, wiretaps, or formal interviews that someone did tell other members he no longer wanted a part of the scheme, this information can be used in his defense.

The burden of proof that the defendant withdrew from the conspiracy ultimately lies with the defendant. This means other members of the conspiracy must be willing to testify that the defendant informed them he no longer wished to be a member of the conspiracy. The likelihood of this is extremely remote; therefore, the only practical way to withdraw from a conspiracy is to reveal it to the police.

Termination of the Conspiracy

Conspiracies are terminated in two ways, either by the object of the conspiracy being completed, or the object of the conspiracy having failed. Knowing when a conspiracy ended is important because, as just mentioned, substantive crimes that are discovered can be charged against members of the conspiracy during the life of that conspiracy, provided they were members of the conspiracy at the time the crimes were committed. Some drug trafficking organizations have been involved in the same conspiracy for decades; others engage in new conspiracies one after another.

When the head of the drug trafficking organization or others are arrested, this does not mean the termination of the conspiracy. The head of the organization may continue to direct the activities of the group from within prison, or another trusted member might take over the vacated leadership role. Either way, unless a member of the conspiracy either formally withdraws or the object of the conspiracy ends in failure, he is liable for all substantive crimes committed to further the object of the conspiracy, even when he is in prison. An example of a conspiracy ending in failure is when a vessel used by a marijuana smuggling organization accidentally sinks before reaching the United States, and its cargo cannot be recovered.

Venue

Venue is where court jurisdiction lies. Under federal law, venue lies in any jurisdiction in which an overt act occurs, or where the agreement was made, or in Washington, D.C. if the agreement or overt acts took place outside the territorial boundaries of the United States. Venue is an important consideration for drug agents since venue is established anywhere an overt act is committed.

Agents may find that members of complex drug conspiracies, who operate throughout a state or region of the country, will commit many overt acts in different counties, states, and court districts. Every time an overt act is identified in another venue, the prosecuting authority has the ability, but not the obligation, to adopt the entire case and can prosecute each member of the conspiracy within its own particular venue.

The advantage to this for drug agents is that one prosecutor may determine that his office does not have the time, enthusiasm, or resources necessary to prosecute a complex conspiracy investigation, while another prosecutor, in another venue where venue exists, may view the same conspiracy as a routine matter.

Drug agents who seek prosecution in a specific venue may legally arrange for an overt act to occur in that venue during an ongoing conspiracy investigation. For example, undercover agents may arrange to take delivery of drugs from a member of the conspiracy in a particular locality for the sole reason of establishing venue. Even if agents orchestrated the event, venue applies. The logistics involved in prosecuting a matter in more than one venue can create challenges that have to be closely coordinated with prosecutors to eliminate duplication and double jeopardy issues.

Duration of the Conspiracy

Conspiracies run from the time of the agreement until it ends in either success or failure.

Statute of Limitations

Under federal law, and in most states, the statute of limitations runs 5 years from the last overt act or when the conspiracy ends, whichever is later.

Types of Conspiracies

There are four basic types of conspiracies modern drug agents will most frequently encounter: ongoing, historical, chain, and wheel.

Ongoing Conspiracies

Ongoing conspiracies are those currently underway and where the object of the conspiracy may not have yet been achieved. These conspiracies most often include an undercover agent or informant who is gathering physical evidence and attempting to identify all members of the criminal organization.

Drug evidence is not necessary in prosecuting an ongoing conspiracy, but every effort should be made to obtain it. These cases are sometimes called *dry,* or *no-dope conspiracies.* A prosecutor's enthusiasm to prosecute such a case seems to increase with the amount of drugs and money seized by agents during the course of the conspiracy investigation.

Historical Conspiracies

Historical conspiracies are those where the object of the conspiracy has already been met. Investigating these conspiracies is done in the same manner as any reported crime, e.g., locating and interviewing witnesses, gathering physical evidence including documents, etc., and interrogating suspects. The main difference is that drug agents are attempting to prove that members of the conspiracy made an unlawful agreement to violate drug laws.

Historical drug conspiracy cases are classic no-dope conspiracies that are initiated when an informant, whether motivated by revenge, greed, fear of prosecution, or some other reason, admits to participating in a past drug transaction.

As a result, these cases do not require, and seldom provide, the opportunity to seize drug evidence or to use undercover agents. They may, however, result in the arrest of a notorious drug trafficker.

Historical drug conspiracy cases require the same techniques used to investigate any other crime. However, the investigation must prove only that an agreement to violate drug laws was reached between two or more persons.[1]

Although the probable cause required to obtain search warrants to seize drug evidence probably will not exist in historical drug conspiracy cases, warrants for documents can be readily justified. Drug traffickers maintain *pay and owe sheets* or meticulous records, which chronicle the details of past drug transactions and can identify other members of the conspiracy. Drugs found during the execution of a document search warrant are admissible as evidence. In fact, historical drug conspiracy cases frequently locate proceeds of drug transactions that are subject to seizure.

Historical conspiracy investigations are usually initiated when a former member of the conspiracy is arrested on unrelated charges and reveals to the police his involvement in the crime. He will attempt to lead drug agents to co-conspirators and may be directed by the drug agents to solicit recorded conversations where they acknowledge their involvement in the crime. The informant may help drug agents obtain documents and other evidence that will corroborate his statements. This corroboration is required since the presumption is that informants, especially those who have never been used as informants in the past, are inherently unreliable and untrustworthy. It is the agent's job to corroborate all aspects of the informant's information in order to boost his credibility and competency.

For example, a recently arrested informant claims that several months ago he met with others in a hotel room to discuss the smuggling of cocaine into the United States. Drug agents need to have the informant identify when and where the meeting took place. Drug agents should check hotel registration records for that date to ascertain the name of the person who rented the room. The telephone records of all calls dialed from the room need to be checked, and the subscribers of those telephone numbers need to be identified.

Once identified, the names of the persons called need to be checked for past criminal history and intelligence regarding their involvement in the drug trade. Each person needs checking for a driver's license, and photographs of these persons through DMV records must be obtained.

The name of the person who signed the hotel registration form also needs to be checked with the state DMV records where his mailing address and photograph can be obtained. The address given on the registration should be checked against DMV records. The photograph of the person who rented the room should be shown to the informant in a six-photograph line up, sometimes called a *six-pack*, to determine if he can be picked out.

The method of payment used to rent the room will further help corroborate the informant's story. If a credit card was used for payment of the room, and the account holder's name is the same as the person who registered the room, this further corroborates the informant's information. Paying cash for the hotel room may raise suspicion with the hotel clerk. The clerk may be able to identify the person in a photographic line up using the card holder's driver's license photo. A hotel employee who has no special interest in the case is an excellent way to corroborate the informant's information.

Seizing the registration card for fingerprints and future handwriting comparison will complete the task of corroborating as much information about the suspect as possible. Agents must anticipate that the suspect will deny being at the hotel, renting the room, signing any registration card, attending any meeting, making any phone calls, knowing the informant, or anyone that was telephoned from the room.

Thoroughness is key to convincing the prosecutor and jury that an agreement to violate drug laws must have taken place since the informant information about the meeting was corroborated. The investigation may further show that people who were called from the room have a history of drug crimes.

If the suspect denies renting the room despite his fingerprints being found to be on the card, a handwriting expert may be able to testify that his handwriting matches that found on the card, further corroborating the informant's information.

The jury will decide for themselves why the suspect rented the room in the first place, and later lied to drug agents. Also why telephone calls were

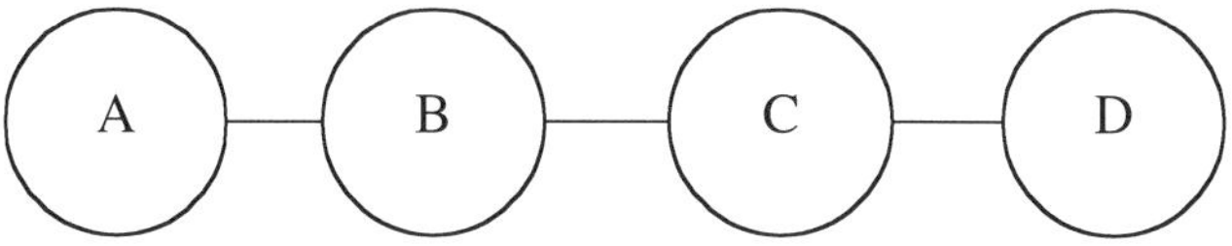

Figure 12.1 Chain conspiracy.

made to known drug traffickers, and why he may have used a fictitious name or paid cash to conceal his identity. Any suspect statements that can be refuted will enhance the credibility of the informant and the prosecutor's theory that he is lying to conceal his involvement in a drug conspiracy.

To further bolster the case, prosecutors can grant selected members of the conspiracy immunity to provide eyewitness testimony about the overt acts, both criminal and noncriminal, that occurred during the life of the conspiracy. Drug agents are cautioned that before initiating any historical conspiracy investigation they should coordinate with their supervisor and local prosecutor to get their opinion and guidance.

Chain Conspiracies

Like the name implies, members of *chain conspiracies* are all connected despite only some of the links interacting with the others. Each link of the chain represents a member of the conspiracy. Link A only knows about the existence of link B, however B knows about A and C. Link C knows about the existence of B and D, but neither of them know anything about A. Not all members know each other, and no single person knows everyone in the conspiracy (see Figure 12.1). Despite this, each can be charged with the criminal acts committed by other members in furtherance of the conspiracy.

Wheel Conspiracies

Wheel conspiracies resemble a wagon wheel in that each spoke represents a member of the conspiracy, with the hub being the leader. The hub knows the identities of each member of the conspiracy; however, the individual members only know of the existence of two other members in addition to the leader. Despite these members knowing only two other members of the conspiracy, they are criminally liable for the actions of other unknown members of the conspiracy.

These types of conspiracies are effective in concealing the identities of other members of the conspiracy by means of compartmentalization. If one or two members of the conspiracy are arrested, they cannot reveal the identities of all the members of the conspiracy because they have purposely been denied that knowledge (see Figure 12.2).

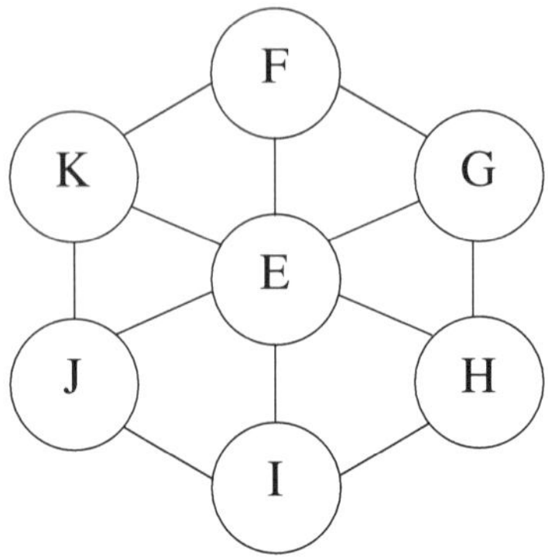

Figure 12.2 Wheel conspiracy.

Combination Wheel and Chain Conspiracies

A *combination wheel and chain* conspiracy is one in which members of a wheel conspiracy and a chain conspiracy frequently interact and eventually become a part of the same conspiracy (see Figure 12.3).

Advantages of Conspiracy Investigations

The biggest advantage to conducting a conspiracy investigation is that it can result in the entire elimination of the criminal organization. Picking-off one or two members of the organization will do nothing to stop it from functioning.

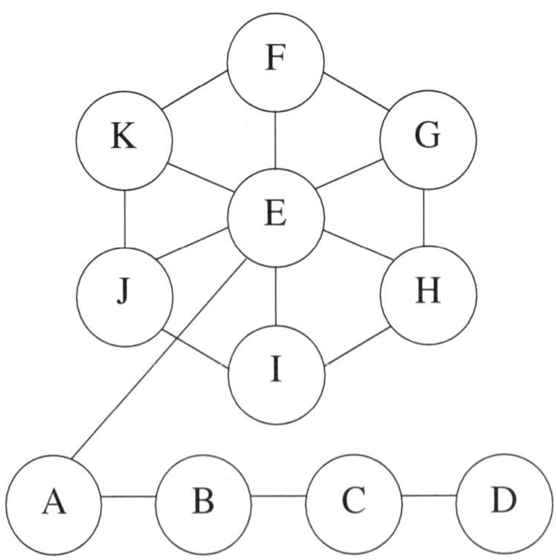

Figure 12.3 Combination wheel and chain conspiracy.

Conducting traditional drug investigations by making controlled purchases from the same defendant eventually can reach the point of diminishing returns. Drug enforcement budgets deplete rapidly when prosecutors, seeking to establish the most compelling case possible to secure a conviction, demand that several buys be made in order to thwart possible entrapment claims by the defendant. Thus, a department's entire "buy money" budget could be exhausted on just one investigation. Further, the jury may interpret additional buys as the agency's attempt to punish the defendant with more prison time. In contrast, drug agents can satisfy the elements of proof for drug conspiracy early on in their investigations, and reap the benefits normally not associated with more traditional investigations.

Simplicity

Prosecutors risk losing cases that are too complicated for the jury to understand. Charging defendants with crimes such as continuing criminal enterprise, and racketeering influence corrupt organization (RICO) statutes may be professionally appealing, but the elements of proof in order to secure a conviction can be overwhelming to a jury. The sheer magnitude of a multi-defendant trial can cause a jury to lose sight of even the simple elements of the crime. During the course of a long and complicated drug trial, the defense has ample opportunity to portray the defendant as the victim of an intrusive, overzealous prosecutor. Conspiracy cases avoid these problems because the jury needs only to recognize that the defendants entered an agreement to commit a crime.

Crime Prevention

Drug conspiracy cases, especially no-dope conspiracies, are a form of crime prevention. To identify and arrest defendants who agreed to sell drugs in the community before they had a chance to do so is a noble goal, one that appeals to any jury.

In addition, in many jurisdictions, the penalty for conspiracy is the same as the penalty for the substantive crime the defendants conspired to commit. Federal law mandates the same punishment in federal cases.[2] Drug conspiracy laws, coupled with mandatory minimum sentences, are powerful crime prevention tools for drug enforcement.

Leverage

Conspiracy cases also give prosecutors added leverage during plea-bargaining, because all members of a conspiracy can be charged with crimes committed by any one member. However, the crime must have been a foreseeable consequence, and in furtherance, of the conspiracy.[5,6]

For example, if one subject steals a boat to transport a drug shipment into the country, everyone in the group can be charged with that crime, if they were members of the conspiracy at the time of the theft. However, if the subject stops at a liquor store and steals a six-pack of beer on the way home from stealing the boat, the others cannot be charged with that theft since it was clearly not committed in furtherance of the conspiracy. In addition, murders often occur in the course of drug transactions. Therefore, the courts consider them foreseeable consequences of conspiracies, and prosecutors can charge each member of the group with murder.

Exception to the Hearsay Rule of Evidence

An added benefit to conspiracy prosecutions is the exception to the hearsay rule of evidence. Because conspiracies are secretive by nature, the rules of evidence allow a cooperating defendant, drug agent, or an informant to testify about the words, deeds, and actions of others, even if they did not actually witness them. In other words, an informant could testify about overhearing the defendants talking about selling drugs.

In contrast, if defendants are charged with aiding or abetting, the hearsay rule attaches, and such evidence would not be admissible. Therefore, prosecutors can help their cases by indicting defendants for conspiracy.

Asset Forfeiture

Asset forfeiture laws apply to drug conspiracy cases just as they do for any other drug law violation. Many civil seizure laws do not require that defendants be convicted of a substantive drug crime in order to make their property subject to seizure.

Although asset forfeiture funds can supplement lean budgets, supervisors in law enforcement agencies must resist the temptation to target drug traffickers based solely upon their assets. The suspect who poses the biggest threat to the community may own little property. The focus of any drug investigation should be people, drugs, and assets, in that order. With people as the primary focus of the investigation, drugs and assets invariably will follow.

Evidence against one defendant is evidence against all. Since each defendant is liable for the actions of each other, the evidence gathered to prove the conspiracy can be used against all the defendants. Conspiracy cases that net a large number of defendants are often handled for prosecution in increments of five or less. Prosecutors will indict a handful of defendants at a time in order to streamline the process. For example, in a 20-defendant conspiracy, four trials of five defendants each may be in order. The evidence used in the first trial can be used in all subsequent trials.

The punishment for conspiracy may be the same as the crime they conspired to commit. Under federal mandatory minimum sentencing guidelines, the punishment for drug conspiracy is the same as if the object of the conspiracy was carried out. Many states have comparable laws, putting teeth into the statute.

Disadvantages of Conspiracy Investigations

Despite the many advantages to conspiracy cases, certain disadvantages have to be considered before undertaking a large-scale, complex investigation.

Conspiracy Investigations Can Be Protracted

Many months can be spent gathering evidence against what could turn out to be numerous members of the conspiracy. As mentioned, multiple venues often pose logistical and sometimes political problems for the agents and prosecutors alike. Prosecutors may not view drug prosecutions as a priority for their office, or they are not willing to devote the time necessary for the case. Or, prosecutors in every area where venue has been established may all want to take the lead on a particular high profile, significant prosecution. Conflicts over venue must be resolved early on in any large-scale conspiracy investigation. In any event, every effort should be made to get a firm commitment from the prosecutor's office to devote the necessary amount of manpower before any long-term conspiracy investigation gets underway.

Some large scale, multi-jurisdiction conspiracy investigations will require extensive manpower expenditures. Supervisors may balk at committing the manpower the case agent requests. The need for vast amounts of manpower will often dampen the enthusiasm of supervisors who may have other priorities.

Verification and Corroboration

Witnesses have to be found, and documentary evidence has to be located, seized, and analyzed. The most damning evidence will come from testimony from co-conspirators; however, the prosecutor, jury, and judge will always view these witnesses as inherently unreliable.

Drug agents will spend a significant amount of time locating evidence that will corroborate the testimony of the informants and co-conspirators. This evidence can range from car rental applications, vehicle registration documents, bank loans, or business licenses. It all must be identified, located, and seized, often in different parts of the country or world, adding to the already mentioned manpower expenditures.

No-Dope Conspiracies

The prosecutor's enthusiasm for filing charges against drug conspirators will be diminished if drugs are not seized during the course of the investigation. Prosecutors need evidence for jury appeal during trials. Lacking drugs, guns, or money sometimes plays into the hands of defense attorneys who ask where the drugs are if this organization is as prolific as the prosecutor contends.

Drug agents must strive to recover drugs during any investigation they conduct, and need to ensure their supervisors and prosecutors that this is one of the objectives of the investigation. Some cases that started off with the promise of huge drug seizures end up with none only because of the incompetence or misfortunes of the conspirators. The drug business is like any other business; sometimes sources of supply cannot deliver as they promised. When that happens, these cases need to be pursued as *dry* or *no-dope* conspiracies since these drug traffickers sincerely intended to sell drugs, and they will not otherwise be deterred from continuing in their illegal conduct.

Conspiracy Case Development

Every investigative technique used in modern criminal investigation is used in conspiracy case development. Often, more and varied investigative techniques are used in drug investigations than in traditional after-the-fact cases.

Confidential Informants

Most drug cases begin with an informant. Nearly every drug case conducted by law enforcement stems from information supplied by either an informant or a co-conspirator already in jail who wants to seek revenge on his fellow conspirators. The other cases are usually historical conspiracies where drugs are found abandoned on a commercial airliner or on a secluded beach, or the suspects are caught in the act of smuggling contraband without benefit of an informant's information.

The drug agent's job is to produce witnesses and evidence to support the prosecution theory that a conspiracy existed. Evidence may consist simply of documents such as car rental agreements, hotel receipts, and phone bills. These seemingly innocent transactions take on a different appearance when witnesses testify the defendant used the hotel room to privately discuss the details of an upcoming drug deal; that phone records revealed the defendant called known drug dealers from the room; that the defendant, using a fictitious name, paid for the room with cash to avoid creating a credit card receipt; and that scientific evidence positively identified the handwriting and fingerprints on the registration card as those belonging to the defendant.

Because conspiracy cases allow for the exception to the hearsay rule of evidence, informants can testify about the words, deeds, and actions of the defendants. However, because the courts and the public view informants as inherently unreliable, their information must be corroborated whenever possible. For example, if an informant claims to have attended a meeting at a hotel on a certain date, drug agents can verify this information through hotel registration records. Hotel employees may further corroborate the informant's testimony and may be able to identify the defendants by viewing a *photo line-up*.

All of these factors tend to corroborate the informant's testimony. The jury can then decide for themselves why an "innocent" person would pay cash to rent a hotel room using a fictitious name and then meet with and telephone drug dealers from that room. Although much of the evidence in itself has no meaning, the totality of the evidence will help in securing the conviction.

Some states require that an overt act take place before the crime of conspiracy is consummated. An overt act is anything that furthers the goal of the conspiracy, such as conducting a meeting or renting a car. The acts need not be criminal in nature or even known by all the participants. Simply stated, overt acts show sincerity and intent by the members of the conspiracy to reach their criminal goal. The greater the number of overt acts uncovered, the easier it is for the jury to conclude that the defendants actually intended to commit the crime. Informants are in a position to help identify many of the overt acts the conspirators committed during the lifetime of the conspiracy.

Undercover Agents

Buy and bust operations employ undercover agents or informants to infiltrate criminal organizations. The same technique applies to drug conspiracy investigations. Undercover officers are expert witnesses who can testify about the events they see or hear. A highly effective way of gathering first hand information about the conspirators, and to move the progress of the case forward rapidly, is through the use of undercover agents.

Informants are often used to introduce undercover agents to significant suspects within the conspiracy. These agents purchase drugs or provide needed services to facilitate the drug conspiracy. Drug agents can legally smooth the path of the criminals for the purpose of arresting them later.

Thorough debriefings of informants are important in analyzing where the criminal organization is most vulnerable. A drug trafficking organization in need of a truck driver to transport drugs from one location to another is an example of an opportunity to interject an undercover agent. Drug organizations work the same way as many legitimate outfits, and they always have the need for dependable, trustworthy employees.

Asset Seizure Inquiries

Members of large-scale drug trafficking organizations amass large amounts of money and property through their dealings. They have to launder their money to give it the appearance of being derived through legitimate means. This laundering process may take the form of purchasing real estate, businesses and other property. Others simply transport their money to a foreign country in an attempt to keep it out of reach of U.S. law enforcement.

Once members of a drug trafficking organization are identified, they should be routinely checked through indices for any property they may either own or occupy. How they acquired that property may lead to the discovery of other crimes such as bank fraud, mail fraud, or tax evasion.

In 1988, in Santa Cruz County, CA, 9 tons of marijuana and numerous vehicles were left abandoned on a secluded beach. Sheriff's deputies had responded there to investigate a tip from a passerby that a possible off-loading of drugs was taking place. Upon arrival, they estimated as many as 50 people had fled the area, mostly on foot. The Coast Guard later that day captured a fishing vessel in Monterey Bay with an additional 5 tons of marijuana aboard.

Through investigation, agents discovered that the registered owner of one of the abandoned pick up trucks had acquired a California driver license after presenting someone else's birth certificate as proof of identity. Further investigation revealed that the abandoned pick-up truck had been purchased at a local new-car dealership and was financed through a federally insured bank. The bank loan was obtained through submitting an application using the name on the fictitious drivers license, thereby committing bank fraud. Since driver licenses in California can only be obtained through the mail, the suspect was also charged with mail fraud. Because of the Pinkerton rule, all members of the conspiracy at the time of the bank and mail frauds were charged with the offenses. Federal agents seized the vehicle as a proceed of drug trafficking that was also used to facilitate the drug crime. Because of the lien on the vehicle, it was returned to the bank.

In the same case, a conspirator admitted to the agents that the off-loading teams used to remove the marijuana from the boat had met at a co-conspirator's home prior to being taken to the beach. The defendant-informant told agents that while on the property, off-loaders were formed into several teams, and they were issued equipment to quickly remove the marijuana from the boat. The owner of the home received a fee for the use of his secluded property. Agents filed an affidavit in support of seizing the property since it was used to facilitate a drug smuggle, in that it was used to conceal the preparation for the event. Agents and U.S. Marshals seized the property after a federal seizure warrant was issued.

Agents should identify potential real property, vehicles, money, and bank accounts that may be subject to seizure during their criminal investigation.

Seizure warrants can be obtained anytime during the course of the investigation when property subject to seizure is identified.

Fixed and Mobile Surveillance

As in any proactive investigation, physical and electronic surveillance of known suspects will frequently identify other members of the conspiracy. Unlike other criminals, drug traffickers assume they are under constant surveillance. Their paranoia forces them to drive their vehicles in such a manner as to disguise what their ultimate destination is. They will frequently drive down cul-de-sacs to see who follows them, and go around city blocks several times before parking, even though plenty of parking spaces were available. Some traffickers will practice these and other driving techniques even when they are merely going to a grocery store or other business.

Patience will pay off for the drug surveillance agent who can successfully follow the trafficker to his ultimate destination. When a meeting between two conspirators ends and there is an insufficient amount of manpower to follow both suspects, then the case agent has to decide which of the two is more important to follow. Suspects have led agents to *stash houses* where drugs and money are stored, homes of other conspirators, travel agencies used by them, and other businesses that provide services to the organization. When given the opportunity, *follow* the money.

Drug agents use fixed surveillance equipment that can be mounted on telephone and power poles disguised as transformers or other apparatus. The development of these devices is only limited by the imagination of the person designing them for use by drug law enforcement (see Chapter 6 for details).

Pen Registers

Also known as dial digit recorders, *pen registers* can be installed to telephone lines servicing a particular telephone number. The device is activated whenever the telephone instrument's receiver is picked up or the telephone is turned on, and it records the time this occurred. The device then records the outgoing telephone numbers dialed by the suspect from that particular phone number, and records the time the hand receiver was returned to the cradle of the phone, or the telephone is turned off. It does not record incoming telephone numbers or voices, only outgoing telephone numbers.

Most of this same information can be captured in telephone company long distance toll information; however, pen registers record all telephone numbers that are dialed, including local calls. The machine also records any numbers dialed while the telephone line is in use. The device frequently captures credit card numbers, prepaid telephone cards, or personal identification numbers. The installation of these devices requires a court order.

Telephone Wiretaps and Technical Listening Devices

Telephone wiretaps and technical listening devices offer a proven way for agents to learn the identities of co-conspirators, how they operate, and who they sell their drugs to. Both federal and state judges have the power to order wiretaps after drug agents establish there is probable cause to believe that not only is the suspect selling drugs, but also is using the telephone to facilitate the crime.

Many drug traffickers, because of their paranoia of being arrested, assume their telephones and other communication devices are constantly monitored by the police. They spend large amounts of money on devices that supposedly will detect the presence of listening devices in their homes and on telephone lines. Many of these devices, thankfully, do not work.

When on the telephone they sometimes speak in code, believing they are clever enough to fool an agent that may be listening. They often substitute the name of a drug with some harmless commodity, like white shirts, green shirts, tires, or something similar. They sometimes get caught up in the code and discuss selling one-half shirt, or one-half tire, as if such a sale is possible. When presented to a jury, this type of recorded evidence solidifies in their minds, in most cases, that the suspects are obviously talking about something illegal.

Conducting a conspiracy investigation involving wiretaps is a long and arduous process that requires many man-hours. There is constant court-mandated reporting, expensive equipment to purchase and maintain, and other requirements that do not always lead to large drug or money seizures.

Despite having a court order, not all phone conversations can be monitored. If the agent determines that the conversation probably does not involve drugs, he or she is obligated to perform *minimization*, and turn off the recording equipment. An example of this may be a conversation between a suspect's wife and her dentist making an appointment.

Once the investigation is over and the recordings have stopped, copies of the tapes are provided to each defendant. Every person recorded who can be identified must be notified that their conversation was captured during the investigation.

The number of wiretaps conducted by law enforcement rose significantly in the 1990s. Agencies have relied more heavily on them than in the past. Wiretaps, however, are not a substitute for old-fashioned police work.

Technical listening devices may be installed in homes, businesses, automobiles, and other places. Their installation requires a court order The mechanics of installing them can be challenging since they must be placed in areas frequented by the conspirators in the hopes of capturing incriminating conversation. Some agencies have technical agents that are trained to enter a building or vehicle, plant the device, and then leave without a trace of them ever being there.

The Grand Jury

In coordination with the U.S. Attorney's Office or local district attorney, drug agents will routinely testify about the findings of their investigation to a grand jury, and seek the *indictment* of the suspects. An indictment means that a suspect is formally accused of committing a crime. *Accusatory grand juries* indict drug suspects, making them *defendants* in criminal matters. Once someone is indicted, an arrest warrant is immediately issued, and the defendant is subject to arrest. An indictment eliminates the need for a preliminary hearing. After the defendant's arraignment, the next step is to go to trial.

Grand juries hear testimony of drug agents and other witnesses brought to it by the prosecuting attorney. Defense attorneys are not allowed to accompany witnesses or potential defendants into the grand jury room during questioning. The testimony of the witnesses is considered secret and cannot be disclosed outside the grand jury room, even to other agents, unless sanctioned by a supervising judge.

Grand juries have the power of subpoena. They hear requests from drug agents to issue subpoenas for records of individuals and businesses. Under the federal system, a grand jury subpeona is required to obtain financial records from banks and other institutions. Once the records are obtained, the agent must return to the grand jury with his or her findings.

Federal grand juries consist of 24 individuals who reside in the district, and usually serve an 18-month term. Drug agents should communicate early in their investigation and often with a grand jury. In complex criminal investigations, the grand jury needs ample opportunity to understand what the investigation has revealed, and who is involved. By explaining the investigation in increments rather than in one long session, the grand jury members become interested and look forward to periodic updates. When the time comes to seek an indictment, the grand jury usually spends little time in making a decision since it is already thoroughly familiar with the situation. Federal and state grand juries make it possible to subpoena suspects involved in drug conspiracies to appear before it and give testimony.

Unindicted co-conspirators and other *material witnesses* can be compelled to testify before the grand jury, locking in their testimony before the trial begins. It also gives the prosecutor an opportunity to learn how good a witness the person is, e.g., is he believable? Or is he totally without credibility? Grand juries also serve as a means to convince reluctant witnesses that they should cooperate with the prosecutor instead of running the risk of being indicted and going to prison.

Coordination with Other Law Enforcement Agencies

Many conspiracy cases will lead drug agents into multiple jurisdictions and venues. They must include the local enforcement agencies in their investigations in order to glean criminal intelligence, obtain manpower assistance, and foster good working relationships between the agencies.

Since drug conspiracies often involve many persons who live in different areas of the state or country, the cooperation of those agencies must be solicited unless there is a compelling reason not to seek that assistance. The DEA routinely solicits the cooperation of local law enforcement in areas where they may be affected. Combating drugs is a mission bigger than any one agent or agency. It requires the cooperation and coordination of all affected enforcement agencies. Agents who frequently share drug information with other law enforcement agencies usually receive similar information in kind, making him or her a more effective criminal investigator.

Analytical Investigative Support/Toll Analysis

Intelligence analysts provide valuable services to any investigation. Through intelligence indices, they can perform the groundwork and uncover background information and raw criminal intelligence about criminal suspects, allowing the agents more time to perform enforcement activities. Their help in conducting telephone toll analysis can show irrefutable evidence of knowledge and association between suspects when they telephone each other.

Analysts can provide link diagrams and flow charts, making it clear which suspects know each other, and those who do not. These charts display circles and squares that represent suspects and businesses with lines connecting them to one another, making it easy for agents and juries alike to understand the relationships between suspects and what their role is in the criminal conspiracy (see Figure 12.1 and Figure 12.2).

Intelligence analysts begin toll analysis by sending subpoenas to various telephone companies that provide long distance or cellular service to the suspect, asking for at least the last 6 months worth of toll calls made from his home, business, and cellular telephones. Once in hand, the analyst can then ask for the subscribers of each of the telephone numbers called. With subscriber information, the analyst can begin criminal history and intelligence records checks on each subscriber and look for telephone calls made by the subscribers to the known suspects. A link diagram can then be made that illustrates which suspects interact with each other and how often. Analysts frequently see telephone activity increasing at the times major drug transactions take place. Many of these analyses serve as the foundation to initiate a wiretap on one or more of these telephone numbers.

Use of Public, Private, and Government Records

Drug agents will use many public and private records during the course of their investigations. When a suspect is followed to an address that has never come up before in the investigation, a check with the local utility company can provide the agent with the name of the person paying the utility bills at the address. This name can then be provided to intelligence analysts or other agents to start the tedious, but necessary process of checking through different indices to search for criminal information on the suspect. The subscriber to the utilities often is connected to the conspiracy.

Public and government records are necessary to determine if a suspect owns a home, land, automobile, or holds any licenses. They reveal if he paid taxes, what his mailing addresses are, and when he was born. Other records show if he is a native or naturalized citizen, where he migrated from, if he holds a passport, if he has ever been granted a U.S. visa, and when it expires. Also where he went to school, who his parents are, and if he is registered to vote.

Private records will reveal where he banks, holds stock and mutual funds, and what his credit rating is. Also what loans he has, how much money he has borrowed, who his doctor is, where he took a commercial airline, what rental car company he used, what hotel he stayed at, and what phone calls he made from his room. Drug agents will routinely review public and private records during the course of their investigations and will rely heavily on them for quick, accurate information.

Polygraph Examinations

A useful tool in criminal investigations is the *polygraph*, sometimes called a *lie detector*. The findings of the device cannot be used in court; however, it is an investigative tool used in interrogations that is highly effective and accurate.

A polygraph simply measures bodily functions, most of which cannot be modified voluntarily. The machine measures the person's breathing, galvanic skin responses, heartbeats, and blood pressure. It operates on the theory that when a person is confronted with danger, certain involuntary physiological things happen within the body to help overcome the danger. The autonomic nervous system automatically transfers blood where it is needed most and regulates breathing.

When someone suddenly encounters a rattlesnake, a person's autonomic nervous system will automatically transfer additional blood to the person's legs and regulate his breathing to ensure a quick getaway. A person taking a polygraph examination, who is asked a question he intends to lie about, goes through these same involuntary physiological changes as a defense mechanism to lying. The machine measures these "fight or flight" responses and, coupled with the skill of the examiner, can tell with much accuracy if the person is being truthful when he answers a certain question using a simple yes or no format.

The examiner fully explains the functions of the polygraph to the defendant before the exam and will reveal exactly what questions will be asked, although they may not be in the same order each time. The questions will directly relate to the matter at hand and not deviate to other topics. Polygraph examinations help drug agents further their conspiracy investigations by using them to discover hidden assets, unknown suspects, and determine if a cooperating defendant is being completely truthful about his and others involvement in the crime.

Any plea-bargain between the prosecutor and a criminal defense attorney on behalf of his client should always be based on the defendant revealing everything he knows about the members of the drug conspiracy and the assets they have accumulated during its existence. These agreements should always state, in writing, that the defendant is subject to more than one polygraph examination that will be administered by a government agent, at his discretion, to determine if the defendant is being truthful with the investigating agents. It is important that prosecutors not agree to allow private examiners working for defense attorneys to administer the polygraph examination since their results may be tainted.

The polygraph should not be used as a bluff, but actually given to determine the truthfulness of a defendant who wants to cooperate with the prosecutor in return for consideration in his legal dilemma. After an initial in-depth debriefing of the defendant, the polygraph should be administered before drug agents act on leads provided by him. A condition of continued consideration in the defendant's legal situation should always be that the examination must be taken, and if the defendant is determined to be deceptive, the prosecutor is not obligated to honor any promises made about legal consideration. Further, the defendant should be informed that if he lies or refuses to take any law enforcement administered polygraph examination, the prosecutor will use any information already obtained from the defendant in future court proceedings against him.

If a small police department does not have qualified polygraphers, they should seek the support of a state or federal agency to have the test administered. Without the services of a qualified polygrapher, the defendant will almost always underexaggerate or lie about his or others involvement in the conspiracy.

Mail Covers

A *mail cover* is a service provided by the U.S. Postal Service in which law enforcement is provided with the names of all senders of first class mail sent to a suspect's address within a 30-day period. A mail cover does not authorize agents to look at the contents of the mail, only to determine who the senders are. Mail covers can accelerate and bolster the investigation by quickly providing numerous investigative leads. The average household receives numerous pieces of mail from various persons, businesses, and organizations during any single month. This mail will most likely include correspondence from the suspect's long distance telephone carrier, brokerage firm, and mutual fund company; advertisements or statements from travel agencies he deals with; credit card billing statements; automobile and mortgage companies; as well as possible property tax bills. Each piece of correspondence gives the drug agent a lead into the personal, financial, and recreational dealings of the suspect.

Once the long-distance telephone carrier is identified through the mail, it can be subpoenaed to provide toll and subscriber information. Brokerage houses and mutual fund companies can be served with grand jury subpoenas for financial information of the suspect that may eventually lead to assets and proceeds of drug trafficking. Travel agencies sending the suspect literature may have arranged for his travel in the past, or in the future, and their records can be queried. Credit card companies can provide information on where and when purchases were made, and may be helpful in determining what traveling the suspect has done, the specific hotel he stayed in and, later, what telephone calls were made from his room.

The postal inspector in charge where the mailbox is located can provide specific instructions on how to obtain a mail cover. Mail covers do not require a court order. They can be accomplished simply by providing a letter from the agency head to the Postal Service outlining the basic facts of the investigation and the reason for the request. In short, information gleaned from mail covers can be found out through other formal methods; however, it serves as a quick and simple way to determine the lifestyle and spending habits of the suspect and may provide enormous investigative leads that may reveal other members of the drug conspiracy.

Trash Runs

Trash runs provide another easy way of determining long-distance toll carriers, bank affiliations, telephone tolls, and travel itineraries. Evidence of crimes may surface when such items as pay-and-owe sheets, packaging materials, empty boxes of cutting agents, and other drug paraphernalia are found. Usually drug agents must wait for the trash to be placed on the curb or common waste receptacle before it can be seized.*

* Under federal law, individuals have no expectation of privacy in trash set at the edge of curtilage for pickup. See *California v. Greenwood*, 108 S.Ct. 1625 (1988). However, officers should check with their local prosecutors to determine the law in their jurisdictions.

Photo Spreads

In order to develop witnesses other than paid informants, drug agents may have an opportunity to display photographs to citizens to verify these suspects were present at a particular location. As an example, an informant describes to agents a meeting that took place at a particular hotel on a certain date to discuss drug trafficking. Agents attempt to corroborate the informant's information by verifying with the hotel that the suspect rented a room. Agents may go so far as to determine if any employees, such as the registration clerk, can identify the suspect among five other photographs, as being the person who rented that particular room. This further verification and corroboration by a citizen, as opposed to another informant or someone else who may have a questionable background, go a long way in convincing the jury that the informant is being truthful. It brings credibility in the eyes of the jury when they realize the prosecutor is not relying solely on the testimony of informants who probably have something to gain by the defendant's conviction.

Technical Listening Equipment

The questions that the officer or informant asks a defendant during recorded conversations* can reveal the truth about a defendant's intent to commit the crime that was the objective of the conspiracy. A skillful undercover agent can elicit responses to the same questions jurors may have during a trial.

For example, a defendant may admit to the undercover agent to having sold drugs hundreds of times, or may boast of an ability to obtain any drug in any amount. When the agent expresses doubt, a defendant sometimes will boast about past drug sales and other crimes.

Such a tape provides evidence that is hard to dispute. Even if the defendant makes no admissions under formal questioning, the recording alone satisfies the elements of proof for conspiracy, because the defendant committed an overt act simply by meeting with the undercover agent. In addition, a defendant's mere admission to engaging in the drug trade with others is sufficient to sustain a conviction for conspiracy[3] even if the co-conspirators are never identified or indicted.[4]

Execution of Search Warrants for Documents

Although probable cause to obtain search warrants to seize drug evidence may not exist, sufficient probable cause may be present to look for *documen-*

* Conversations recorded with the consent of at least one involved party do not require a warrant. However, because consensual eavesdropping rules vary, officers should consult with their state's attorney's office before using this technique.

tary evidence. In historical conspiracy investigations, warrants for documents are commonly justified. Drug agents know, through training and experience, that traffickers maintain meticulous records chronicling past drug transactions that may identify other members of the conspiracy. If drugs are found during the execution of a documentary search warrant, the drug evidence is admissible in court. Historical drug conspiracy cases also frequently locate proceeds from drug transactions that are subject to seizure.

Coordination with the Prosecutor

Although charging defendants with conspiracy can simplify most cases, some investigations require extraordinary means to achieve its goals. Any investigation can be streamlined if the drug agent and the prosecutor come to a mutual understanding before the case is initiated. Prosecutors know the legal community and sitting judges best. They know what sitting judge will be receptive to multi-defendant trials where there is little to no drug evidence.

Agents and prosecutors should conduct strategy meetings to determine the goal and scope of the investigation, the availability of potential witnesses and evidence, the means of its collection, and the anticipated legal defense tactics. Together, agents and prosecutors can formulate a viable plan of attack.

A way to "pitch" the case to the local prosecutor is to give him or her a realistic view of the potential of the investigation. Are there too many potential defendants or not enough? These numbers will vary widely depending on the policies and resources of the prosecutor's office. Before embarking on any long-term conspiracy investigation, the drug agent is well advised to consult with his or her local prosecutor. Prosecutors know the make up of the juries in the district best and can gauge the probable outcome of a trial. Some deputy district attorneys and assistant U.S. attorneys have wide discretion on who to prosecute, others are restricted by the elected or appointed officials above them. If an agent finds an aggressive career prosecutor willing to try a case on less than substantial physical and circumstantial evidence, he or she should consider himself or herself fortunate. Many prosecutors will reject conspiracy cases because they lack drug evidence. This is why agents must strive to submit the best quality investigation they can with as much drug, documentary, physical, and testimonial evidence as possible.

Crimes Committed by Conspirators

Drug agents who have thorough knowledge of state and federal criminal statutes will prepare the most accurate criminal indictments possible. A complete listing of all violations uncovered during the course of the conspiracy investigation should be used to facilitate plea bargaining agreements and may add to the punishment the defendant will receive. The following are examples of federal statutes that are usually duplicated in state penal codes. Drug agents will discover that members of a drug conspiracy frequently commit these violations of law in addition to drug crimes:

- 18 U.S. Code 4 — Misprision of felony (requires persons knowledgeable of crimes to inform law enforcement authorities)
- 18 U.S. Code 111 — Assaulting, resisting, or impeding federal officers
- 18 U.S. Code 924 (C) — Use or possession of a firearm during and in relation to a federal drug trafficking crime (5 year mandatory minimum)
- 18 U.S. Code 1001 — False statements
- 18 U.S. Code 1071 — Concealing person from arrest (harboring a fugitive)
- 18 U.S. Code 1073 — Flight to avoid prosecution or giving testimony
- 18 U.S. Code 1341 — Mail fraud
- 18 U.S. Code 1503 — Influencing or injuring officer or juror
- 18 U.S. Code 1504 — Influencing a juror by writing
- 18 U.S. Code 1510 — Obstruction of criminal investigations
- 18 U.S. Code 1511 — Obstruction of state or local law enforcement
- 18 U.S. Code 1512 — Tampering with a witness, victim, or informant
- 18 U.S. Code 1513 — Retaliating against a witness, victim, or informant
- 18 U.S. Code 1542 — False statement in application and use of passport
- 18 U.S. Code 1543 — Forgery or false use of passport
- 18 U.S. Code 1952 — Interstate and foreign travel or transportation in aid of a racketeering enterprise
- 18 U.S. Code 1956 — Laundering of monetary instruments
- 18 U.S. Code 1957 — Engaging in monetary transactions in property derived from specified unlawful activity
- 18 U.S. Code 1621 — Perjury
- 18 U.S. Code 1622 — Subornation of perjury
- 21 U.S. Code 841(a)(2) — Distribution of counterfeit substance
- 21 U.S. Code 841(e)(1) — Booby traps on federal property
- 21 U.S. Code 843 (b) — Use of communication facility to facilitate a drug crime (a.k.a. phone counts. Does not matter if agent initiated telephone contact with defendant)
- 21 U.S. Code 849 — Distribution within 1000 feet of rest or truck stop (doubles sentence)
- 21 U.S. Code 859 — Distribution to persons under age 21 (sentence is doubled)

- 21 U.S. Code 860 — Distribution or manufacturing in or near schools and colleges (within 1000 feet of property doubles sentence)
- 21 U.S. Code 861 — Employment of persons under 18 years of age in drug crime (doubles sentence)
- 21 U.S. Code 953 — Exportation of a controlled substance (e.g., cocaine already in the U.S. in exchange for Canadian marijuana)

Each defendant identified during the course of the investigation should be charged with all crimes committed by the other members after they entered the conspiracy.[5] It should be clear in their minds what their potential sentence is if they are convicted on all counts. This is a way of enticing defendants to cooperate in the prosecutor's case and to testify against other defendants. (See section on immunity for more details.)

Agents should be cognizant that because of the secretive nature and size of some criminal conspiracies, not all members of the conspiracy will know the existence of every other member. Nor will they know what overt acts or crimes the other members of the conspiracy committed. However, many defendants will know some of the other co-conspirators. Drug agents investigating a conspiracy may be the only ones who actually know all the members of the conspiracy and what overt acts and crimes each member committed.

Sealed Indictments

A prosecutor can ask the court to seal the indictments of the defendants. This will prevent the premature disclosure of the existence of the investigation to the defendants. However, once any member of the conspiracy is arrested, the seal is broken, and the existence of indictments and arrest warrants stemming from the investigation becomes public knowledge.

Arrest Warrants

Warrants for the arrests of those participating in a conspiracy should be obtained once a decision to prosecute the individuals has been made. Arrest warrants provide the case agent more flexibility in planning case strategy and is required for the extradition of fugitives, either domestic or foreign. It also provides other law enforcement agents protection from civil liability when making the arrests. Prosecutors should request the court issue sealed arrest warrants in order to not alert the suspects they are subject to arrest.

Grand Jury Subpoenas

Grand jury subpoenas are required to obtain financial records. Administrative subpoenas, like those issued by the DEA and other U.S. government agencies, are not honored at banks or other financial institutions. An agent must appear before the grand jury to request a subpoena. After the service of the subpoena, the agent must return to the grand jury and inform them of the results.

Grand jurors are curious about ongoing criminal investigations, and like most people, want to be made to feel they are a part of the procedure, which they most certainly are. They may sometimes ask agents irrelevant questions, but the prosecutor will be there to guide them in obtaining the relevant facts before an indictment or *true bill* is requested.

Periodic visits to the grand jury will keep them apprised of a complex ongoing investigation and will often facilitate the expeditious securing of criminal indictments. The prosecutor may ask that a true bill be returned on suspects as they are identified through an ongoing or historical criminal investigation. This can greatly expedite grand jury proceedings and make the management of the prosecution easier.

In multi-defendant cases, prosecutors may try suspects in increments of five or less in order to make the prosecution more manageable. These defendants are usually members of a conspiracy that had comparable roles, as opposed to mixing a supervisor or manager with defendants that only had minor roles.

Immunity

Prosecutors grant immunity to select defendants sparingly and only after being guided by department policy and input from the case agent. Immunity may provide a valuable witness otherwise not available. Before a defendant is offered immunity, he should be thoroughly debriefed by the case agents during what is called a *proffer*. A proffer, or formal offer of information, should reveal exactly the involvement and knowledge of the defendant, and help the prosecutor determine if this defendant will make a credible witness. If the prosecutor agrees that the defendant's testimony is essential to receiving guilty pleas from other defendants or help the jury fully understand the entire scope of the conspiracy, serious consideration should be given to offering immunity. Conditions should attach that the defendant must fully cooperate throughout the entire trial phase, and that his reneging will subject him to prosecution as well.

Multiple Venues

Coordination between different U.S. Attorney/District Attorney Offices is required to consolidate cases, avoid duplication of effort, and double jeopardy issues.

Asset Seizures

Frequently, real property and other assets of the defendants involved in a conspiracy are located in different venues. Close coordination is required to ensure that all known assets subject to seizure are identified and that civil proceedings are initiated. A single polygraph examination may determine if all assets known by a particular defendant have been identified.

Material Witness Warrants

The court is sometimes asked to issue a *material witness warrant* for a person to insure his presence during future crucial judicial proceedings. The witness is required to post a bond to insure his appearance. This technique is usually reserved for unindicted co-conspirators who may flee to avoid testifying or fear being arrested. The witness may even be incarcerated if a bond is not posted.

Defense Attorney Trial Tactics

Drug agents at all levels will experience a variety of legal defenses launched by criminal defense attorneys who specialize in drug cases. Some of these attorneys will not represent clients who have agreed to cooperate with drug agents in return for consideration in their legal matter. Agents may think that the extent a defense attorney will go to come up with a legal defense for his client is only limited by his imagination.

Agents, who are cognizant of defense attorney trial tactics, can conduct their investigations in such a manner to avoid their use. This essentially takes away the tools of the defense attorney to defend their clients. The following are some of the most common legal tactics criminal defense attorneys who usually specialize in drug cases use that drug agents are likely to encounter.

Defendant Withdrew from the Conspiracy

In court, the defendant readily concedes his involvement in the conspiracy; however, he claims he withdrew from the conspiracy long before the object of the conspiracy was met. By doing this, the defense attorney shields his client from criminal liability for crimes committed by other members of the conspiracy during its lifetime (see Pinkerton Theory of Vicarious Liability).

Drug agents need to focus on exactly when a defendant entered into a conspiracy, and exactly when, if applicable, he took affirmative steps to withdraw from it. Conspirators can only withdraw from a criminal conspiracy by doing something affirmative. One way a defendant can withdraw from a conspiracy is for him to either inform all known members of his intentions to withdraw. This means the other defendants would have to testify on his behalf to corroborate his claim, something not likely to occur. The other method of withdrawing is for the defendant to inform the police of his involvement in the conspiracy. This usually only occurs after the defendant has been arrested.

While questioning suspects in any conspiracy case, agents should focus on exactly when a particular conspirator entered into the agreement and more importantly, if the conspirator legally withdrew from it. This way defendants cannot later falsely claim they were no longer a member of the conspiracy when in reality they made no efforts to legally withdraw. Carefully interviewing the defendant and his co-defendants with these things in mind will help thwart this legal defense.

Outrageous Government Conduct

Criminal defense attorneys will sometimes claim that the conduct of the drug agents and prosecutors during the investigation or trial was so outrageous as to warrant an acquittal or dismissal. Here the defense attorney readily admits his client's involvement in the crime. However, he wants the judge or jury to believe that the agents and prosecutor conducted themselves in such an outrageous manner, that to deter them from repeating it in the future, and to punish them for it now, the defendant should be acquitted of all charges. Drug agents need to remember that it only takes one juror to agree with this defense theory to create a hung jury that cannot convict.

Drug agents need to discuss with a prosecutor, in detail, any unusual techniques they intend to use during the conduct of their conspiracy investigation. Any controversial technique used by drug agents that may be perceived by jurors as *outrageous*, although perfectly legal, should be avoided, if possible. A prosecutor may want to educate the jury by having a drug agent testify as an expert in drug trafficking investigations, and explain that lying to the suspects during an undercover operation is a routinely deployed investigative technique. A skilled defense attorney can make any investigative technique appear underhanded and give the false impression that agents were relentless in sending an innocent person to prison.

Examples of outrageous conduct may include a female informant having sexual relations with one or more defendants or when the star witness in the prosecutor's case, usually the informant, has a criminal history of multiple arrests and convictions for crimes against women and children.

Prosecutors should be as forthright with jurors as soon as possible when using an informant to testify about the words, deeds, and actions of the defendants. They need to have the informant admit their past crimes to the jury, in open court, in order to steal the thunder of the defense attorney who will make the witness appear to be worse than he may be. The prosecutor needs to also educate the jury that informants in the drug world come from within it, and good citizens do not normally possess the information needed to infiltrate drug conspiracies, leaving law enforcement with little option but to work with them.

Taking the Fall for Others

This is where the defendants coerce one particular defendant to take the blame for the crimes committed by the other conspirators, thereby exonerating them. This usually occurs in the middle of a lengthy trial that is going badly for the defendants. Suddenly, one defendant changes his plea from not guilty to guilty. His defense attorney announces that the defendant feels guilt and shame for having gotten his "friends" into a legal jam since they had absolutely nothing to do with the crime (despite overwhelming evidence to the contrary). The truth of the matter is that all the defendants are equally guilty; however, this one defendant was either threatened by the others or promised that his family will be well taken care of while he is in prison and that they will receive a stipend if he pleads guilty and, essentially, takes the fall for the others.

Entrapment

The *entrapment defense* tactic sometimes is presented in conjunction with *outrageous government conduct*. This is the most common form of defense in drug cases. This describes a situation where a drug agent, or the confidential informant, convinces the suspect to commit a drug crime when he would not normally be predisposed to do so, solely for the purpose of arresting him.

The defense attorney will attempt to show that the idea of selling drugs to the undercover agent or informant was planted there by them, not the defendant. The defense will attempt to show that agents and informants convinced the defendant he could make a lot of money with very little effort and few risks involved. The defense will imply the defendant knew nothing about the drug business, and if he did, he did not know enough to sell the quantity of drugs the drug agent or informant convinced him to sell to them.

This legal defense can usually be defeated when multiple-buys of controlled substances are made from the suspect to show that not only was he predisposed to commit the crime, but that he had connections to obtain increasingly larger amounts of drugs to sell to the agent or informant. Drug agents should be careful to ensure their informants are not targeting individuals who truly are not engaged in the drug business.

Mistaken Identity

The defense attorney maintains that his client simply is not the person named in the indictment. In some cultures, defendants will pay others to pose as them and serve their sentences.

Fabrication of Exculpatory Evidence

A real sign of desperation on the part of the defense is when he fabricates exculpatory evidence. *Exculpatory evidence* is evidence that tends to prove the defendant is innocent. Here the defense attorney calls an alleged *expert witness* to the stand who directly contradicts the testimony of an agent or the informant. Examples include an expert witness who testifies that certain audio or video tape recordings made by the agents or informant are entirely fabricated, edited, or altered in some way to convict an otherwise innocent person. The defense may introduce a recently made tape recording of a telephone conversation that supposedly took place months earlier between two of the defendants, in which one informs the other of his intention to withdraw from the conspiracy. The expert witness authenticates the recording as being genuine, when in reality it is a fabrication and the so-called expert lacks any expertise to conduct such an examination or draw this conclusion.

The defense might introduce a private-sector polygraph examiner as a witness who will testify that he conducted a polygraph examination of the defendant showing him to be completely truthful when he denied any involvement in the drug conspiracy. Other expert witness may include someone who has a so-called "critical ear," and hears the defendant's words on a taped confession differently from the police transcripts of the recording. Despite having a tape recording of the defendant saying, "I murdered the man," an expert may be found to testify that after listening to the tape, he concluded that the defendant actually said, "I did *not* murder the man." Other expert witnesses may be recently fired or retired drug agents who are prepared to testify that the procedures followed by the agents are either unsound, unprofessional, or in contrast to the department's manual.

Many expert witnesses for the defense are legitimate and possess the academic training and experience to render such opinions, however, there are an ever-increasing number of people who claim to possess an expertise in an area they clearly do not. These people offer their services to anyone who is willing to pay for them, and after being briefed on the case, in an indirect or roundabout way, will suggest they can testify to exactly what the defense was hoping for, no matter how unbelievable it may be.

When drug agents first learn that an expert witness will be introduced, they should immediately request the witness's resumé and investigate each claim of education, knowledge, employment, and experience in the field. Many of these witnesses assume that no one will check out their qualifications, or if it happens, it will be too late for the prosecutor to recover from the damage done to its case by the expert witness.

Agents need to find legitimate expert witnesses in the same field who can recreate the examination conducted by the defense expert witness, and testify why his findings are in error. The federal government, especially the

FBI and military, employ experts with impeccable credentials and world-class expertise who, if applicable, can contradict the findings of any self-educated expert witness who is essentially nothing more than a hired gun for the defense, used to kill the credibility of the prosecutor's witnesses.

Some criminal defense attorneys will intentionally seek out unethical expert witnesses to bolster an otherwise dismal legal defense. Others are victims of consumer fraud, or are simply convinced that drug agents, and the police in general, routinely fabricate evidence to make innocent persons appear guilty. They firmly believe these expert witnesses validate their prejudices and provide a real service by helping ferret out corruption within the ranks of the police. Drug agents should never underestimate the powerful testimony these witnesses provide. Some are extremely convincing, especially when they exhibit the right body language and bring props into the courtroom to conduct demonstrations.

Placing the Agent on Trial

This is sometimes done in conjunction with the outrageous government conduct defense, and especially when a defense expert witness challenges the findings of the prosecutor. Defense attorneys have employed private investigators to look into the personal lives of drug agents and informants to ascertain their financial situation and lifestyle, simply to imply they are living above their means and may be taking bribes or selling drugs themselves.

Others will attack drug agents directly on the stand insinuating they are incompetent, immoral, unethical, or are only interested in seeking big headlines and big promotions. Agents need to remain professional and maintain their composure when they are being accused of these things, and try not to exhibit body language indicative of being irritated with this line of questioning.

Defense attorneys may exploit an overlooked procedure as the grounds to attack the agent. For example, the agent collects certain writings by the defendant that tend to show he is involved in the drug conspiracy. The agent obtains handwriting exemplars of the defendant for comparison with the handwriting on the documents. A prosecution expert concludes positively, that the defendant wrote the documents in question. The defense attorney may ask the agent if any fingerprints were found on the document. When the agent responds he or she did not request a fingerprint examination since the handwriting analysis showed the defendant wrote the document, the attorney will seize the moment by stating that *if* the document had been examined for fingerprints, the defendant's fingerprints would not be there. This may be contrary to logic, but the defense attorney is attempting to convince at lease one juror that the agent is incompetent because a fingerprint examination was not requested. He is also implying that the defendant did not write the incriminating document since his fingerprints were not found on it, completely ignoring the questioned documents expert's findings.

Defense attorneys realize that the extent of a juror's knowledge of criminalistics is what they have seen on television or read in novels, and that if a person's fingerprints are not on a document, then obviously he did not touch it, and therefore he could not have authored it. The prosecutor needs to re-establish that a handwriting expert positively concluded that the defendant wrote the document in question, and that fingerprint analysis would have been redundant. Drug agents can avoid these situations by being as thorough as possible, and to conduct of as many scientific examinations of the evidence as possible to limit the defense attorney's ability to attack the findings and the agent's professional conduct.

Defendant Was Involved in an Entirely Different Conspiracy

The defense attorney acknowledges that the defendant is a criminal involved in the drug trade; however, he was involved in an entirely different conspiracy, not the one for which he was indicted. This is a legal maneuver designed to overturn a conviction during an appeal. Drug agents need to amass as much evidence as possible and be specific when testifying about the role of each defendant in the conspiracy to counter such claims.

The Blind Mule

This defense is commonly used by defendants who are caught in the act of transporting drugs in privately owned vehicles, rental cars, commercial airlines, buses, or trains. The defendant claims he had no knowledge that the drugs found in his suitcase or car were there. He claims to be a victim who was used by drug dealers to unwittingly transport drugs for them.

Drug agents can easily counter such defense claims by gathering facts and offering expert testimony that drug dealers lose control of their product when they secret it in a conveyance over which they have no control. If a rental car had drugs in it prior to the defendant renting it, how did the drug dealers know where the rental car would be going? If drug dealers secreted drugs in the defendant's suitcase, there is no guarantee the suitcase would not be stolen since they have no control over the security of the bag.

Some drug couriers who are asked by drug agents if they can search their carry-on luggage will cite giving their consent is evidence they did not know drugs were there. Drug agents can counter this by explaining that through training and experience they know that drug couriers firmly believe that if they give consent: (1) the agent will believe he is innocent; (2) drug agents are lazy, and will not go through the entire bag looking for drugs if he gives consent; or (3) that the drugs are so well concealed that drug agents have no chance of locating them. Drug agents should never pass up the opportunity to search someone who has given them consent to do so.

Summary

Drug agents know through training and experience that it is virtually impossible to commit a drug crime alone. Conspiracy laws allow drug law enforcement agents to bring these co-conspirators to justice. Without U.S. conspiracy laws, federal authorities could not indict, arrest, and try suspected international drug criminals who conspire to violate U.S. drug laws outside America's borders.

A conspiracy is simply two or more persons who enter an agreement to commit a crime. The only thing the agent has to prove is that an agreement was made between the parties to commit a crime, and that they committed overt acts in furtherance of the goal of the conspiracy. Since it is impractical that an undercover agent or confidential informant (CI) will be present at the moment a conspiracy is hatched, the courts allow circumstantial evidence in trial to convict conspirators involved in the drug crime.

Advantages to enforcing conspiracy statues include the dismantling of entire criminal organizations, the ability to charge each member with the crimes committed by any member of the conspiracy to further the goal of the conspiracy, and allows for an exception to the hearsay rule of evidence. Conspiracy is a separate and distinct offense from the substantive crime they agreed to commit. Even if the goal of the conspiracy is never realized, the members can still be charged with the separate crime of conspiracy, which in many cases carries the same penalty as the crime they conspired to commit. Seizing drug evidence during the investigation is not necessary to charge the suspects with conspiracy, but it should always be the goal. Historical conspiracy cases are investigated the same way as any other reported or after-the-fact crime.

Most drug conspiracy cases are initiated through information provided by CIs. Every investigative technique in traditional investigations can be utilized, and some are used extensively in drug enforcement, such as undercover. Drug agents need to coordinate with prosecutors before any large-scale investigation is launched. Conspiracy investigations can be time consuming and manpower intensive.

References

1. *Iannelli v. United States*, 420 U.S. 770, 1975.
2. U.S. Sentencing Commission, *Guidelines Manual*, Sec. 2D1.4(a)Nov 1991.
3. *United States v. Figueroa*, 720 F.2d 1239, 1983.

4. *United States v. Goodwin*, 492 F.2d 1141, 1974.
5. *Pinkerton v. United States*, 328 U.S. 640, 66 S. Ct. 1180, 90 L.Ed. 1489, 1946.
6. *United States v. Gutierrez*, 978 F.2d 1463, 7th Cir., 1992.

13 Clandestine Laboratories

The vast majority of clandestine laboratories discovered in the United States manufacture methamphetmine. According to the DEA, 2155 of these laboratories were seized in the United States in 1999 compared to 1627 in 1998. This trend will most likely continue until the popularity of the drug levels off or drops. The vast majority of these labs were found in California, far more than any other state; however, many other states are catching up. Most of the labs were only capable of producing less than 10 pounds of methamphetamine at one time, but 10% were *super labs*, as the DEA refers to them, and were only capable of producing well beyond 10 pounds, possibly as much as 100 pounds per manufacturing session.

The manufacture of methamphetamine requires precursor, or necessary chemicals, such as ephedrine, red phosphorus, and Freon® to make the finished product. Often these chemicals are federally controlled and require the vendor to document the sale and the identity of the buyer. This documentation requirement has forced laboratory operators to find other sources for their chemicals.

Ephedrine is a highly sought after precursor chemical for the finished products of methamphetamine and crystal methamphetamine. Ephedrine is the active ingredient of a noncontrolled substance found in many over-the-counter cold remedies called pseudoephedrine. Ephedrine by itself is not manufactured in the United States, but elsewhere. Laboratory operators have found ways of chemically extracting the ephedrine from pseudoephedrine's binding agents. These *extraction laboratories* usually go to work before the assembly of the laboratory that will be used to make the methamphetamine. Suspects who are found with huge quantities of cold remedy tablets containing pseudoephedrine, or their empty containers, should be suspected of methamphetamine manufacturing.

Volatile clandestine methamphetamine laboratories are found in rural, suburban, and even densely populated settings. Traffickers will often set up their labs in rented hotel rooms or apartment complexes exposing occupants to the dangers of chemicals, fire, and explosions.

Specialty within Drug Law Enforcement

The investigation of clandestine laboratories, or *clan labs*, is a specialty within drug enforcement. Drug agents that are not trained and certified in the dismantling of such labs, and are not wearing special breathing apparatuses and protective clothing should not enter any dwelling or building where a suspected laboratory may be. Many chemicals that are found in these laboratories are corrosive or flammable. Vapors from them can create chemical reactions that attack mucous membranes, eyes, skin, and the respiratory tract. Some chemicals can react with water or other chemicals that will cause a fire or explosion.

Those with the training and experience of dismantling clan labs must undergo periodic physical examinations to insure they have not been exposed to toxic chemicals. Female drug agents are particularly at risk to exposure to these chemicals as they may have an effect on fetal development. The DEA as well as a number of state police organizations, including the California Bureau of Narcotic Enforcement (BNE), conduct weeks long special schooling on the detection and dismantling of clandestine laboratories.

Booby-Traps

As if the exposure to chemicals was not bad enough, many clan labs are found to be booby-trapped by the operators. Some booby-traps and protective measures found by drug agents over the years include:

- Light switches wired to flammable liquid containers, booby-trapped light bulbs, or other explosive devices
- Internal refrigerator light bulbs wired to detonate with explosives when door is opened
- Videotape cassettes altered to detonate an internal explosive when placed into a video player
- Monofilament trip lines connected to chemical or explosive booby-traps or fishing hooks
- Attack dogs
- Poisonous snakes
- Pipe bombs
- Weapons
- Other obvious devices

Countering Booby-Traps

Drug agents can counter most booby-traps by carefully visually checking everything before touching it. Furniture should not be used until examined. Light switches or interior lights should not be switched on while inside a building, and doors to refrigerators should not be opened. Electrically operated appliances should be unplugged.

A container should not be opened without first giving it a thorough exterior inspection before touching it. Food or drink should never be consumed at any laboratory site since chemical contamination can occur through air particulate matter. Drug agents need to stay alert and let their senses guide them.

Recognizing Clan Labs

Clandestine laboratories are not always found in buildings. Some have been discovered in recreational vehicles, houseboats, small trailers, and other conveyances. The most common lab sites are buildings within industrial or commercial complexes, self-storage facilities, and residences. The biggest clue to where a clan lab may be located is from the peculiar odors they produce. Some of these odors have been described as ether- or vinegar-like, as well as pungent, acrid, sour, or ammonia-like. These odors frequently cause eye, nose, and throat irritations.

If a drug agent responds to a location where a clan lab is believed to be, he should look for exterior clues, including unusual fortifications at the residence or commercial building and unusual waste or containers in receptacles. Further clues may be the discoloration of pavement due to chemical spills or a general unkempt appearance of the lawn or landscape. Neighbors may also report the unusual or furtive behavior of the occupants of the home or building during late evening hours.

Obvious clues are the discovery of laboratory equipment, not unlike that found in chemistry classrooms in high schools and colleges. Commonly found are plastic buckets and containers with labels indicating corrosive chemicals, and small pits created in yards where laboratory waste may have been disposed of.

When agents enter the suspected lab site, they may find a *boxed lab* where all the ingredients and equipment necessary to manufacture controlled substances is present, but not set up at the moment. Boxed laboratories often emit strong chemical smells. Drug agents or police patrol officers who find an operational laboratory should immediately leave the location and call the DEA or another agency equipped to handle such an event.

Chemicals and Products Commonly Found at Clan Lab Sites

Many every day products can be found at clan lab sites in addition to the chemical precursors that are needed to produce the finished product. The following is a listing of commonly found products and chemicals found at these sites:

Commercial Products	Chemicals	Hazards	Uses
Aluminum foil	Aluminum	Nonhazardous	Forms metal complex
Camera batteries	Lithium	Water reactive	Forms metal complex
Charcoal lighter fluid	Petroleum distillates	Flammable	Oil extraction
Denatured alcohol	Mixture of alcohols	Flammable	Tablet extraction
Epsom salts	Magnesium sulfate	Nonhazardous	Absorbs water
Gasoline	Petroleum distillates	Highly flammable	Oil extraction
Heet®	Methyl alcohol	Flammable	Tablet extraction
Iodine crystals/7% tincture of iodine	Iodine	Irritant	Forms complex with ephedrine/pseudo-ephedrine
Kerosene	Petroleum distillates	Highly flammable	Oil extraction
Lacquer thinner	Petroleum distillates	Flammable	Oil extraction
Mineral spirits	Petroleum distillates	Flammable	Oil extraction
Muriatic acid	Hydrochloric acid	Corrosive acid	Converts oil to white powder
Red Devil lye	Sodium hydroxide	Corrosive base	Adjusts pH
Roto Rooter/drain cleaner/battery acid	Sulfuric acid	Corrosive acid	Reacts with table salt
Starting fluid	Ethyl ether	Highly flammable	Oil extraction
Striker plate/match heads	Phosphorus	Flammable	Source of red phosphorus
Table salt	Sodium chloride	Nonhazardous	Reacts with sulfuric acid to form hydrochloric acid gas
Over-the-counter cold medicine	Ephedrine/pseudo-ephedrine	Nonhazardous	Required for synthesis
Coffee filters	N/A	N/A	Separates liquids from solids
Pots, pans, bowls	N/A	N/A	Cooking utensil
Stove top, oven, microwave	N/A	N/A	Sources of heat
Iced tea jars/drinking water dispensers	N/A	N/A	Mixes sulfuric acid with table salt to form hydrochloric acid gas

Other Clan Lab Indicators

Upon entering a residence, business, or vehicle, a drug agent may see and smell things that may be indications that a clan laboratory is either in the process of manufacturing methamphetamine or another drug, or may have just completed the process. Agents need to be cognizant of items commonly found in such labs and household items that may be used during the manufacturing process.

Since the precursor chemical ephedrine is not readily available in the United States, large amounts of cold tablets containing pseudoephedrine are used as a substitute. Chemists seek large bottles of the tablets that are in easy to open containers to expedite the process. Empty boxes that contained individual jars of the tablets may be in or around the lab site.

Some other indicators may be:

- Neighbors or surveillance observing the occupants of the dwelling or building going outside to smoke
- Jars, bottles, or other glassware with rubber tubing attached to them
- Red phosphorus jars or jars containing a fine dark red or purple powder
- Glassware of jars containing a clear liquid with a white colored solid on the bottom
- Common coffee filters with a white pasty substance, a dark red sludge, or small amounts of white crystals
- Iodine jars or other jars containing dark shiny metallic purple crystals
- Bottles of hydrochloric acid or sulfuric acid
- Strong smell of chemicals such as ether, acetone, or ammonia, or any combination of the same
- Many Coleman or other brands of camping stove fuel, starting fluid, acetone, paint thinner, lighter fluid, Red Devil lye, drain cleaners containing sulfuric acid, or bottles containing muriatic acid
- Large amounts of ice
- Numerous lithium batteries and their packaging, many of which are stripped or in the process of being so
- Frying pans, pots, and other cookware that contain residue of powder
- Numerous rolls of aluminum foil, some possibly in a liquid solution of oil or kerosene
- Propane tanks inside of building or dwelling

Operational Laboratories

Anytime laboratory equipment such as flasks, condenser columns, reflux or distillation apparatus and the like are found with liquids, coupled with the strong odor of chemicals, drug agents should contain the scene and immediately call for assistance from clan lab specialists and take the following actions:

- Local police officers should be summoned to contain the scene and keep spectators away. Neighbors in the immediate vicinity should be evacuated.
- Movement within the controlled area should be restricted, and the media should not be allowed in.
- The fire department should be summoned to stand by in the event of an explosion or fire.
- If children are present, child social service representatives should be called to take custody of them. Animal control officers need to respond to the presence of any pets or animals at the scene.
- A command post should be established upwind from the laboratory site, ready to move in the event of a change of wind direction.
- Hazardous material teams, known as HAZMAT teams, need to respond to evaluate the situation and initiate clean up upon completion of the safe dismantling of the laboratory.

Summary

Clandestine laboratory investigations can prove to be one of the most dangerous endeavors in which any drug agent will be engaged. The presence of hazardous and toxic chemicals can kill or injure those around them, and should never be taken lightly by law enforcement personnel who happen upon them. Many clan lab sites are booby-trapped to discourage pilferers or drug law enforcement agents. These booby-traps are designed to maim or kill. Drug agents need to be aware of the chemicals used in the manufacture of methamphetamine, which is the most prevalent drug processed by clan labs. If police officers or drug agents happen upon an operational laboratory, they need to make immediate and specific notifications in order to maintain the integrity of the crime scene as well as remove the elements of explosion and fire.

Transportation Hub Interdiction Operations

14

Drug traffickers have long used commercial airlines and other means of public transportation as a way to transport drugs and drug proceeds from one place in the country, or world, to another. To combat this, drug enforcement agents are assigned to international and domestic airports, bus terminals, and train stations throughout the country. Each year, thousands of pounds of controlled substances and millions of dollars in drug proceeds are seized making it one of the most successful operations ever conducted by drug law enforcement. None of these seizures came as a result of utilizing traditional drug investigation methods such as undercover. The procedures originally used at airports are now routinely deployed at bus terminals and train stations since couriers will often use alternative means of transportation to avoid detection, especially since airport security has increased following the terrorist events of September 11, 2001.

Courier Profiling

Drug couriers come in each gender and in all races, shapes, and sizes; however, they generally exhibit certain characteristics that will alert an experienced drug agent that they may be couriers. One way to detect couriers is by using proven courier profiling techniques.

Some couriers are more experienced than others, and others are better at concealing their emotions and nervousness than others. However, drug agents have seen a pattern of activity that remains consistent with people engaged in transporting drugs on airplanes, trains, and busses. When agents detect one or more of these traits in a passenger, they have to make a decision whether or not to approach the person and make an initial inquiry. The drug agent's objective is to obtain certain information, voluntarily from the suspect, that will give the agent probable cause to either arrest the person for possession of drugs or seek a search warrant for the person and his luggage.

Approaching a suspected drug courier cold at an airport, train station, or bus terminal is not unlike a patrol officer who stops a suspicious pedestrian on the street to inquire why the person is there. Several U.S. Supreme Court decisions have had a direct effect on what drug agents can do during interdiction operations.

The U.S. Supreme Court in the famous 1968 decision, *Terry v. Ohio*, 392 U.S. 1, 30, (1968), distinguished between an investigative stop and an arrest and between a frisk and a full-blown search requiring a warrant. A decision in 1989, *U.S. v. Sokolow*, 490 U.S. 1, affirmed the method drug agents used when conducting investigative stops of potential drug couriers. (See Appendix C for the complete court's ruling.)

In the Sokolow case, DEA agents stopped Sokolow when he arrived in Los Angeles from Miami enroute to the Honolulu International Airport, finding 1063 grams of cocaine (approximately one kilogram) in his carry-on luggage. Before confronting Sokolow, the agents knew through their preliminary investigation that he had paid $2100 for two round-trip plane tickets from a roll of $20 bills; that he was traveling under a fictitious name that did not match the name under which his telephone number was listed; that his original flight destination was Miami, a source city for illicit drugs; that Sokolow appeared nervous during his trip; and that he did not check in any of his luggage.

Sokolow was taken to the DEA office where a drug-trained K-9 reacted to his carry on luggage. Due to the late hour, search warrants were obtained and the cocaine was found the next day. Sokolow was arrested and indicted in Hawaii for possession with intent to distribute cocaine. The district court denied his motion to suppress the evidence, finding that the stop was justified by a reasonable suspicion that he was engaged in criminal activity, as required by the Fourth Amendment. However, the 9th Circuit Court of Appeals disagreed and reversed Sokolow's conviction.

The Supreme Court ruled that the stop and arrest was reasonable. Chief Justice Rehnquist said the following in his opinion for the court: "The process does not deal with hard certainties, but with probabilities. Long before the law of probabilities was articulated as such, practical people formulated certain common-sense conclusions about human behavior; jurors as factfinders are permitted to do the same — and so are law enforcement officers."

The DEA special agent who arrested Sokolow is Richard Kempshall, who has since retired and is now the executive director of the International Narcotics Interdiction Association (INIA). This outstanding organization provides specialized drug law enforcement training for drug agents who work at transportation nodes throughout the world. More information on the INIA can be found at www.inia.org.

In 2002, the U.S. Supreme Court ruled in the case *U.S. v. Drayton,* 231 F. 3d 787, that police conducting interdiction operations are not required to inform passengers they wish to question or search that they have the right to refuse to cooperate. This ruling gives considerable latitude to drug agents so long as they can show the questioning and search was clearly voluntary.

Some of the traits drug agents look for when profiling passengers are:

- Passenger's ticket was purchased with cash, not a credit card
- Ticket is good for one way only
- Ticket was purchased the day of travel or the night before
- Ticket was purchased through a travel agent in a city not near where he resides, or would be inconvenient to his residence or work address
- Passenger has little to no luggage
- Passenger has excessive amounts of luggage
- Passenger makes an excessive number of phone calls from cellular phone or a public phone booth at the terminal before leaving or upon arriving at the airport
- Airline records reflect an erratic pattern of travel between his departure point and destination; length of stay varies
- Passenger has a return ticket the following day from a city where the length of stay would normally be longer due to distance traveled e.g., Los Angeles to New York or Miami to Honolulu
- Passenger lives out of the normal service area of the airport where the flight originates
- Passenger does not remember how he got to the airport
- Passenger cannot remember the name or address of the friend he is visiting
- Passenger does not know if his friend will be picking him up at his final destination
- Passenger appears exceedingly nervous, furtive, or evasive
- Passenger does not know the combination to the lock on his suitcase
- Passenger cannot recall the name of the travel agency where he supposedly purchased his ticket
- Narcotics detection K-9 reacts to the presence of controlled substances in the passenger's checked in or carry-on luggage
- He is the first one on the airplane to be seated
- He is the last passenger off the airplane once it lands
- Baggage has nametags that are different than those of the ticketed passenger

- Passenger claims to live in one state, but has a drivers' license from another
- Passenger is extremely uncooperative
- Passenger is extremely cooperative
- Passenger's heart rate and breathing increase significantly; he begins to perspire and to shake once confronted

Approaching the Passenger

Drug agents must keep in mind they have no legal authority to open a suspect's bag, or search his person for tickets, passports, and other travel documents without a search warrant, or incidental to an arrest. The object is for the drug agent to solicit the traveler's cooperation and eventual granting of permission to search his luggage.

How a drug agent initially approaches a person suspected of being a drug courier may well determine if he or she will be successful in obtaining permission to search the person or their luggage. Tact is extremely important. A chess game of sorts takes place once the drug agent makes the initial contact, and he or she must be prepared to handle what is often a fluid situation. Drug agents should never approach a suspect alone, but always have a partner with them to offer protection, as well as be a good observer and witness.

When approaching a suspected courier, the agents should be courteous and professional. They need to communicate to the suspect that they are soliciting his cooperation voluntarily. After asking to see the suspect's airline ticket, many questions will be asked once it is examined. Agents working airports generally know airline codes that are indicative of special restrictions and conditions that may not be obvious on the ticket itself.

Many suspected couriers will either claim not to know or lie about how they received their ticket, why it was purchased a certain way, or whom they will be visiting.

The totality of the circumstances will dictate what actions the drug agents will take. If a narcotic detection K-9 is available, the dog should be allowed to examine the suspect's bag without opening it. In the event the dog reacts to controlled substances inside, the passenger and his luggage can be held at the airport office while a search warrant is being sought.

If a K-9 is not available and the passenger does not allow the agents to search the bags and insists on leaving, agents have the option of calling the airport where the passenger will be arriving to have other agents further observe the suspect's actions and with whom he meets. During the passenger's flight to his ultimate destination, the original agents can run a series of record checks for any drug intelligence that may exist about the person, as well as any criminal record he may have. He or she can also request that the other agents arrange for a drug detection K-9 to be available upon the suspect's arrival.

Other Considerations

Drug couriers have been arrested from every racial and ethnic group. However, from experience, drug agents know that statistically, certain groups are more frequently drug couriers than others. To counter this, organizers of drug courier and smuggling rings believe that conservatively dressed caucasians, especially women, are the least likely to be approached or noticed by drug enforcement agents at transportation nodes. Drug agents need to be cognizant that smuggling rings often employ caucasians for this very reason, however no matter how innocent looking these people may be, they will still exhibit other profile traits such as nervousness, cash purchase of tickets, and the like. Drug agents should not be lulled into believing that only non-whites are involved in the drug smuggling trade.

Drug agents know from training and experience that selling drugs requires the concerted effort of many people. When a lone courier is arrested, his pocket litter and personal belongings should be thoroughly examined for clues concerning where the drugs were to be delivered, where they came from, and who else is involved. Any address book found should be photocopied for later analysis. Every courier case is an instant conspiracy investigation waiting to be launched through the investigative skills of the agents.

Hotel Profiling

Drug agents may not want to approach a suspect at a transportation terminal and elect to follow the person to his hotel or other destination to further observe his activity. Through the years, airport interdiction agents have developed characteristics of people staying in hotels that may be involved in the drug trade. Often these people are not noticed when arriving at an airport, train, or bus station, but were picked up later by a source of information working as a hotel clerk, who in turn notifies drug agents.

Drug agents will ask their hotel sources of information to look for guests who check in either without a reservation or who made one very recently. These couriers have a tendency to pay cash for their stay, order room service instead of going out or eating in the hotel restaurant, refuse daily maid service, and receive few visitors. These suspects usually remain in their room for inordinate periods of time, and may stay at the hotel for a week or more with no apparent reason for being there. Drug agents know from experience that this profile of a hotel guest may be indicative of a drug courier either waiting to have suitcases with drugs delivered to them, or having drug-laden suitcases picked up in his room. Other times, they may have money instead of drugs, or may have delivered drugs, and are now waiting for money to take back with them on their return trip.

When alerted, drug agents can conduct a preliminary investigation into the identity of the person, how they got to their destination, and what telephone calls they are making from the hotel room. Further analysis can determine if the name of the traveler and telephone numbers he is calling are known to have a history of involvement in drug trafficking. The results of the drug agents' inquiries will determine whether or not the hotel guest should be placed under surveillance to see what develops. Hotel profiling has been highly successful in identifying courier routes, members of drug smuggling organizations, and has been responsible for the recovery of large amounts of drugs and drug proceeds.

Summary

Observant agents working at the nation's major transportation hubs have been responsible for interdicting large amounts of drugs and money without the use of undercover informants or agents. They develop their skills from interaction with passengers who appear to be out of the ordinary and cannot provide details about their trip. From their years of experience working at transportation centers in the country, drug agents have developed characteristics that likely couriers for major drug organizations possess.

Through the years the U.S. Supreme Court has made some favorable rulings for law enforcement in drug interdiction cases. Any drug courier arrested is part of a conspiracy. His pocket litter and personal belongings must be examined to render clues about who the drugs were intended for, and where they came from. Transportation hub interdiction has developed into the profiling of hotel guests that exhibit the same behavior as passengers. These interdictions have also been proven to be highly successful.

Smuggling and Smugglers 15

Definition of Smuggling

Smuggling is the secretive movement of controlled substances or other contraband over an international border. Smuggling has been going on around the world for thousands of years and is not likely to stop so long as there is a demand for the products being smuggled, and money to be made smuggling it. Most of the drugs abused in the United States originate in foreign countries and have to be smuggled into this country to reach consumers.

Agencies Conducting Smuggling Investigations

Many federal agencies investigate drug smuggling organizations, but the primary responsibility lies with the Drug Enforcement Administration (DEA).

Drug Enforcement Administration

The DEA is the lead organization when it comes to drug smuggling. Memoranda of understanding exist between the DEA and the FBI, Bureau of Immigration and Customs Enforcement, Border Patrol, and other agencies that may bring information pertaining to the smuggling of drugs to the DEA's attention for its action. The DEA frequently delegates the responsibility of the investigation to the agency that discovers the crime, but still maintains the right to assume the investigation later.

The DEA is the lead agency in the management of the *El Paso Intelligence Center* (EPIC). This multi-agency federal law enforcement entity has representatives from all federal and many military law enforcement organizations that pool their information in an effort to interdict smuggling as it occurs. From monitoring private plane radio traffic to analyzing information received from CIs, EPIC has been highly successful in the interdiction of thousands of pounds of drugs before they entered the United States.

The DEA also has special agents and intelligence analysts assigned at over 70 offices in over 56 countries around the world including Bogotá, Colombia; Bangkok, Thailand; Mexico City, Mexico; and Islamabad, Pakistan. These agents carry diplomatic status; gather drug intelligence; and help their host nation counterparts in drug enforcement training, sharing of intelligence, and case development.

Many agents are instrumental in the seizing of large quantities of drugs at their source, and often arrange *controlled deliveries* into the United States to identify the recipients and other members of their criminal organization (see Chapter 16 for more details).

The DEA also conducts special operations in Central America, South America, and the Caribbean in the interdiction of shipments of drugs to the United States. These initiatives have resulted in the seizure of tons of cocaine and marijuana prior to reaching the shores of the country.

Bureau of Immigration and Customs Enforcement

The U.S. Immigration and Naturalization Service and U.S. Customs Service merged with the creation of the Department of Homeland Security. The agency's new name is the Bureau of Immigration and Customs Enforcement (ICE). Until the merger, the U.S. Customs Service was one of the oldest law enforcement organizations in the nation.

ICE brings together approximately 14,000 federal employees to focus on the enforcement of immigration and customs laws within the United States, the protection of specified federal buildings, and air and marine enforcement. By unifying previously fragmented investigative functions, the ICE strives to deliver effective and comprehensive enforcement. An Assistant Secretary heads the bureau who reports directly to the Undersecretary for Border and Transportation Security.

The bureau derives its authority to investigate drug smuggling from its border search authority. The old Customs Service was formed primarily to assess customs duty on goods being imported into the United States, and these duties were at one time the primary source of revenue for the U.S. government. As a result of the events of September 11, 2001, this new agency became a front line defense against undocumented aliens and illegal goods and contraband entering the country.

ICE's customs enforcement mission is not limited to conducting investigations. The Air and Marine Interdiction Division (AMID) maintains a large fleet of aircraft and vessels strategically located throughout the United

States, including Puerto Rico and the Virgin Islands. AMID's mission is to detect and intercept suspect air and marine targets and to provide surveillance support to investigative entities. Because of their extensive capability, AMID has provided airspace security coverage over Washington, D.C. to protect facilities of national interest during heightened terrorist alerts.

ICE's customs-related investigative and interdiction enforcement is complemented with an extensive intelligence component. The intelligence division is responsible for coordinating intelligence activities including managing the collection, analysis, and dissemination of intelligence; conducting intelligence-related liaison activities with the intelligence and law enforcement community; and providing contributions to Department of Homeland Security intelligence assessments and reports.

Operational and tactical control of investigative and intelligence operations are divided geographically by areas of responsibility and are managed by special agents in charge (SACs). The SACs are responsible for the administration and management of all investigative related customs enforcement activities within the geographic countries of the office. The SACs develop, coordinate, and implement enforcement strategies to ensure conformance with national policies and procedures and support national intelligence programs. Similarly, AMID has a number of air and marine branches that provide the same control within their areas of responsibility (Figure 15.1).

ICE is obligated to notifying the DEA whenever they seize drugs or investigate a case that may lead to a domestic drug seizure since the DEA has

Figure 15.1 U.S. Customs inspector conducts secondary inspection of airline passenger. (Courtesy of the Bureau of Immigration and Customs Enforcement.)

the primary jurisdiction over the matter. The DEA often works jointly with ICE against drug smuggling organizations. ICE has special agents serving in many different foreign countries and maintains an intelligence database called TECS, the Treasury enforcement computer system.

ICE can also determine if a person has recently entered the United States and filed a customs declaration, or if what is called a *cash transaction report* (CTR) has been filed. A CTR is required whenever anyone either brings in or leaves the country with more than $10,000 in cash or negotiable instruments such as a bearer bond. It is not a crime to possess the money. It is a federal crime to not declare having the money. If a person fails to declare the money, it can be seized and forfeited to the U.S. Treasury. Many drug smugglers conceal large amounts of cash when coming into and out of the country, which are usually proceeds of drug trafficking activity. During the course of any investigation, ICE can provide drug agents with this information.

ICE can also enter someone into their computer system to look for individuals under a *silent lookout*. If the person in question is located at a point of entry, he will be allowed to proceed unmolested by ICE agents, but the law enforcement organization requesting the lookout will be notified that the person was located and where. Contrasting this, ICE can look for wanted persons entering the country and arrest or detain them for other law enforcement agencies.

ICE can also perform what is known as an *extension of the border search*. ICE agents with prior information about a particular person, vehicle, or other conveyance that is smuggling contraband into the country, will allow the person to enter the country without benefit of an inspection. The person is followed continuously to his intended destination, at which time ICE exerts their authority to conduct a warrantless search. ICE has the authority to conduct this type of search due to its border search authority.

U.S. Border Patrol

A part of the newly formed Department of Homeland Security, the U.S. Border Patrol, whose members are referred to as agents, are uniformed officers primarily stationed along both the southwest border with Mexico and the northern border with Canada. Border Patrol agents are also assigned to the interior of the country in order to search for illegal immigrants near the nation's borders and are truly the nation's front line defense.

The Border Patrol makes more individual seizures of drugs than any other agency due to their frequency of encounters with illegal aliens attempting to cross the international border with contraband. The agency also has border search authority, which has been delegated to them by ICE. Each year the Border Patrol is responsible for seizing tons of controlled substances, along with hundreds of thousands of illegal aliens attempting to cross the borders illegally.

Federal Aviation Administration

The FAA has a program by which they track lookouts of suspect aircraft across the country that may be involved in moving contraband from one location to another. They also provide lookouts for specific aircraft entering the United States from a foreign country.

Frequently, law enforcement agencies will get court orders to install transponders in suspect aircraft to determine where it is during a drug smuggling investigation. The FAA will monitor these transponders and notify the agency where the aircraft is at any given time.

U.S. Coast Guard

Another agency affected by the creation of the Department of Homeland Security is the U.S. Coast Guard, which makes up the third line of defense of the nation's borders and coastlines. The Coast Guard also makes a significant number of arrests for drug violations due to the frequency of contact with suspect vessels attempting to enter the territorial waters of the United States carrying drugs and other illegal contraband.

Coast Guardsmen can conduct boating safety inspections that often lead to the discovery of contraband. These inspections can take place in territorial waters where the vessel may not be suspected of international smuggling.

The Coast Guard maintains a force of special agents that investigate foreign counter-intelligence matters as well as international smuggling organizations. They also maintain a listing of all contacts made between the Coast Guard and boats in both territorial and international waters. This system may help drug agents in determining the identities of the crewmembers and the whereabouts of a particular vessel if it is suspected of being involved in drug smuggling.

Federal Bureau of Investigation

Because the FBI shares Title 21 (CSA) authority with the DEA, it can initiate drug smuggling investigations. However since the events of September 11, 2001, the FBI has trimmed back the number of agents devoted to drug enforcement investigations in order to use them to investigate terrorist organizations. The FBI still maintains a large presence in the high intensity drug trafficking area task forces (HIDTA) throughout the country. These HIDTA task forces, which comprise of federal, state, and local law enforcement agencies, has been effective in combating drug trafficking in their particular geographical areas.

Military Joint Task Forces (JTFs)

In the late 1980s, the Department of Defense was designated as the lead agency for the detecting and monitoring air and maritime shipments of illegal drugs in transit to the United States. In that regard, a number of JTFs were formed.

JTFs are strategically located around the United States to help law enforcement track smugglers. They also share military equipment with law enforcement agencies when appropriate. Military technology is also deployed to help track vessels during long journeys from one part of the globe to another. This often includes the use of submarines, surface vessels, and satellites. The different military services, especially the National Guard, have intelligence analysts who are often loaned to DEA domestic and international offices, to provide analytical support on specific investigations. These JTFs can also provide training to foreign governments in the identification and apprehension of individuals involved in smuggling.

Since September 11, 2001, many of the JTFs have been diverted to anti-terrorism operations.

U.S. Postal Service

The U.S. Postal Service has a police force that employs drug detection dogs within domestic and international mail centers to screen mail destined for the United States. The Postal Inspection Service will provide inspectors to pose as mail carriers and deliver suspect parcels to addresses in what is called a *controlled delivery* (CD). Upon delivering the package, the recipient will be arrested for possession of the contraband. CDs have been highly effective in identifying members of international drug smuggling organizations operating within the United States (see Chapter16 on controlled deliveries for further details).

Methods of Smuggling

Smugglers use a variety of means to transport illegal drugs and contraband to the United States. They are only limited by their imagination when it comes to methods of concealment. Conveyances of every kind have been used in smuggling via air, land, and sea.

Air

Private aircraft are extensively used due to speed and load capabilities. Extended ranges can be obtained by using auxiliary fuel tanks. Crews and passengers on commercial airlines have been known to smuggle contraband. Baggage handlers, maintenance personnel, and ground crews are often involved with smuggling organizations. Baggage handlers have been known to place contraband into several suitcases that will be spotted by a

Figure 15.2 Container being x-rayed by Bureau of Immigration and Customs Enforcement inspectors. (Courtesy of the Bureau of Immigration and Customs Enforcement.)

baggage handler accomplice who will be unloading the plane. The luggage is then separated from the rest of the plane's cargo without benefit of inspection by ICE.

Land

Anything on wheels can be used to conceal and transport contraband into the United States. Recreational vehicles, cars, and tractor-trailer rigs are frequently used to haul large amounts of drugs. ICE randomly x-rays entire tractor-trailer rigs for hidden contraband (Figure 15.2). Beasts of burden are still used to transport drugs over the rough terrain that still exists along the southwest border of the United States with Mexico. Camels are used extensively in Pakistan, Afghanistan, and Iran to move large amounts of hashish and raw opium to markets in western Europe.

Sea

Smugglers have used anything that floats to smuggle drugs. Pleasure craft with hidden compartments are a long-time favorite. Fishing trawlers, "go-fast" boats, tugboats, and barges are other frequently used vessels that offer huge, multi-ton load capacities.

Smugglers will frequently forge or alter bills of lading and change the seals on containerized cargo shipments in order to disguise the true point of origin for the shipment. A containerized shipment from a drug-source country may initially arrive in a nondrug source port, only to have its bills of lading changed and reshipped to a U.S. port of entry. It is not unusual for a containerized shipment containing drugs or other contraband to take up to

Figure 15.3 Container ship at U.S. port. (Courtesy of the Bureau of Immigration and Customs Enforcement.)

18 months to arrive at its intended destination due to the many stops it may make on the way. Once in the United States or other intended country, the smugglers will often have the shipment transported to a storage facility where it will sit for several more weeks in the event of law enforcement surveillance. They may conduct counter-surveillance hoping to detect the presence of drug or customs agents who may show an interest in the container. By waiting this extra period of time, the smugglers hope to wear out surveillance agents who will then shift to other priorities (Figure 15.3).

Crews aboard cruise ships have long smuggled cocaine and other contraband aboard ships from the Caribbean. Colombian drug traffickers were once discovered with all the parts necessary to assemble a Russian submarine they intended to use for smuggling.

Go-Fast Boats

A frequently encountered method of sea smuggling cocaine into Mexico from Colombia for ultimate delivery into the United States is through the use of *go-fast* boats. These speedboats, which vary from 25 to 40 feet in length, can carry between 2 to 4 tons of contraband. They are modified with additional bladder style fuel tanks and depart from the west coast of Colombia for their journey to Mexico (Figure 15.4).

The smugglers will hire commercial fishing vessels to situate themselves along the route of travel to replenish these go-fast boats with fuel to continue their journey. These *logistical supply vessels* not only serve as floating gas stations, but also act as lookout platforms for maritime law enforcement in the area, and communicate with the crews of the go-fast boats during their cruise.

Figure 15.4 U.S. Customs helicopter encourages go-fast boat to stop. (Courtesy of the Bureau of Immigration and Customs Enforcement.)

When stopped and seized on Mexico's west coast, the crewmembers of these vessels will often deny that the cocaine found on their go-fast was destined for the United States. This denial, absent information from a CI, may result in the U.S. Attorney's Office declining prosecution since a nexus to the United States cannot be established. Without a nexus, there is no crime against the United States. Venue must be established before an arrest or prosecution can occur. Crewmembers must be interviewed or interrogated to determine where the contraband was ultimately intended to arrive.

Drug agents should, at a minimum, check for markings on kilo-size packages that may be identical to previously seized cocaine packages in the United States. The DEA maintains a library of documentation and photographs of previously seized markings on cocaine kilo packages and can provide other expertise.

Methods of Concealment

The following is only a partial listing of devices that have been used by smugglers to conceal drugs or money (Figure 15.5 through Figure 15.9):

- Shoes
- Canned goods
- Surgical implants
- Flower shipments
- Scuba tanks

- False bottom suitcases
- Dead human bodies
- Body cavities
- Surfboards
- Soft drink containers
- Inflated tires
- Artificial limbs
- Diplomatic pouches
- Gasoline tanks
- Live animals
- Hollowed out wood products and lumber
- Strapped to bodies of passengers
- Household good shipments
- Automobile upholstery
- Antiques
- Ice chests

Unwitting Accomplices

Smugglers have been known to solicit the help of people to transport a suitcase or package containing drugs, without alerting them to the presence of the contraband. Often they will say the package is for a relative who will pick it up upon their arrival at the airport or hotel room.

Swallowers

These are smugglers who will swallow small balloons or condoms containing cocaine or heroin. Customs will discover the foreign objects in the stomachs of the smugglers through x-rays and have to wait until nature takes its course to retrieve the evidence. Many smugglers who use this method have died when the balloon or condom bursts inside the stomach wall, causing almost instantaneous death from a drug overdose.

Smugglers' Profile

Successful smugglers possess common traits and skills. They are cleaver, resourceful, and understand organization and management. Above all, they are risk takers. Smuggling is a risky business and the smuggler must face dangers such as being arrested as well as being cheated, betrayed, or killed by accomplices and drug suppliers alike. Besides the vast amounts of cash they

Figure 15.5 U.S. Customs inspector readies to inspect containerized shipment. (Courtesy of the Bureau of Immigration and Customs Enforcement.)

Figure 15.6 U.S. Customs discover 40 kilograms of marijuana in body of car under the back seat. (Courtesy of the Bureau of Immigration and Customs Enforcement.)

Figure 15.7 Concealment devices used by individuals. (Courtesy of the U.S. Drug Enforcement Administration.)

Figure 15.8 A *swallower* is led away by ICE inspectors. (Courtesy of the Bureau of Immigration and Customs Enforcement.)

may earn, boat captains and pilots often engage in the business to seek adventure. They often live the role of adventurers and often have a "big money" lifestyle. They exhibit a beat-the-system attitude and are highly mobile. Many smugglers are highly skilled pilots and sailors who will take precautions such as changing the color, registration, or name of their vessel or airplane to avoid detection. Professional smugglers will have many aliases and have access to

Figure 15.9 Pseudoephedrine tablets concealed in gas tank of car. (Courtesy of the U.S. Drug Enforcement Administration.)

false passports and documents. They sometimes report their passports lost in order to conceal the foreign destinations they have traveled.

After meeting with their drug source of supply in a known drug source country, some smugglers have been known to fly to either Mexico City, Mexico or Vancouver, Canada in order to avoid contact with ICE. They will then take a domestic flight to a border city where they will mail their passport to their residence before crossing over the border on foot to the United States.

Characteristics of Drug Smuggling Organizations

Sophisticated smuggling organizations have operated for years without detection. These organizations possess certain characteristics that may reveal their existence to drug agents.

Possess and Use State-of-the-Art Equipment

Established drug smuggling organizations can earn massive amounts of money from just one successful smuggling operation. Because money is no object when avoiding detection, supervisors, managers, and other decision-makers within the organization will routinely purchase state-of-the-art equipment to facilitate their trade. It is not unusual for them to possess complex navigational equipment, vehicles, boats, and airplanes. When hauling heavy loads of marijuana, only vehicles that have had their suspension systems modified to conceal the heavy load will be used. Heavy-duty six-wheel dually trucks are often used. Many pick-up trucks will be equipped with camper shells with curtained or blacked-out windows to discourage curious onlookers. Recreational vehicles are often purchased or rented to serve as mobile command posts during an off-loading operation. Many will use scanners to monitor police radio transmissions. The use of walkie-talkies and cellular telephones is common.

Well Organized

These smuggling groups are successful because they are well organized and close knit. They recruit people that are known to be involved in criminal activity, specifically drug sales or use, and compartmentalize information to limit the knowledge any one individual smuggler or off-loader may possess. Only a few trusted people will know the identities or even the existence of other members of the drug smuggling organization.

Well-Defined Roles

In a large off-loading operation, each member of the organization will be assigned a specific task in order to remove the drugs as quickly as possible. One group may be assigned to off-load a boat's starboard side, while another is assigned the port side. Others will shuttle the load to awaiting pick-up trucks that will leave immediately upon being loaded so as to not create a caravan from the location. Lookouts are usually deployed for the presence of police or surveillance agents.

Large Number of Members

A smuggling organization investigated by the DEA in Monterey, CA had 62 members identified. They had been in operation for 10 years and used the same Santa Cruz County, CA beach to off-load multi-ton amounts of marijuana on 12 separate occasions. Other off-load sites up and down California's 1000 mile coastline had also been used by this group. The organization's leaders owned some of these sites. The organization was dismantled after a citizen walking on the beach notified the sheriff's department about a fishing trawler being off-loaded by a number of persons. Because this information was passed to the responding uniformed deputies by mouth rather than radio, the suspects were caught completely off guard.

The investigation identified the ultimate source of supply in Thailand along with all members of the organization. Only three members knew more than five others involved in the same scheme due to the compartmentalization of this information.

Use of Private Investigators

Sophisticated smuggling organizations sometimes deploy unscrupulous private investigators to investigate the backgrounds and pending legal matters of current or perspective members of the organization. Some of these private investigators may administer polygraph examinations to insure members are not working for law enforcement or that perspective members are not undercover drug agents. Smugglers know that drug agents will often solicit cooperation and information from recently arrested persons in return for assistance in their legal situation.

Top Legal Help

The prior successes of the drug smuggling organization can sometimes be measured by the quality of private legal counsel retained by them. High-dollar attorneys are frequently used as defense councils for successful drug smuggling organizations.

Drug Smuggling Case Initiation

Drug smuggling investigations can be initiated through a variety of means. The use of CIs is not always possible. Developing good sources of information can alert drug agents to the planning of a smuggling operation. Sources of information specifically for smuggling cases include:

- Boat captains
- Pilots
- Flight service station employees
- Airplane rental agencies and retailers
- Marine suppliers
- Yacht club employees and bartenders
- Harbor masters
- Recreational vehicle rental companies

Methods of Investigating Smuggling Cases

Virtually every investigative technique normally used in criminal investigations will be utilized during a smuggling case.

- Physical surveillance of persons, places, and things
- Electronic surveillance in the form of wire tapes, pen registers, and transponders
- Undercover operations conducted by drug agents and informants
- Grand jury subpoenas and search warrants
- Locating assets
- Witness interviews

Summary

The primary agency responsible for investigating the smuggling of drugs into the United States is the DEA. ICE and other agencies interdict not only drugs, but also many other items of contraband. But when it comes to drugs, the DEA has the primary responsibility. The DEA, ICE, Border Patrol, FAA, U.S. Coast Guard, the FBI, Military JTFs, and the Postal Service work in concert to uncover smuggling operations.

Smugglers are only limited by their imagination when it comes to concealment methods in their trade. Smuggling groups, in order to transport contraband, use anything that can travel over land, in the air, or on the sea. Smugglers use many everyday items to conceal drugs, and many risk death by swallowing drugs in balloons and condoms.

Smugglers are risk takers. They are often adventurers and thrill seekers. They live the big money lifestyle and can easily afford to use state-of-the-art equipment in their craft. Some have used private investigators to ferret out informants and check out undercover agents.

Drug smuggling cases can be initiated by using sources of information that most likely will first detect the activities of smuggling organizations. Some of these include flight service station employees, yacht club employees, and harbor masters. Virtually every investigative technique normally used in criminal investigations will be utilized during smuggling cases.

Controlled Deliveries 16

Definition of Controlled Delivery

A *controlled delivery* (CD) is a proven investigative technique that is used by the Drug Enforcement Administration (DEA) to identify recipients of shipments of drugs and other contraband coming into the United States. The technique is equally effective in both domestic and international settings when a drug-laden package is either mailed or privately delivered from one part of the country or the world to another.

CDs, whether it be international or domestic, require that a law enforcement agency monitor the delivery of the drugs to their intended recipient. Once the delivery is made, the decision can be made to affect an arrest. CDs are one of the few occasions when drug agents will investigate a drug crime without the help of a confidential informant (CI).

Internationally Controlled Delivery Scenario

In an international setting, police in foreign countries routinely seize packages determined to have drugs secreted in them. When it is determined a package is addressed to the United States, the DEA or, in some cases, the Bureau of Immigration and Customs Enforcement (ICE) and the U.S. Postal Inspectors are notified.

When a foreign police agency discovers drugs within a package destined for the United States, they will contact the DEA or the regional security officer directly at the U.S. embassy. The DEA country attaché will direct an agent to immediately commence coordination with the host country counterparts to secure permission for the package to be removed from the country and delivered to the United States for the purpose of a CD.

Many nations are reluctant to allow the removal of such packages, fearing it will become lost or stolen. In many cases the foreign officials do not want their country to develop a reputation for being a supplier of drugs to the United States. Some nations routinely cooperate, others not at all. Once the permission is secured, the package is delivered to the DEA, where a special agent will hand carry it to the United States to maintain a solid chain of custody as evidence.

The DEA or ICE office handling the CD must also coordinate with their offices in the city and state the package is destined for. Drug agents in the United States will begin to determine what type of residence or business exists at the address listed on the package, as well as who lives there, or is associated with the business, and if they have a history of involvement in drug trafficking. The DEA will also coordinate with the local police department to involve them if the matter should later be prosecuted in a state court setting because it does not meet the threshold for federal prosecution.

Methods of Delivery

Many packages with drugs are designed to appear legitimate. Many are sent by international courier services such as DHL or Emery. Others may choose UPS or Federal Express. No matter what courier service is used, their assistance is required to make the delivery. Tracking systems maintained by these couriers can be accessed over the Internet, and any delay in the delivery may cause the recipient to refuse to take delivery of the package fearing law enforcement intervention. Unnecessary delays must be avoided in order to maintain the appearance of normalcy.

When the actual delivery takes place, drug agents will usually pose as an employee of the courier service by driving one of their vehicles while wearing an official uniform and knocking on the door to personally deliver the package to the addressee. In the event there is no answer at the door, an alternative is to leave a written notice from the courier service indicating a delivery was attempted, and that they should telephone their office to reschedule delivery or arrange for the package to be picked up at their offices. The courier will notify the DEA if they have been contacted to make a second delivery attempt.

Before a delivery is attempted, drug agents will often remove all but a small amount of the controlled substance from the package and then reseal it after placing a battery powered electronic alert device inside. Once the recipient opens the package, the alert will transmit a signal to a receiver surveillance agents are monitoring. At that time, agents will quickly serve a previously obtained anticipatory search warrant to recover the package before the suspect discovers the alert device and disposes of the drug evidence.

Figure 16.1 Kilogram quantities of cocaine are sometimes seized during controlled deliveries. (Courtesy of the Drug Enforcement Administration.)

Domestic Controlled Deliveries

Many traffickers use the U.S. Postal Service to transport drugs to various parts of the country. When a CD is going to be attempted using the mail, a postal inspector will dress as a mail carrier and deliver the package to the intended address. Private express courier services are also often used to deliver drugs domestically. Coordination with their security departments will assist in obtaining their cooperation (Figure 16.1).

Mail Drops

Often drug traffickers will list the address where the package is to be delivered as a private post office box. Drug agents are often reluctant to solicit the help of the owner of the business since they have been known to alert their customers about drug agents inquiring about them.

If the owner of the business cooperates with drug agents, he can advise the agents if the customer inquires about any packages delivered to his address. Many recipients will allow the package to remain in their private box for several days before retrieving it, in an attempt to wear down drug agents during any surveillance operation they may be conducting to determine who picks up the package.

With the cooperation of the owner of the private mail drop, drug agents may place a small camera inside to record who opens the mailbox and retrieves the package. Once the package is picked up, agents will usually follow the suspect to see who he meets with and will arrest him before he has a chance to elude surveillance.

Using a Ruse

In one CD investigation conducted by the DEA, the agents seized a package containing SWA heroin and left a note in the private mailbox for the intended recipient. The note said that the writer was an employee of the store and knew what was in the package. The writer went on to say that if the reader of the note wanted to see his package, he should call him at a given telephone number.

The agent received a telephone call from the man and an undercover meeting took place where the agent said that he wanted to buy the drugs in the package and receive more in the future. The agent said he would pay the man upon delivery of a second package. The suspect agreed. During the undercover meeting, the man laid out the heroin distribution operation leading to the identities of other suspects. When a second package arrived, the suspect was arrested and an equal amount of heroin was seized.

Physical Evidence

When a package is seized, the packaging itself becomes physical evidence of the crime. The package needs to be collected and placed in a nondrug evidence property room for evaluation as evidence. A thorough examination of the package may reveal who the sender was. It is highly unlikely, although possible, that the sender will use his actual address as the return address on the package. The package should be examined for latent fingerprints, and if stamps or other items were licked and adhered to the package, it may be possible to obtain saliva for DNA analysis.

Traffickers have been known to visit source countries and then mail a package to themselves using a mail drop. Handwriting analysis of the address on the package should be compared to that of the recipient if it is suspected that he mailed the package to himself or another person living with him. Items sent through domestic courier services can also have handwritten shipping documents examined for handwriting comparison. Other items within the package itself may offer clues to the identity of the sender as well.

Summary

Controlled deliveries, or CDs, have been used by drug law enforcement for years to identify the receivers of drug shipments from either within the country or from foreign addresses. Packages delivered to the addressee can be fitted with electronic alerts to inform drug agents when the package has been opened; an important element in proving the person knew that drugs were contained within the package.

The key to a successful CD is speed. Any delays in the delivery of the package to the addressee can alert the suspect that law enforcement may have seized the package and are in the process of conducting a CD. Modern Internet tracking programs can alert suspects quickly where their packages are, and any unexplained delay may prompt the suspect to refuse to take delivery when it arrives.

Control delivery investigations are one of the few times drug agents will not be working with a CI. They should, however, attempt to solicit the cooperation of any person arrested in order to expand their investigation.

Drug Intelligence

17

Intelligence is much more than mere information. Intelligence is the product of vetted, analyzed, and assessed information that can be applied to make accurate conclusions and take appropriate action. The more intelligence a police organization has, the better equipped it is to solve crime. Small police drug units, as well as organizations devoted entirely to drug law enforcement, benefit from timely intelligence about drug trafficking organizations, their membership, smuggling methods, and prices charged for controlled substances.

Intelligence is gathered by a variety of means, such as surveillance, debriefings, and telephone toll analyses. More on this will be covered later in the chapter. Other intelligence comes in anonymously as raw data that is filed as such to indicate it has not been substantiated. An example of this may be a caller who says his next-door neighbor sells drugs. All intelligence developed should be cataloged and filed for easy retrieval. Most police departments and investigative agencies have computerized retrieval systems that sort intelligence by name, address, telephone number, associates, occupation, date of birth, and the like. This intelligence is usually cross-referenced for easy retrieval.

The DEA has the narcotics and dangerous drug intelligence system (NADDIS). *NADDIS* contains all the above intelligence plus summaries of reports concerning different events. Other DEA systems allow the user access to the FBI's National Crime Information Center, the national law enforcement teletype system, individual states' department of motor vehicles, and other unique databases. The system is designed to provide special agents and intelligence analysts with timely and historical information about an individual and his associates.

The Intelligence Analyst

The intelligence analyst is an important member of the investigative team. They often work for federal, state, and sometimes local law enforcement agencies. In many cases, drug agents perform analytical functions for their own cases. The intelligence analyst role is to study case data to determine the relationships between people and events. Their role is to develop meaning from collected data gathered by drug agents. Analysts also prepare charts and other documents to aid in the understanding of complex investigations. These graphical representations frequently aid in clarifying and enhancing the understanding of the case for drug agents and eventually prosecutors and juries.

Intelligence analysts often provide substantial benefits during an investigation. They can provide new insights and theories of a case that may require further investigation. This analysis often provides for a more efficient and effective investigative process. Intelligence analysts frequently develop comprehensive background information on the known or suspected members of a drug conspiracy; create charts showing the relationships between known or suspected conspirators; perform telephone toll analysis; and create spreadsheets and timelines that aid in the thorough understanding of the case.

Drug trends in a particular country, state, or city can potentially change rapidly. Intelligence analysts conduct studies of the current major drugs of abuse in a given area, their primary source of supply, and identify the primary methods of distribution.

Informant Debriefings

The key to obtaining quality intelligence is through a network of drug informants. Once someone is established as an informant, a drug agent can send him or her on assignments to collect specific intelligence on individuals or whole organizations. The informant is then debriefed by drug agents and, if available, analysts, and the intelligence is documented in reports and entered into a computerized database for future use. The intelligence entered into any database is only as good as the information received. The saying "garbage in, garbage out" accurately describes a drug intelligence program that lacks timely, quality intelligence.

The DEA publishes a Source Debriefing Guide.[1] It is extremely useful in debriefing informants to gain knowledge about specific information on all aspects of drug trafficking. Most informants or suspects that are questioned after their arrest will not know the answer to every question, but through a series of interviews and debriefings, a better picture of a drug trafficking organization emerges. This type of specific questioning works well with defendants during a proffer in which they offer to share information about drug traffickers in return for consideration in their legal matters.

The following general questions, as outlined in the DEA's Source Debriefing Guide, should be asked of a cooperating defendant who is being debriefed for the first time:

1. What illegal drugs have you used, sold, or transported? Are there any brands or trademarks on the drugs?
2. Who is your source of supply? Where is the person located? Where did the person obtain the drugs? Who are his U.S. distributors? Who are the foreign distributors?
3. Who else is involved in the trafficking system?
4. Do you know of any locations where drugs are cultivated, manufactured, processed, or stored?
5. Do you have any knowledge of the smuggling of drugs across the U.S. border? If so, where are the entry points? Do you know of smuggling across other international borders? For end use or transit?
6. Do you have any knowledge of methods used to transport drugs?
7. Describe the method of concealment, type of conveyance, and persons involved in drug smuggling.
8. Are false documents used to conceal the identity of smugglers or couriers? How are documents obtained? How are they falsified, and by whom? What types of documents are used?
9. What are the prices and purity of the drugs upon entering the United States? Do you know prices and purities at other stages of trafficking?
10. Have you ever seen or been told of opium poppy, coca, cannabis, or mescal cultivation in or outside the United States?
11. Do you have any knowledge of heroin, cocaine, hashish oil, crack, or dangerous drug laboratories within or outside the United States?
12. Who finances the drug trafficking operations?
13. How are the drugs paid for? Is the money paid up front, or are the drugs sold on consignment or exchanged for other goods? If in currency, identify it. If payment is in exchange, identify other goods.
14. How are funds to pay for the drugs moved? Cash? Letter of credit? Bank deposits? Bank wire transfer? International checks? Traditional "underground" banking systems?
15. Do you know how or where the proceeds of any drug transaction have been hidden or invested? Who controls laundered drug funds?
16. Do you know the associates or businesses of any drug trafficker?
17. Do you have knowledge of any drug transactions?
18. What types of ledgers, journals, classified ads, computers, bulletin boards, or other documents or mechanisms are used to manage drug transactions? Are codes used?

19. Are you familiar with any other areas of the United States or the world? Describe. Have you ever lived in these areas? When? For how long?
20. Do you know of any other smuggling activity into or out of the United States? Are drugs exchanged for other goods? Do you know of non-U.S. international smuggling activity?
21. Is there an exchange of one drug for another, for example, cocaine for heroin? Are arms being traded for narcotics? Identify the source and recipient of the arms and the drugs.
22. Is there any official corruption involved? Who? Paid by whom? How much? For how long? What major traffickers are they associated with?
23. What is the principle ethnic group involved in the drug activity? What syndicates or organizations, multi-national or national, are involved? Will the traffickers deal outside their group or organization?
24. What languages do you speak?
25. What special skills do you have? Pilot, ham radio operator, chemist, photographer, money launderer, other?
26. Have you ever worked as a CI? For whom? Give dates and current status.
27. Have you been involved in nondrug criminal activity? Give dates of involvement.
28. Have you been confined in prison or any other institution? Give names, dates, locations, and reason for confinement.

Although the topics for these questions are general in nature, they are specific when it comes to who, what, when, where, and why. This same form of questioning can be applied to any drug enforcement topic including clandestine laboratories, smuggling activities, diversion of legitimate drugs, and money laundering activities.

Telephone Subscriber Information

Drug traffickers rely on the telephone as their primary means of communication. In order for a drug organization to thrive, it must communicate with its members at all levels to provide guidance and direction. Telephone service providers, whether for landline or cellular, document these telephone calls. Landline telephone companies only document toll, or long distance calls; however, every call made on a cellular service is documented. These records are vital in expanding drug investigations by identifying other members of the drug trafficking organization. When conducting undercover operations, phone usage tends to increase as the time for the delivery of drugs nears.

Drug agents frequently learn the cellular and residential telephone numbers of a targeted trafficker from a CI. The informant may not know the true identity of the trafficker, but the telephone number will assist greatly in this regard. Agents and analysts may also query the landline or cell phone companies for a list of all phones associated with a specific phone, residence, or individual. Armed with the power of a subpoena, court order, or search warrant, drug agents and analysts routinely request that the telephone service provider furnish them with the name of the subscriber of a given telephone number, where the phone is installed, credit information on the subscriber, all telephone numbers associated with the subscriber's account, and the person or business paying the bill.

A further check of the individual subscriber can often reveal prior criminal histories and involvement in drug trafficking. When the suspect's long distance tolls or cellular telephone bills are requested, the telephone numbers that he dialed are revealed. Subscriber and toll information on each of these telephone numbers will reveal the names and addresses the subject is calling and exactly when these calls were made. The names of the subscribers can be further queried through various databases to include open sources of information, in order to further identify the subscriber and any potential users of the phone. These databases can also reveal persons who have previously used that address, neighbors of addressee, etc. This information is important when one of the persons dialed by the drug trafficker denies any knowledge of the person under investigation. Denying knowing the person is fruitless when agents prove that the main suspect has received numerous telephone calls from his phone. Thorough investigations require that analysts or agents obtain the subscribers of each telephone number called by the primary target of the investigation, as well as the telephone numbers dialed by each of the persons they called in the past several months. The amount of phone calls made to and from the primary target's phone often reveals the importance of these other individuals to the drug trafficking organization.

Drug traffickers will frequently attempt to disguise themselves as the subscriber of a cellular telephone number by obtaining telephone service from independent mom-and-pop venders who do not, or will not, check identification or require credit background checks. Many, but certainly not all of these outlets, knowingly provide services to known drug traffickers. Other drug traffickers use prepaid cellular telephones and phone cards to further disguise their illegal activities.

Telephone Toll Analysis

One of the most important tools of a drug agent or intelligence analyst is the analysis of telephone tolls of phones linked to drug traffickers and their associates. Through this painstaking analysis, with the help of dedicated computer programs, analysts and agents can deduce associates of the trafficker, the recipients of the drugs, distribution points, and where the drug proceeds are destined.

After obtaining the cellular and landline toll numbers called from the main suspect's telephones, the intelligence analyst will ask the subscribers for those numbers. In the next step, the analyst will then ascertain the tolls and cellular telephone numbers these people have called. In the final step, the analyst will request the subscribers of these telephones. From the telephone numbers gathered, the agent or analyst can conduct an analysis of the numbers and their subscribers to see who is calling whom and how frequently. An increase in calling activity may be apparent just before, during, and immediately after a drug transaction has taken place. The frequency of the calls between numbers may be a clue to the identities of leaders, managers, and supervisors of a drug conspiracy. Through this process, the analyst can determine who knows each other, and there is a good chance all members of the drug criminal organization will be identified.

Intelligence analysts will also obtain driver license photos, criminal histories, immigration files, and other indices for each of the subscribers. Each telephone number called should be handled as an investigative lead that can potentially identify other members of the criminal conspiracy.

Wiretaps

Investigations that incorporate the use of monitoring telephone conversations obtain real time intelligence about the internal workings of drug organizations. Drug agents who obtain court-ordered wire intercept authority enhance their chances of identifying other members of the criminal conspiracy, as well as learning of future drug transactions, storage facilities, and the future plans of traffickers. Federal authorities have long used wiretaps to expand their ongoing investigations, and many state police organizations have recently been given the statutory authority to implement this type of investigative technique. The prerequisites for a particular jurisdiction must be met before such authority is granted. The requirements can be arduous, and agents must closely coordinate with their prosecutors to obtain such permission.

Many drug traffickers assume they are constantly under government surveillance. If drug agents know that the target of a potential wiretap investigation disciplines himself to not talk about drugs on the telephone, or frequently changes cellular telephone service providers, this must be weighed against the time, expense, and manpower requirements required to perform such an operation.

Conducting wiretaps require specially trained agents who possess specialized equipment in order to capture and record the conversations being recorded. Start up costs and manpower requirements to conduct wiretaps often prevent many law enforcement agencies from conducting them. When a smaller agency has a viable candidate as the target of a wiretap, they should coordinate with state investigators or the DEA for help and guidance.

Summary

Intelligence is much more than mere information. It is the product of vetted, analyzed, and assessed information that can be applied to make accurate conclusions and take appropriate action. The more intelligence any investigative unit possesses, the more effective it is. Drug intelligence is gathered in various ways including the debriefing of CIs/sources of information and the capturing of telephone numbers called by drug trafficking operations. Telephone long-distance toll information has proven to be an effective way of gathering information leading to the identities of other members of the trafficking organization. Analyzing these telephone numbers can lead to not only co-conspirators, but also the source of drugs as well as customers, money launders, and other facilitators.

References

1. Source Debriefing Guide, U.S. Department of Justice, Drug Enforcement Administration.

Asset Forfeiture and Money Laundering

18

Federal Civil and Criminal Forfeitures

To take the profit out of the drug business, federal and many state law enforcement agents have the lawful authority to seize property, money, and tools used to facilitate drug trafficking and money laundering, as well as many other specific crimes such as customs, explosives, and counterfeit violations. It has become an especially effective weapon against drug traffickers and those who launder their illegally gotten gains. Money, vehicles, real estate, and other items can be seized federally either through civil or criminal forfeiture proceedings.

The principal purposes of forfeiture laws is to deter drug trafficking by depriving criminals of the profits of their criminal activities and weaken criminal enterprises by removing funding of the crime. Another purpose is to enhance cooperation among federal, state, and local law enforcement agencies by sharing the proceeds of drug traffickers with those agencies that participated in the investigation that led to the seizure of the assets. However, the most important reasons for federal seizure laws are to promote drug law enforcement and deter drug crime. The federal program designed to seize drug trafficker assets and share them with state and local law enforcement agencies is known as the *equitable sharing program*.

The concept of asset forfeiture law originated in American jurisprudence during the Revolutionary War period when the young nation confiscated tea and other commodities that were smuggled into the country to avoid paying customs duties. The ships that smuggled these goods were seized by the government as well. The same concept applies to civil forfeiture proceedings today.

By way of example, drug agents conduct undercover meetings with a drug trafficker to arrange for the purchase of a quantity of drugs indicative of resale. In other words, the quantity of drugs could not be construed as an amount for personal use. After several undercover meetings, the trafficker delivers the drugs to the agent in a privately owned vehicle, and he is immediately arrested. Besides making the arrest, drug agents have the duty to confiscate the trafficker's automobile because it was used in the *facilitation of a drug crime*. After adjudication, the vehicle can later either be placed in service of the law enforcement agency or sold to generate money that is deposited into an asset forfeiture fund for drug investigation expenses and to pay confidential informants (CIs). Vehicles seized by local law enforcement organizations through federal forfeiture procedures are either returned to the police agency for their use or sold. The money from the sale of the vehicle is given to the agency for future use in drug enforcement.

In the above example, no mention is made of the vehicle having a lien on it from a bank lender, or if the vehicle was borrowed from the owner who had no idea that it was going to be used in a drug deal. Further, whether or not the suspect was convicted of the drug crime is not addressed. Under the original concept of the law, and, until recently, under federal law, these particulars made no difference. The law, in its purest form, allows federal agents to seize these items without regard to ownership, because the item, not a person, had committed the wrong, and to prevent it from happening again, it is subject to seizure. The moment the property is used in the crime, or purchased with proceeds from drug trafficking, the item becomes property subject to seizure by the U.S. government. A conviction of the suspect is not always required; however, agents must develop *probable cause* that the item was used in a drug crime, or the money came as a result of drug sales. In fact, the suspect could be acquitted, but his vehicle would still be subject to civil forfeiture proceedings if the probable cause standard is met. Even foreign commercial airliners that bring drugs into the United States with the knowledge or consent of the pilot in command can and have been seized by federal drug agents.

Differences between the law, and the policy of the individual agency can be substantial. These policies differ between federal and state law enforcement agencies, but they have always taken into account the possibility of an *innocent owner*. Until the turn of this century, under federal law, the burden of proof was on the innocent owner to show he did not have any knowledge his vehicle was being used to facilitate a drug deal. Federal law now requires this burden be placed on the agency involved in the confiscation.

Even real property, e.g., houses, commercial buildings, ranches, farms, etc., are subject to seizure if purchased with drug proceeds or used to facilitate a drug crime. Examples are a marijuana cultivator who uses his land to grow a crop he intends to sell and a homeowner who takes compensation from drug traffickers to allow them to use the house to conduct meetings to discuss future smuggling operations.

Lien holders also have a legitimate claim to have the confiscated items returned to them as innocent owners, and these claims are consistently honored. Most policies provide that there be a certain percentage of equity in the property before initiating forfeiture procedures. If the drug dealer owes more on the car than it is worth, the lien holder will most likely be awarded the vehicle by the drug agency. If there is a substantial amount of equity in the vehicle, the balance of the loan is usually paid off from the asset forfeiture fund, and the vehicle is either placed into service or sold at auction to replenish the fund.

Federal and state drug enforcement agencies have seized billions of dollars in recent years. Many assets seized by federal agencies are shared with state counterparts and are used to purchase equipment and provide overtime payments for drug agents. The DEA now seizes, on average, enough money and assets to almost equal its annual budget, making it essentially a cost-free agency.

There are two ways for drug agents to have property forfeited, either through civil or criminal forfeiture proceedings.[1] There is no general forfeiture law in the United States. Unless there is a specific law that addresses the forfeiture of property that was used or gained from a certain crime, there can be no federal forfeiture.

Civil forfeiture proceedings can either be done through *administrative* or *judicial* procedures. The value of the property generally determines which method of civil forfeiture will be used. Civil administrative forfeitures apply only where the property has a value less than $500,000 except real property, which must be forfeited judicially. Automobiles, boats, or planes used to import, export, transport, or store any controlled substances; or any monetary instrument as defined in 31 U.S. Code § 5312(a)(3) are forfeited under civil administrative forfeiture proceedings.

Judicial Forfeitures

Civil forfeitures, either judicial or administrative, are actions *in rem*, or against the property, since the government contends it is tainted because it is the fruits of criminal conduct, the property is traceable to criminal proceeds, or the property was used to facilitate or otherwise was involved in a drug offense. Drug agents have a 90-day limit to take legal action against the property once it has been seized.

The government must establish that the property is subject to forfeiture action by meeting a *preponderance of the evidence* standard, not the *beyond a reasonable doubt* standard used in a criminal trial.[2]

A civil forfeiture can be conducted even if the owner of the property is a fugitive, has died, or is unknown. There is no requirement to convict the owner or anyone else of any crime in order to initiate civil forfeiture proceedings. The government bears the burden, by a preponderance of the evidence, to demonstrate either that the property is subject to forfeiture, or that the owners had knowledge of the criminal activity that led to the forfeiture; in other words, that they are not *innocent owners* in that they have given permission for their property to be used in the crime. An example of an innocent owner might be someone who loaned his automobile to a friend to visit a sick relative, but instead the friend transported drugs in the vehicle and delivered them to an undercover agent. Even if an undercover agent suggests to the trafficker that he deliver the drugs in his Mercedes instead of his Toyota, the vehicle can be seized since it was used to facilitate the crime.

All civil forfeiture actions are entirely separate from any criminal prosecutions connected to the property. The civil forfeiture action cannot be joined with a criminal prosecution. Normally, a civil forfeiture is completed only after the related criminal prosecution because the civil forfeiture is commonly stayed during the course of any related criminal prosecution.

Administrative Forfeitures

By far the most common, administrative civil forfeiture proceedings make up the bulk of seizures conducted by drug agents under the provisions of Title 21 U.S. Code § 881. The primary provisions of this statute are:

1. Conveyances (§ 881(a)(4)). All conveyances, including aircraft, vehicles, or vessels, which are used, or are intended for use, to transport, or in any manner facilitate the transportation, sale, receipt, possession, or concealment of property described in paragraph (1), (2), or (9).
2. Proceeds (§ 881(a)(6)). All moneys, negotiable instruments, securities, or other things of value furnished or intended to be furnished by any person in exchange for a controlled substance or listed chemical in violation of this subchapter, all proceeds traceable to such an exchange, and all moneys, negotiable instruments, and securities used or intended to be used to facilitate any violation of this subchapter.
3. Real Property (§ 881(a)(7)). All real property, including any right, title, and interest (including any leasehold interest) in the whole of any lot or tract of land and any appurtenances or improvements, which is used, or intended to be used, in any manner or part, to commit, or to facilitate the commission of, a violation of this subchapter punishable by more than one year's imprisonment.

The secondary provisions* of the statute are:

1. Drug Paraphernalia (§ 881(a)(8)) (as defined in 21 U.S. Code § 863)
2. Firearms (§ 881(a)(11)) used or intended to be used to facilitate the transportation, sale, receipt, possession, or concealment of controlled substances or raw materials, products, and equipment of any kind used or intended for use in manufacturing, compounding, processing, delivering, importing or exporting any controlled substances or listed chemical and any proceeds traceable to such property.
3. Controlled Substances (§§ 881(a)(1) and (8)) that have been illegally manufactured, distributed, dispensed, acquired, or possessed.
4. Raw Materials, Products, Equipment (§§ 881(a)(2) and (a)(9)) used or intended to be used in illegally manufacturing, compounding, processing, delivering, importing, or exporting any controlled substance or listed chemical and listed chemicals, drug manufacturing equipment, tableting machines, encapsulating machines, and gelatine capsules, which have been or are intended to be illegally imported, exported, manufactured, possessed, distributed, dispensed, or acquired.
5. Containers (§ 881(a)(3)) used or intended for use as a container for property identified in categories #3 and 4 (except containers used or intended for use only in the possession of a controlled substances) except where the container qualifies as drug paraphernalia.
6. Plants (§ 853(a)(1)) from which controlled substances in schedules I and II may be derived, which have been planted or cultivated in violation of federal drug law, or of which the owners or cultivators are unknown, or which are wild growths.

Administrative seizures only require the government to have a preponderance of evidence to believe that a conveyance or other item was either a proceed of drug trafficking or was used to facilitate a drug crime before these item(s) can be seized. An example is a trafficker delivering drugs to an undercover agent or informant in a "borrowed" vehicle that also contains a large amount of cash. If the owner of the property takes no action, the item(s) are automatically forfeited to the government. However, if the owner of the conveyance or property contests the seizure and provides a *cost and claim bond*, the matter is elevated to a civil forfeiture proceeding and the government must again show that the preponderance of evidence is that he was not an "innocent" owner as he claims.

* None of the listed "secondary provisions" includes a statutory "innocent owner" defense.

In civil proceedings, hearsay evidence is not allowed, and drug agents may have to produce a knowledgeable confidential informant to testify in the matter. Police agencies must weigh the exposure of a credible informant in open court against the value of the property in question.

If the property owner does not provide a cost and claim bond, but instead files a *petition for remission* with the DEA claiming he is an innocent owner, a special agent will investigate the facts and the DEA chief counsel will be the deciding official of whether or not the property should be returned to the owner. A vast majority of petitions for remission are rejected, and the property is forfeited to the government.

Policy Considerations

As shown, the most common instrumentalities of drug crimes are listed in these statutes. Drug agents frequently seize vehicles, money, and real property that is either a proceed of drug trafficking, or used in the commission of the crime. State and local law enforcement agencies should note that when they refer a seizure action to the DEA for federal asset forfeiture, policy might preclude the seizure if the value of the property does not meet the threshold amount for a particular federal judicial district, or if there is an existing duplicate state forfeiture law. However, the DEA commonly adopts bank accounts, money, and property seizures made by state and local agencies, even though the DEA did not participate in the investigation.

The DEA's policy of adopting a state or local law enforcement agency seizure includes the following:

- The state drug law violated is also a federal violation.
- Federal law provides for the forfeiture of the property in question.
- The object of the adoption must meet the monetary thresholds the DEA and the U.S. Attorney's Office has established at the time of the seizure. Currently, in most cases, vehicles must have $2500 in equity or value, vessels and aircraft must have $5000 in equity or value, and real property must have greater than $10,000 in equity or 20% of equity of the appraised value.
- All other property, e.g., currency, monetary instruments, bank accounts, or jewelry must be valued at least $1000.

State and local law enforcement agencies are advised to consult with their local DEA office to determine the current policy on adopted seizures. The policy is designed to foster cooperation between federal and local law enforcement agencies. Many state and local agencies refer seizures to the DEA simply because their own state forfeiture laws are weak in comparison to the federal statutes. The FBI also has the ability to adopt seizures made by state and local law enforcement.

It should also be noted that unless waived, the DEA automatically takes 20% of the net value of the property being seized as part of an administrative fee. This money is used to cover administrative costs associated with the seizure, and it is deposited into a fund for future drug enforcement operations.

State and local law enforcement agencies must submit a completed form DAG-71 to the DEA, along with all police reports that clearly articulate the probable cause for the seizure, within 60 days of the federal adoption or when the property was seized. The DEA then opens a separate case file that is submitted to the U.S. Attorney's Office for action.

Notice

In administrative forfeiture actions, the DEA must provide *notice* within 60 days from the seizure date unless the government files a civil complaint; or names the seized property in a criminal indictment. Notice is usually accomplished through the publishing of a description of the property that was seized in a national publication, such as the *Wall Street Journal.* In cases where the DEA has adopted the seizure from a state or local law enforcement agency, notice must be sent within 90 days of the seizure. Failure in being timely in providing notice to the owner of the property to be seized will result in the property being returned, although, in some cases, the property can be seized again. If the owner of the property is incarcerated, notice must be provided to the prisoner via U.S. mail to the facility in which he is housed.

Criminal Forfeiture Procedures

Criminal forfeiture is an action *in personam*, or personally against property of a criminal defendant. As with civil forfeiture, the property is tainted because it is the proceeds of criminal behavior or is the proceeds of drug trafficking, or the property was used to facilitate or somehow was involved in the drug crime.

Federal prosecutors can seize property used in the drug crime by indicting the property as well as the defendant in the criminal matter, eliminating the need to have a separate civil action. The major disadvantage to criminal forfeiture proceedings is that the defendant must be convicted. If the defendant is acquitted, there can be no criminal forfeiture.

21 U.S. Code § 853 governs criminal forfeiture:

1. Scope of Forfeiture
    a. Proceeds (§ 853(a)(1)). Any property — any real property or tangible or intangible personal property — constituting or derived

from any proceeds the person obtains directly or indirectly, as a result of a drug offense of conviction.

   b. Facilitating property (§ 853(a)(2)). Any property — any real property or tangible or intangible personal property — used, or intended for use, in any manner or part, to commit, or to facilitate the commission of a drug offense of conviction.
   c. Continuing criminal enterprise (CCE) Property (§ 853(a)(3)). Any interest in, claim against, and property or contractual rights affording a source of control over the CCE.*
2. Statutory exemptions from forfeiture (21 U.S. Code § 853(n)).
   a. The interest of any nondefendant third-party owner who establishes that, at the time the offense of conviction was committed, his interest in the property was superior to that of the defendant.
   b. The interest of any nondefendant third-party owner who acquired an interest in the property after the offense of conviction was committed and who establishes that he is a bona fide purchaser for value who was, at the time of the purchase, reasonably without cause to believe that the property was subject to forfeiture.

Advantages of Criminal Forfeitures

There are many advantages to criminal forfeitures, including receiving a judgment against the defendant for the value of the property acquired during the conduct of drug trafficking even if the property was either destroyed, transferred to an innocent owner, or is somehow or otherwise unavailable. Convicted codefendants are equally liable for satisfying any money judgment of forfeiture. The prosecutor may enforce its money judgment of forfeiture against the deep pockets in a conspiracy. Convicted defendants can also be compelled to return assets held out of the country to satisfy the criminal forfeiture judgment. This provision is unavailable to the prosecutor in civil forfeiture actions. If the defendant is convicted for drug conspiracy or CCE, the law allows full forfeiture of the indicted property.

Equitable Sharing Program

State and local law enforcement agencies are encouraged to seize drug proceeds from traffickers in order to take the profit out of the crime. Currently, the U.S. Justice Department and Treasury Department manage federal asset

* Applies only to persons convicted of continuing criminal enterprise (CCE) offense under 21 U.S.C. § 848.

forfeiture programs that include other agencies such as the Department of Agriculture, Postal Inspection Service, Food and Drug Administration, and the Coast Guard.

Those state and local law enforcement agencies that directly participated in a drug investigation that resulted in the seizure of forfeited assets can request a share of the assets seized during an investigation in which a federal agency participated. The seized money or assets (which can be sold) that is returned to the state or local agency must be used for drug enforcement purposes. In many cases, even the expenses for investigators overtime can be reimbursed to the state or local agency.

This is particularly true if the state or local agency participated in an investigation designated as an *organized crime drug enforcement task force* (OCDETF) case. OCDETF is a Justice Department program that started in 1982. The program strives to dismantle large-scale drug trafficking organizations using the combined manpower and resources of federal, state, and local law enforcement agencies. The assets seized from these investigations are shared with the participating agencies, including some manpower overtime expense reimbursements.

The DEA maintains many offices that are manned by *task force officers* who, when deputized as a federal agent, receive training and the same authority DEA special agents enjoy. The state and local law enforcement agencies employing these officers are eligible to share the assets seized during any investigation conducted by the task force. Their agencies agree to the sharing formula that exists, and the agency head must sign a federal equitable sharing agreement that is valid for 3 years.

Those agencies participating in an OCDETF investigation submit an annual certification report that is due 60 days after the end of the federal fiscal year, as well as a federal equitable sharing agreement that is valid for 3 years. The application for sharing the assets seized is made via the DAG 71 form, which can be obtained at any DEA office.

Determining Who Gets What

Sharing assets is based on the *net* amount of money and property seized during the course of the investigation minus the 20% held by the DEA. The shared amount is calculated by the degree of direct participation by the state or local law enforcement agency. This calculation takes into account the number of man-hours expended during the course of the investigation. Qualitative factors are considered when a particular agency either initiated the investigation, or provided unique or indispensable assistance. An example of this may be an investigator playing a key undercover role, or controlling the informant who provided the initial information.

Depending on the amount of money to be shared, various decision makers come into play. DEA group supervisors, resident agents in charge, or special agents in charge sometimes make decisions on administrative seizures valued under $1,000,000. Amounts over that are referred to the Deputy Attorney General of the United States. On judicial forfeitures under $1,000,000, the U.S. Attorney's Office will make the final determination with input from the DEA. Judicial seizures over $1,000,000 are referred to the Deputy Attorney General.

Permissible Uses of the Money

State and local agencies must agree that the money they receive from the program will be used exclusively for law enforcement purposes. This includes activities that will enhance future investigations, law enforcement operations, training, equipment, and facilities. Money can also be used for drug education and awareness programs.

Money received from the program cannot be used for nonlaw enforcement expenses such as parks and recreation or deposited into a general fund. The uses of the money must be specified in the submitted DAG-71 form.

Seized funds can be used to fund the first year salary for new or temporary positions. They can also be used for the salary of an officer who replaces the officer assigned to the DEA managed state and local task force. Further, the funds may be used to pay the salary of an officer assigned to nontraditional functions such as the *Drug Abuse Resistance Education*, or DARE program, as well as other expressly authorized federal matching share programs and grants. The money cannot be used to supplant appropriated funds.

Up to 15% of the funds can be used for community-based drug abuse treatment, drug and crime prevention education, housing, and job skills programs if approved by the chief law enforcement officer of the affected state or local government.

Further information on federal asset forfeitures can be obtained from the Asset Forfeiture and Money Laundering Section of the U.S. Department of Justice, 1400 New York Avenue, NW, Washington, D.C. 20530 (202) 514-1263, or by e-mail: criminal.division@usdoj.gov. This e-mail address is linked to the criminal division's website: www.usdoj.gov/criminal/afmls.html.

Money Laundering

Money laundering is simply the steps drug traffickers take to make illegally gotten gains appear to come from legitimate sources. The steps they sometimes take, however, cannot be simply described. All drug money that is laundered is subject to federal seizure.

Drug agents need to understand that major drug trafficking organizations have firmly entrenched themselves in the United States and anywhere in the world drug sales flourish. These organizations devote a major portion of their energies in moving vast amounts of money out of the United States to foreign countries. Many countries including the Cayman Islands, Panama, United Arab Emirates, Singapore, Switzerland, and others have become havens for these drug proceeds, many of which have bank secrecy laws protecting account information. Once money is deposited into a foreign bank, frequently in the name of a fictitious or *shelf company* these proceeds can then be wire transferred to the United States and elsewhere to be spent as seemingly legitimate funds. A shelf company is one that exists only on paper. Unscrupulous attorneys attempt to show legitimacy of a company that does not produce goods, services, or income. They exist only in a binder maintained on the shelf at the attorney's office. These laundered funds are often invested in real estate, failing cash businesses, commercial property, and the like to be used to further launder money for drug organizations.

Money can also either be physically smuggled out of the country or moved through well-established banking systems and other means. As drug law enforcement becomes aware of the methods used by these drug organizations, they quickly change to more diverse and imaginative ways of moving the money. Drug agents must work within established guidelines and deal with the bureaucracies in the banking industry throughout the world to combat this crime; however, drug money launderers operate as though the world is seamless and without borders. This chapter will explain how some organizations have been highly successful in moving drug proceeds out of the country undetected, as well as methods of operation that exist in the 21st century.

Methods of Investigation

The basic law enforcement techniques for financial investigations are identical to those used in drug enforcement. Undercover, surveillance, informants, electronic monitoring, and use of intelligence are all methods used in both arenas. The only true difference is that financial investigations focus on the money, whereas unsophisticated traditional drug investigations only focus on the contraband. Drug agents need to strive to focus on both in order to be more effective against either large or small drug trafficking organizations.

Assets vs. Liability

Drug agents can request the Internal Revenue Service (IRS) to conduct what is known as an *assets versus liability* study of a particular drug trafficker. The

IRS will review past tax returns, and based on declared income, as evidenced by filed tax returns, will determine if the filer is living within his or her means. By way of example, a person files tax returns documenting that he or she has earned $50,000 in the past 5 calendar years; an investigation is conducted that reveals the filer lives in a home that is valued at $1,000,000 and drives several vehicles that collectively cost over $100,000. The IRS will calculate whether a person earning $50,000 can possibly afford such expenses, and if they cannot, conclude that the taxpayer obviously has other sources of income (probably drug proceeds) not reported on their federal income tax return. Filing a false income tax return is a felony, and the person can be prosecuted in federal court. Often the IRS can bring a trafficker to justice with much less time and effort than drug agents spend on the same violator.

Follow the Money

The focus of any money laundering investigation is the money. Drug agents know that if they can effectively follow the money in any given organization, they will end up at the top or near the top management of the group.

In any organization, whether it be a Fortune 500 company, the Sicilian mafia, or a large-scale drug cartel, a disproportionate amount of the money always goes to the top or head of the organization. Drug agents need to understand that money is evidence, it is intelligence, it is an investigative tool, and money is a liability for traffickers. It is the reason why drug traffickers are in the business.

Federally, money laundering is a separate crime itself in addition to being a part of a larger drug conspiracy. Money laundering statutes carry heavy penalties, and the money itself is subject to federal forfeiture procedures. The two most frequently used federal statutes against money launderers are:

- 18 U.S. Code 1956 — Laundering of monetary instruments. This is a specific element crime where drug agents need to prove that the defendant knew the financial transaction involved the proceeds of some form of unlawful activity, e.g., drug trafficking.
- 18 U.S. Code 1957 — Engaging in monetary transactions in property derived from specified unlawful activity. Here the specific unlawful activity can be drug trafficking or many other crimes related to drug trafficking.

Drug agents have the task of convincing juries that those engaged in money laundering were disguising the actual source of the income and that they knew, or should have known, that the money derived from the sale of drugs.

Typical Exchanges of Money

Many drug trafficking organizations are made up of hundreds of individuals who make up *cells* within the organization throughout the country. When a substantial amount of drug proceeds is accumulated and needs to be moved to the drug organization's home country, a chain of events takes place to move the money as well as isolate those involved from being identified by drug law enforcement.

A home or apartment may be used as a money stash house that contains hundreds of thousands of dollars, and possibly a million dollars or more. The cell member charged with the security of the money will typically receive an electronic page with a code number signifying who to call, or he will receive a cellular telephone call from a mid-level manager within the organization. The manager will instruct the member of the money-laundering cell to take a specific amount of money to a certain location at a particular time and meet with another cell member he does not know. These meetings typically take place in a public parking lot of a business or shopping mall.

The two men will park side-by-side and exchange the keys to their vehicles. The man who is to receive the money will drive away in the other man's car back to his nearby money stash house, leaving his own car with the man behind. He will place the money in the vehicle, usually hidden inside common items like a laundry detergent box or gym bag. He will immediately return to the parking lot where they will again exchange keys and each drive away. This method further keeps the money stash house and the participant's identities secret. The man who received the money may now add this currency to a larger load being readied for a bulk shipment out of the country, or it may be deposited in a bank for wire transfer to a foreign bank account.

Money Laundering Methods

There are four basic methods of money laundering: bulk shipments, financial institutions, nonfinancial, and underground banking system.

Bulk Shipments

To move money out of the country, traffickers may simply drive over the border, secret it in cargo, or use couriers who smuggle currency by attaching it to their person or packing it in their baggage (Figure 18.1). When smuggling U.S. currency out of the country, drug agents need to be aware of how much weight and bulk there is when a large amount of money is involved. As an example, each U.S. note weighs 1 gram. Thus, 1 kilogram, or 1000 grams (2.2 pounds) of \$20 bills equals \$20,000; 1 kilogram of \$100 bills equals

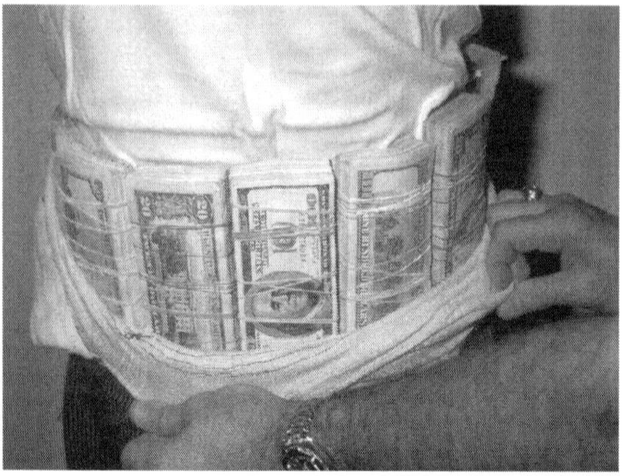

Figure 18.1 U.S. Customs seizes drug money proceeds from a smuggler. (Courtesy of the Bureau of Immigration and Customs Enforcement.)

$100,000. Fifty kilograms of $20 bills equals $1,000,000; if it were $100 bills, it would equal $5,000,000. One hundred kilograms of $20 bill notes equal $2,000,000; $100 notes would equal $10,000,000. A stack of $100 bills hardly larger than a ream of photocopy paper can contain as much as $300,000. It is not unusual for drug agents to seize $1,000,000 or more at one time from drug traffickers in any city in the United States (Figure 18.2 and Figure 18.3).

Financial Institutions

Drug traffickers and money launderers have long circumvented established reporting requirements set by the federal government. Federal law requires persons entering or leaving the country with more than $10,000 in cash or negotiable instruments, to declare them to the U.S. Bureau of Immigration

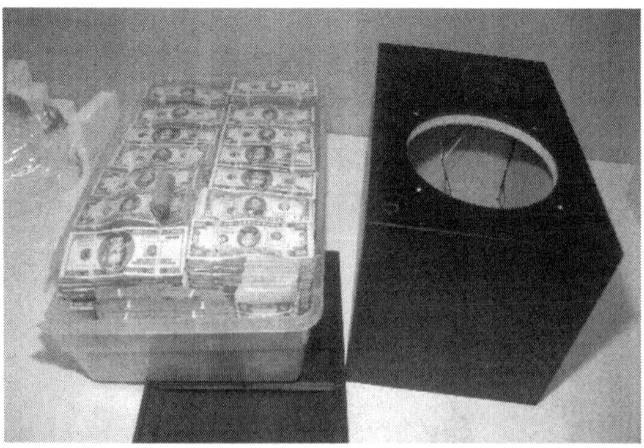

Figure 18.2 Currency found inside speakers about to leave the country. (Courtesy of the Bureau of Immigration and Customs Enforcement.)

Figure 18.3 Currency concealed in walls of ice chest. (Courtesy of the Bureau of Immigration and Customs Enforcement.)

and Customs Enforcement. A *cash transaction report* or *CTR* is also required for anyone who deposits in a bank or makes a purchase with over $10,000 in cash. Even deposits less than $10,000 that appear suspicious or an obvious attempt to circumvent the reporting requirement requires a suspicious activity report (SAR). Some businesses are exempted from this reporting requirement.

Money launderers have been known to come up with innovative ways to circumvent the reporting requirements. They have paid corrupt bank employees a percentage of the cash they take there to be deposited in amounts under $10,000. They have hired scores of people, known as *smurfs*, to make deposits under $10,000 to a specific bank account. This type of activity is known as structuring. Smurfs are known to be employed to purchase postal money orders, bank checks, and to send Western Union wire money transfers in varying amounts just under $10,000 to avoid mandatory reporting requirements (Figure 18.4).

Nonfinancial Institutions

Many different nonfinancial businesses are used to launder drug money, including some precious metal companies where traffickers will purchase gold coins or platinum bars to smuggle out of the country and later trade them for cash. Other examples are:

- Jewelry companies sell expensive diamonds and jewelry that can later be sold on the wholesale market.
- Legal gambling casinos are required to document a player's large winnings for tax purposes as income, when in reality there was none.
- Corrupt car dealers will sell automobiles for cash and register them in fictitious names for drug traffickers.

Figure 18.4 Money launderer being arrested by DEA special agents. (Courtesy of the U.S. Drug Enforcement Administration.)

- Real estate agents may arrange for traffickers to purchase properties in fictitious names, or knowingly allow someone to be the *straw purchaser* for the transaction. A straw purchaser is someone who is paid to pose as the buyer of a piece of real property. He also allows his name to be listed on the title of the real property, even though he has no financial interest or investment in it. Straw purchasers are used primarily to disguise whose money is actually being used to purchase the property.
- Mortgage companies may take cash or numerous money orders as payment for real estate.
- Money order/check cashing services will take cash for payment of money orders that smurfs can later deposit in banks.
- Some travel agencies will knowingly sell airline tickets in fictitious names to traffickers and will take cash in payment.
- Failing businesses are often used as fronts for money launderers to report huge profits on business tax forms in an effort to disguise the true source of income.
- Any business that deals in cash such as barber shops, beauty parlors, and automobile repair shops have the potential of being used by drug traffickers to launder illegal drug proceeds.
- Western Union offices take cash and will wire transfer it to another office for a fee.
- Post offices sell numerous money orders that are purchased in cash making the movement of money easier and much less bulky.

Underground Banking Networks

Terrorists and drug traffickers of Chinese, Indian, and Pakistani ethnicity all practice a systematic method of removing money from one country to another called the *Hawala underground banking network*. It works much the same way a money wire transfer is conducted by a company such as Western Union. It works this way: drug traffickers or terrorists in one country want to move a large sum of money to their homeland or a third country. They provide a trusted member of their ethnic community with the money they want transferred to another country. That person will provide them with a chit receipt, and then telephone or fax instructions to their contacts in the other country to provide the sum of money to the customer's contact when he arrives. The person requesting the transaction pays a fee, usually a percentage, for the service. These businesses exist based on trust or family ties to the drug trafficker or terrorist.

Summary

Asset forfeiture laws are designed to take the profit out of drug crimes and to deter people from becoming involved in drug trafficking. All money, property, and other assets accumulated or used by drug traffickers and their organizations is subject to federal seizure. These seizures can be made two different ways: civilly through judicial and administrative procedures, or criminally in conjunction with a criminal indictment.

The money derived from federal seizures is commonly shared with state and local law enforcement agencies that participated in the investigation that led to the seizure. The money is used for specific purposes, including some salary reimbursement, law enforcement, and drug prevention programs. The DEA maintains many task forces in which the participating state and local task force officers' departments automatically receive an agreed upon portion of the assets recovered through investigations conducted by the task forces.

Money is the sole reason why people become involved in the drug business. Traffickers do not exist to provide a service to the drug user community. They are in it for the money, and billions of dollars are earned every year through drug trafficking, making it an attractive crime for many people who think they can become rich quickly and are willing to take the risk of being caught.

Drug asset forfeiture laws allow law enforcement agencies to seize the profits of drug trafficking organizations and seek their forfeiture criminally or civilly. The intent of these laws is to take the profit out of the crime, and they act as a deterrence for those inclined to get involved in this multi-billion-dollar enterprise.

Money laundering is simply giving illegally gotten gains the appearance of originating from legitimate sources. Many innovative schemes have been devised to accomplish this; however, drug law enforcement has discovered many of these techniques, enabling them to seize assets that derive from drug trafficking activities.

Some drug trafficking organizations use well-established methods of transferring drug proceeds from one point of the world to another. These methods, used extensively in the Far and Middle East, are based on trust, and are extremely hard for drug agents to penetrate.

Traffickers have been known to convert cash into highly valuable commodities such as gold and diamonds. These items are easily transported, and it is difficult to prove where the money to purchase them originated.

References

1. The Civil Asset Forfeiture Reform Act of 2000, Pub. L. No. 106-185, 114 Stat. 202.
2. 18 U.S. Code § 983(c), 114 Stat. 205.

Shared Traits of Drug Traffickers and Terrorists

19

International terrorist organizations and drug traffickers share many similar traits that may not be obvious at first. Terrorists, specifically Osama Bin Laden's al-Qaida network and international drug dealers, plan, stage, and execute their crimes shrouded in secrecy. Both have cells established around the world to achieve their goals. They rely on compartmentalization for operational security, and exhibit ingenious ways to smuggle co-conspirators, explosives, drugs, equipment, money, weapons, and other contraband long distances from one country to another.

By virtue of their crimes, both are engaged in ongoing criminal conspiracies. Counter-terrorism and drug agents investigate their respective crimes *as they occur* as opposed to traditional reactive, after-the-fact, criminal investigations.

For many years the Drug Enforcement Administration (DEA) special agents have recognized that terrorist organizations rely on drug traffickers as a straightforward, easy source of income to finance their political agendas. Drug traffickers, in turn, rely on the terrorists to provide protection for their laboratory and drug distribution endeavors. Through protection rackets, extortion, or "taxation" of drug traffickers, terrorists receive the funds necessary to carry out their violent acts.

An important distinction between the two organizations is that all terrorists are criminals, but not all criminals are terrorists. Criminals are motivated solely by profit, and they do not plan on dying in the process like a suicide bomber does. Terrorists, on the other hand, commit violent crimes to make a political statement, and sometimes make it a point to proclaim their group's involvement. But, what distinguishes them from common criminals is that they are sometimes willing to die for their cause, making their capture moot. Intelligence analysts need to be careful not to lump the two into the same category since the motivation behind their acts is always what drives these criminals to do what they do. A violent act may initially appear to have been carried out by terrorists; however, if a detailed analysis does not expose a political agenda, the perpetrators are most probably mere criminals.

Organizational Structure

Most terrorist organizations and large-scale international drug trafficking organizations are managed from the top down. The leaders of these organizations give the orders and rarely delegate. They give the orders and expect them to be followed. They discourage innovation by their members, and do not tolerate disloyalty.

Both have individual *cells* of their organizations in many countries throughout the world. For operational security purposes, the members of both drug and terrorism cells do not know the identities of other members within the same cell. This compartmentalization has proven to be highly effective. It prevents an arrested cell member from disclosing to law enforcement the identities of the other members of their own and other cells operating within a particular geographic region.

Often the leader of the cell is the only person who knows the number and identities of the other members. He may know that other cells exist elsewhere, but he has purposely been excluded from this information in case he is arrested and interrogated by law enforcement or intelligence officials. Both drug trafficking and terrorist organizations are structured in such a way that if one cell were to be dismantled the other cells and the organization survive.

Drug and Terrorism Source Countries

Both drug and terrorism organizations thrive in countries that lack strong central governments and whose law enforcement officials are ineffective and highly susceptible to corruption. Endemic corruption is probably the single most contributing factor in these organizations' ability to flourish. Pakistan, Afghanistan, and Colombia are examples of countries that have both terrorist and drug traffickers operating within their borders. These organizations operate freely after establishing partnerships with corrupt officials to facilitate their criminal enterprises.

Money Laundering

Drug traffickers require a way to launder their ill-gotten gains to give them the appearance of legitimacy, whereas terrorists, in addition to traditional money laundering activities, often convert seemingly honest money from donations to so-called charitable organizations and use it to finance their operations. Both go through elaborate schemes to disguise the true source of the money or its intended purpose. Terrorist front organizations around the world, particularly in the United States, and sometimes play the race or religion card to gain sympathy from the public. Drug cartels have been known to build housing and infrastructure for members of the communities they operate in for the same purpose.

Drug dealers and terrorist organizations use *straw purchasers* to buy property, weapons, vehicles, and the like. A straw purchaser is someone who is paid to buy something, like real property, for someone else in order to disguise the true owner. Straw purchasers are also used to rent items such as apartments, cars, boats, and trucks. They are never told the real intended purpose of the purchase in order to ensure they cannot reveal it to law enforcement. They are paid for their silence.

Communications

Drug traffickers rely on secure communications such as encrypted email and code words over unsecured telephone lines to thwart law enforcement and intelligence agencies from learning their intentions. They will often purchase off-the-shelf items at novelty spy stores that purport to detect radio transmitters or determine if their telephones and rooms are tapped or bugged. Some of these stores sell voice stress analysis machines that supposedly tell the owner if the person he is talking to on the telephone is telling the truth. Fortunately, many of these items do not work as advertised, however some do. Terrorists have been known to use many of these same items. However, terrorists that are state sponsored may have sophisticated espionage equipment at their disposal that definitely works.

Many terrorist organizations and drug dealers communicate with their co-conspirators throughout the world using satellite and cellular telephones. They are handy to check on the progress of shipments of drugs or weapons from one part of the world to another, as well as the health and welfare of their members. To disguise the subscriber of the telephone service, both terrorists and drug dealers have been known to prepay large amounts of airtime, and then discipline themselves to only telephone co-conspirators when necessary using these phones. Drug traffickers and terrorists have long used prepaid telephone calling cards, Internet connections at libraries and Internet cafes, as well as disposable telephones to disguise their identities. They do not want a record of phone calls or emails being documented as being made by them.

Training Manuals

Large drug trafficking organizations have furnished lower-level members of their organization detailed training manuals on how to perform their jobs and assimilate into American culture. Documents seized by the DEA during search warrants of modest middle-class homes in neighborhoods in America revealed detailed instructions to the occupants on how to not draw attention to themselves. These occupants are hired by drug cartels to live in the residence and provide security for the multi-hundred kilograms of drugs stored there. Seized instruction manuals train the persons in charge of the stash houses to cut the lawn and register their children in the local schools. They are also encouraged to have backyard barbeques and be friendly with their neighbors, as well as to have a cover story to explain odd working hours.

These manuals also instruct the occupants to be conscious of surveillance by the police, and what to do in emergencies. Recovered al-Qaida training manuals also instruct its members on how to do many of the same things. It specifically has chapters on how to perform counter-surveillance operations before any planned meetings to avoid police surveillance.

Immigration Fraud and False Identity Documents

A large percentage of international drug traffickers operating in the United States and other consumer nations are foreign nationals. These traffickers want to show a legitimate reason for traveling to the country, so they fraudulently represent themselves to be tourists, professional athletics, students, asylum seekers, or businessmen. Once in the country, they overstay their visas and continue operating until they are caught or ordered back to their home countries by top management of the drug cartel. Terrorist organizations do the same thing in order to insert their personnel into a given country. Terrorists and drug smugglers often use forged passports of countries not believed to be synonymous with terrorism or drugs.

International terrorists also have the dilemma of overcoming U.S. immigration law. Claims of religious or political persecution, attending school, or accepting employment have been successful ruses to gain entry. However, once in the country, they will obtain false documentation in another name to keep law enforcement off balance. Some of the airline hijackers who attacked the United States on September 11, 2001, had fraudulently obtained genuine Virginia State identity cards.

Drug traffickers also use either genuine government-issued identification, issued in a false name, or counterfeit IDs in order to avoid detection. Both drug dealers and terrorists have long realized that having multiple identities enhance their likelihood of success.

Smuggling Techniques

Drug smugglers often transport multi-ton amounts of controlled substances to the United States and Europe. Terrorists have been known to smuggle weapons and people from one country to another, often using established drug smuggling routes. Smugglers often use commercial shipping to transport contraband into the United States disguised as legitimate cargo. Although only about 2% of all commercial shipping is inspected by U.S. Customs authorities when it arrives, the smugglers still want to increase the odds in their favor. Pakistani drug smugglers will often ship a container from the port city of Karachi to a nondrug source country where the bill of lading and seal are changed. The shipment then proceeds to another part of the world where other co-conspirators again change the bill of lading and seal to prepare it for another shipment. This layering of bills of lading and seals disguises the country of origin and may take the container over a year to finally arrive at its intended destination. Once the container arrives at a port in the United States, the smugglers will hire a company to have it transported to a rented storage area where they will abandon it for several weeks. They will then conduct occasional surveillance on the container to see if it has drawn the attention of law enforcement. Only after they are reasonably certain the container is safe will they finally open it and distribute the contents. This technique has proven to be highly successful for drug traffickers, and works equally well for terrorist organizations. Terrorists, many of whom work in concert with drug traffickers to earn money for their activities, have been known to rely on drug smugglers to transport weapons and other contraband from one part of the world to another.

Airport Profiling

DEA special agents and their task force partners have long recognized certain characteristics that smugglers exhibit when using commercial air transportation to move drugs and money around the country and the world. In their attempt to disguise their motives and true identities, smugglers often raise red flags. Terrorists may also exhibit many of these characteristics:

- Purchasing tickets with cash
- Purchasing tickets shortly before departure
- Changing air carriers to the same destination shortly before departure
- Using a travel agency suspected of facilitating criminal activity
- Carrying little to no luggage, or only having a carry-on bag
- Not having a logical explanation for their travel

- Not knowing the name, address, or telephone number of the person the traveler is supposedly visiting
- Having a return ticket within 24 to 36 hours of their departure
- Making frequent phone calls just before departure, and immediately after arriving
- Making a point to be the last person to deplane

No single characteristic is positive proof of either terrorism or the smuggling of drugs, explosives, or hazardous material on board an aircraft. But, taken in totality, these characteristics may lead law enforcement officials to initiate contact with the traveler to further investigate.

Human Sources of Information

The intelligence community and federal law enforcement agencies both use information they receive from a variety of diverse confidential sources to meet their objectives. With 78 offices in 56 foreign countries, the DEA probably has one of the single-most comprehensive network of human intelligence sources available to the U.S. government. These drug sources are sometimes linked directly or indirectly to terrorist organizations and their international drug trafficking partners. The information they provide is readily available to U.S. intelligence and other federal law enforcement agencies. This worldwide network of informants has been used to target international terrorist and drug trafficking organizations.

Parallel Investigative Techniques

The techniques used in investigating drug trafficking organizations are largely the same as those used in terrorism investigation. Both drug and terrorist organizations engage in continuing criminal enterprises and commit many overt acts to accomplish their goals. Drug investigations are almost always conducted as the crime is occurring. Proactive terrorism investigations also investigate ongoing conspiracies that have led to the prevention of many terrorist acts. Both drug and terrorism investigations use confidential informants (CIs), electronic and physical surveillance, wiretaps, mail covers, trash runs, and telephone toll analysis to identify members of these criminal organizations. Search warrants for documents, surveillance video tapes of potential targets, illegal contraband, computer hard drives, weapons, bomb making materials, etc. have proven to be fruitful in uncovering future plans of terrorists and drug traffickers. Using federal grand jury subpoenas to obtain financial records has long been used by drug enforcement. These subpoenas are equally effective in terrorism investigations leading to the discovery of bank accounts and the identities of some so-called charitable organizations that funnel money into terrorist organizations.

Telephone toll analysis is used extensively in both terrorism and drug investigations. The analysis of telephone toll calls and emails is probably the single most effective way of identifying members and associates of both drug and terrorist organizations. Many times, a nexus between terrorists and drug traffickers is discovered through this analysis (see Chapter 17 for details).

Intelligence analysts will also obtain driver license photos, criminal histories, immigration files, and other records and dossiers for each of the subscribers.

Comparisons of Terrorist and Drug Trafficking Organizations

Terrorist Organizations	Drug Trafficking Organizations
1. Engage in conspiracies that are investigated as they occur	1. Engage in conspiracies that are investigated as they occur
2. Suspects operate in cells	2. Suspects operate in cells
3. Suspects compartmentalize information on pending operations	3. Suspects compartmentalize information on pending operations
4. Top-down management style	4. Top-down management style
5. Members use sophisticated communication devices	5. Members use sophisticated communication devices
6. Members launder money to disguise source of income	6. Members launder money to disguise source of income
7. Vulnerable to infiltration by informants	7. Vulnerable to infiltration by informants
8. Commit crimes to meet their objectives	8. Commit crimes to meet their objectives
9. Partner up with drug criminals	9. Partner up with terrorists
10. Use established drug smuggling methods of operation	10. Use established drug smuggling methods of operation
11. Use forged identity documents	11. Use forged identity documents
12. Publish training manuals for its members	12. Publish training manuals for its members
13. Vulnerable to profiling by law enforcement	13. Vulnerable to profiling by law enforcement
14. Flourish in corrupt countries	14. Flourish in corrupt countries
15. Driven by political agendas	15. Profit motivated
16. Extensive use of telephones and computers to communicate	16. Extensive use of telephones and computers to communicate
17. Often resort to violence to achieve their goals	17. Often resort to violence to achieve their goals

Summary

Terrorist and drug trafficking organizations possess many similarities. All terrorists are criminals, but not all criminals are terrorists. The DEA recognized long ago that a nexus often exists between international drug and terrorism organizations. Due to the nature of their crimes and the way these organizations operate, the techniques used to investigate international drug and terrorist organizations are frequently similar, if not identical. Drug traffickers and terrorists often use the same methods of operation to achieve their goals. The sharing of intelligence information between law enforcement and the intelligence community will alert agents if they are dealing with drug dealers, terrorists, or both.

Nexus between Drugs and Terrorism 20

The evidence is clear. There is a direct connection between drug trafficking organizations and terrorism. Terrorist organizations have been funded for years by the profits of drug traffickers, and it is likely to continue in the future, especially when state-sponsored support is eroded by political or military action. Drug users unwittingly contribute funds to terrorist organizations throughout the world every time they buy drugs. Terrorists use drug sales profits to fund operations to destabilize governments around the world, including the United States. The methods they use to achieve their goals are similar to those used by drug traffickers (see Chapter 19 for details).

Glenn Levant, president and founding director of Drug Abuse Reduction Education (D.A.R.E) said, "As a nation, we must recognize that those who buy and consume illicit drugs are ultimately supporting acts of terror and violence. Consequently, our strategic war plans and national resolve must also focus on a continued and broadened strategy to eliminate this major source of funds for terrorism."

President George W. Bush said in regard to the nexus of drugs and terrorism: "It's so important for Americans to know that the traffic in drugs finances the work of terror, sustaining terrorists, that terrorists use drug profits to fund their cells to commit acts of murder. If you quit drugs, you join the fight against terror in America." Drug agents can further the cause of drug demand reduction in their communities by emphasizing the nexus of drugs to terrorist organizations.

This nexus between drug traffickers and terrorists directly threatens the United States and other nations. It has the potential of creating regional instability and threatening national security as well as the future of America's youth. This linkage also directly harms U.S. interests and citizens around the world.

The U.S. Department of State has identified 12 of 28 terrorist organizations that traffic drugs to raise funding.[1] These groups include:

- Abu Sayyaf Group. An extremist separatist group operating in the Philippines that seeks an independent Islamic state. They are known to grow marijuana for resale and have close ties to Osama Bin Laden's al-Qaida terrorist organization.
- Basque Fatherland and Liberty. Dedicated to a separate homeland apart from Spain, this violent group traffics in a variety of drugs to fund their goals.
- Hezbollah. This Lebanese based, highly violent group is comprised of two wings, a political and guerrilla military force. Hezbollah conceived the tactic of suicide bombing in its goal to expel Israel from southern Lebanon. It was heavily backed by Iran until the war on terrorism in 2001 because of fears of reprisal from the United States, which may result in increased drug trafficking in opium and hashish to secure funds. The group is responsible for the bombing of the U.S. embassy in Lebanon in 1993, killing 63 people, including 17 Americans. It also drove an explosive-laden truck into a U.S. Marine barracks outside Beirut, killing 241 servicemen in 1983, and kidnapped and killed William Buckley, the CIA station chief in Beirut a few years later. It has also been tied to numerous other acts of terror throughout the world, primarily against Israeli interests. Hezbollah is believed to be closely aligned with the al-Qaida organization to achieve their mutual goals.[2]
- Islamic Movement of Uzbekistan. Involved in drug trafficking.
- Kurdistan Workers Party. Sandwiched between northern Iraq and southern Turkey, this group has long used violence to achieve their goal of a separate Kurdish state. Known to traffic in heroin.
- Liberation Tigers of Tamil Eelam. Based in Sri Lanka, this group has fought for years to achieve an independent state. Known to act as drug couriers, primarily in Pakistani hashish.
- National Liberation Army. Involved in all aspects of drug trafficking except international movement.
- Palestinian Islamic Jihad. Involved in trafficking hashish and heroin to achieve a Palestinian state.
- Al Qaida. Headed by Osama Bin Laden and was responsible for the original attack on the World Trade Center in 1993, a truck bombing of a U.S. military barracks in Saudi Arabia in 1996, attacks on U.S. embassies in eastern Africa in 1998, the USS Cole in 2000, and the commercial airline hijackings and suicide crashes into the World Trade Center and The Pentagon in 2001. Known to traffic opium and heroin in Afghanistan.

- Revolutionary Armed Forces of Colombia (FARC). Primarily a communist revolutionary movement for many decades, they traffic in cocaine and provide protection for Colombian drug cartels to raise funding to overthrow the established democratic government in Colombia. Also perform kidnappings and extortion to raise funds. Believe to earn $300 million dollars annually in criminal and drug activities.
- Shining Path. Provide protection for cocaine growers and laboratories.
- United Self-Defense Forces of Colombia (AUC). The AUC is a right-wing paramilitary organization Involved in all aspects of cocaine trafficking to counter the advances of the FARC. Estimates have them receiving 40 to 70% of their revenues derived from the drug trade.

Drug agents who investigate and arrest heroin and cocaine traffickers are contributing to winning the fight against the global war on terrorism. Names of suspects believed to have clear international connections should be run against established *watch lists* the FBI maintains of known or suspected terrorists operating in the United States and elsewhere.

Afghanistan

Throughout the lifetime of the Taliban, proceeds from drug cultivators and traffickers have funded their operations. As outlined in Chapter 2, Afghanistan is a major source of heroin in the world and in 2000, supplied 70% of the world's supply of opium, which is the essential ingredient of heroin.

By taxing farmers and others who cultivate, transport, and sell opium, the Taliban raised significant funding, estimated to be between $40 and $50 million dollars, to further their regime. Since the Taliban protected Osama Bin Laden's al-Qaida terrorist network, it benefited directly from the tax revenues generated from opium farmers. The farmers produce opium because of a strong demand for heroin that exists throughout the world, especially in western Europe.

The DEA has generated multiple-source information that Osama Bin Laden himself has been involved in the financing and facilitation of heroin-trafficking activities. In September 2002, two Pakistanis and an American were arrested after being indicted in San Diego, CA for conspiring to trade 1320 pounds of heroin and 5 tons of hashish for four Stinger shoulder fired anti-aircraft missiles. The three men told undercover FBI agents they intended to sell the Stinger missiles to members of the Taliban, an organization that the defendants indicated was the same as al Qaida, according to the indictment.

Colombia

There are three groups operating within the country that have been designated by the U.S. Department of State as being terrorist organizations: the *Revolutionary Armed Forces of Colombia (FARC)*, the *National Liberation Army (ELN)*, and the paramilitary group, the *United Self-Defenses of Colombia* (AUC). The FARC and AUC have been heavily involved in protecting cocaine laboratories and engaging in cocaine trafficking, and they receive enormous funding for their causes.

In November 2002, four AUC members negotiated with undercover DEA and FBI agents in Panama to purchase 9000 assault rifles, submachine guns, sniper rifles, 300 pistols, rocket propelled grenade launchers, shoulder fired missiles, 300,000 grenades, and about 60 million rounds of ammunition in exchange for cash and cocaine.

"This multimillion-dollar cocaine-for-arms deal is yet another example of the convergence of violence and terrorism with drug trafficking," Drug Enforcement Administration chief Asa Hutchison said. "We have demonstrated that drug traffickers and terrorists work out of the same jungle, they plan in the same cave and they train in the same desert." The U.S. Attorney's Office in Houston, TX described the AUC as an umbrella organization that consolidated local and regional paramilitary groups in Colombia.[3]

The FARC is the military wing of the Colombian Communist Party and was established in 1964. It has been named by the U.S. State Department as the most dangerous international terrorism group based in the western hemisphere. In 2002, the DEA successfully indicted three members of the 16th Front of the FARC, including their co-leader, on charges of conspiracy to transport and later distribute cocaine in the United States. This marked the first time members of a known terrorist organization have been indicted on drug trafficking charges.

The 16th Front operates out of a remote village in eastern Colombia. The revenues generated from cocaine sales goes to purchasing weapons, equipment, and supplies. The State Department estimates that the FARC receives $300 million annually from cocaine trafficking to finance their political agenda through terrorism.

In 2002, the government of Colombia decided to recapture a previously established demilitarized zone occupied by the FARC. When the Colombian army arrived, they discovered two major cocaine laboratories and seized five tons of processed cocaine. They also destroyed a 200-foot communications tower the FARC operated to communicate with their members. Evidence suggests the FARC not only provides protection to established Colombian cartels in their manufacturing and distribution activities, but it is also independently involved in drug trafficking in an effort to make even more money.

Since 1990, narco-terrorists in Colombia have kidnapped more than 50 U.S. citizens, mostly for extortion to generate revenue and, since 1995, they have murdered 12 other Americans.

The AUC's leader, Carlos Castaño, admitted in a published book[4] that his paramilitary group used funds derived from cocaine trafficking activities to carry out their own agendas. He has admitted that upwards of 70% of his organization's funding derives from the drug trade. The AUC has enough funding to operate a website, http://colombia-libre.org/colombialibre/pp.asp.

Peru

Peru is the home of the Shining Path terrorist organization, a revolutionary communist organization. It has also historically benefited by taxing cocaine traffickers and providing them protection to further their political agenda against the established government.

Middle East

Middle Eastern drug traffickers operating in the United States and Canada, predominately from Lebanon, have been responsible for the distribution of multiton quantities of pseudoephedrine to supply methamphetamine laboratories in California and elsewhere. Many of these traffickers have known or suspected connections with terrorist groups operating in the Middle East.

The DEA, U.S. Customs Service, Internal Revenue Service, and the Royal Canadian Mounted Police conducted a massive investigation in 2002 called Operation Mountain Express, in which over the course of three phases, 30 tons of pseudoephedrine was seized. The vast majority of the suspects arrested were of Middle Eastern descent, and the monies earned through their illegal activities were sent to the Middle East and believed to be used to fund various terrorist organizations.

During all the three phases of Operation Mountain Express, the seized pseudoephedrine would have produced about 37,000 pounds of methamphetamine, predominately by Mexican laboratory operators. This is significant in that, in 2001, U.S. authorities reported only 6000 pounds of methamphetamine seized nationwide.

Summary

The nexus between drug trafficking and terrorism is clear. The U.S. State Department has identified 12 of 28 known terrorist organizations that traffic in drugs. Drug agents who investigate and arrest heroin and cocaine traffickers contribute to winning the global war on terrorism.

When Afghanistan's ruling Taliban was in power, they funded many of their activities through taxing opium farmers. Al-Qaida also profited from the direct sales of heroin. In South America, the FARC and the AUC operate freely, earning multi-millions of dollars to finance and advance their political agendas. In Peru, the Shining Path furthers their political beliefs through terrorism financed directly from cocaine trafficking. Middle Easterners with direct and indirect ties to terrorist organizations have demonstrated their ability to profit from drug trafficking by smuggling multi-ton quantities of pseudoephedrine into the United States from Canada to feed Mexican-controlled methamphetamine laboratories.

References

1. Report on Foreign Terrorists Organizations, U.S. Department of State, October 2001.
2. Priest, D. and Farah, D.,Terror Alliance Has U.S. Worried, *The Washington Post*, June 30, 2002.
3. Vartabedian, R., U.S. Officials Announce 2 Terrorism Indictments, *Los Angeles Times*, November 7, 2002.
4. Molina, M.A., Mi Confesión (My Confession: Carlos Castaño Reveals His Secrets), *Los Angeles Times*, November 7, 2002.

21 Talking Points against Drug Legalization

Each year drug abuse takes the lives of about 14,000 Americans and costs taxpayers nearly $70 billion. The use of drugs incites child and spousal abuse, violence, property crimes, the spread of AIDS and other diseases, and costs employers millions of dollars in accidents, absenteeism, and loss of productivity. Despite this, concerted efforts are being made through state ballot initiatives to legalize marijuana and other drugs. Many prodrug advocates use the guise of medicine to advance their agenda. The issues surrounding drug legalization are complex and sometimes emotional. Law enforcement officers must be totally familiar with the facts so they will feel comfortable discussing the issue.

Drug legalization issues are being discussed around the country with little input from law enforcement officials. With the passage of propositions legalizing certain drugs in Arizona and California, and the attempt by other states, law enforcement officials should give their opinions about legalization initiatives. Police officers experience first hand the tremendous damage to individuals and entire communities that are caused by drugs and violence associated with their abuse. Without the facts about the impact drugs have on society, and the positive results of their enforcement efforts, they may hesitate to participate in a public forum about this important issue. What follows are ten undeniable facts that can be used to help defeat prodrug legislation.

Ten Undeniable Facts

Undeniable Fact 1

The United States has made significant progress in fighting drug use and drug trafficking in America. Now is certainly not the time to abandon our efforts. Legalization advocates claim that the war on drugs cannot be won. However, overall drug use is down by more than a third in the last 20 years, while cocaine use has dropped by an astounding 70%! Ninety-five percent of Americans do not use drugs. This is an outstanding success by any measure. To abandon current national and international strategies now would reverse this trend and lead to more harmful effects against the citizens law enforcement officers strive to protect. Dedicated drug agents would like nothing better than to work themselves out of a job.

Undeniable Fact 2

A balanced approach of prevention, enforcement, and treatment is the key in winning the war on drugs. A successful drug policy must apply a balanced approach of prevention through education, enforcement, and treatment. All three aspects are crucial. Enforcement is necessary to reduce or eliminate the availability of drugs so new users will not start and current users will quit. For those who end up hooked on drugs, there are innovative programs, like drug treatment courts, that offer nonviolent users the option of seeking treatment. Drug treatment courts provide court mandatory supervision, unlike voluntary treatment centers. It is often the only way an addicted person gets drug treatment. If drug use became as unpopular in our society as smoking cigarettes, people would opt not to use them, and the drug cartels would move on to other customer-rich countries to peddle their deadly wares. Since this is not the case, youths must be taught not to use drugs, enforcement must continue at a vigorous rate, and treatment must be provided for those who seek it.

Undeniable Fact 3

Illegal drugs are illegal because they are harmful. You bet they are! People who abuse drugs often claim they can stop at any time. They are just kidding themselves. They know that stopping drug use is a monumental task. They are addictive. Heroin addicts transfer their energies from being productive people in society to focusing only on getting their supply for that day. The euphoric effects gradually leads to *maintenance* to cope with their heroin addiction in order to avoid withdrawal symptoms that are extremely harsh. For them, the euphoric effect is gone, and they have to keep using heroin to stay "normal." There is a growing misconception that some illegal drugs can be taken safely. For example, savoir-faire Ecstasy drug dealers have learned to market drugs, especially to youth, by claiming it has no harmful effects. Tell that to the thousands of teenagers who have been hospitalized in the last year after attending a Rave event where Ecstasy was sold. Some in the legalization lobby even claim such drugs have medical value, despite the lack of conclusive scientific evidence. The evidence is clear. Drugs like Ecstasy lead to instant brain damage. Illegal drugs are illegal simply because they are harmful and because of the lack of scientific foundation showing they are not. When you add up all the destroyed lives that would otherwise have been productive ones, the cost of using drugs is enormous.

Undeniable Fact 4

Smoking marijuana has not been scientifically approved as a form of medication. According to the Institute of Medicine, there is no future in smoking marijuana as medicine. However, the prescription drug Marinol — a legal and safe version of medical marijuana that isolates the active ingredient of THC — has been studied and approved by the FDA as a safe medicine. The difference is that you do not get the euphoric effects of smoking marijuana with Marinol, and you have to get a prescription for it from a licensed physician. The legalization crowd is merely attempting to normalize marijuana as an everyday substance that everyone should be allowed to enjoy.

Undeniable Fact 5

Drug control spending is a fraction of the U.S. budget. Compared to the social costs of drug abuse and addiction, government spending on drug control is minimal. The United States spent about $18 billion dollars on the war on drugs on 2003. That is less money than it budgeted for foreign aid! The legalization lobby would like you to believe that the United States has wasted billions of dollars in its antidrug efforts. But for those children and their families who were saved from drug addiction, this is hardly a waste of money. Moreover, the fight against drug abuse is an ongoing struggle that should be treated the same as other social problems. Should we give up on education or the war on poverty simply because we have not eliminated all of the problems associated with it? Compared to the social costs of drug abuse and addiction — whether in taxpayer dollars or in pain and suffering — government spending on drug control is paltry by comparison.

Undeniable Fact 6

Legalization of drugs will lead to increased use and increased levels of addiction. Of course it will! If there are no consequences for using illegal drugs, then the number of people who will experience harmful drugs will increase tremendously, adding to social ills. Legalization has been tried before in Alaska and failed miserably. Alaska's experiment with legalization in the 1970s led to the state's teenagers using marijuana at more than twice the rate of other youths nationally. Remember, this is a gateway drug to more harmful substances. This led Alaska's voters to recriminalize marijuana in 1990.

Reducing illegal drug use is not an impossible task. Illicit drug use by Americans fell from an estimated 24 million users in 1979 to 13 million users in 1994. Education, leadership by example, and vigorous enforcement of the law made the difference. This combination can make the difference again.

Law enforcement leaders are responsible members of society who know that important issues affecting the well being of their community cannot be ignored. Prolegalization advocates never consider or discuss issues that they know will adversely affect our citizens.

If the prolegalization crowd had their way, would all drugs be legalized? Who determines who gets access?

Who is liable for damages caused by drug use and the activities of those taking drugs?

How will society care for and pay for the social costs of increased drug use, including family disintegration and child neglect?

Can anyone, regardless of age or physical or medical conditions, purchase drugs?

These are hard questions the prolegalization crowd refuses to answer.

Undeniable Fact 7

Crime, violence, and drug use go hand-in-hand. People under the influence of drugs commit six times as many homicides as those who are looking for money to buy drugs. People trying to pay for drugs do not commit most drug crimes; people under the influence of drugs do.

For example, in 1998 an estimated 61,000 convicted jail inmates said they committed their offense to get money for drugs. Of convicted property and drug offenders, about one in four had committed their crimes to get money for drugs. A higher percentage of drug offenders in 1996 (24%) than in 1989 (14%) were in jail for a crime committed to raise money for drugs.[1]

The Uniform Crime Reporting Program of the Federal Bureau of Investigation reported that in 2000, 4.4% of the 12,943 homicides in which circumstances were known were drug related. Murders committed specifically during a drug felony, such as drug trafficking or manufacturing, are considered drug related.

In a 1997 survey of inmates in state and federal correctional facilities, 33% of state prisoners and 22% of federal prisoners said they had committed their offense while under the influence of drugs. Drug offenders (42%) and property offenders (37%) reported the highest incidence of drug use at the time of the offense.[2,3]

In recent years, we have seen a decrease in the violent crime rate in many communities, such as New York City, Boston, and Houston, which is attributable to aggressive law enforcement efforts and the increase in incarceration of criminals. We know that vigorous law enforcement actions aimed at criminal activity, including illegal drug use, have a material effect on reducing violent crime in our communities.

Our struggle with drug abuse has taught us a sobering lesson: drug use increases dramatically when society reinforces the acceptability of drug use. In 1962, fewer than 4 million Americans had ever tried drugs; by 1995, almost 74 million had. During the intervening years, many prolegalization and decriminalization proponents actively sought to broaden public acceptance of drug use, and our society saw the number of drug users and societal problems increase steadily.

In the late 1970s, drug tolerance and leniency reached a peak in the United States. Not surprisingly, drug use among children skyrocketed, reaching a high point in 1979 when one in ten high school seniors was high on marijuana every day of the week. Two out of three high school seniors had tried marijuana. In 1979 over 56 million people had tried illegal drugs; in 1985, that number rose to 66 million.

After a period of aggressive and consistent law enforcement, antidrug education, and a societal shift of public opinion away from drugs, the number of regular users of illegal drugs was reduced by 50% between 1985 and 1995 (from 23.3 million to 12.8 million).

Currently, our nation is seeing an increase in marijuana use among young people, with a doubling of use since 1992. In some measure, this increase is due to diminished perceptions of risk, reductions in the frequency of network news coverage of the dangers of drugs, and ambivalence about drug use on the part of baby boomer parents.

The legalization movement, and the growing destigmatization of drugs, along with the confusing messages about the beneficial properties of substances like marijuana, can result in further decreases in the perceptions of risk, and a concurrent increase in drug use.

Increased drug availability and use will worsen our crime problems. Law enforcement officials know that numerous government studies clearly demonstrate that drug users are more likely to be involved in criminal activities than nondrug users. In 1986, during the midst of the crack epidemic, violent crime reached a level of 617 violent crimes per 100,000 people. As we experienced a continuing escalation of drug-related violence, this figure rose in 1993 to 746 violent crimes for every hundred thousand inhabitants.

Outraged public and governmental leaders joined together to challenge the escalating violent crime. As a result of their efforts, vigorous new enforcement programs were implemented in the 1990s that have begun to reverse this trend. After making progress against violent crime during the past decade, we should not erode these gains by instituting policies such as decriminalization and legalization that will surely increase drug use and drug-related crime.

Undeniable Fact 8

Alcohol has caused significant health, social, and crime problems in this country, and legalized drugs would only make the situation worse. The legalization lobby claims drugs are no more dangerous than alcohol. But drunk driving is one of the primary killers of Americans. Do we want our bus drivers, nurses, and airline pilots to be able to take drugs one evening, and operate freely at work the next day? Do we want to add to the destruction by making drugged driving another primary killer?

Undeniable Fact 9

Europe's more liberal drug policies are not the right model for America. Legalization advocates claim that the European model of the drug problem is successful. However, since the legalization of marijuana in Holland, heroin addiction levels have tripled, and Needle Park seems like a poor model for America. Law enforcement officers know that marijuana is a gateway drug that often leads to the abuse of other, more harmful substances like cocaine and heroin. Police officers know that not all people who smoke marijuana will go on to using heroin, but heroin addicts will often tell you they got their start in drug abuse by smoking marijuana.

Undeniable Fact 10

Most nonviolent drug users get treatment, not jail time. The legalization lobby claims that America's prisons are filling up with users. Truth is, only about 5% of inmates in federal prison are there because of simple possession. Most drug criminals are in jail — even on possession charges — because they have plea-bargained down from major trafficking offenses or more violent drug crimes.

A Law Enforcement Officer's Approach to the Problem

Personalize the impact of drugs — Just as citizen groups successfully personalized drunk driving tragedies, we can put faces and lives with the antidrug message. The harmful effects of marijuana are not only harmful to the users, but to those around them and should be illustrated. An effective message should show young people whose lives were destroyed by marijuana, by their own use or that of others. Demonstrate the tragic results of fatalities involving users under the influence of drugs.

It is not "just marijuana" — One of the early challenges was persuading the public that beer is as lethal as hard liquor. In much the same way, the public needs to be informed that marijuana, its short- and long-term impact, is a very dangerous drug.

Credible role models and spokespersons — Credible role models and spokespersons, especially those personally touched by drunk driving, were instrumental in helping to turn around public opinion. You may wish to consider a similar approach using those who have had their lives impacted by drug abuse.

Cultivate civic and watchdog groups — Organizations that are effective in setting out a no-use or antimarijuana legalization message include: educational institutions and organizations; business, industry, or professional organizations; community associations; media; neighborhood groups; religious organizations, service organizations and clubs; youth groups; and social service organizations.

Grassroots political drive — Legislators must hear from their constituents. Police chiefs, law enforcement, and civic group leaders and members should communicate to the offices of their governors, lieutenant governors, state legislators, mayors, and national congressmen and representatives their views against drug legalization.

Law enforcement leadership — Federal, state, and local law enforcement leaders can inform and influence public opinion. Law enforcement leaders could deliver keynote addresses in town hall meetings; talk radio interview programs; and contribute articles to local and civic newsletters, newspaper editorials, etc.

Law enforcement expertise — Law enforcement officials are easy targets for critics who claim that they are being self-serving and parochial in their opposition to legalization. "They're cops, of course they oppose legal drugs," is an often repeated statement. In reality, law enforcement leaders are in an excellent position to explain why these drugs are dangerous and the terrible consequences that will follow if they are legalized.

Maintain a good relationship with the local media — Establish sound relationships with your local media. Periodic meetings with the editorial boards of local papers or with station managers will present you with the opportunity to speak out on drug legalization.

Help support programs to build young leaders who take strong anti-drug positions — Work with organizations such as the Boys and Girls Clubs,

Police Athletic Leagues (PAL), the CYO, YMCA, scouting organizations, and sports teams promoting antidrug messages.

Support antidrug programs, such as Drug Abuse Resistance Education (D.A.R.E.) in your local schools — Know your state's referendum process and understand how it works.

By understanding the mechanisms available to prolegalization groups to change state drug laws, you will know what to expect and can work with citizen groups and others to properly respond to these issues.

Where to Go for Additional Help

Antidrug Organizations

Partnership for a Drug-Free America
405 Lexington Avenue
New York, NY, 10174
(212) 922-1560

The Partnership for a Drug-Free America is a coalition of volunteers from the communications industry. The American Association of Advertising Agencies formed it in 1986, and its objective is to combine the creativity of advertising agencies with the power of the media to address drug abuse prevention. The Partnership has become the largest public service campaign in history with over 250 advertising agencies contributing work with the nation's media donating over $2.3 billion in time and space to the campaign. The goal of the Partnership is to set out a message to change society's attitude about drugs to denormalize their use and to prevent the use of illegal drugs based on the logic that if fewer people try them, fewer will fall into addiction.

Community Anti-Drug Coalitions of America (CADCA)
901 North Pitt Street
Suite 300
Alexandria, VA 22314
(800) 54-CADCA

CADCA is the principal national substance abuse prevention organization working with community-based coalitions and representing their interests at the national level. The organization supports coalition members with technical assistance and training, public policy work, media strategies and marketing programs, conferences and special events, implementation of

"Drugs Don't Work" workplace programs, and the creation of mobilization strategies surrounding current drug-related national issues. CADCA's 1-800-DRUGS-50 toll-free number informs individuals about pertinent substance abuse issues and allows them to be connected directly to their representatives to give input on pending congressional action.

Drug Watch International
P.O. Box 1454
Elmhurst, IL 60126-2127
(708) 530-8999

A drug information network designed to track policy and to counteract what it calls "misinformation distributed by pro-drug legalization advocates." They bring information, policy recommendations, and research about drugs to the public, news media, Congress, and international governments and organizations. They are dedicated to the support of demand reduction programs and combating the idea of legalizing drugs.

National Families in Action
2296 Henderson Mill Road
Suite 300
Atlanta, GA 30345
(404) 934-6364

National Families in Action is a direct education and prevention organization that seeks to educate society about the dangers of alcohol, tobacco, and other drugs by disseminating accurate information and to help citizens use that information to identify and resolve problems that contribute to substance abuse.

Parents' Resource Institute for Drug Education (PRIDE)
The Hurt Building, Suite 210
50 Hurt Plaza
Atlanta, GA 30103
www.prideusa.org

This is a membership organization that assists parents, young people, and community organizations in the prevention of alcohol and other drug problems. In addition to educational efforts and program support aimed at these constituencies, PRIDE is the source of a major annual report on the extent of drug use by American youth.

Resources and Publications

Resources

Bureau of Justice Statistics Clearinghouse
Box 179
Annapolis Junction, MD 20701-0179
(800) 732-3277

Community Anti-Drug Coalitions of America (CADCA)
901 North Pitt Street, #301
Alexandria, VA 22314
(800) 542-2322

National Highway Traffic Safety Administration
Office of Program Development and Evaluation
400 Seventh Street, SW
Washington, D.C. 20590
(202) 366-0123

Publications

Survey of State Prison Inmates, 1991, Drugs, Crime and the Justice System
California Narcotic Officers Association
24509 Walnut Street, #201
Santa Clarita, CA 91321
(805) 287-0195

The Myths of Drug Legalization
Center on Addiction and Substance Abuse (CASA)
Columbia University
152 West 57th Street
New York, NY 10019-3310
(212) 841-5200

Legalization: Panacea or Pandora's Box
Citizens Against Drug Impaired Driving (CANDID)
P. O. Box 17705
Milwaukee, WI 53217-0705
(414) 352-2043

Say It Straight: The Medical Myths of Marijuana
The Council on Crime in America
c/o The Manhattan Institute
52 Vanderbilt Place
New York, NY 10017
(212) 599-7000

The State of Violent Crime in America
Drug Enforcement Administration
Washington, D.C. 20537
(202) 307-7936

Speaking Out Against Legalization
Drug Abuse Warning Network (DAWN) Emergency Room Report
Drug & Crime Clearinghouse of the Office of National Drug Control Policy
1600 Research Boulevard
Rockville, MD 20850
(800) 666-3332

Drug Use Forecasting (DUF) Annual Report on Adult and Juvenile Arrestees
National Association of Police Athletic Leagues
618 North U.S. Highway 1, Suite 201
North Palm Beach, FL 33408
(561) 844-1823

National Highway Traffic Safety Administration
Office of Program Development & Evaluation
400 Seventh Street, SW
Washington, D.C. 20590
(202) 366-0123

Drugs in Crashes and Impaired Driving Arrests
The Incidence and Role of Drugs in Fatally Injured Drivers
Marijuana Effects on Actual Driving Performance
Impact of the Drug Evaluation and Classification Program on Enforcement and Adjudication
National Institute of Justice
National Criminal Justice Reference Service
Box 6000
Rockville, MD 20849-6000
(800) 851-3420

Summary

The prolegalization lobby has been successful in California and Arizona in making drug use more acceptable in society. More efforts will be made in other states, and successes could prove to be destructive to many of the citizens law enforcement officers are sworn to protect. There has been little input by law enforcement in the prolegalization debate. They should be more involved and be armed with the facts that will counter such arguments by pointing out the correlation between drug abuse and violent crime, and the fact marijuana is often a gateway drug for other more dangerous drugs of abuse.

References

1. Source: Bureau of Justice Statistics (BJS), *Profile of Jail Inmates, 1996*, NCJ 164620, April 1998.
2. *Drug Use, Testing, and Treatment in Jails*, NCJ 179999, May 2000.
3. BJS, Substance Abuse and Treatment, State and Federal Prisoners, 1997, NCJ 172871, January 1999.

Glossary of Terms Common to Drug Law Enforcement

ACISS An automated date analysis system.

ADA Assistant District Attorney. Attorney who acts under the authority of the District Attorney's office to represent the state in all criminal matters within a particular jurisdiction, typically a county.

AMA Dump A common term for a cellular telephone company.

APB All points bulletin; advisory police board. General policy of the FBI is recommended by the APB that operates under the principles of the National Crime Information Center (NCIC). It is comprised of member law enforcement agencies across the United States.

ASAC Assistant special agent in charge. The term is used by the DEA, FBI, U.S. Secret Service, and most other federal agencies.

ATF Commonly used to reference the U.S. Department of Justice's Bureau of Alcohol, Tobacco, and Firearms; formerly a part of the Department of Treasury.

AUSA Assistant U.S. Attorney. A federal prosecutor who handles criminal and civil matters for the U.S. government.

Activity flowcharting Used to pinpoint patterns of activity as sequential events.

Administrative subpena The DEA, FBI, and other agencies are authorized by statute to issue subpenas for records, including telephone subscriber and toll information. They cannot be used to obtain bank records. A grand jury subpoena is required for bank records. Note the different spelling of *subpoena* when referring to administrative subpenas.

Affidavit A sworn written statement made under oath before an individual authorized by law to certify the statement. Affidavits are used in support for an application for a search warrant.

Affiant The law enforcement official who files a sworn affidavit in support of the application for a search or arrest warrant.

Analysis The function of developing meaning from collected data or information.

Analyst Notebook® A commonly used software program to aid in the analysis of data and to construct link diagrams and flow charts.

Association matrix The first step in the link analysis process. Shows the raw data about people and organizations associated with known or suspected criminal activity. It is an effort to organize this information into a systematic or logical order.

BATF Bureau of Alcohol, Tobacco, and Firearms. Now a part of the Department of Justice, it is responsible for the enforcement and administration of laws related to alcohol, tobacco, firearms, explosives, arson, and other destructive devices.

C3I Command, control, communication, and intelligence. A division of the Bureau of Immigration and Customs Enforcement of the U.S. Customs Service responsible for ground- and aerial-based tracking radars. It is the main clearinghouse for detecting suspicious aircraft involved in smuggling.

CALEA Communication Assistance for Law Enforcement Act enacted in 1994, which allows the government to use technology that is reasonably available during the course of an investigation.

CI Confidential informant. Sometimes called confidential source (CS) or cooperating witness (CW). Used in drug investigations due to their specific and intimate information related to drug trafficking activity.

CIA Central Intelligence Agency. Operates the Crime and Narcotics Center. Monitors, reviews, and delivers information about international drug trafficking and international organized crime to government leaders and law enforcement agencies.

CID The Criminal Investigation Division of the Internal Revenue Service (IRS). Also the Criminal Investigation Command of the U. S. Army. IRS CID is a member agency of the OCDETF program.

CPIC Canadian Police Information Centre. Operates similarly to the FBI's NCIC.

CS Confidential source. Sometimes called confidential informant (CI) or cooperating witness (CW). Used in drug investigations due to their specific and intimate information related to drug trafficking activity.

CSA Controlled Substance Act. Title 21 of the U.S. Code that created the DEA and contains criminal statutes related to federal drug violations.

CTA Control terminal agency. The message switcher used in each state for NCIC traffic.

CTR Currency transaction report.

CW Cooperating witness or confidential witness. Sometimes called confidential source (CS) or confidential informant (CI). Used in drug investigations due to their specific and intimate information related to drug trafficking activity.

Cell site Cellular telephones emit a signal that can be traced back to a particular cellular tower. Each cell site has a numerical identifier called a cell site.

Circuit court A court that has jurisdiction over several counties, districts, or states. A circuit court holds sessions in all these areas.

Commodities In general terms, something of common value for trade or commerce. A tangible good such as products or merchandise, other than a service. In the drug trade, a commodity could be the drug itself, weapons, money, or other services which may be provided.

Commodities flowcharting Graphic illustration showing the flow of a commodity, either tangible or intangible during a criminal activity.

Consumers In the drug trade, this person is an addicted individual who buys small quantities of drugs for personal use.

Controlled Substance Act Also known as the CSA. Title 21 of the U.S. Code that created the DEA and contains criminal statutes related to federal drug violations.

Control terminal Message center for delivering messages to the NCIC and retrieving messages from the CTA. Each state has a version of this messaging system.

Corroborate To strengthen and support with evidence. As in *corroborating* the information provided by a CI.

Court order A written direction, instruction, or command handed down by a judge. Also known as a judicial order.

Customs A common term for the former U.S. Customs Service, which is now the Bureau of Immigration and Customs Enforcement (ICE) within the Department of Homeland Security. ICE has the authority to search any person, vehicle, or container entering or leaving the United States without a warrant.

DEA Drug Enforcement Administration. A part of the U.S. Department of Justice, it has the responsibility of enforcing the Controlled Substance Act (CSA). Member agency of the OCDETF program.

DNR Dialed number recorder. Device that is attached to a telephone line and provides real time information about numbers dialed by the target phone. Also known as a pen register. They do not provide the content of the telephone conversation, but do provide information on the time, date, and duration of the call, as well as the number dialed. A court order is required to install such a device.

DO District office. Term used by the DEA for an office subordinate to a field division, but superior to a resident office.

Detective Criminal investigator for a local police department.

District Attorney A local public official who is elected or appointed to represent the state in all criminal matters in a particular jurisdiction, usually a county.

District Court A trial court which has general jurisdiction in a specific judicial district. The United States has 92 district courts located throughout the country and its territories.

EPIC The El Paso Intelligence Center. Joint federal organization managed by the Drug Enforcement Administration, located in Fort Bliss, TX. It is a national repository of criminal information related to drugs, alien smuggling and weapons. Serves as a one-stop-shop for member agencies to run individuals through multiple federal databases.

Event flowcharting Provides a graphical depiction of a series of events in order of occurrence.

Extension of the border search An investigative technique used by ICE where a vehicle entering the United States that is believed to be carrying drugs or other contraband is followed and then searched upon its arrival at its initial stopping place. A search warrant is not required for this search.

FBI Federal Bureau of Investigation. Investigates a variety of violations of U.S. Code. Has concurrent Title 21 (CSA) authority with the DEA. Member agency of OCDETF.

FBI-AIS Federal Bureau of Investigation Automatic Identification System. Automated system for identifying record fingerprints.

FBI-III Federal Bureau of Investigation Interstate Identification Index.

FINCEN Financial Crimes Enforcement Network. FINCEN was established as a multi-agency, multi-source financial intelligence and analytical network to serve as a source of systematic identification, collation, and analysis of information related to financial crimes.

FMS search A common term for a cellular telephone provider.

Federal Appellate Court A circuit court that may overturn or uphold the standings of a federal trial court within its jurisdiction.

Federal court A court which has federal jurisdiction. Federal courts include the U.S. Supreme Court, Courts of Appeals, district courts, bankruptcy courts, and tax courts.

Flow charting Used to show a relationship between activities, events, and commodities. Shows a progression of activities over a period of time.

Flipping a suspect The process of convincing a freshly arrested drug suspect to become a confidential informant.

FAA Federal Aviation Administration. Provides information pertaining to pilots, mechanics, and the registration and history of aircraft. Member agency of OCDETF.

FSN Foreign service national. An employee of a U.S. embassy who is a local national of the host country. The DEA employs many vetted FSN investigators at their more than 78 offices worldwide.

Friendly A person who is a confidential informant.

G/J Refers to a grand jury.

G/S Group supervisor. Term used for a supervisory special agent of the DEA.

Grand jury A body of citizens who are impaneled at random and who serve for at least a month, sometimes up to a year or more, and who in proceedings outside of the courtroom, decides where to issue indictments. A true bill of indictment is issued if the grand jury decides that evidence in a certain case is strong enough to charge a suspect with a specific crime. Grand juries are usually comprised of 24 persons.

Grand jury subpoena A writ issued by a grand jury to obtain records, including bank and other financial records.

HIDTA High intensity drug trafficking area. This program is funded by the Office of National Drug Control Policy (ONDCP) to provide resources to locations that have been designated as having critical drug trafficking problems. HIDTAs are located throughout the United States, predominately in large metropolitan centers.

HIFCA High-intensity money laundering and related crime area. Similar to HIDTAs; however, its focus is on major money-laundering organizations operating within a specific geographical area.

IA or **I/A** (1) Intelligence analyst. (2) Investigative assistant. (3) Internal affairs.

IRS U.S. Internal Revenue Service. Responsible for enforcing the tax codes of the United States. IRS special agents can seize property and money believed to be derived from drug trafficking. A part of the U.S. Treasury Department that investigates, through its Criminal Investigation Division (CID), persons who evade paying income taxes through profits from legal and illegal business, such as the drug trade. IRS CID is a member of the OCDETF program.

In camera When confidential or sensitive information is examined outside of the court session to determine whether it can become public record.

Indictment A formal accusation of a specific crime brought by a prosecutor and returned by a grand jury. An indictment can be in lieu of a pretrial hearing.

Intelligence analyst Also known as an I/A. A member of an investigative team whose responsibility is to determine relationships between people and events.

INTERPOL The International Police Organization. An international law enforcement and criminal intelligence association with more than 125 member nations. Contact with INTERPOL is made through different member federal agencies, including the FBI and DEA.

Interstate Crossing a state line, outside the borders of a state.

JIATF Joint Interagency Task Force. Currently there are two, West, located in Oakland, CA and South, located in Key West, FL. Both provide military assets in drug interdiction operations in the Pacific, Atlantic, Gulf of Mexico, and Caribbean.

JTF Joint task force. A joint military operation in participation with the DEA, FBI, and ICE. It is designed to provide analytical and logistic support in counter-drug operations.

Jurisdiction The territory or limitations in which political or judicial authority may be exercised.

Key Refers to a kilo.

Kilo A metric unit of measurement equaling 1000 grams and weighing approximately 2.2 pounds.

LEA Law enforcement agency.

LEIU Law enforcement intelligence unit. Located in California, this unit is a nationwide organization with members from state, county, and local agencies. Also included is Canada.

Lane check A check the Bureau of Immigration and Customs Enforcement makes to determine if a particular person has recently entered the United States. See Silent lookout.

Link analysis An investigative tool to graphically illustrate known and suspected associates of individuals, businesses, and other entities in a complex drug conspiracy investigations. Used for one set period of time only.

MAGLOCLEN Middle Atlantic Great Lakes Organized Crime Law Enforcement Network. A part of the Regional Information Sharing System (RISS), located in Pennsylvania.

MSOCIC Mid States Organized Crime Information Center. A part of the RISS, located in Missouri.

MTF Multi-jurisdictional task forces. MTFs are sponsored by federal agencies that federally deputize state and local task force officers (TFO) who may need to cross outside their jurisdiction in the course of a criminal investigation.

Mag Ct U.S. magistrate court.

Measured Service Telephone calls made on a payment per call basis.

Mule An individual who is hired to smuggle drugs or money. A drug smuggler.

NADDIS Narcotics and Dangerous Drugs Information System. Maintained by the DEA, covering over three million records with worldwide information archived and current drug related investigations, names, addresses, and telephone numbers.

NCIC National Crime Information Center. Standardizes data for the FBI and participating states on information related to people, vehicles, properties, and securities. Also contains the U.S. Secret Service's protective files.

NCIS Naval Criminal Investigation Service. Responsible for handling all investigations for naval counter-intelligence and security.

NDIC National Drug Intelligence Center. Located in Johnstown, PA, this agency collects comprehensive information from 88 different agencies to gain global strategic information about drug related activity. Provides analytical products and support for large-scale federal drug investigations. Reports directly to the Deputy Attorney General of the United States.

NESPIN New England State Police Information Network. A part of the RISS located in Massachusetts.

NLETS National Law Enforcement Telecommunication System. A nationwide system of telecommunication that assists in the exchange of information between states and to Canada (through INTERPOL).

OCDETF Organized Crime Drug Enforcement Task Forces program. Federal program initiated in 1982, which provides funding and expertise for selected investigations concerning organized drug traffickers. Member agencies include the DEA, U.S. Marshals Service, U.S. Coast Guard, FBI, FAA, IRS, and ICE.

ONDCP Office of National Drug Control Policy. ONDCP falls under the executive office of the President of the United States and was established to oversee the implementation of drug control strategies and advises the National Security Council (NSC) on drug related policy.

ORI Originating agency identifier. A nine character code used by the U.S. Justice Department through the FBI NCIC, to identify law enforcement/criminal justice agencies.

OSI Air Force Office of Investigations. Responsible for criminal investigations and counter-intelligence matters affecting the U.S. Air Force.

Ounce A unit of measurement, approximately 28 grams.

PC Probable cause. A requirement for search and seizure and arrest warrants. Requires that sufficient knowledge and facts be present to reasonably believe that a crime has been committed or that property is connected with a criminal act.

POD Post of duty. Term used by the DEA for an office subordinate to a resident office. Usually staffed with two or three special agents.

Penlink® A commonly used software program used by intelligence analysts to download and receive telephone numbers.

Pen register Also known as a dialed number recorder (DNR). Device that is attached to a telephone line and provides real time information about numbers dialed on the target phone. The equipment does not provide the content of the telephone conversation, but do provide information on the time, date, and duration of the call, as well as the number dialed. A court order is required to install such a device.

Pipeline stop Refers to Operation Pipeline. When a state trooper stops a driver because he and his vehicle exhibit characteristics indicative of being a cross-country drug courier.

Posse comitatus The Posse Comitatus Act of 1878 was passed by Congress in response to military interference with a civil election. The act restricts the power of the military in regards to enforcing civilian law. Revisions to this act have expanded the military's role in providing assistance to civilian law enforcement personnel combating drug related criminal activity.

Producers Individuals or organizations that produce and distribute a drug to wholesalers who have distribution networks in place.

Prosecution summary A summary prepared by the prosecuting attorney who outlines the major events of a case.

RA Resident agency. Term used by the FBI and other federal agencies to identify an office that is subordinate to a field division.

RAC Resident agent in charge. Term used by the DEA for the supervisory special agent in charge of a resident office (RO).

RO Resident office. Term used by the DEA to signify an office subordinate to a district office or field division.

RISS Regional Information Sharing Systems. This program is federally funded to support law enforcement agencies in their efforts to combat organized crime, drug trafficking, gang activity, and violent crime. This program is made up of six regional projects covering all 50 states. These regional projects are: MAGELOCEN, MOCIC, NESPIN, RMIN, ROCIC, and WSIN.

RMIN Rocky Mountain Information Network. A part of the RISS program located in Arizona.

ROCIC Regional Organized Crime Information Center. A part of the RISS program located in Tennessee.

Reasonable suspicion Facts or other information that would cause a reasonable person to believe that a crime has been or was about to be committed.

Retailers Street level drug dealers who deal in small quantities.

SA or S/A Special agent. Term used by most federal agencies to designate a criminal investigator.

SAC Special agent in charge.

SSA Supervisory special agent.

SSRA Supervisory senior resident agent. Term used by the FBI to designate the agent in charge of a resident agency (RA).

Significant violator A major drug trafficker who may be an organizer, manager, or supervisor for a large a criminal organization.

Silent lookout ICE will tell a requesting law enforcement agency when a particular suspect or his vehicle enters the United States. ICE inspectors will not harass or otherwise alert the suspect he is being scrutinized.

Subpoena A court ordered writ demanding that an individual (1) appear in a court proceeding to testify, and (2) produce documents or other items in a court proceeding, under penalty of prosecution.

2DetectML A money-laundering detection system used by the DEA, ICE, and the IRS that monitors financial transactions to detect the presence of money laundering. It is manufactured by Actionable Intelligence Technologies.

TECS Treasury Enforcement Computer System. Maintained by ICE; records pilot and flight records in and out of the country. It also records boat registrations and look out lists of boats and aircrafts transiting in and out of the country.

TFO Task force officer.

TSA Transportation Security Administration. A part of the Department of Homeland Security charged with providing air marshals and luggage screeners at airports throughout the United States.

Target The subject of a drug investigation.

Telephone debit cards Cards that provide prepaid telephone service. Often used by drug traffickers because there is no record of the sale of the cards. However, if found on a drug dealer, the company that issued the card can provide a listing of telephone numbers called from the card number.

Telephone toll analysis The act of analyzing telephone toll records to establish a link between individuals in an investigation. Can show links in a criminal conspiracy. It is one of the most effective methods of collecting evidence in a drug investigation.

Title III Sometimes called T-3. The portion of federal law that governs the use of wiretaps.

Trial court The court that has the original jurisdiction, and where the evidence is first considered.

Transporting groups Networks that have transportation channels to specific and strategically located distribution points. At the distribution points, they sell wholesale quantities to a chain of distributors.

UC (1) Undercover. (2) Undercover agent.

UMS search A common term for a cellular telephone company.

U.S. Attorney Appointed by the President, the U.S. Attorney for each of the 92 federal judicial districts represents the United States in all criminal and civil matters that fall under federal jurisdiction.

USCG United States Coast Guard. Among other duties, the USCG conducts drug interdiction missions and have the authority to arrest drug smugglers attempting to introduce contraband into the United States. It is now a part of the Department of Homeland Security.

USMS United States Marshals Service. Part of the U.S. Department of Justice, these federal officers carry out the orders of the federal courts. They provide courtroom security in federal court, and arrest federal fugitives, many of which are wanted for drug violations.

USSS United States Secret Service. Responsible for protecting the President; Secret Service agents prevent and investigate counterfeiting, and investigate criminal activity related to money transfers and computer fraud.

U.S. Court of Appeals A federal appellate court that has jurisdiction over the 13 judicial districts, District of Columbia, and federal circuit court. Cases from these districts can be stayed or overturned by the U.S. Court of Appeals.

WSIN Western States Information Network. A part of the RISS program located in California.

Wall-off An investigative technique in drug cases in which the involvement of a federal agency is disguised in order to not alert the drug traffickers there is a federal interest in their illegal activities.

Wholesalers Drug dealers who have distribution networks in place. Wholesalers can be small or extensive organizations.

Appendix A: Controlled Substance Act Schedules*

This document is a general reference and not a comprehensive list. This list describes the basic or parent chemical and does not describe the salts, isomers and salts of isomers, esters, ethers and derivatives which may also be controlled substances.

Schedule I

Substance	DEA Number	Non-Narcotic	Other Names
1-(1-Phenylcyclohexyl) pyrrolidine	7458	N	PCPy, PHP, rolicyclidine
1-(2-Phenylethyl)-4-phenyl-4-acetoxypiperidine	9663		PEPAP, synthetic heroin
1-[1-(2-Thienyl) cyclohexyl] piperidine	7470	N	TCP, tenocyclidine
1-[1-(2-Thienyl) cyclohexyl] pyrrolidine	7473	N	TCPy
1-Methyl-4-phenyl-4-propionoxypiperidine	9661		MPPP, synthetic heroin
2,5-Dimethoxy-4-ethylamphetamine	7399	N	DOET
2,5-Dimethoxyamphetamine	7396	N	DMA, 2,5-DMA
3,4,5-Trimethoxyamphetamine	7390	N	TMA
3,4-Methylenedioxyamphetamine	7400	N	MDA, Love Drug
3,4-Methylenedioxymethamphetamine	7405	N	MDMA, Ecstasy, XTC
3,4-Methylenedioxy-*N*-ethylamphetamine	7404	N	*N*-ethyl MDA, MDE, MDEA
3-Methylfentanyl	9813		China White, fentanyl
3-Methylthiofentanyl	9833		Chine White, fentanyl
4-Bromo-2, 5-dimethoxyamphetamine	7391	N	DOB, 4-bromo-DMA
4-Bromo-2, 5-dimethoxyphenethylamine	7392	N	Nexus, 2-CB, has been sold as Ecstasy, i.e., MDMA
4-Methoxyamphetamine	7411	N	PMA
4-Methyl-2, 5-dimethoxyamphetamine	7395	N	DOM, STP
4-Methylaminorex (*cis* isomer)	1590	N	U4Euh, McN-422

Note: N = nonnarcotic

* Drug Enforcement Administration

Schedule I (continued)

Substance	DEA Number	Non-Narcotic	Other Names
5-Methoxy-3, 4-methylenedioxyamphetamine	7401	N	MMDA
Acetorphine	9319		
Acetyl-alpha-methylfentanyl	9815		
Acetyldihydrocodeine	9051		Acetylcodone
Acetylmethadol	9601		Methadyl acetate
Allylprodine	9602		
Alphacetylmethadol except levo-alphacetylmethadol	9603		
Alpha-Ethyltryptamine	7249	N	ET, Trip
Alphameprodine	9604		
Alphamethadol	9605		
Alpha-Methylfentanyl	9814		China White, fentanyl
Alpha-Methylthiofentanyl	9832		China White, fentanyl
Aminorex	1585	N	Has been sold as methamphetamine
Benzethidine	9606		
Benzylmorphine	9052		
Betacetylmethadol	9607		
Beta-Hydroxy-3-methylfentanyl	9831		China White, fentanyl
Beta-Hydroxyfentanyl	9830		China White, fentanyl
Betameprodine	9608		
Betamethadol	9609		
Betaprodine	9611		
Bufotenine	7433	N	Mappine, *N, N*-dimethylserotonin
Cathinone	1235	N	Constituent of khat plant
Clonitazene	9612		
Codeine methylbromide	9070		
Codeine-*N*-oxide	9053		
Cyprenorphine	9054		
Desomorphine	9055		
Dextromoramide	9613		Palfium, Jetrium, Narcolo
Diampromide	9615		
Diethylthiambutene	9616		
Diethyltryptamine	7434	N	DET
Difenoxin	9168		Lyspafen
Dihydromorphine	9145		
Dimenoxadol	9617		
Dimepheptanol	9618		
Dimethylthiambutene	9619		
Dimethyltryptamine	7435	N	DMT
Dioxaphetyl butyrate	9621		
Dipipanone	9622		Dipipan, phenylpiperone HCl, Diconal, Wellconal

Schedule I (continued)

Substance	DEA Number	Non-Narcotic	Other Names
Drotebanol	9335		Metebanyl, oxymethebanol
Ethylmethylthiambutene	9623		
Etonitazene	9624		
Etorphine (except HCl)	9056		
Etoxeridine	9625		
Fenethylline	1503	N	Captagon, amfetyline, ethyltheophylline amphetamine
Furethidine	9626		
Gamma Hydroxybutyric Acid (GHB)	2100	N	GHB, gamma hydroxybutyrate, sodium oxybate
Heroin	9200		Diacetylmorphine, diamorphine
Hydromorphinol	9301		
Hydroxypethidine	9627		
Ibogaine	7260	N	Constituent of *Tabernanthe iboga* plant
Ketobemidone	9628		Cliradon
Levomoramide	9629		
Levophenacylmorphan	9631		
Lysergic acid diethylamide	7315	N	LSD, lysergide
Marihuana	7360	N	Cannabis, marijuana
Mecloqualone	2572	N	Nubarene
Mescaline	7381	N	Constituent of peyote cacti
Methaqualone	2565	N	Quaalude, Parest, Somnafac, Opitimil, Mandrax
Methcathinone	1237	N	*N*-Methylcathinone, cat
Methyldesorphine	9302		
Methyldihydromorphine	9304		
Morpheridine	9632		
Morphine methylbromide	9305		
Morphine methylsulfonate	9306		
Morphine-*N*-oxide	9307		
Myrophine	9308		
N, *N*-Dimethylamphetamine	1480	N	
N-Ethyl-1-phenylcyclohexylamine	7455	N	PCE
N-Ethyl-3-piperidyl benzilate	7482	N	JB 323
N-Ethylamphetamine	1475	N	NEA
N-Hydroxy-3,4-methylenedioxyamphetamine	7402	N	*N*-hydroxy MDA
Nicocodeine	9309		
Nicomorphine	9312		Vilan

Schedule I (continued)

Substance	DEA Number	Non-Narcotic	Other Names
N-Methyl-3-piperidyl benzilate	7484	N	JB 336
Noracymethadol	9633		
Norlevorphanol	9634		
Normethadone	9635		Phenyldimazone
Normorphine	9313		
Norpipanone	9636		
Para-Fluorofentanyl	9812		China White, fentanyl
Parahexyl	7374	N	Synhexyl,
Peyote	7415	N	Cactus which contains mescaline
Phenadoxone	9637		
Phenampromide	9638		
Phenomorphan	9647		
Phenoperidine	9641		Operidine, Lealgin
Pholcodine	9314		Copholco, Adaphol, Codisol, Lantuss, Pholcolin
Piritramide	9642		Piridolan
Proheptazine	9643		
Properidine	9644		
Propiram	9649		Algeril
Psilocybin	7437	N	Constituent of "magic mushrooms"
Psilocyn	7438	N	Psilocin, constituent of "magic mushrooms"
Racemoramide	9645		
Tetrahydrocannabinols	7370	N	THC, Delta-8 THC, Delta-9 THC and others
Thebacon	9315		Acetylhydrocodone, Acedicon, Thebacetyl
Thiofentanyl	9835		Chine white, fentanyl
Tilidine	9750		Tilidate, Valoron, Kitadol, Lak, Tilsa
Trimeperidine	9646		Promedolum

Schedule II

Substance	DEA Number	Non-Narcotic	Other Names
1-Phenylcyclohexylamine	7460	N	Precusor of PCP
1-Piperidinocyclohexanecarbonitrile	8603	N	PCC, precusor of PCP
Alfentanil	9737		Alfenta
Alphaprodine	9010		Nisentil

Schedule II (continued)

Substance	DEA Number	Non-Narcotic	Other Names
Amobarbital	2125	N	Amytal, Tuinal
Amphetamine	1100	N	Dexedrine, Biphetamine
Anileridine	9020		Leritine
Benzoylecgonine	9180		Cocaine metabolite
Bezitramide	9800		Burgodin
Carfentanil	9743		Wildnil
Coca leaves	9040		
Cocaine	9041		Methyl benzoylecgonine, crack
Codeine	9050		Morphine methyl ester, methyl morphine
Dextropropoxyphene, bulk (non-dosage forms)	9273		Propoxyphene
Dihydrocodeine	9120		Didrate, Parzone
Diphenoxylate	9170		
Diprenorphine	9058		M50-50
Ecgonine	9180		Cocaine precursor, in coca leaves
Ethylmorphine	9190		Dionin
Etorphine HCl	9059		M 99
Fentanyl	9801		Innovar, Sublimaze, Duragesic
Glutethimide	2550	N	Doriden, Dorimide
Hydrocodone	9193		Dihydrocodeinone
Hydromorphone	9150		Dilaudid, dihydromorphinone
Isomethadone	9226		Isoamidone
Levo-alphacetylmethadol	9648		LAAM, long acting methadone, levomethadyl acetate
Levomethorphan	9210		
Levorphanol	9220		Levo-Dromoran
Meperidine	9230		Demerol, Mepergan, pethidine
Meperidine intermediate-A	9232		Meperidine precursor
Meperidine intermediate-B	9233		Meperidine precursor
Meperidine intermediate-C	9234		Meperidine precursor
Metazocine	9240		

Schedule II (continued)

Substance	DEA Number	Non-Narcotic	Other Names
Methadone	9250		Dolophine, Methadose, Amidone
Methadone intermediate	9254		Methadone precursor
Methamphetamine	1105	N	Desoxyn, D-desoxyephedrine, ICE, Crank, Speed
Methylphenidate	1724	N	Ritalin
Metopon	9260		
Moramide-intermediate	9802		
Morphine	9300		MS Contin, Roxanol, Duramorph, RMS, MSIR
Nabilone	7379	N	Cesamet
Opium extracts	9610		
Opium fluid extract	9620		
Opium poppy	9650		Papaver somniferum
Opium tincture	9630		Laudanum
Opium, granulated	9640		Granulated opium
Opium, powdered	9639		Powdered opium
Opium, raw	9600		Raw opium, gum opium
Oxycodone	9143		OxyContin, Percocet, Tylox, Roxicodone, Roxicet,
Oxymorphone	9652		Numorphan
Pentobarbital	2270	N	Nembutal
Phenazocine	9715		Narphen, Prinadol
Phencyclidine	7471	N	PCP, Sernylan
Phenmetrazine	1631	N	Preludin
Phenylacetone	8501	N	P2P, phenyl-2-propanone, benzyl methyl ketone
Piminodine	9730		
Poppy straw	9650		Opium poppy capsules, poppy heads
Poppy straw concentrate	9670		Concentrate of poppy straw, CPS
Racemethorphan	9732		
Racemorphan	9733		Dromoran
Remifentanil	9739		Ultiva
Secobarbital	2315	N	Seconal, Tuinal
Sufentanil	9740		Sufenta

Schedule II (continued)

Substance	DEA Number	Non-Narcotic	Other Names
Thebaine	9333		Precursor of many narcotics

Schedule III

Substance	DEA Number	Non-Narcotic	Other Names
Amobarbital and noncontrolled active ingredient	2126	N	Amobarbital/ephedrine capsules
Amobarbital suppository dosage form	2126	N	
Anabolic steroids	4000	N	Body building drugs
Aprobarbital	2100	N	Alurate
Barbituric acid derivative	2100	N	Barbiturates not specifically listed
Benzphetamine	1228	N	Didrex, Inapetyl
Boldenone	4000	N	Equipoise, Parenabol, Vebonol, dehydrotestosterone
Butabarbital	2100	N	Butisol, Butibel
Butalbital	2100	N	Fiorinal, Butalbital with aspirin
Chlorhexadol	2510	N	Mechloral, Mecoral, Medodorm, Chloralodol
Chlorotestosterone (same as clostebol)	4000	N	If 4-chlorotestosterone then clostebol
Chlorphentermine	1645	N	Pre-Sate, Lucofen, Apsedon, Desopimon
Clortermine	1647	N	Voranil
Clostebol	4000	N	Alfa-Trofodermin, Clostene, 4-chlorotestosterone
Codeine and isoquinoline alkaloid 90 mg/du	9803		Codeine with papaverine or noscapine
Codeine combination product 90 mg/du	9804		Empirin, Fiorinal, Tylenol, ASA or APAP w/codeine
Dehydrochlormethyltestosterone	4000	N	Oral-Turinabol
Dihydrocodeine combination product 90 mg/du	9807		Synalgos-DC, Compal
Dihydrotestosterone (same as stanolone)	4000	N	See stanolone
Dronabinol in sesame oil in soft gelatin capsule	7369	N	Marinol, synthetic THC in sesame oil/soft gelatin
Drostanolone	4000	N	Drolban, Masterid, Permastril

Schedule III (continued)

Substance	DEA Number	Non-Narcotic	Other Names
Ethylestrenol	4000	N	Maxibolin, Orabolin, Durabolin-O, Duraboral
Ethylmorphine combination product 15 mg/du	9808		
Fluoxymesterone	4000	N	Anadroid-F, Halotestin, Ora-Testryl
Formebolone (incorrect spelling in law)	4000	N	Esiclene, Hubernol
Hydrocodone and isoquinoline alkaloid 15 mg/du	9805		Dihydrocodeinone+papaverine or noscapine
Hydrocodone combination product 15 mg/du	9806		Tussionex, Tussend, Lortab, Vicodin, Hycodan, Anexsia ++
Ketamine	7285	N	Ketaset, Ketalar, Special K, K
Lysergic acid	7300	N	LSD precursor
Lysergic acid amide	7310	N	LSD precursor
Mesterolone	4000	N	Proviron
Methandienone (see Methandrostenolone)	4000	N	
Methandranone	4000	N	
Methandriol	4000	N	Sinesex, Stenediol, Troformone
Methandrostenolone	4000	N	Dianabol, Metabolina, Nerobol, Perbolin
Methenolone	4000	N	Primobolan, Primobolan Depot, Primobolan S
Methyltestosterone	4000	N	Android, Oreton, Testred, Virilon
Methyprylon	2575	N	Noludar
Mibolerone	4000	N	Cheque
Morphine combination product/50 mg/100 ml or gm	9810		
Nalorphine	9400		Nalline
Nandrolone	4000	N	Deca-Durabolin, Durabolin, Durabolin-50
Norethandrolone	4000	N	Nilevar, Solevar
Opium combination product 25 mg/du	9809		Paregoric, other combination products
Oxandrolone	4000	N	Anavar, Lonavar, Provitar, Vasorome
Oxymesterone	4000	N	Anamidol, Balnimax, Oranabol, Oranabol 10
Oxymetholone	4000	N	Anadrol-50, Adroyd, Anapolon, Anasteron, Pardroyd

Schedule III (continued)

Substance	DEA Number	Non-Narcotic	Other Names
Pentobarbital and noncontrolled active ingredient	2271	N	FP-3
Pentobarbital suppository dosage form	2271	N	WANS
Phendimetrazine	1615	N	Plegine, Prelu-2, Bontril, Melfiat, Statobex
Secobarbital and noncontrolled active ingred	2316	N	Various
Secobarbital suppository dosage form	2316	N	Various
Stanolone	4000	N	Anabolex, Andractim, Pesomax, dihydrotestosterone
Stanozolol	4000	N	Winstrol, Winstrol-V
Stimulant compounds previously excepted	1405	N	Mediatric
Sulfondiethylmethane	2600	N	
Sulfonethylmethane	2605	N	
Sulfonmethane	2610	N	
Talbutal	2100	N	Lotusate
Testolactone	4000	N	Teslac
Testosterone	4000	N	Android-T, Androlan, Depotest, Delatestryl
Thiamylal	2100	N	Surital
Thiopental	2100	N	Pentothal
Tiletamine and Zolazepam combination product	7295	N	Telazol
Trenbolone	4000	N	Finaplix-S, Finajet, Parabolan
Vinbarbital	2100	N	Delvinal, vinbarbitone

Schedule IV

Substance	DEA Number	Non-Narcotic	Other Names
Alprazolam	2882	N	Xanax
Barbital	2145	N	Veronal, Plexonal, barbitone
Bromazepam	2748	N	Lexotan, Lexatin, Lexotanil
Butorphanol	9720	N	Stadol, Stadol NS, Torbugesic, Torbutrol
Camazepam	2749	N	Albego, Limpidon, Paxor
Cathine	1230	N	Constituent of "Khat" plant
Chloral betaine	2460	N	Beta Chlor
Chloral hydrate	2465	N	Noctec

Schedule IV

Substance	DEA Number	Non-Narcotic	Other Names
Chlordiazepoxide	2744	N	Librium, Libritabs, Limbitrol, SK-Lygen
Clobazam	2751	N	Urbadan, Urbanyl
Clonazepam	2737	N	Klonopin, Clonopin
Clorazepate	2768	N	Tranxene
Clotiazepam	2752	N	Trecalmo, Rize
Cloxazolam	2753	N	Enadel, Sepazon, Tolestan
Delorazepam	2754	N	
Dexfenfluramine	1670	N	Redux
Dextropropoxyphene dosage forms	9278		Darvon, propoxyphene, Darvocet, Dolene, Propacet
Diazepam	2765	N	Valium, Valrelease
Dichloralphenazone	2467	N	Midrin, dichloralantipyrine
Diethylpropion	1610	N	Tenuate, Tepanil
Difenoxin 1 mg/25 µg AtSO4/du	9167		Motofen
Estazolam	2756	N	ProSom, Domnamid, Eurodin, Nuctalon
Ethchlorvynol	2540	N	Placidyl
Ethinamate	2545	N	Valmid, Valamin
Ethyl loflazepate	2758	N	
Fencamfamin	1760	N	Reactivan
Fenfluramine	1670	N	Pondimin, Ponderal
Fenproporex	1575	N	Gacilin, Solvolip
Fludiazepam	2759	N	
Flunitrazepam	2763	N	Rohypnol, Narcozep, Darkene, Roipnol
Flurazepam	2767	N	Dalmane
Halazepam	2762	N	Paxipam
Haloxazolam	2771	N	
Ketazolam	2772	N	Anxon, Loftran, Solatran, Contamex
Loprazolam	2773	N	
Lorazepam	2885	N	Ativan
Lormetazepam	2774	N	Noctamid
Mazindol	1605	N	Sanorex, Mazanor
Mebutamate	2800	N	Capla
Medazepam	2836	N	Nobrium
Mefenorex	1580	N	Anorexic, Amexate, Doracil, Pondinil
Meprobamate	2820	N	Miltown, Equanil, Deprol, Equagesic, Meprospan
Methohexital	2264	N	Brevital
Methylphenobarbital (mephobarbital)	2250	N	Mebaral, mephobarbital

Schedule IV

Substance	DEA Number	Non-Narcotic	Other Names
Midazolam	2884	N	Versed
Modafinil	1680	N	Provigil
Nimetazepam	2837	N	Erimin
Nitrazepam	2834	N	Mogadon
Nordiazepam	2838	N	Nordazepam, Demadar, Madar
Oxazepam	2835	N	Serax, Serenid-D
Oxazolam	2839	N	Serenal, Convertal
Paraldehyde	2585	N	Paral
Pemoline	1530	N	Cylert
Pentazocine	9709	N	Talwin, Talwin NX, Talacen, Talwin compound
Petrichloral	2591	N	Pentaerythritol chloral, Periclor
Phenobarbital	2285	N	Luminal, Donnatal, Bellergal-S
Phentermine	1640	N	Ionamin, Fastin, Adipex-P, Obe-Nix, Zantryl
Pinazepam	2883	N	Domar
Pipradrol	1750	N	Detaril, Stimolag Fortis
Prazepam	2764	N	Centrax
Quazepam	2881	N	Doral, Dormalin
Sibutramine	1675	N	Meridia
SPA	1635	N	1-dimethylamino-1, 2-diphenylethane, Lefetamine
Temazepam	2925	N	Restoril
Tetrazepam	2886	N	
Triazolam	2887	N	Halcion
Zaleplon	2781	N	Sonata
Zolpidem	2783	N	Ambien, Stilnoct, Ivadal

Schedule V

Substance	DEA Number	Non-Narcotic	Other Names
Buprenorphine	9064		Buprenex, Temgesic
Codeine preparations 200 mg/100 ml or 100 gm			Cosanyl, Robitussin A-C, Cheracol, Cerose, Pediacof
Difenoxin preparations 0.5 mg/25 μg AtSO4/du			Motofen

Schedule V

Substance	DEA Number	Non-Narcotic	Other Names
Dihydrocodeine preparations 10 mg/100 ml or 100 gm			Cophene-S, various others
Diphenoxylate preparations 2.5 mg/25 μg AtSO4			Lomotil, Logen
Ethylmorphine preparations 100 mg/100 ml or 100 gm			
Opium preparations 100 mg/100 ml or gm			Parepectolin, Kapectolin PG, Kaolin Pectin P.G.
Pyrovalerone	1485	N	Centroton, Thymergix

Appendix B: Controlled Substances Alphabetically*

A

Acetorphine

DEA Number	9319
CSA Schedule	I
Classification	Narcotic
Other Names	

Acetyl-alpha-methylfentanyl

DEA Number	9815
CSA Schedule	I
Classification	Narcotic
Other Names	

Acetyldihydrocodeine

DEA Number	9051
CSA Schedule	I
Classification	Narcotic
Other Names	Acetylcodone

Acetylmethadol

DEA Number	9601
CSA Schedule	I
Classification	Narcotic
Other Names	Methadyl acetate

* Drug Enforcement Administration

Alfentanil

DEA Number	9737
CSA Schedule	II
Classification	Narcotic
Other Names	Alfenta

Allylprodine

DEA Number	9602
CSA Schedule	I
Classification	Narcotic
Other Names	

Alphacetylmethadol except levo-alphacetylmethadol

DEA Number	9603
CSA Schedule	I
Classification	Narcotic

Alpha-Ethyltryptamine

DEA Number	7249
CSA Schedule	I
Classification	Nonnarcotic
Other Names	ET, Trip

Alphameprodine

DEA Number	9604
CSA Schedule	I
Classification	Narcotic
Other Names	

Alphamethadol

DEA Number	9605
CSA Schedule	I
Classification	Narcotic
Other Names	

Alpha-Methylfentanyl

DEA Number	9814
CSA Schedule	I
Classification	Narcotic
Other Names	China White, fentanyl

Alpha-Methylthiofentanyl

DEA Number	9832
CSA Schedule	I
Classification	Narcotic
Other Names	China White, fentanyl

Alphaprodine

DEA Number	9010
CSA Schedule	II
Classification	Narcotic
Other Names	Nisentil

Alprazolam

DEA Number	2882
CSA Schedule	IV
Classification	Nonnarcotic
Other Names	Xanax

Aminorex

DEA Number	1585
CSA Schedule	I
Classification	Nonnarcotic
Other Names	Has been sold as methamphetamine

Amobarbital

DEA Number	2125
CSA Schedule	II
Classification	Nonnarcotic
Other Names	Amytal, Tuinal

Amobarbital and noncontrolled active ingredient

DEA Number	2126
CSA Schedule	III
Classification	Nonnarcotic
Other Names	Amobarbital/ephedrine capsules

Amobarbital suppository dosage form

DEA Number	2126
CSA Schedule	III
Classification	Nonnarcotic
Other Names	

Amphetamine

DEA Number	1100
CSA Schedule	II
Classification	Nonnarcotic
Other Names	Dexedrine, Adderall, Obetrol

Anabolic steroids

DEA Number	4000
CSA Schedule	III
Classification	Nonnarcotic
Other Names	Body building drugs

Anileridine

DEA Number	9020
CSA Schedule	II
Classification	Narcotic
Other Names	Leritine

Aprobarbital

DEA Number	2100
CSA Schedule	III
Classification	Nonnarcotic
Other Names	Alurate

B

Barbital

DEA Number	2145
CSA Schedule	IV
Classification	Nonnarcotic
Other Names	Veronal, Plexonal, barbitone

Barbituric acid derivative

DEA Number	2100
CSA Schedule	III
Classification	Nonnarcotic
Other Names	Barbiturates not specifically listed

Benzethidine

DEA Number	9606
CSA Schedule	I
Classification	Narcotic
Other Names	

Benzoylecgonine

DEA Number	9180
CSA Schedule	II
Classification	Narcotic
Other Names	Cocaine metabolite

Benzphetamine

DEA Number	1228
CSA Schedule	III
Classification	Nonnarcotic
Other Names	Didrex, Inapetyl

Benzylmorphine

DEA Number	9052
CSA Schedule	I
Classification	Narcotic
Other Names	

Betacetylmethadol

DEA Number	9607
CSA Schedule	I
Classification	Narcotic
Other Names	

Beta-Hydroxy-3-methylfentanyl

DEA Number	9831
CSA Schedule	I
Classification	Narcotic
Other Names	China White, fentanyl

Beta-Hydroxyfentanyl

DEA Number	9830
CSA Schedule	I
Classification	Narcotic
Other Names	China White, fentanyl

Betameprodine

DEA Number	9608
CSA Schedule	I
Classification	Narcotic
Other Names	

Betamethadol

DEA Number	9609
CSA Schedule	I
Classification	Narcotic
Other Names	

Betaprodine

DEA Number	9611
CSA Schedule	I
Classification	Narcotic
Other Names	

Bezitramide

DEA Number	9800
CSA Schedule	II
Classification	Narcotic
Other Names	Burgodin

Boldenone

DEA Number	4000
CSA Schedule	III
Classification	Nonnarcotic
Other Names	Equipoise, Parenabol, Vebonol, Dehydrotestosterone

Bromazepam

DEA Number	2748
CSA Schedule	IV
Classification	Nonnarcotic
Other Names	Lexotan, Lexatin, Lexotanil

4-Bromo-2, 5-dimethoxyamphetamine

DEA Number	7391
CSA Schedule	I
Classification	Nonnarcotic
Other Names	DOB, 4-bromo-DMA

4-Bromo-2, 5-dimethoxyphenethylamine

DEA Number	7392
CSA Schedule	I
Classification	Nonnarcotic
Other Names	Nexus, 2-CB, has been sold as Ecstasy, i.e., MDMA

Bufotenine

DEA Number	7433
CSA Schedule	I
Classification	Nonnarcotic
Other Names	Mappine, N, N-dimethylserotonin

Buprenorphine

DEA Number	9064
CSA Schedule	V
Classification	Narcotic
Other Names	Buprenex, Temgesic

Butabarbital

DEA Number	2100
CSA Schedule	III
Classification	Nonnarcotic
Other Names	Secbutababital, Butisol, Butibel

Butalbital

DEA Number	2100
CSA Schedule	III
Classification	Nonnarcotic
Other Names	Fiorinal, Butalbital with aspirin

Butobarbital

DEA Number	2100
CSA Schedule	III
Classification	Nonnarcotic
Other Names	Butethal, Soneryl

Butorphanol

DEA Number	9720
CSA Schedule	IV
Classification	Nonnarcotic
Other Names	Stadol, Stadol NS, Torbugesic, Torbutrol

C

Camazepam

DEA Number	2749
CSA Schedule	IV
Classification	Nonnarcotic
Other Names	Albego, Limpidon, Paxor

Carfentanil

DEA Number	9743
CSA Schedule	II
Classification	Narcotic
Other Names	Wildnil

Cathine

DEA Number	1230
CSA Schedule	IV
Classification	Nonnarcotic
Other Names	Constituent of "Khat" plant

Cathinone

DEA Number	1235
CSA Schedule	I
Classification	Nonnarcotic
Other Names	Constituent of "Khat" plant

Chloral betaine

DEA Number	2460
CSA Schedule	IV
Classification	Nonnarcotic
Other Names	Beta Chlor

Chloral hydrate

DEA Number	2465
CSA Schedule	IV
Classification	Nonnarcotic
Other Names	Noctec

Chlordiazepoxide

DEA Number	2744
CSA Schedule	IV
Classification	Nonnarcotic
Other Names	Librium, Libritabs, Limbitrol, SK-Lygen

Chlorhexadol

DEA Number	2510
CSA Schedule	III
Classification	Nonnarcotic
Other Names	Mechloral, Mecoral, Medodorm, Chloralodol

Chlorotestosterone (same as clostebol)

DEA Number	4000
CSA Schedule	III
Classification	Nonnarcotic
Other Names	If 4-chlorotestosterone then clostebol

Chlorphentermine

DEA Number	1645
CSA Schedule	III
Classification	Nonnarcotic
Other Names	Pre-Sate, Lucofen, Apsedon, Desopimon

Clobazam

DEA Number	2751
CSA Schedule	IV
Classification	Nonnarcotic
Other Names	Urbadan, Urbanyl

Clonazepam

DEA Number	2737
CSA Schedule	IV
Classification	Nonnarcotic
Other Names	Klonopin, Clonopin

Clonitazene

DEA Number	9612
CSA Schedule	I
Classification	Narcotic
Other Names	

Clorazepate

DEA Number	2768
CSA Schedule	IV
Classification	Nonnarcotic
Other Names	Tranxene

Clortermine

DEA Number	1647
CSA Schedule	III
Classification	Nonnarcotic
Other Names	Voranil

Clostebol

DEA Number	4000
CSA Schedule	III
Classification	Nonnarcotic
Other Names	Alfa-Trofodermin, Clostene, 4-chlorotestosterone

Clotiazepam

DEA Number	2752
CSA Schedule	IV
Classification	Nonnarcotic
Other Names	Trecalmo, Rize, Clozan, Veratran

Cloxazolam

DEA Number	2753
CSA Schedule	IV
Classification	Nonnarcotic
Other Names	Akton, Lubalix, Olcadil, Sepazon

Coca Leaves

DEA Number	9040
CSA Schedule	II
Classification	Narcotic
Other Names	

Cocaine

DEA Number	9041
CSA Schedule	II
Classification	Narcotic
Other Names	Methyl benzoylecgonine, crack

Codeine

DEA Number	9050
CSA Schedule	II
Classification	Narcotic
Other Names	Morphine methyl ester, methyl morphine

Codeine and isoquinoline alkaloid 90 mg/du

DEA Number	9803
CSA Schedule	III
Classification	Narcotic
Other Names	Codeine with papaverine or noscapine

Codeine combination product 90 mg/du

DEA Number	9804
CSA Schedule	III
Classification	Narcotic
Other Names	Empirin, Fiorinal, Tylenol, ASA or APAP w/codeine

Codeine methylbromide

DEA Number	9070
CSA Schedule	I
Classification	Narcotic
Other Names	

Codeine preparations 200 mg/100 ml or 100 gm

DEA Number	Pending
CSA Schedule	V
Classification	Narcotic
Other Names	Cosanyl, Robitussin A-C, Cheracol, Cerose, Pediacof

Codeine-*N*-oxide

DEA Number	9053
CSA Schedule	I
Classification	Narcotic
Other Names	

Cyprenorphine

DEA Number	9054
CSA Schedule	I
Classification	Narcotic
Other Names	

D

Dehydrochlormethyltestosterone

DEA Number	4000
CSA Schedule	III
Classification	Nonnarcotic
Other Names	Oral-Turinabol

Delorazepam

DEA Number	2754
CSA Schedule	IV
Classification	Nonnarcotic
Other Names	

Desomorphine

DEA Number	9055
CSA Schedule	I
Classification	Narcotic
Other Names	

Dexfenfluramine

DEA Number	1670
CSA Schedule	IV
Classification	Nonnarcotic
Other Names	Redux

Dextromoramide

DEA Number	9613
CSA Schedule	I
Classification	Narcotic
Other Names	Palfium, Jetrium, Narcolo

Dextropropoxyphene dosage forms

DEA Number	9278
CSA Schedule	IV
Classification	Narcotic
Other Names	Darvon, propoxyphene, Darvocet, Propacet

Dextropropoxyphene, bulk (nondosage forms)

DEA Number	9273
CSA Schedule	II
Classification	Narcotic
Other Names	Propoxyphene

Diampromide

DEA Number	9615
CSA Schedule	I
Classification	Narcotic
Other Names	

Diazepam

DEA Number	2765
CSA Schedule	IV
Classification	Nonnarcotic
Other Names	Valium, Valrelease, Diastat

Dichloralphenazone

DEA Number	2467
CSA Schedule	IV
Classification	Nonnarcotic
Other Names	Midrin, dichloralantipyrine

Diethylpropion

DEA Number	1610
CSA Schedule	IV
Classification	Nonnarcotic
Other Names	Tenuate, Tepanil

Diethylthiambutene

DEA Number	9616
CSA Schedule	I
Classification	Narcotic
Other Names	

Diethyltryptamine

DEA Number	7434
CSA Schedule	I
Classification	Nonnarcotic
Other Names	DET

Difenoxin

DEA Number	9168
CSA Schedule	I
Classification	Narcotic
Other Names	Lyspafen

Difenoxin 1 mg/25 ug AtSO4/du

DEA Number	9167
CSA Schedule	IV
Classification	Narcotic
Other Names	Motofen

Difenoxin preparations 0.5 mg/25 ug AtSO4/du

DEA Number	Pending
CSA Schedule	V
Classification	Narcotic
Other Names	Motofen

Dihydrocodeine

DEA Number	9120
CSA Schedule	II
Classification	Narcotic
Other Names	Didrate, Parzone

Dihydrocodeine combination product 90 mg/du

DEA Number	9807
CSA Schedule	III
Classification	Narcotic
Other Names	Synalgos-DC, Compal

Dihydrocodeine preparations 10 mg/100 ml or 100 gm

DEA Number	
CSA Schedule	V
Classification	Narcotic
Other Names	Cophene-S, various others

Dihydroetorphine

DEA Number	9334
CSA Schedule	II
Classification	Narcotic
Other Names	

Dihydromorphine

DEA Number	9145
CSA Schedule	I
Classification	Narcotic
Other Names	

Dihydrotestosterone (same as stanolone)

DEA Number	4000
CSA Schedule	III
Classification	Nonnarcotic
Other Names	See stanolone

Dimenoxadol

DEA Number	9617
CSA Schedule	I
Classification	Narcotic
Other Names	

Dimepheptanol

DEA Number	9618
CSA Schedule	I
Classification	Narcotic
Other Names	

2,5-Dimethoxyamphetamine

DEA Number	7396
CSA Schedule	I
Classification	Nonnarcotic
Other Names	DMA, 2,5-DMA

2,5-Dimethoxy-4-ethylamphetamine

DEA Number	7399
CSA Schedule	I
Classification	Nonnarcotic
Other Names	DOET

Dimethylthiambutene

DEA Number	9619
CSA Schedule	I
Classification	Narcotic
Other Names	

Dimethyltryptamine

DEA Number	7435
CSA Schedule	I
Classification	Nonnarcotic
Other Names	DMT

Dioxaphetyl butyrate

DEA Number	9621
CSA Schedule	I
Classification	Narcotic
Other Names	

Diphenoxylate

DEA Number	9170
CSA Schedule	II
Classification	Narcotic
Other Names	

Diphenoxylate preparations 2.5 mg/25 μg AtSO4

DEA Number	Pending
CSA Schedule	V
Classification	Narcotic
Other Names	Lomotil, Logen

Dipipanone

DEA Number	9622
CSA Schedule	I
Classification	Narcotic
Other Names	Dipipan, phenylpiperone HCl, Diconal, Wellconal

Diprenorphine

DEA Number	9058
CSA Schedule	II
Classification	Narcotic
Other Names	M50-50

Dronabinol in sesame oil in soft gelatin capsule

DEA Number	7369
CSA Schedule	III
Classification	Nonnarcotic
Other Names	Marinol, synthetic THC in sesame oil/soft gelatin capsule

Drostanolone

DEA Number	4000
CSA Schedule	III
Classification	Nonnarcotic
Other Names	Drolban, Masterid, Permastril

Drotebanol

DEA Number	9335
CSA Schedule	I
Classification	Narcotic
Other Names	Metebanyl, oxymethebanol

E

Ecgonine

DEA Number	9180
CSA Schedule	II
Classification	Narcotic
Other Names	Cocaine precursor, in coca leaves

Estazolam

DEA Number	2756
CSA Schedule	IV
Classification	Nonnarcotic
Other Names	ProSom, Domnamid, Eurodin, Nuctalon

Ethchlorvynol

DEA Number	2540
CSA Schedule	IV
Classification	Nonnarcotic
Other Names	Placidyl

Ethinamate

DEA Number	2545
CSA Schedule	IV
Classification	Nonnarcotic
Other Names	Valmid, Valamin

Ethyl loflazepate

DEA Number	2758
CSA Schedule	IV
Classification	Nonnarcotic
Other Names	

Ethylestrenol

DEA Number	4000
CSA Schedule	III
Classification	Nonnarcotic
Other Names	Maxibolin, Orabolin, Durabolin-O, Duraboral

Ethylmethylthiambutene

DEA Number	9623
CSA Schedule	I
Classification	Narcotic
Other Names	

Ethylmorphine

DEA Number	9190
CSA Schedule	II
Classification	Narcotic
Other Names	Dionin

Ethylmorphine combination product 15 mg/du

DEA Number	9808
CSA Schedule	III
Classification	Narcotic
Other Names	

Ethylmorphine preparations 100 mg/100 ml or 100 gm

DEA Number	
CSA Schedule	V
Classification	Narcotic
Other Names	

Etonitazene

DEA Number	9624
CSA Schedule	I
Classification	Narcotic
Other Names	

Etorphine (except HCl)

DEA Number	9056
CSA Schedule	I
Classification	Narcotic
Other Names	

Etorphine HCl

DEA Number	9059
CSA Schedule	II
Classification	Narcotic
Other Names	M 99

Etoxeridine

DEA Number	9625
CSA Schedule	I
Classification	Narcotic
Other Names	

F

Fencamfamin

DEA Number	1760
CSA Schedule	IV
Classification	Nonnarcotic
Other Names	Reactivan

Fenethylline

DEA Number	1503
CSA Schedule	I
Classification	Nonnarcotic
Other Names	Captagon, amfetyline, ethyltheophylline amphetamine

Fenfluramine

DEA Number	1670
CSA Schedule	IV
Classification	Nonnarcotic
Other Names	Pondimin, Ponderal

Fenproporex

DEA Number	1575
CSA Schedule	IV
Classification	Nonnarcotic
Other Names	Gacilin, Solvolip

Fentanyl

DEA Number	9801
CSA Schedule	II
Classification	Narcotic
Other Names	Innovar, Sublimaze, Duragesic, Oralet, Actiq

Fludiazepam

DEA Number	2759
CSA Schedule	IV
Classification	Nonnarcotic
Other Names	

Flunitrazepam

DEA Number	2763
CSA Schedule	IV
Classification	Nonnarcotic
Other Names	Rohypnol, Narcozep, Darkene, Roipnol

Fluoxymesterone

DEA Number	4000
CSA Schedule	III
Classification	Nonnarcotic
Other Names	Anadroid-F, Halotestin, Ora-Testryl

Flurazepam

DEA Number	2767
CSA Schedule	IV
Classification	Nonnarcotic
Other Names	Dalmane

Formebolone (incorrect spelling in law)

DEA Number	4000
CSA Schedule	III
Classification	Nonnarcotic
Other Names	Esiclene, Hubernol

Furethidine

DEA Number	9626
CSA Schedule	I
Classification	Narcotic
Other Names	

G

Gamma Hydroxybutyric Acid (GHB)

DEA Number	2010
CSA Schedule	I
Classification	Nonnarcotic
Other Names	GHB, gamma hydroxybutyrate, sodium oxybate

Glutethimide

DEA Number	2550
CSA Schedule	II
Classification	Nonnarcotic
Other Names	Doriden, Dorimide

H

Halazepam

DEA Number	2762
CSA Schedule	IV
Classification	Nonnarcotic
Other Names	Paxipam

Haloxazolam

DEA Number	2771
CSA Schedule	IV
Classification	Nonnarcotic
Other Names	

Heroin

DEA Number	9200
CSA Schedule	I
Classification	Narcotic
Other Names	Diacetylmorphine, diamorphine

Hydrocodone

DEA Number	9193
CSA Schedule	II
Classification	Narcotic
Other Names	Dihydrocodeinone

Hydrocodone and isoquinoline alkaloid 15 mg/du

DEA Number	9805
CSA Schedule	III
Classification	Narcotic
Other Names	Dihydrocodeinone+papaverine or noscapine

Hydrocodone combination product 15 mg/du

DEA Number	9806
CSA Schedule	III
Classification	Narcotic
Other Names	Tensioned, Lorcet, Lortab, Norco, Vicodin, Vicoprofen

Hydromorphinol

DEA Number	9301
CSA Schedule	I
Classification	Narcotic
Other Names	

Hydromorphone

DEA Number	9150
CSA Schedule	II
Classification	Narcotic
Other Names	Dilaudid, dihydromorphinone

Hydroxypethidine

DEA Number	9627
CSA Schedule	I
Classification	Narcotic
Other Names	

I

Ibogaine

DEA Number	7260
CSA Schedule	I
Classification	Nonnarcotic
Other Names	Constituent of Tabernanthe iboga plant

Isomethadone

DEA Number	9226
CSA Schedule	II
Classification	Narcotic
Other Names	Isoamidone

K

Ketamine

DEA Number	7285
CSA Schedule	III
Classification	Nonnarcotic
Other Names	Ketaset, Ketalar, Special K, K

Ketazolam

DEA Number	2772
CSA Schedule	IV
Classification	Nonnarcotic
Other Names	Anxon, Loftran, Solatran, Contamex

Ketobemidone

DEA Number	9628
CSA Schedule	I
Classification	Narcotic
Other Names	Cliradon

L

Levo-alphacetylmethadol

DEA Number	9648
CSA Schedule	II
Classification	Narcotic
Other Names	LAAM, long-acting methadone, levomethadyl acetate

Levomethorphan

DEA Number	9210
CSA Schedule	II
Classification	Narcotic
Other Names	

Levomoramide

DEA Number	9629
CSA Schedule	I
Classification	Narcotic
Other Names	

Levophenacylmorphan

DEA Number	9631
CSA Schedule	I
Classification	Narcotic
Other Names	

Levorphanol

DEA Number	9220
CSA Schedule	II
Classification	Narcotic
Other Names	Levo-Dromoran

Loprazolam

DEA Number	2773
CSA Schedule	IV
Classification	Nonnarcotic
Other Names	

Lorazepam

DEA Number	2885
CSA Schedule	IV
Classification	Nonnarcotic
Other Names	Ativan

Lormetazepam

DEA Number	2774
CSA Schedule	IV
Classification	Nonnarcotic
Other Names	Noctamid

Lysergic acid

DEA Number	7300
CSA Schedule	III
Classification	Nonnarcotic
Other Names	LSD precursor

Lysergic acid amide

DEA Number	7310
CSA Schedule	III
Classification	Nonnarcotic
Other Names	LSD precursor

Lysergic acid diethylamide

DEA Number	7315
CSA Schedule	I
Classification	Nonnarcotic
Other Names	LSD, lysergide

M

Marijuana

DEA Number	7360
CSA Schedule	I
Classification	Nonnarcotic
Other Names	Cannabis, marijuana

Mazindol

DEA Number	1605
CSA Schedule	IV
Classification	Nonnarcotic
Other Names	Sanorex, Mazanor

Mebutamate

DEA Number	2800
CSA Schedule	IV
Classification	Nonnarcotic
Other Names	Capla

Mecloqualone

DEA Number	2572
CSA Schedule	I
Classification	Nonnarcotic
Other Names	Nubarene

Medazepam

DEA Number	2836
CSA Schedule	IV
Classification	Nonnarcotic
Other Names	Nobrium

Mefenorex

DEA Number	1580
CSA Schedule	IV
Classification	Nonnarcotic
Other Names	Anorexic, Amexate, Doracil, Pondinil

Meperidine

DEA Number	9230
CSA Schedule	II
Classification	Narcotic
Other Names	Demerol, Mepergan, pethidine

Meperidine intermediate-A

DEA Number	9232
CSA Schedule	II
Classification	Narcotic
Other Names	Meperidine precursor

Meperidine intermediate-B

DEA Number	9233
CSA Schedule	II
Classification	Narcotic
Other Names	Meperidine precursor

Meperidine intermediate-C

DEA Number	9234
CSA Schedule	II
Classification	Narcotic
Other Names	Meperidine precursor

Meprobamate

DEA Number	2820
CSA Schedule	IV
Classification	Nonnarcotic
Other Names	Miltown, Equanil, Micrainin, Equagesic, Meprospan

Mescaline

DEA Number	7381
CSA Schedule	I
Classification	Nonnarcotic
Other Names	Constituent of peyote cacti

Mesterolone

DEA Number	4000
CSA Schedule	III
Classification	Nonnarcotic
Other Names	Proviron

Metazocine

DEA Number	9240
CSA Schedule	II
Classification	Narcotic
Other Names	

Methadone

DEA Number	9250
CSA Schedule	II
Classification	Narcotic
Other Names	Dolophine, Methadose, Amidone

Methadone intermediate

DEA Number	9254
CSA Schedule	II
Classification	Narcotic
Other Names	Methadone precursor

Methamphetamine

DEA Number	1105
CSA Schedule	II
Classification	Nonnarcotic
Other Names	Desoxyn, D-desoxyephedrine, ICE, Crank, Speed

Methandienone (see Methandrostenolone)

DEA Number	4000
CSA Schedule	III
Classification	Nonnarcotic
Other Names	

Methandranone

DEA Number	4000
CSA Schedule	III
Classification	Nonnarcotic
Other Names	

Methandriol

DEA Number	4000
CSA Schedule	III
Classification	Nonnarcotic
Other Names	Sinesex, Stenediol, Troformone

Methandrostenolone

DEA Number	4000
CSA Schedule	III
Classification	Nonnarcotic
Other Names	Dianabol, Metabolina, Nerobol, Perbolin

Methaqualone

DEA Number	2565
CSA Schedule	I
Classification	Nonnarcotic
Other Names	Quaalude, Parest, Somnafac, Opitimil, Mandrax

Methcathinone

DEA Number	1237
CSA Schedule	I
Classification	Nonnarcotic
Other Names	*N*-Methylcathinone, “cat”

Methenolone

DEA Number	4000
CSA Schedule	III
Classification	Nonnarcotic
Other Names	Primobolan, Primobolan Depot, Primobolan S

Methohexital

DEA Number	2264
CSA Schedule	IV
Classification	Nonnarcotic
Other Names	Brevital

4-Methoxyamphetamine

DEA Number	7411
CSA Schedule	I
Classification	Nonnarcotic
Other Names	PMA

5-Methoxy-3, 4-methylenedioxyamphetamine

DEA Number	7401
CSA Schedule	I
Classification	Nonnarcotic
Other Names	MMDA

4-Methylaminorex (*cis* isomer)

DEA Number	1590
CSA Schedule	I
Classification	Nonnarcotic
Other Names	U4Euh, McN-422

Methyldesorphine

DEA Number	9302
CSA Schedule	I
Classification	Narcotic
Other Names	

Methyldihydromorphine

DEA Number	9304
CSA Schedule	I
Classification	Narcotic
Other Names	

4-Methyl-2, 5-dimethoxyamphetamine

DEA Number	7395
CSA Schedule	I
Classification	Nonnarcotic
Other Names	DOM, STP

3, 4-Methylenedioxyamphetamine

DEA Number	7400
CSA Schedule	I
Classification	Nonnarcotic
Other Names	MDA, Love Drug

3, 4-Methylenedioxymethamphetamine

DEA Number	7405
CSA Schedule	I
Classification	Nonnarcotic
Other Names	MDMA, Ecstasy, XTC

3, 4-Methylenedioxy-N-ethylamphetamine

DEA Number	7404
CSA Schedule	I
Classification	Nonnarcotic
Other Names	*N*-ethyl MDA, MDE, MDEA

3-Methylfentanyl

DEA Number	9813
CSA Schedule	I
Classification	Narcotic
Other Names	China White, fentanyl

Methylphenidate

DEA Number	1724
CSA Schedule	II
Classification	Nonnarcotic
Other Names	Ritalin, Concerta

Methylphenobarbital (mephobarbital)

DEA Number	2250
CSA Schedule	IV
Classification	Nonnarcotic
Other Names	Mebaral, mephobarbital

1-Methyl-4-phenyl-4-propionoxypiperidine

DEA Number	9661
CSA Schedule	I
Classification	
Other Names	MPPP, synthetic heroin

Methyltestosterone

DEA Number	4000
CSA Schedule	III
Classification	Nonnarcotic
Other Names	Android, Oreton, Testred, Virilon

3-Methylthiofentanyl

DEA Number	9833
CSA Schedule	I
Classification	Narcotic
Other Names	China White, fentanyl

Methyprylon

DEA Number	2575
CSA Schedule	III
Classification	Nonnarcotic
Other Names	Noludar

Metopon

DEA Number	9260
CSA Schedule	II
Classification	Narcotic
Other Names	

Mibolerone

DEA Number	4000
CSA Schedule	III
Classification	Nonnarcotic
Other Names	Cheque

Midazolam

DEA Number	2884
CSA Schedule	IV
Classification	Nonnarcotic
Other Names	Versed

Modafinil

DEA Number	1680
CSA Schedule	IV
Classification	Nonnarcotic
Other Names	Provigil

Moramide-intermediate

DEA Number	9802
CSA Schedule	II
Classification	Narcotic
Other Names	

Morpheridine

DEA Number	9632
CSA Schedule	I
Classification	Narcotic
Other Names	

Morphine

DEA Number	9300
CSA Schedule	II
Classification	Narcotic
Other Names	MS Contin, Roxanol, Oramorph, RMS, MSIR

Morphine combination product/50 mg/100 ml or gm

DEA Number	9810
CSA Schedule	III
Classification	Narcotic
Other Names	

Morphine methylbromide

DEA Number	9305
CSA Schedule	I
Classification	Narcotic
Other Names	

Morphine methylsulfonate

DEA Number	9306
CSA Schedule	I
Classification	Narcotic
Other Names	

Morphine-N-oxide

DEA Number	9307
CSA Schedule	I
Classification	Narcotic
Other Names	

Myrophine

DEA Number	9308
CSA Schedule	I
Classification	Narcotic
Other Names	

N

N, *N*-Dimethylamphetamine

DEA Number	1480
CSA Schedule	I
Classification	Nonnarcotic
Other Names	

Nabilone

DEA Number	7379
CSA Schedule	II
Classification	Nonnarcotic
Other Names	Cesamet

Nalorphine

DEA Number	9400
CSA Schedule	III
Classification	Narcotic
Other Names	Nalline

Nandrolone

DEA Number	4000
CSA Schedule	III
Classification	Nonnarcotic
Other Names	Deca-Durabolin, Durabolin, Durabolin-50

N-Ethyl-1-phenylcyclohexylamine

DEA Number	7455
CSA Schedule	I
Classification	Nonnarcotic
Other Names	PCE

N-Ethyl-3-piperidyl benzilate

DEA Number	7482
CSA Schedule	I
Classification	Nonnarcotic
Other Names	JB 323

N-Ethylamphetamine

DEA Number	1475
CSA Schedule	I
Classification	Nonnarcotic
Other Names	NEA

N-Hydroxy-3, 4-methylenedioxyamphetamine

DEA Number	7402
CSA Schedule	I
Classification	Nonnarcotic
Other Names	*N*-hydroxy MDA

Nicocodeine

DEA Number	9309
CSA Schedule	I
Classification	Narcotic
Other Names	

Nicomorphine

DEA Number	9312
CSA Schedule	I
Classification	Narcotic
Other Names	Vilan

Nimetazepam

DEA Number	2837
CSA Schedule	IV
Classification	Nonnarcotic
Other Names	Erimin

Nitrazepam

DEA Number	2834
CSA Schedule	IV
Classification	Nonnarcotic
Other Names	Mogadon

N-Methyl-3-piperidyl benzilate

DEA Number	7484
CSA Schedule	I
Classification	Nonnarcotic
Other Names	JB 336

Noracymethadol

DEA Number	9633
CSA Schedule	I
Classification	Narcotic
Other Names	

Nordiazepam

DEA Number	2838
CSA Schedule	IV
Classification	Nonnarcotic
Other Names	Nordazepam, Demadar, Madar

Norethandrolone

DEA Number	4000
CSA Schedule	III
Classification	Nonnarcotic
Other Names	Nilevar, Solevar

Norlevorphanol

DEA Number	9634
CSA Schedule	I
Classification	Narcotic
Other Names	

Normethadone

DEA Number	9635
CSA Schedule	I
Classification	Narcotic
Other Names	Phenyldimazone

Normorphine

DEA Number	9313
CSA Schedule	I
Classification	Narcotic
Other Names	

Norpipanone

DEA Number	9636
CSA Schedule	I
Classification	Narcotic
Other Names	

O

Opium combination product 25 mg/du

DEA Number	9809
CSA Schedule	III
Classification	Narcotic
Other Names	Paregoric, other combination products

Opium extracts

DEA Number	9610
CSA Schedule	II
Classification	Narcotic
Other Names	

Opium fluid extract

DEA Number	9620
CSA Schedule	II
Classification	Narcotic
Other Names	

Opium poppy

DEA Number	9650
CSA Schedule	II
Classification	Narcotic
Other Names	Papaver somniferum

Opium preparations - 100 mg/100 ml or gm

DEA Number	Pending
CSA Schedule	V
Classification	Narcotic
Other Names	Parepectolin, Kapectolin PG, Kaolin Pectin P.G.

Opium tincture

DEA Number	9630
CSA Schedule	II
Classification	Narcotic
Other Names	Laudanum

Opium, granulated

DEA Number	9640
CSA Schedule	II
Classification	Narcotic
Other Names	Granulated opium

Opium, powdered

DEA Number	9639
CSA Schedule	II
Classification	Narcotic
Other Names	Powdered opium

Opium, raw

DEA Number	9600
CSA Schedule	II
Classification	Narcotic
Other Names	Raw opium, gum opium

Oxandrolone

DEA Number	4000
CSA Schedule	III
Classification	Nonnarcotic
Other Names	Anavar, Lonavar, Provitar, Vasorome

Oxazepam

DEA Number	2835
CSA Schedule	IV
Classification	Nonnarcotic
Other Names	Serax, Serenid-D

Oxazolam

DEA Number	2839
CSA Schedule	IV
Classification	Nonnarcotic
Other Names	Serenal, Convertal

Oxycodone

DEA Number	9143
CSA Schedule	II
Classification	Narcotic
Other Names	OxyContin, Percocet, Endocet, Roxicodone, Roxicet

Oxymesterone

DEA Number	4000
CSA Schedule	III
Classification	Nonnarcotic
Other Names	Anamidol, Balnimax, Oranabol, Oranabol 10

Oxymetholone

DEA Number	4000
CSA Schedule	III
Classification	Nonnarcotic
Other Names	Anadrol-50, Adroyd, Anapolon, Anasteron, Pardroyd

Oxymorphone

DEA Number	9652
CSA Schedule	II
Classification	Narcotic
Other Names	Numorphan

P

Para-Fluorofentanyl

DEA Number	9812
CSA Schedule	I
Classification	Narcotic
Other Names	China White, fentanyl

Parahexyl

DEA Number	7374
CSA Schedule	I
Classification	Nonnarcotic
Other Names	Synhexyl

Paraldehyde

DEA Number	2585
CSA Schedule	IV
Classification	Nonnarcotic
Other Names	Paral

Pemoline

DEA Number	1530
CSA Schedule	IV
Classification	Nonnarcotic
Other Names	Cylert

Pentazocine

DEA Number	9709
CSA Schedule	IV
Classification	Nonnarcotic
Other Names	Talwin, Talwin NX, Talacen, Talwin Compound

Pentobarbital

DEA Number	2270
CSA Schedule	II
Classification	Nonnarcotic
Other Names	Nembutal

Pentobarbital and noncontrolled active ingredient

DEA Number	2271
CSA Schedule	III
Classification	Nonnarcotic
Other Names	FP-3

Pentobarbital suppository dosage form

DEA Number	2271
CSA Schedule	III
Classification	Nonnarcotic
Other Names	WANS

Petrichloral

DEA Number	2591
CSA Schedule	IV
Classification	Nonnarcotic
Other Names	Pentaerythritol chloral, Periclor

Peyote

DEA Number	7415
CSA Schedule	I
Classification	Nonnarcotic
Other Names	Cactus which contains mescaline

Phenadoxone

DEA Number	9637
CSA Schedule	I
Classification	Narcotic
Other Names	

Phenampromide

DEA Number	9638
CSA Schedule	I
Classification	Narcotic
Other Names	

Phenazocine

DEA Number	9715
CSA Schedule	II
Classification	Narcotic
Other Names	Narphen, Prinadol

Phencyclidine

DEA Number	7471
CSA Schedule	II
Classification	Nonnarcotic
Other Names	PCP, Sernylan

Phendimetrazine

DEA Number	1615
CSA Schedule	III
Classification	Nonnarcotic
Other Names	Plegine, Prelu-2, Bontril, Melfiat, Statobex

Phenmetrazine

DEA Number	1631
CSA Schedule	II
Classification	Nonnarcotic
Other Names	Preludin

Phenobarbital

DEA Number	2285
CSA Schedule	IV
Classification	Nonnarcotic
Other Names	Luminal, Donnatal, Bellergal-S

Phenomorphan

DEA Number	9647
CSA Schedule	I
Classification	Narcotic
Other Names	

Phenoperidine

DEA Number	9641
CSA Schedule	I
Classification	Narcotic
Other Names	Operidine, Lealgin

Phentermine

DEA Number	1640
CSA Schedule	IV
Classification	Nonnarcotic
Other Names	Ionamin, Fastin, Adipex-P, Obe-Nix, Zantryl

Phenylacetone

DEA Number	8501
CSA Schedule	II
Classification	Nonnarcotic
Other Names	P2P, phenyl-2-propanone, benzyl methyl ketone

1-Phenylcyclohexylamine

DEA Number	7460
CSA Schedule	II
Classification	Nonnarcotic
Other Names	Precusor of PCP

1-(1-Phenylcyclohexyl) pyrrolidine

DEA Number	7458
CSA Schedule	I
Classification	Nonnarcotic
Other Names	PCPy, PHP, rolicyclidine

1-(2-Phenylethyl)-4-phenyl-4-acetoxypiperidine

DEA Number	9663
CSA Schedule	I
Classification	Narcotic
Other Names	PEPAP, synthetic heroin

Pholcodine

DEA Number	9314
CSA Schedule	I
Classification	Narcotic
Other Names	Copholco, Adaphol, Codisol, Lantuss, Pholcolin

Piminodine

DEA Number	9730
CSA Schedule	II
Classification	Narcotic
Other Names	

Pinazepam

DEA Number	2883
CSA Schedule	IV
Classification	Nonnarcotic
Other Names	Domar

1-Piperidinocyclohexanecarbonitrile

DEA Number	8603
CSA Schedule	II
Classification	Nonnarcotic
Other Names	PCC, precusor of PCP

Pipradrol

DEA Number	1750
CSA Schedule	IV
Classification	Nonnarcotic
Other Names	Detaril, Stimolag Fortis

Piritramide

DEA Number	9642
CSA Schedule	I
Classification	Narcotic
Other Names	Piridolan

Poppy straw

DEA Number	9650
CSA Schedule	II
Classification	Narcotic
Other Names	Opium poppy capsules, poppy heads

Poppy straw concentrate

DEA Number	9670
CSA Schedule	II
Classification	Narcotic
Other Names	Concentrate of poppy straw, CPS

Prazepam

DEA Number	2764
CSA Schedule	IV
Classification	Nonnarcotic
Other Names	Centrax

Proheptazine

DEA Number	9643
CSA Schedule	I
Classification	Narcotic
Other Names	

Properidine

DEA Number	9644
CSA Schedule	I
Classification	Narcotic
Other Names	

Propiram

DEA Number	9649
CSA Schedule	I
Classification	Narcotic
Other Names	Algeril

Psilocybin

DEA Number	7437
CSA Schedule	I
Classification	Nonnarcotic
Other Names	Constituent of "magic mushrooms"

Psilocyn

DEA Number	7438
CSA Schedule	I
Classification	Nonnarcotic
Other Names	Psilocin, constituent of "magic mushrooms"

Pyrovalerone

DEA Number	1485
CSA Schedule	V
Classification	Nonnarcotic
Other Names	Centroton, Thymergix

Q

Quazepam

DEA Number	2881
CSA Schedule	IV
Classification	Nonnarcotic
Other Names	Doral, Dormalin

R

Racemethorphan

DEA Number	9732
CSA Schedule	II
Classification	Narcotic
Other Names	

Racemoramide

DEA Number	9645
CSA Schedule	I
Classification	Narcotic
Other Names	

Racemorphan

DEA Number	9733
CSA Schedule	II
Classification	Narcotic
Other Names	Dromoran

Remifentanil

DEA Number	9739
CSA Schedule	II
Classification	Narcotic
Other Names	Ultiva

S

Secobarbital

DEA Number	2315
CSA Schedule	II
Classification	Nonnarcotic
Other Names	Seconal, Tuinal

Secobarbital and noncontrolled active ingredient

DEA Number	2316
CSA Schedule	III
Classification	Nonnarcotic
Other Names	Various

Secobarbital suppository dosage form

DEA Number	2316
CSA Schedule	III
Classification	Nonnarcotic
Other Names	Various

Sibutramine

DEA Number	1675
CSA Schedule	IV
Classification	Nonnarcotic
Other Names	Meridia

SPA

DEA Number	1635
CSA Schedule	IV
Classification	Nonnarcotic
Other Names	1-dimethylamino-1, 2-diphenylethane, Lefetamine

Stanolone

DEA Number	4000
CSA Schedule	III
Classification	Nonnarcotic
Other Names	Anabolex, Andractim, Pesomax, dihydrotestosterone

Stanozolol

DEA Number	4000
CSA Schedule	III
Classification	Nonnarcotic
Other Names	Winstrol, Winstrol-V

Stimulant compounds previously excepted

DEA Number	1405
CSA Schedule	III
Classification	Nonnarcotic
Other Names	Mediatric

Sufentanil

DEA Number	9740
CSA Schedule	II
Classification	Narcotic
Other Names	Sufenta

Sulfondiethylmethane

DEA Number	2600
CSA Schedule	III
Classification	Nonnarcotic
Other Names	

Sulfonethylmethane

DEA Number	2605
CSA Schedule	III
Classification	Nonnarcotic
Other Names	

Sulfonmethane

DEA Number	2610
CSA Schedule	III
Classification	Nonnarcotic
Other Names	

T

Talbutal

DEA Number	2100
CSA Schedule	III
Classification	Nonnarcotic
Other Names	Lotusate

Temazepam

DEA Number	2925
CSA Schedule	IV
Classification	Nonnarcotic
Other Names	Restoril

Testolactone

DEA Number	4000
CSA Schedule	III
Classification	Nonnarcotic
Other Names	Teslac

Testosterone

DEA Number	4000
CSA Schedule	III
Classification	Nonnarcotic
Other Names	Android-T, Androlan, Depotest, Delatestryl

Tetrahydrocannabinols

DEA Number	7370
CSA Schedule	I
Classification	Nonnarcotic
Other Names	THC, Delta-8 THC, Delta-9 THC and others

Tetrazepam

DEA Number	2886
CSA Schedule	IV
Classification	Nonnarcotic
Other Names	

Thebacon

DEA Number	9315
CSA Schedule	I
Classification	Narcotic
Other Names	Acetylhydrocodone, Acedicon, Thebacetyl

Thebaine

DEA Number	9333
CSA Schedule	II
Classification	Narcotic
Other Names	Precursor of many narcotics

Thiamylal

DEA Number	2100
CSA Schedule	III
Classification	Nonnarcotic
Other Names	Surital

1-[1-(2-Thienyl) cyclohexyl] piperidine

DEA Number	7470
CSA Schedule	I
Classification	Nonnarcotic
Other Names	TCP, tenocyclidine

1-[1-(2-Thienyl) cyclohexyl] pyrrolidine

DEA Number	7473
CSA Schedule	I
Classification	Nonnarcotic
Other Names	TCPy

Thiofentanyl

DEA Number	9835
CSA Schedule	I
Classification	Narcotic
Other Names	China white, fentanyl

Thiopental

DEA Number	2100
CSA Schedule	III
Classification	Nonnarcotic
Other Names	Pentothal

Tiletamine and Zolazepam combination product

DEA Number	7295
CSA Schedule	III
Classification	Nonnarcotic
Other Names	Telazol

Tilidine

DEA Number	9750
CSA Schedule	I
Classification	Narcotic
Other Names	Tilidate, Valoron, Kitadol, Lak, Tilsa

Trenbolone

DEA Number	4000
CSA Schedule	III
Classification	Nonnarcotic
Other Names	Finaplix-S, Finajet, Parabolan

Triazolam

DEA Number	2887
CSA Schedule	IV
Classification	Nonnarcotic
Other Names	Halcion

Trimeperidine

DEA Number	9646
CSA Schedule	I
Classification	Narcotic
Other Names	Promedolum

3,4,5-Trimethoxyamphetamine

DEA Number	7390
CSA Schedule	I
Classification	Nonnarcotic
Other Names	TMA

V

Vinbarbital

DEA Number	2100
CSA Schedule	III
Classification	Nonnarcotic
Other Names	Delvinal, vinbarbitone

Z

Zaleplon

DEA Number	2781
CSA Schedule	IV
Classification	Nonnarcotic
Other Names	Sonata

Zolpidem

DEA Number	2783
CSA Schedule	IV
Classification	Nonnarcotic
Other Names	Ambien, Stilnoct, Stilnox, Ivadal

Appendix C: U.S. Supreme Court Decision: *U.S. v. Sokolow*

U.S. v. SOKOLOW, 490 U.S. 1 (1989)

490 U.S. 1
U.S. v. SOKOLOW
CERTIORARI TO THE UNITED STATES COURT OF APPEALS FOR THE NINTH CIRCUIT
No. 87-1295.

Argued January 10, 1989
Decided April 3, 1989

Drug Enforcement Administration (DEA) agents stopped respondent upon his arrival at Honolulu International Airport. The agents found 1,063 grams of cocaine in his carry-on luggage. When respondent was stopped, the agents knew, inter alia, that (1) he paid $2,100 for two round-trip plane tickets from a roll of $20 bills; (2) he traveled under a name that did not match the name under which his telephone number was listed; (3) his original destination was Miami, a source city for illicit drugs; (4) he stayed in Miami for only 48 hours, even though a round-trip flight from Honolulu to Miami takes 20 hours; (5) he appeared nervous during his trip; and (6) he checked none of his luggage. Respondent was indicted for possession with intent to distribute cocaine. The District Court denied his motion to suppress the evidence, finding that the stop was justified by a reasonable suspicion that he was engaged in criminal activity, as required by the Fourth Amendment. The Court of Appeals disagreed and reversed respondent's conviction, applying a two-part test for determining reasonable suspicion. First, ruled the court, at least one fact describing "ongoing criminal activity" — such as the use of an alias or evasive movement through an airport — was always necessary to support a reasonable-suspicion finding. Second, "probabilistic" facts describing "personal characteristics" of drug couriers — such as the cash payment for tickets, a short trip to a major source city for drugs, nervousness, type of attire, and unchecked luggage — were only relevant if there was evidence of "ongoing criminal activity" and the Government [490 U.S. 1, 2] offered "[e]mpirical documentation" that the combination of facts at issue did not describe the behavior of "significant numbers of innocent persons." The Court of Appeals held the agents' stop impermissible, because there was no evidence of ongoing criminal behavior in this case.

Held:

On the facts of this case, the DEA agents had a reasonable suspicion that respondent was transporting illegal drugs when they stopped him. Pp. 7-11.

(a) Under *Terry v. Ohio*, 392 U.S. 1, 30, the police can stop and briefly detain a person for investigative purposes if they have a reasonable suspicion supported by articulable facts that criminal activity "may be afoot," even if they lack probable cause under the Fourth Amendment. Reasonable suspicion entails some minimal level of objective justification for making a stop — that is, something more than an inchoate and unparticularized suspicion or "hunch," but less than the level of suspicion required for probable cause. P. 7.

(b) The Court of Appeals' two-part test creates unnecessary difficulty in dealing with one of the relatively simple concepts embodied in the Fourth Amendment. Under this Court's decisions, the totality of the circumstances must be evaluated to determine the probability, rather than the certainty, of criminal conduct. *U.S. v. Cortez*, 449 U.S. 411, 417. The Court of Appeals' test draws an unnecessarily sharp line between types of evidence, the probative value of which varies only in degree. While traveling under an alias or taking an evasive path through an airport may be highly probative, neither type of evidence has the sort of ironclad significance attributed to it by the Court of Appeals, because there are instances in which neither factor would reflect ongoing criminal activity. On the other hand, the test's "probabilistic" factors also have probative significance. Paying $2,100 in cash for airline tickets from a roll of $20 bills containing nearly twice that amount is not ordinary conduct for most business travelers or vacationers. The evidence that respondent was traveling under an alias, although not conclusive, was sufficient to warrant consideration. Of similar effect is the probability that few Honolulu residents travel for 20 hours to spend 48 hours in Miami during July. Thus, although each of these factors is not by itself proof of illegal conduct and is quite consistent with innocent travel, taken together, they amount to reasonable suspicion that criminal conduct was afoot. Pp. 7-10.

(c) The fact that the agents believed that respondent's behavior was consistent with one of the DEA's "drug courier profiles" does not alter this analysis, because the factors in question have evidentiary significance regardless of whether they are set forth in a "profile." P. 10.

(d) The reasonableness of the decision to stop does not, as respondent contends, turn upon whether the police used the least intrusive means [490 U.S. 1, 3] available to verify or dispel their suspicions. Such a rule would unduly hamper the officers' ability to make on-the-spot decisions — here, respondent was about to enter a taxicab — and would require courts to indulge in unrealistic second-guessing. *Florida v. Royer*, 460 U.S. 491, 495, distinguished. Pp. 10-11.

831 F.2d 1413, reversed and remanded.

REHNQUIST, C. J., delivered the opinion of the Court, in which WHITE, BLACKMUN, STEVENS, O'CONNOR, SCALIA, and KENNEDY, JJ., joined. MARSHALL, J., filed a dissenting opinion, in which BRENNAN, J., joined, post, p. 11.

Paul J. Larkin, Jr., argued the cause for the United States. With him on the briefs were Solicitor General Fried, Acting Assistant Attorney General Dennis, Deputy Solicitor General Bryson, and Patty Merkamp Stemler.

Robert P. Goldberg argued the cause and filed a brief for respondent.

CHIEF JUSTICE REHNQUIST delivered the opinion of the Court.

Respondent Andrew Sokolow was stopped by Drug Enforcement Administration (DEA) agents upon his arrival at Honolulu International Airport. The agents found 1,063 grams of cocaine in his carry-on luggage. When respondent was stopped, the agents knew, inter alia, that (1) he paid $2,100 for two airplane tickets from a roll of $20 bills; (2) he traveled under a name that did not match the name under which his telephone number was listed; (3) his original destination was Miami, a source city for illicit drugs; (4) he stayed in Miami for only 48 hours, even though a round-trip flight from Honolulu to Miami takes 20 hours; (5) he appeared nervous during his trip; and (6) he checked none of his luggage. A divided panel of the United States Court of Appeals for the Ninth Circuit held that the DEA agents did not have a reasonable suspicion to stop respondent, as required by the Fourth Amendment. 831 F.2d 1413 (1987). We take the contrary view. [490 U.S. 1, 4]

This case involves a typical attempt to smuggle drugs through one of the Nation's airports, Footnote 1. On a Sunday in July 1984, respondent went to the United Airlines ticket counter at Honolulu Airport, where he purchased two round-trip tickets for a flight to Miami leaving later that day. The tickets were purchased in the names of "Andrew Kray" and "Janet Norian" and had open return dates. Respondent paid $2,100 for the tickets from a large roll of $20 bills, which appeared to contain a total of $4,000. He also gave the ticket agent his home telephone number. The ticket agent noticed that respondent seemed nervous; he was about 25 years old; he was dressed in a black jumpsuit and wore gold jewelry; and he was accompanied by a woman, who turned out to be Janet Norian. Neither respondent nor his companion checked any of their four pieces of luggage.

After the couple left for their flight, the ticket agent informed Officer John McCarthy of the Honolulu Police Department of respondent's cash purchase of tickets to Miami. Officer McCarthy determined that the telephone number respondent gave to the ticket agent was subscribed to a "Karl Herman," who resided at 348-A Royal Hawaiian Avenue in Honolulu. Unbeknownst to McCarthy (and later to the DEA agents), respondent was Herman's roommate. The ticket agent identified respondent's voice on the answering machine at Herman's number. Officer McCarthy was unable to find any listing under the name "Andrew Kray" in Hawaii. McCarthy subsequently learned that return reservations from Miami to Honolulu had been made in the names of Kray and Norian, with their arrival scheduled for July 25, three days after respondent and his companion had left. He also learned that Kray and Norian were scheduled to make stopovers in Denver and Los Angeles. [490 U.S. 1, 5]

On July 25, during the stopover in Los Angeles, DEA agents identified respondent. He "appeared to be very nervous and was looking all around the waiting area." App. 43-44. Later that day, at 6:30 p. m., respondent and Norian arrived in Honolulu. As before, they had not checked their luggage. Respondent was still wearing a black jumpsuit and gold jewelry. The couple proceeded directly to the street and tried to hail a cab, where Agent Richard Kempshall and three other DEA agents approached them. Kempshall displayed his credentials, grabbed respondent by the arm, and moved him back onto the sidewalk. Kempshall asked respondent for his airline ticket and identification; respondent said that he had neither. He told the agents that his name was "Sokolow," but that he was traveling under his mother's maiden name, "Kray."

Respondent and Norian were escorted to the DEA office at the airport. There, the couple's luggage was examined by "Donker," a narcotics detector dog, which alerted on respondent's brown shoulder bag. The agents arrested respondent. He was advised of his constitutional rights and declined to make any statements. The agents obtained a warrant to search the shoulder bag. They found no illicit drugs, but the bag did contain several suspicious documents indicating respondent's involvement in drug trafficking. The agents had Donker reexamine the remaining luggage, and this time the dog alerted on a medium-sized Louis Vuitton bag. By now, it was 9:30 p. m., too late for the agents to obtain a second warrant. They allowed respondent to leave for the night, but kept his luggage. The next morning, after a second dog confirmed Donker's alert, the agents obtained a warrant and found 1,063 grams of cocaine inside the bag.

Respondent was indicted for possession with the intent to distribute cocaine in violation of 21 U.S.C. 841(a)(1). The United States District Court for Hawaii denied his motion to suppress the cocaine and other evidence seized from his luggage, finding that the DEA agents had a reasonable suspicion [490 U.S. 1, 6] that he was involved in drug trafficking when they stopped him at the airport. Respondent then entered a conditional plea of guilty to the offense charged.

The United States Court of Appeals for the Ninth Circuit reversed respondent's conviction by a divided vote, holding that the DEA agents did not have a reasonable suspicion to justify the stop. 831 F.2d, at 1423, Footnote 2. The majority divided the facts bearing on reasonable suspicion into two categories. In the first category, the majority placed facts describing "ongoing criminal activity," such as the use of an alias or evasive movement through an airport; the majority believed that at least one such factor was always needed to support a finding of reasonable suspicion. Id., at 1419. In the second category, it placed facts describing "personal characteristics" of drug couriers, such as the cash payment for tickets, a short trip to a major source city for drugs, nervousness, type of attire, and unchecked luggage. Id., at 1420. The majority believed that such characteristics, "shared by drug couriers and the public at large," were only relevant if there was evidence of ongoing criminal behavior and the Government offered "[e]mpirical documentation" that the combination of facts at issue did not describe the behavior of "significant numbers of innocent persons." Ibid. Applying this two-part test to the facts of this case, the majority found that there was no evidence of ongoing criminal behavior, and thus that the agents' stop was impermissible. The dissenting judge took the view that the majority's approach was "overly mechanistic" and "contrary to the case-by-case determination of reasonable articulable suspicion based on all the facts." Id., at 1426. [490 U.S. 1, 7]

We granted certiorari to review the decision of the Court of Appeals, 486 U.S. 1042 (1988), because of its serious implications for the enforcement of the federal narcotics laws. We now reverse.

The Court of Appeals held that the DEA agents seized respondent when they grabbed him by the arm and moved him back onto the sidewalk. 831 F.2d, at 1416. The Government does not challenge that conclusion, and we assume — without deciding — that a stop occurred here. Our decision, then, turns on whether the agents had a reasonable suspicion that respondent was engaged in wrongdoing when they encountered him on the sidewalk. In *Terry v. Ohio*, 392 U.S. 1, 30 (1968), we held that the police can stop and briefly detain a person for investigative purposes if the officer has a reasonable suspicion supported by articulable facts that criminal activity "may be afoot," even if the officer lacks probable cause.

The officer, of course, must be able to articulate something more than an "inchoate and unparticularized suspicion or 'hunch.'" Id., at 27. The Fourth Amendment requires "some minimal level of objective justification" for making the stop. *INS v. Delgado*, 466 U.S. 210, 217 (1984). That level of suspicion is considerably less than proof of wrongdoing by a preponderance of the evidence. We have held that probable cause means "a fair probability that contraband or evidence of a crime will be found," *Illinois v. Gates*, 462 U.S. 213, 238 (1983), and the level of suspicion required for a Terry stop is obviously less demanding than that for probable cause, see *U.S. v. Montoya de Hernandez*, 473 U.S. 531, 541, 544 (1985).

The concept of reasonable suspicion, like probable cause, is not "readily, or even usefully, reduced to a neat set of legal rules." Gates, supra, at 232. We think the Court of Appeals' effort to refine and elaborate the requirements of "reasonable suspicion" in this case creates unnecessary difficulty in dealing with one of the relatively simple concepts embodied [490 U.S. 1, 8] in the Fourth Amendment. In evaluating the validity of a stop such as this, we must consider "the totality of the circumstances — the whole picture." *U.S. v. Cortez*, 449 U.S. 411, 417 (1981). As we said in Cortez:

"The process does not deal with hard certainties, but with probabilities. Long before the law of probabilities was articulated as such, practical people formulated certain common-sense conclusions about human behavior; jurors as factfinders are permitted to do the same — and so are law enforcement officers." Id., at 418.

The rule enunciated by the Court of Appeals, in which evidence available to an officer is divided into evidence of "ongoing criminal behavior," on the one hand, and "probabilistic" evidence, on the other, is not in keeping with the quoted statements from our decisions. It also seems to us to draw a sharp line between types of evidence, the probative value of which varies only in degree. The Court of Appeals classified evidence of traveling under an alias, or evidence that the suspect took an evasive or erratic path through an airport, as meeting the test for showing "ongoing criminal activity." But certainly instances are conceivable in which traveling under an alias would not reflect ongoing criminal activity: for example, a person who wished to travel to a hospital or clinic for an operation and wished to conceal that fact. One taking an evasive path through an airport might be seeking to avoid a confrontation with an angry acquaintance or with a creditor. This is not to say that each of these types of evidence is not highly probative, but they do not have the sort of ironclad significance attributed to them by the Court of Appeals.

On the other hand, the factors in this case that the Court of Appeals treated as merely "probabilistic" also have probative significance. Paying

$2,100 in cash for two airplane tickets is out of the ordinary, and it is even more out of the ordinary to pay that sum from a roll of $20 bills containing nearly twice that amount of cash. Most business travelers, we feel confident, purchase airline tickets by credit card or check so as to [490 U.S. 1, 9] have a record for tax or business purposes, and few vacationers carry with them thousands of dollars in $20 bills. We also think the agents had a reasonable ground to believe that respondent was traveling under an alias; the evidence was by no means conclusive, but it was sufficient to warrant consideration, Footnote 3. While a trip from Honolulu to Miami, standing alone, is not a cause for any sort of suspicion, here there was more: surely few residents of Honolulu travel from that city for 20 hours to spend 48 hours in Miami during the month of July.

Any one of these factors is not by itself proof of any illegal conduct and is quite consistent with innocent travel. But we think taken together they amount to reasonable suspicion. See *Florida v. Royer*, 460 U.S. 491, 502 (1983) (opinion of WHITE, J.); id., at 515-516 (BLACKMUN, J., dissenting); id., at 523-524 (REHNQUIST, J., dissenting), Footnote 4. We said in *Reid v. Georgia*, 448 U.S. 438 (1980) (per curiam), "there could, of course, be circumstances in which wholly lawful conduct might justify the suspicion that criminal activity was afoot." Id., at 441, Footnote 5. Indeed, Terry itself involved "a series of acts, [490 U.S. 1, 10] each of them perhaps innocent" if viewed separately, "but which taken together warranted further investigation." 392 U.S., at 22; see also Cortez, supra, at 417-419. We noted in Gates, 462 U.S., at 243-244, n. 13, that "innocent behavior will frequently provide the basis for a showing of probable cause," and that "[i]n making a determination of probable cause the relevant inquiry is not whether particular conduct is `innocent' or `guilty,' but the degree of suspicion that attaches to particular types of noncriminal acts." That principle applies equally well to the reasonable suspicion inquiry.

We do not agree with respondent that our analysis is somehow changed by the agents' belief that his behavior was consistent with one of the DEA's "drug courier profiles," Footnote 6. Brief for Respondent 14-21. A court sitting to determine the existence of reasonable suspicion must require the agent to articulate the factors leading to that conclusion, but the fact that these factors may be set forth in a "profile" does not somehow detract from their evidentiary significance as seen by a trained agent.

Respondent also contends that the agents were obligated to use the least intrusive means available to verify or dispel their suspicions that he was smuggling narcotics. Id., at 12-13, 21-23. In respondent's view, the agents should have simply approached and spoken with him, rather than forcibly detaining him. He points to the statement in *Florida v. Royer*, supra, at 500 (opinion of WHITE, J.), that "the investigative [490 U.S. 1, 11] methods employed should be the least intrusive means reasonably available to verify or dispel the officer's suspicion in a short period of time." That statement, however, was directed at the length of the investigative stop, not at whether the police had a less intrusive means to verify their suspicions before stopping Royer. The reasonableness of the officer's decision to stop a suspect does not turn on the availability of less intrusive investigatory techniques. Such a rule would unduly hamper the police's ability to make swift, on-the-spot decisions — here, respondent was about to get into a taxicab — and it would require courts to "indulge in 'unrealistic second-guessing.'" Montoya de Hernandez, 473 U.S., at 542, quoting *U.S. v. Sharpe*, 470 U.S. 675, 686, 687 (1985).

We hold that the agents had a reasonable basis to suspect that respondent was transporting illegal drugs on these facts. The judgment of the Court of Appeals is therefore reversed, and the case is remanded for further proceedings consistent with our decision.

It is so ordered.

Footnotes

[Footnote 1] The facts in this case were developed at suppression hearings held in the District Court over three separate days. The parties also stipulated to certain facts.

[Footnote 2] In an earlier decision, the Court of Appeals also reversed the District Court, but on the basis of different reasoning. 808 F.2d 1366, vacated, 831 F.2d 1413 (1987). The Court of Appeals' second decision was issued after the Government petitioned for rehearing on the ground that the court had erred in considering each of the facts known to the agents separately rather than in terms of the totality of the circumstances.

[Footnote 3] Respondent also claims that the agents should have conducted a further inquiry to resolve the inconsistency between the name he gave the airline and the name, "Karl Herman," under which his telephone number was listed. Brief for Respondent 26. This argument avails respondent nothing; had the agents done further checking, they would have discovered not only that respondent was Herman's roommate but also that his name was "Sokolow" and not "Kray," the name listed on his ticket.

[Footnote 4] In Royer, the police were aware, inter alia, that (1) Royer was traveling under an assumed name; (2) he paid for his ticket in cash with a number of small bills; (3) he was traveling from Miami to New York; (4) he put only his name and not an address on his checked luggage; and (5) he seemed nervous while walking through Miami airport. 460 U.S., at 493, n. 2, 502 (opinion of WHITE, J.).

[Footnote 5] In Reid, the Court held that a DEA agent stopped the defendant without reasonable suspicion. At the time of the stop, the agent knew that (1) the defendant flew into Atlanta from Fort Lauderdale, a source city for cocaine; (2) he arrived early in the morning, when police activity was believed to be at a low ebb; (3) he did not check his luggage; and (4) the defendant [490 U.S. 1, 10] and his companion appeared to be attempting to hide the fact that they were together. The Court held that the first three of these facts were not sufficient to supply reasonable suspicion, because they "describe a very large category of presumably innocent travelers," while the last fact was insufficient on the facts of that case to establish reasonable suspicion. 448 U.S., at 441.

[Footnote 6] Agent Kempshall testified that respondent's behavior "had all the classic aspects of a drug courier." App. 59. Since 1974, the DEA has trained narcotics officers to identify drug smugglers on the basis of the sort of circumstantial evidence at issue here.

JUSTICE MARSHALL, with whom JUSTICE BRENNAN joins, dissenting.

Because the strongest advocates of Fourth Amendment rights are frequently criminals, it is easy to forget that our interpretations of such rights apply to the innocent and the guilty alike. *Illinois v. Gates*, 462 U.S. 213, 290 (1983) (BRENNAN, J., dissenting). In the present case, the chain of events set in motion when respondent Andrew Sokolow was stopped by Drug Enforcement Administration (DEA) agents at Honolulu International Airport led to the discovery of cocaine and, ultimately, to Sokolow's conviction for drug trafficking. But in sustaining this conviction on the ground that the agents reasonably suspected Sokolow of ongoing criminal activity, the Court diminishes the rights of all citizens "to be secure in their persons," U.S. Const., Amdt. 4, as they [490 U.S. 1, 12] traverse the Nation's airports. Finding this result constitutionally impermissible, I dissent.

The Fourth Amendment cabins government's authority to intrude on personal privacy and security by requiring that searches and seizures usually be supported by a showing of probable cause. The reasonable-suspicion standard is a derivation of the probable-cause command, applicable only to those brief detentions which fall short of being full-scale searches and seizures and which are necessitated by law enforcement exigencies such as the need to stop ongoing crimes, to prevent imminent crimes, and to protect law enforcement officers in highly charged situations. *Terry v. Ohio*, 392 U.S. 1, 30 (1968). By requiring reasonable suspicion as a prerequisite to such seizures, the Fourth Amendment protects innocent persons from being subjected to "overbearing or harassing" police conduct carried out solely on the basis of imprecise stereotypes of what criminals look like, or on the basis of irrelevant personal characteristics such as race. Id., at 14-15, and n. 11 (citation omitted).

To deter such egregious police behavior, we have held that a suspicion is not reasonable unless officers have based it on "specific and articulable facts."

Id., at 21; see also *U.S. v. Brignoni-Ponce*, 422 U.S. 873, 880 (1975). It is not enough to suspect that an individual has committed crimes in the past, harbors unconsummated criminal designs, or has the propensity to commit crimes. On the contrary, before detaining an individual, law enforcement officers must reasonably suspect that he is engaged in, or poised to commit, a criminal act at that moment. See, e.g., *Brown v. Texas*, 443 U.S. 47, 51 (1979) (to detain, officers must "have a reasonable suspicion, based on objective facts, that the individual is involved in criminal activity"); Terry, supra, at 30 (reasonable suspicion exists only where policeman reasonably concludes, inter alia, "that criminal activity may be afoot"). The rationale for permitting brief, warrantless seizures is, after all, that it is impractical to demand strict compliance [490 U.S. 1, 13] with the Fourth Amendment's ordinary probable-cause requirement in the face of ongoing or imminent criminal activity demanding "swift action predicated upon the on-the-spot observations of the officer on the beat." Terry, supra, at 20. Observations raising suspicions of past criminality demand no such immediate action, but instead should appropriately trigger routine police investigation, which may ultimately generate sufficient information to blossom into probable cause.

Evaluated against this standard, the facts about Andrew Sokolow known to the DEA agents at the time they stopped him fall short of reasonably indicating that he was engaged at the time in criminal activity. It is highly significant that the DEA agents stopped Sokolow because he matched one of the DEA's "profiles" of a paradigmatic drug courier. In my view, a law enforcement officer's mechanistic application of a formula of personal and behavioral traits in deciding whom to detain can only dull the officer's ability and determination to make sensitive and fact-specific inferences "in light of his experience," Terry, supra, at 27, particularly in ambiguous or borderline cases. Reflexive reliance on a profile of drug courier characteristics runs a far greater risk than does ordinary, case-by-case police work of subjecting innocent individuals to unwarranted police harassment and detention. This risk is enhanced by the profile's "chameleon-like way of adapting to any particular set of observation." 831 F.2d 1413, 1418 (CA9 1987). Compare, e. g., *U.S. v. Moore*, 675 F.2d 802, 803 (CA6 1982) (suspect was first to deplane), cert. denied, 460 U.S. 1068 (1983), with *U.S. v. Mendenhall*, 446 U.S. 544, 564 (1980) (last to deplane), with *U.S. v. Buenaventura-Ariza*, 615 F.2d 29, 31 (CA2 1980) (deplaned from middle); *U.S. v. Sullivan*, 625 F.2d 9, 12 (CA4 1980) (one-way tickets), with *U.S. v. Craemer*, 555 F.2d 594, 595 (CA6 1977) (round-trip tickets), with *U.S. v. McCaleb*, 552 F.2d 717, 720 (CA6 1977) (nonstop flight), with *U.S. v. Sokolow*, 808 F.2d 1366, 1370 (CA9), vacated, 831 F.2d 1413 [490 U.S. 1, 14] (1987) (case below) (changed planes); Craemer, supra, at 595 (no luggage), with *U.S. v. Sanford*, 658 F.2d 342, 343 (CA5 1981) (gym bag), cert. denied, 455 U.S. 991 (1982), with Sullivan, supra, at

12 (new suitcases); *U.S. v. Smith*, 574 F.2d 882, 883 (CA6 1978) (traveling alone), with *U.S. v. Fry*, 622 F.2d 1218, 1219 (CA5 1980) (traveling with companion); *U.S. v. Andrews*, 600 F.2d 563, 566 (CA6 1979) (acted nervously), cert. denied sub nom. *Brooks v. United States*, 444 U.S. 878 (1979), with *U.S. v. Himmelwright*, 551 F.2d 991, 992 (CA5) (acted too calmly), cert. denied, 434 U.S. 902 (1977). In asserting that it is not "somehow" relevant that the agents who stopped Sokolow did so in reliance on a prefabricated profile of criminal characteristics, ante, at 10, the majority thus ducks serious issues relating to a questionable law enforcement practice, to address the validity of which we granted certiorari in this case, Footnote 1.

That the factors comprising the drug courier profile relied on in this case are especially dubious indices of ongoing criminal activity is underscored by *Reid v. Georgia*, 448 U.S. 438 (1980), a strikingly similar case. There, four facts, encoded in a drug courier profile, were alleged in support of the DEA's detention of a suspect at the Atlanta Airport. First, Reid had arrived from Fort Lauderdale, Florida, a source city for cocaine. Second, he arrived in the early morning, when law enforcement activity is diminished. Third, he and his companion appeared to have no luggage other than their shoulder bags. And fourth, he and his companion appeared to be trying to conceal the fact that they were traveling together. Id., at 440-441.

This collection of facts, we held, was inadequate to support a finding of reasonable suspicion. All but the last of these facts, we observed, "describe a very large category of presumably [490 U.S. 1, 15] innocent travelers, who would be subject to virtually random seizures were the Court to conclude that as little foundation as there was in this case could justify a seizure." Id., at 441. The sole fact that suggested criminal activity was that Reid "preceded another person and occasionally looked backward at him as they proceeded through the concourse." Ibid. This observation did not of itself provide a reasonable basis for suspecting wrongdoing, for inferring criminal activity from such evidence reflected no more than an "'inchoate and unparticularized suspicion or "hunch."'" Ibid., quoting *Terry*, 392 U.S., at 27, Footnote 2.

The facts known to the DEA agents at the time they detained the traveler in this case are scarcely more suggestive of ongoing criminal activity than those in *Reid*. Unlike traveler Reid, who sought to conceal the fact that he was traveling with a companion, and who even attempted to run away after being approached by a DEA agent, 448 U.S., at 439, traveler Sokolow gave no indications of evasive activity. On the contrary, the sole behavioral detail about Sokolow noted by the DEA agents was that he was nervous. With news accounts proliferating of plane crashes, near collisions, and air terrorism, there are manifold and good reasons for being agitated while awaiting a flight, reasons that have nothing to do with one's involvement in a criminal endeavor.

The remaining circumstantial facts known about Sokolow, considered either singly or together, are scarcely indicative of criminal activity. Like the information disavowed in *Reid* as nonprobative, the fact that Sokolow took a brief trip to a [490 U.S. 1, 16] resort city for which he brought only carry-on luggage also "describe[s] a very large category of presumably innocent travelers." Id., at 441. That Sokolow embarked from Miami, "a source city for illicit drugs," ante, at 3, is no more suggestive of illegality; thousands of innocent persons travel from "source cities" every day and, judging from the DEA's testimony in past cases, nearly every major city in the country may be characterized as a source or distribution city. See, e.g., Buenaventura-Ariza, 615 F.2d, at 31, n. 5. That Sokolow had his phone listed in another person's name also does not support the majority's assertion that the DEA agents reasonably believed Sokolow was using an alias; it is commonplace to have one's phone registered in the name of a roommate, which, it later turned out, was precisely what Sokolow had done, Footnote 3. That Sokolow was dressed in a black jumpsuit and wore gold jewelry also provides no grounds for suspecting wrongdoing, the majority's repeated and unexplained allusions to Sokolow's style of dress notwithstanding. Ante, at 4, 5. For law enforcement officers to base a search, even in part, on a "pop" guess that persons dressed in a particular fashion are likely to commit crimes not only stretches the concept of reasonable suspicion beyond recognition, but also is inimical to the self-expression which the choice of wardrobe may provide.

Finally, that Sokolow paid for his tickets in cash indicates no imminent or ongoing criminal activity. The majority "feel[s] confident" that "[m]ost business travelers... purchase airline tickets by credit card or check." Ante, at 8. Why the majority confines its focus only to "business travelers" I do not know, but I would not so lightly infer ongoing crime from the use of legal tender. Making major cash purchases, while surely less common today, may simply reflect the traveler's aversion to, or inability to obtain, plastic [490 U.S. 1, 17] money. Conceivably, a person who spends large amounts of cash may be trying to launder his proceeds from past criminal enterprises by converting them into goods and services. But, as I have noted, investigating completed episodes of crime goes beyond the appropriately limited purview of the brief, Terry-style seizure. Moreover, it is unreasonable to suggest that, had Sokolow left the airport, he would have been gone forever and thus immune from subsequent investigation. Ante, at 11. Sokolow, after all, had given the airline his phone number, and the DEA, having ascertained that it was indeed Sokolow's voice on the answering machine at that number, could have learned from that information where Sokolow resided.

The fact is that, unlike the taking of patently evasive action, *Florida v. Rodriguez*, 469 U.S. 1, 6 (1984), the use of an alias, *Florida v. Royer*, 460 U.S. 491, 502 (1983), the casing of a store, *Terry*, supra, at 6, or the provision of a reliable report from an informant that wrongdoing is imminent, *Illinois v. Gates*, 462 U.S., at 225-227, nothing about the characteristics shown by airport traveler Sokolow reasonably suggests that criminal activity is afoot. The majority's hasty conclusion to the contrary serves only to indicate its willingness, when drug crimes or antidrug policies are at issue, to give short shrift to constitutional rights. See, e.g., *Skinner v. Railway Labor Executives' Assn.*, 489 U.S. 602, 636 (1989) (MARSHALL, J., dissenting), Footnote 4. In requiring that seizures be based on at least some evidence of criminal conduct, 831 F.2d, at 1419, the Court of Appeals was faithful to the Fourth Amendment principle that law enforcement officers [490 U.S. 1, 18] must reasonably suspect a person of criminal activity before they can detain him. Because today's decision, though limited to its facts, ante, at 11, disobeys this important constitutional command, I dissent.

Footnotes

[Footnote 1] Even if such profiles had reliable predictive value, their utility would be short lived, for drug couriers will adapt their behavior to sidestep detection from profile-focused officers.

[Footnote 2] Nor was Reid a close case: eight Members of the Court found the challenged detention insupportable, five of whom saw fit to dispose of the case by reversing the court below in a per curiam opinion. In a separate concurrence, Justice Powell, joined by Chief Justice Burger and JUSTICE BLACKMUN, agreed that "the fragmentary facts apparently relied on by the DEA agents" provided "no justification" for Reid's detention. 448 U.S., at 442, n. 1. Only then — JUSTICE REHNQUIST, the author of today's majority opinion, dissented, on the ground that the police conduct involved did not implicate Reid's constitutional rights. Id., at 442.

[Footnote 3] That Sokolow was, in fact, using an alias was not known to the DEA agents until after they detained him. Thus, it cannot legitimately be considered as a basis for the seizure in this case.

[Footnote 4] The majority also contends that it is not relevant that the DEA agents, in forcibly stopping Sokolow rather than simply speaking with him, did not "use the least intrusive means available." Ante, at 10. On the contrary, the manner in which a search is carried out — and particularly whether law enforcement officers have taken needlessly intrusive steps — is a highly important index of reasonableness under Fourth Amendment doctrine. See, e.g., *Winston v. Lee*, 470 U.S. 753, 760-761 (1985). [490 U.S. 1, 19]

Index

J

K

L

M

N

O

P

T

U